公式 TOEIC®
Listening & Reading
問題集

9

一般財団法人 国際ビジネスコミュニケーション協会

はじめに

　本書は『公式 TOEIC® Listening & Reading 問題集』シリーズの第9弾です。2016年5月実施の公開テストから加わった新しい出題形式に対応し、実際と同じテスト形式で2回分の問題を掲載しています。TOEIC® Listening & Reading Test の受験準備にお使いください。

本シリーズの特長

- 問題は全て、ETSが実際のテストと同じプロセスで制作しています。
- サンプル問題とテスト2回分の問題(200問×2回、計400問)を掲載し、リスニングセクションはTOEIC®公式スピーカーによる音声が収録されています。
  - ＊実際のテストでは、担当スピーカーや発音の種類(どの国の発音か)の割合が変更される場合があります。
- 素点から参考スコア範囲が算出可能です。
- 正解を導くための詳しい解説の他、学習の助けとなる語注「Words & Phrases」(Part 3、4、6、7)や表現紹介のコーナー「Expressions」(Part 6、7)を掲載しています。

付属CD・特典の音声について

- CDは一般的なプレーヤーで再生できます。また、CDの音声をパソコンなどの機器に取り込んで再生することもできます。
- 『公式TOEIC® Listening & Reading問題集9』の特典として、TEST 1、2のリーディングセクションの以下の音声をダウンロードすることができます。問題に解答した後の学習用教材としてご活用ください。
  - 正解が入った問題音声(Part 5、6)
  - 文書の音声(Part 7)

音声ダウンロードの手順：　＊株式会社 Globee が提供するサービス abceed への会員登録(無料)が必要です。

1. パソコン・スマートフォンで音声ダウンロード用のサイトにアクセスします。
   (右のQRコードまたはブラウザから https://app.abceed.com/audio/iibc-officialprep へ)
2. 表示されたページから、abceed の新規会員登録を行います。既に会員の場合は、ログイン情報を入力して上記1.のサイトへアクセスします。
3. 上記1.のサイトにアクセス後、本教材の画像をクリックします。クリックすると、教材詳細画面へ遷移します。
4. スマートフォンの場合は、アプリ「abceed」の案内が出ますので、アプリからご利用ください。パソコンの場合は、教材詳細画面の「音声」のアイコンからご利用ください。

   ＊音声は何度でもダウンロード・再生ができます。ダウンロードについてのお問い合わせは下記へ
   　Eメール:support@globeejphelp.zendesk.com (お問い合わせ窓口の営業日：祝日を除く月～金曜日)
   ＊特典音声は、必ず一度TEST 1、2 のリーディングセクションの問題に解答した後に、ご利用ください。詳しい使い方は、
   　別冊『解答・解説』p.200 をご参照ください。

　本書が、TOEIC® Listening & Reading Testの出題形式の理解と受験準備、そして皆さまの英語学習のお役に立つことを願っております。

2022年10月
一般財団法人 国際ビジネスコミュニケーション協会

目　次

本誌

*解答用紙は112ページの後ろに綴じ込まれています。

別冊 『解答・解説』

TOEIC® Listening & Reading Test について

TOEIC® Listening & Reading Test とは？

TOEIC® Listening & Reading Test（以下、TOEIC® L&R）は、TOEIC® Programのテストの一つで、英語における Listening（聞く）と Reading（読む）の力を測定します。結果は合格・不合格ではなく、リスニングセクション 5〜495 点、リーディングセクション 5〜495 点、トータル 10〜990 点のスコアで評価されます。スコアの基準は常に一定であり、 英語能力に変化がない限りスコアも一定に保たれます。知識・教養としての英語ではなく、オフィスや日常生活における英語によるコミュニケーション能力を幅広く測定するテストです。特定の文化を知らないと理解できない表現を排除しているので、誰もが公平に受けることができる「グローバルスタンダード」として活用されています。

問題形式

● リスニングセクション（約 45 分間・100 問）とリーディングセクション（75 分間・100 問）から成り、約 2 時間で 200 問に解答します。

● テストは英文のみで構成されており、英文和訳や和文英訳といった設問はありません。

● マークシート方式の一斉客観テストです。

● リスニングセクションにおける発音は、米国・英国・カナダ・オーストラリアが使われています。

＊テスト中、問題用紙への書き込みは一切禁じられています。

<table>
<tr><th colspan="4">リスニングセクション（約 45 分間）</th></tr>
<tr><th>パート</th><th>Part Name</th><th>パート名</th><th>問題数</th></tr>
<tr><td>1</td><td>Photographs</td><td>写真描写問題</td><td>6</td></tr>
<tr><td>2</td><td>Question-Response</td><td>応答問題</td><td>25</td></tr>
<tr><td>3</td><td>Conversations</td><td>会話問題</td><td>39</td></tr>
<tr><td>4</td><td>Talks</td><td>説明文問題</td><td>30</td></tr>
</table>

<table>
<tr><th colspan="4">リーディングセクション（75 分間）</th></tr>
<tr><th>パート</th><th>Part Name</th><th>パート名</th><th>問題数</th></tr>
<tr><td>5</td><td>Incomplete Sentences</td><td>短文穴埋め問題</td><td>30</td></tr>
<tr><td>6</td><td>Text Completion</td><td>長文穴埋め問題</td><td>16</td></tr>
<tr><td>7</td><td>• Single passages
• Multiple passages</td><td>1 つの文書
複数の文書</td><td>29
25</td></tr>
</table>

開発・運営団体について

TOEIC® L&Rは、ETSによって開発・制作されています。ETSは、米国ニュージャージー州プリンストンに拠点を置き、TOEIC® Program や TOEFL、GRE（大学院入学共通試験）を含む約 200 のテストプログラムを開発している世界最大の非営利テスト開発機関です。

日本における TOEIC® L&R を含む TOEIC® Program の実施・運営は、一般財団法人 国際ビジネスコミュニケーション協会（IIBC）が行っています。IIBCは、公式教材の出版やグローバル人材育成など、「人と企業の国際化」の推進に貢献するための活動を展開しています。

本書の構成と使い方

本書は、本誌と別冊に分かれています。それぞれの主な内容は以下の通りです。
- 本誌 …… 「サンプル問題」「TEST 1」「TEST 2」「解答用紙」
- 別冊『解答・解説』…… 「参考スコア範囲の算出方法」「正解一覧」「解答・解説」「CDトラック・特典音声ファイル 一覧表」「音声を使った学習例の紹介」

本誌

サンプル問題（29問）[本誌p.8-27] 全パートから合計29問を掲載しています。

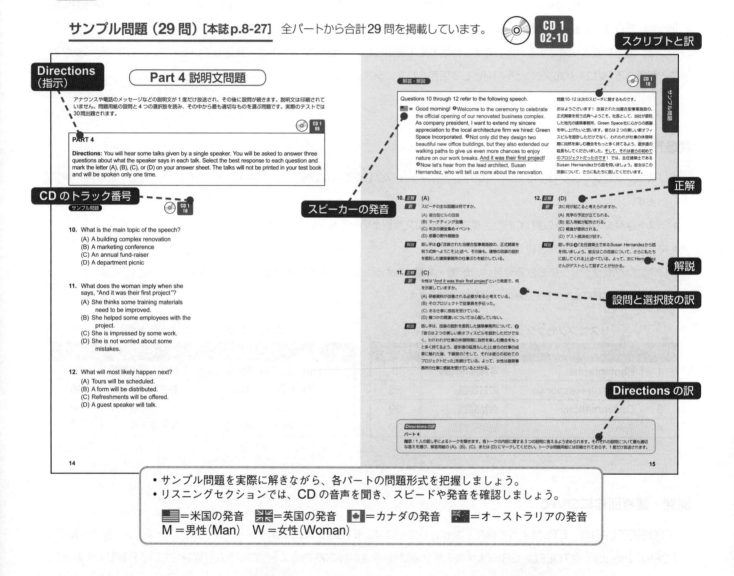

- サンプル問題を実際に解きながら、各パートの問題形式を把握しましょう。
- リスニングセクションでは、CDの音声を聞き、スピードや発音を確認しましょう。

＝米国の発音　＝英国の発音　■＝カナダの発音　■＝オーストラリアの発音
M＝男性（Man）　W＝女性（Woman）

TEST 1 [本誌p.29-70]　CD 1 11-92　　TEST 2 [本誌p.71-111]　CD 2 01-82

TEST 1、2ともに、実際のテストと同じ、合計200問で構成されています。

リスニングセクション	100問	約45分間
リーディングセクション	100問	75分間

予行演習として時間を計って解答し、時間配分の参考にしたり、伸ばしたい分野や弱点を把握したり、使い方を工夫してみましょう。

別冊『解答・解説』

参考スコア範囲の算出方法 ［別冊 p.4］

正解数を基に、参考スコア範囲を算出できます。

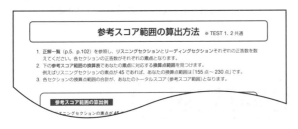

正解一覧 ［TEST 1 ➡ 別冊 p.5　TEST 2 ➡ 別冊 p.102］

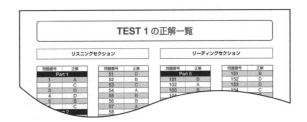

解答・解説 ［TEST 1 ➡ 別冊 p.6-101　TEST 2 ➡ 別冊 p.103-197］

表記の説明は、別冊 p.2-3 をご覧ください。

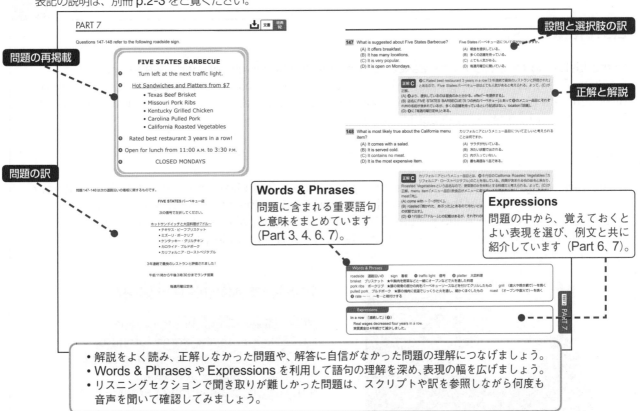

- 解説をよく読み、正解しなかった問題や、解答に自信がなかった問題の理解につなげましょう。
- Words & Phrases や Expressions を利用して語句の理解を深め、表現の幅を広げましょう。
- リスニングセクションで聞き取りが難しかった問題は、スクリプトや訳を参照しながら何度も音声を聞いて確認してみましょう。

CDトラック・特典音声ファイル 一覧表

［別冊 p.198-199］

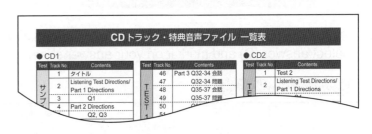

サンプル問題

TOEIC® Listening & Reading Test（以下、TOEIC® L&R）の問題形式を、サンプル問題を使ってご紹介します。サンプル問題は、全部で29問（リスニングセクション12問、リーディングセクション17問）です。問題の番号は連番になっており、実際のテストの問題番号とは異なります。

TOEIC® L&Rのリスニングセクションは4つ、リーディングセクションは3つのパートに分かれています。問題用紙には、各パートの最初にDirectionsが英文で印刷されています。

Part 1 写真描写問題

1枚の写真について4つの短い説明文が1度だけ放送されます。説明文は印刷されていません。4つのうち写真を最も適切に描写しているものを選ぶ問題です。実際のテストでは6問出題されます。

CD 1
02

LISTENING TEST

In the Listening test, you will be asked to demonstrate how well you understand spoken English. The entire Listening test will last approximately 45 minutes. There are four parts, and directions are given for each part. You must mark your answers on the separate answer sheet. Do not write your answers in your test book.

PART 1

Directions: For each question in this part, you will hear four statements about a picture in your test book. When you hear the statements, you must select the one statement that best describes what you see in the picture. Then find the number of the question on your answer sheet and mark your answer. The statements will not be printed in your test book and will be spoken only one time.

Look at the example item below.

Now listen to the four statements.
(A) They're moving some furniture.
(B) They're entering a meeting room.
(C) They're sitting at a table.
(D) They're cleaning the carpet.

Statement (C), "They're sitting at a table," is the best description of the picture, so you should select answer (C) and mark it on your answer sheet.

Now Part 1 will begin.

＊上記枠内の網掛けの部分は音声のみで、問題用紙には印刷されていません。

1.

解答・解説

1. Look at the picture marked number 1 in your test book.

　M　(A) A truck is stopped at a stoplight.
　　　(B) A man is using a gardening tool.
　　　(C) Some people are sitting on the grass.
　　　(D) Some workers are cutting down a tree.

正解　**(B)**

解説　gardeningは「造園、園芸」、toolは「用具、道具」という意味。

訳 問題用紙にある問題1の写真を見てください。

　(A) トラックが停止信号で止まっている。
　(B) 男性が造園用具を使っている。
　(C) 何人かの人々が芝生の上に座っている。
　(D) 何人かの作業員が木を切り倒している。

Directionsの訳

リスニングテスト

リスニングテストでは、話されている英語をどのくらいよく理解しているかが問われます。リスニングテストは全体で約45分間です。4つのパートがあり、各パートにおいて指示が与えられます。答えは、別紙の解答用紙にマークしてください。問題用紙に答えを書き込んではいけません。

パート1

指示: このパートの各設問では、問題用紙にある写真について、4つの説明文を聞きます。説明文を聞いて、写真の内容を最も適切に描写しているものを選んでください。そして解答用紙の該当する問題番号にあなたの答えをマークしてください。説明文は問題用紙には印刷されておらず、1度だけ放送されます。

下の例題を見てください。

では4つの説明文を聞きましょう。
　(A) 彼らは家具を動かしている。
　(B) 彼らは会議室に入ろうとしている。
　(C) 彼らはテーブルのところに座っている。
　(D) 彼らはカーペットを掃除している。

(C)の文、"They're sitting at a table"(彼らはテーブルのところに座っている)がこの写真を最も適切に描写しているので、(C)を選び、解答用紙にマークします。

ではパート1が始まります。

Part 2 応答問題

1つの質問または発言と、3つの応答がそれぞれ1度だけ放送されます。質問も応答も印刷されていません。質問に対して最も適切な応答を選ぶ問題です。実際のテストでは25問出題されます。

CD 1 04

PART 2

Directions: You will hear a question or statement and three responses spoken in English. They will not be printed in your test book and will be spoken only one time. Select the best response to the question or statement and mark the letter (A), (B), or (C) on your answer sheet.

Now let us begin with question number 2.

＊上記枠内の網掛けの部分は音声のみで、問題用紙には印刷されていません。

サンプル問題

CD 1 05

2. Mark your answer on your answer sheet.

3. Mark your answer on your answer sheet.

解答・解説

2. W Are you taking an international or a domestic flight?

 M (A) I'd prefer a window seat.
(B) He moved there last year.
(C) I'm flying internationally.

正解 **(C)**

解説 *A or B*? の形で、国際線と国内線のどちらの便に乗るのかを尋ねているのに対し、「国際線の飛行機で行く」と答えている (C) が正解。

訳 あなたは国際線の便に乗りますか、それとも国内線の便ですか。
(A) 私は窓側の席を希望します。
(B) 彼は昨年、そこへ引っ越しました。
(C) 私は国際線の飛行機で行きます。

3. M Shouldn't we hire more salespeople?

 W (A) I'm glad they went.
(B) A higher profit.
(C) Let's look at the budget.

正解 **(C)**

解説 「もっと販売員を雇った方がいいのではないか」という男性の発言に対し、「予算を見てみよう」と雇用の検討を示唆している (C) が正解。

訳 私たちはもっと販売員を雇った方がいいのではありませんか。
(A) 私は、彼らが行ってうれしいです。
(B) より高い利益です。
(C) 予算を見てみましょう。

Directions の訳

パート2

指示：英語による1つの質問または発言と、3つの応答を聞きます。それらは問題用紙には印刷されておらず、1度だけ放送されます。質問または発言に対して最も適切な応答を選び、解答用紙の (A)、(B)、または (C) にマークしてください。

では、問題2から始めましょう。

問題の訳

答えを解答用紙にマークしてください。

Part 3 会話問題

会話が1度だけ放送され、その後に設問が続きます。会話は印刷されていません。問題用紙の設問と4つの選択肢を読み、その中から最も適切なものを選ぶ問題です。実際のテストでは39問出題されます。

 CD 1 06

PART 3

Directions: You will hear some conversations between two or more people. You will be asked to answer three questions about what the speakers say in each conversation. Select the best response to each question and mark the letter (A), (B), (C), or (D) on your answer sheet. The conversations will not be printed in your test book and will be spoken only one time.

サンプル問題 CD 1 07   CD 1 08

4. Which department is the man most likely calling?

   (A) Receiving
   (B) Catering
   (C) Security
   (D) Finance

5th Annual Agricultural Fair

Day 1–Vegetables
Day 2–Dairy
Day 3–Flowers
Day 4–Baked goods

---

5. Why does the man apologize?

   (A) He has forgotten his badge.
   (B) His report will be late.
   (C) A meeting location has to be changed.
   (D) A shipment must be delivered after business hours.

7. Why do the speakers want to attend the fair?

   (A) To advertise a new business
   (B) To find local food suppliers
   (C) To sell some products
   (D) To participate in a workshop

6. What does the woman say she will do?

   (A) Arrange additional workspace
   (B) Publish some materials
   (C) Issue a temporary pass
   (D) Ask staff to work late

8. What does the man say he has downloaded?

   (A) An electronic book
   (B) A mobile phone application
   (C) Some photographs
   (D) Some tickets

9. Look at the graphic. Which day do the speakers decide to attend the fair?

   (A) Day 1
   (B) Day 2
   (C) Day 3
   (D) Day 4

CD 1
07

Questions 4 through 6 refer to the following conversation.

🇦🇺 M Hello. ❶I'm expecting an extra-large load of clothing racks delivered to the store today, and they'll arrive after business hours. Are you the person I should inform about this?

🇬🇧 W Yes, ❷I'm head of Receiving. But ❸you're supposed to have suppliers make deliveries during business hours.

🇦🇺 M ❹I'm sorry, but this is the only time the supplier can deliver them, and we need the racks for a fashion show we're having tomorrow.

🇬🇧 W I understand. ❺I'm not sure which of my staff members is working tonight, but I'll ask one of them to stay late to accept the delivery.

問題4-6は次の会話に関するものです。

もしもし。今日お店に、洋服ラックの特大の積み荷が配達される予定ですが、それらは営業時間の後に着きます。あなたがこの件についてお知らせすべき方でしょうか。

はい、私が荷受け部門の責任者です。でも、供給業者には、営業時間中に配達してもらうことになっているはずですが。

申し訳ありません。しかし、これが、供給業者がそれらを配達できる唯一の時間帯で、私たちが明日開催するファッションショーには、そのラックが必要なんです。

分かりました。今夜うちのスタッフの誰が勤務するのか定かではありませんが、配達物を受け取るために遅くまで残るよう、彼らのうちの1人に頼みます。

4. 正解 **(A)**

訳 男性はどの部署に電話をかけていると考えられますか。
(A) 荷受け
(B) ケータリング
(C) 警備
(D) 財務

解説 男性からの電話に応答した女性は❷「私が荷受け部門の責任者だ」と答え、その後も2人は配達物の受け取りについて話をしている。

5. 正解 **(D)**

訳 男性はなぜ謝罪していますか。
(A) 自分のバッジを忘れたから。
(B) 報告書が遅れるから。
(C) 会議の場所が変更されなければならないから。
(D) 荷物が営業時間の後に配達されざるを得ないから。

解説 ❶「積み荷が配達される予定だが、それらは営業時間の後に着く」という男性の報告に対し、女性が❸「供給業者には、営業時間中に配達してもらうことになっているはず」と指摘している。それに対して男性は❹で、「申し訳ない」と謝罪後「これが、供給業者がそれらを配達できる唯一の時間帯で、私たちが明日開催するファッションショーには、そのラックが必要だ」と事情を説明している。よって、正解は(D)。

6. 正解 **(D)**

訳 女性は何をすると言っていますか。
(A) 追加の作業スペースを手配する。
(B) 資料を公表する。
(C) 臨時の通行証を発行する。
(D) スタッフに遅くまで勤務するよう頼む。

解説 女性は❺「今夜うちのスタッフの誰が勤務するのか定かではないが、配達物を受け取るために遅くまで残るよう、彼らのうちの1人に頼む」と述べている。stay lateをwork late「遅くまで勤務する」と表した(D)が正解。

Directionsの訳

パート3

指示：2人あるいはそれ以上の人々の会話を聞きます。各会話の内容に関する3つの設問に答えるよう求められます。それぞれの設問について最も適切な答えを選び、解答用紙の(A)、(B)、(C)、または(D)にマークしてください。会話は問題用紙には印刷されておらず、1度だけ放送されます。

Questions 7 through 9 refer to the following conversation and schedule.

🇺🇸 W Pedro, ❶I know we're still looking for local fresh food suppliers for our new restaurant. We should check out the Agricultural Fair next month.

🇨🇦 M That's a good idea. It's a major event, so many local farmers will be there. ❷I downloaded the fair's mobile phone application. The app has a lot of helpful information, including a schedule. Which day do you think we should go?

🇺🇸 W Well, it looks like they'll have dairy vendors on the second day.

🇨🇦 M Hmm, I just contacted a dairy company that might work for us. ❸We really need a vegetable supplier though…

🇺🇸 W Oh, OK. ❹They have a day for showcasing vegetable farmers. Let's go then.

問題7-9は次の会話と予定表に関するものです。

Pedro、私たちはまだ、うちの新しいレストランのために、地元の生鮮食品の供給業者を探しているわよね。来月の農業フェアを見てみるべきだわ。

それは良い考えだね。大きなイベントだから、多数の地元の農業経営者たちがそこにいるだろう。僕はフェアの携帯電話用アプリをダウンロードしたよ。このアプリには、予定表を含め、役立つ情報がたくさんあるんだ。僕たちはどの日に行くべきだと思う？

そうね、乳製品の販売業者は2日目にいるみたいね。

うーん、僕はうちに合いそうな乳製品会社に連絡を取ったばかりなんだ。僕たちには野菜の供給業者はぜひとも必要だけど…。

ああ、分かったわ。野菜農家の出展日があるわ。そのときに行きましょう。

---

7. 正解 **(B)**

訳 なぜ話し手たちはフェアに行きたいと思っていますか。

(A) 新しい店を宣伝するため。
(B) 地元の食品供給業者を見つけるため。
(C) 製品を販売するため。
(D) 講習会に参加するため。

解説 女性は❶「私たちはまだ、うちの新しいレストランのために、地元の生鮮食品の供給業者を探している。来月の農業フェアを見てみるべきだ」と提案し、男性もそれに同意している。よって、(B)が適切。

8. 正解 **(B)**

訳 男性は何をダウンロードしたと言っていますか。

(A) 電子書籍
(B) 携帯電話用アプリ
(C) 数枚の写真
(D) 数枚のチケット

解説 男性は❷「僕はフェアの携帯電話用アプリをダウンロードした」と述べている。

9. 正解 **(A)**

訳 図を見てください。話し手たちはどの日にフェアへ行くことに決めますか。

(A) 1日目
(B) 2日目
(C) 3日目
(D) 4日目

解説 ❸「僕たちには野菜の供給業者がぜひとも必要だ」という男性の発言に対し、女性は❹「野菜農家の出展日がある。そのときに行こう」と提案している。予定表から、野菜農家が集まる日は1日目だと分かる。予定表のbaked goodsはクッキーやパンなどのオーブンで焼いた食品を指す。

図の訳

第5回　年次農業フェア
1日目 ── 野菜
2日目 ── 乳製品
3日目 ── 花
4日目 ── パン・焼き菓子

Part 4 説明文問題

アナウンスや電話のメッセージなどの説明文が1度だけ放送され、その後に設問が続きます。説明文は印刷されていません。問題用紙の設問と4つの選択肢を読み、その中から最も適切なものを選ぶ問題です。実際のテストでは30問出題されます。

PART 4

Directions: You will hear some talks given by a single speaker. You will be asked to answer three questions about what the speaker says in each talk. Select the best response to each question and mark the letter (A), (B), (C), or (D) on your answer sheet. The talks will not be printed in your test book and will be spoken only one time.

サンプル問題

10. What is the main topic of the speech?

   (A) A building complex renovation
   (B) A marketing conference
   (C) An annual fund-raiser
   (D) A department picnic

11. What does the woman imply when she says, "And it was their first project"?

   (A) She thinks some training materials need to be improved.
   (B) She helped some employees with the project.
   (C) She is impressed by some work.
   (D) She is not worried about some mistakes.

12. What will most likely happen next?

   (A) Tours will be scheduled.
   (B) A form will be distributed.
   (C) Refreshments will be offered.
   (D) A guest speaker will talk.

14

Questions 10 through 12 refer to the following speech.

問題10-12 は次のスピーチに関するものです。

🇺🇸 w Good morning! ❶Welcome to the ceremony to celebrate the official opening of our renovated business complex. As company president, I want to extend my sincere appreciation to the local architecture firm we hired: Green Space Incorporated. ❷Not only did they design two beautiful new office buildings, but they also extended our walking paths to give us even more chances to enjoy nature on our work breaks. And it was their first project! ❸Now let's hear from the lead architect, Susan Hernandez, who will tell us more about the renovation.

おはようございます！ 改装された当複合型事業施設の、正式開業を祝う式典へようこそ。社長として、当社が委託した地元の建築事務所、Green Space 社に心からの感謝を申し上げたいと思います。彼らは2つの美しい新オフィスビルを設計しただけでなく、われわれが仕事の休憩時間に自然を楽しむ機会をもっと多く持てるよう、遊歩道の延長もしてくださいました。そして、それは彼らの初めてのプロジェクトだったのです！ では、主任建築士であるSusan Hernandezから話を伺いましょう。彼女はこの改装について、さらに私たちに話してくださいます。

10. 正解 **(A)**

訳 スピーチの主な話題は何ですか。

(A) 複合型ビルの改装
(B) マーケティング会議
(C) 年次の資金集めイベント
(D) 部署の野外親睦会

解説 話し手は❶「改装された当複合型事業施設の、正式開業を祝う式典へようこそ」と述べ、その後も、建物の改装の設計を委託した建築事務所の仕事ぶりを紹介している。

11. 正解 **(C)**

訳 女性は "And it was their first project" という発言で、何を示唆していますか。

(A) 研修資料が改善される必要があると考えている。
(B) そのプロジェクトで従業員を手伝った。
(C) ある仕事に感銘を受けている。
(D) 幾つかの間違いについては心配していない。

解説 話し手は、改装の設計を委託した建築事務所について、❷「彼らは2つの美しい新オフィスビルを設計しただけでなく、われわれが仕事の休憩時間に自然を楽しむ機会をもっと多く持てるよう、遊歩道の延長もした」と彼らの仕事の成果に触れた後、下線部の「そして、それは彼らの初めてのプロジェクトだった」を続けている。よって、女性は建築事務所の仕事に感銘を受けていると分かる。

12. 正解 **(D)**

訳 次に何が起こると考えられますか。

(A) 見学の予定が立てられる。
(B) 記入用紙が配布される。
(C) 軽食が提供される。
(D) ゲスト講演者が話す。

解説 話し手は❸「主任建築士であるSusan Hernandezから話を伺いましょう。彼女はこの改装について、さらに私たちに話してくれる」と述べている。よって、次にHernandezさんがゲストとして話すことが分かる。

Directionsの訳

パート4

指示：1人の話し手によるトークを聞きます。各トークの内容に関する3つの設問に答えるよう求められます。それぞれの設問について最も適切な答えを選び、解答用紙の (A)、(B)、(C)、または (D) にマークしてください。トークは問題用紙には印刷されておらず、1度だけ放送されます。

Part 5 短文穴埋め問題

4つの選択肢の中から最も適切なものを選び、不完全な文を完成させる問題です。実際のテストでは30問出題されます。

READING TEST

In the Reading test, you will read a variety of texts and answer several different types of reading comprehension questions. The entire Reading test will last 75 minutes. There are three parts, and directions are given for each part. You are encouraged to answer as many questions as possible within the time allowed.

You must mark your answers on the separate answer sheet. Do not write your answers in your test book.

PART 5

Directions: A word or phrase is missing in each of the sentences below. Four answer choices are given below each sentence. Select the best answer to complete the sentence. Then mark the letter (A), (B), (C), or (D) on your answer sheet.

サンプル問題

13. Before ------- with the recruiter, applicants should sign in at the personnel department's reception desk.

   (A) meets
   (B) meeting
   (C) to meet
   (D) was met

14. Stefano Linen Company suggests requesting a small fabric ------- before placing your final order.

   (A) bonus
   (B) sample
   (C) feature
   (D) model

13. 正解 (B)

訳 採用担当者と会う前に、応募者の方々は人事部の受付で署名して到着を記録してください。

(A) 動詞の三人称単数現在形
(B) 動名詞
(C) to不定詞
(D) 受動態の過去形

解説 選択肢は全て動詞meet「会う」の変化した形。文頭からカンマまでの部分に主語と動詞がないため、Beforeは前置詞と考えられる。前置詞に続く空所には名詞の働きをする語句が入るので、動名詞の (B) meeting が適切である。sign in「署名して到着を記録する」。

14. 正解 (B)

訳 Stefanoリネン社は、お客さまが最終的な注文をなさる前に、小さな布地見本をご要望になることをお勧めしています。

(A) 特別手当
(B) 見本
(C) 特徴
(D) 模型

解説 選択肢は全て名詞。空所の後ろは「お客さまが最終的な注文をする前に」という意味。(B) sample「見本」を空所に入れるとsmall fabric sample「小さな布地見本」となり、注文前に要望するものとして適切で、意味が通る。

Directionsの訳

リーディングテスト

リーディングテストでは、さまざまな文章を読んで、読解力を測る何種類かの問題に答えます。リーディングテストは全体で75分間です。3つのパートがあり、各パートにおいて指示が与えられます。制限時間内に、できるだけ多くの設問に答えてください。

答えは、別紙の解答用紙にマークしてください。問題用紙に答えを書き込んではいけません。

パート5

指示：以下の各文において語や句が抜けています。各文の下には選択肢が4つ与えられています。文を完成させるのに最も適切な答えを選びます。そして解答用紙の (A)、(B)、(C)、または (D) にマークしてください。

4つの選択肢の中から最も適切なものを選び、不完全な文書を完成させる問題です。実際のテストでは16問出題されます。

PART 6

Directions: Read the texts that follow. A word, phrase, or sentence is missing in parts of each text. Four answer choices for each question are given below the text. Select the best answer to complete the text. Then mark the letter (A), (B), (C), or (D) on your answer sheet.

サンプル問題

Questions 15-18 refer to the following article.

❶ SAN DIEGO (May 5)—Matino Industries has just bolstered its image with environmentally conscious customers thanks to its ------- to reduce its use of nonrenewable energy to less
15.
than 20 percent within five years. -------. Best practices guidelines are already being revised
16.
------- powering down and disconnecting equipment when not in use. In addition, solar-panel
17.
arrays are slated for installation on-site as early as next year. When weather ------- are clear,
18.
these panels will offset Matino's reliance on the power grid, as they already do for a growing list of companies.

＊❶は解説の中で説明している文書中の段落番号等を示しています。問題用紙には印刷されていません。

15. (A) product
    (B) commitment
    (C) contest
    (D) workforce

16. (A) Discounts on all its products have increased Matino's customer base.
    (B) Management predicts that the takeover will result in a net financial gain.
    (C) To achieve this goal, the company will begin by improving its energy efficiency.
    (D) The initial step will involve redesigning the company's logo and slogans.

17. (A) been encouraging
    (B) have encouraged
    (C) encourages
    (D) to encourage

18. (A) conditions
    (B) instructions
    (C) views
    (D) reports

問題15-18は次の記事に関するものです。

サンディエゴ（5月5日）——Matino 産業社は、同社の再生不能エネルギーの使用を5年以内に20パーセント未満に削減するという公約のおかげで、環境意識の高い顧客にとっての同社のイメージを強化したところである。*この目標を達成するために同社は、自社のエネルギー効率を改善することから始める予定だ。機器を使用していないときには電源を落として接続を切ることを推奨するために、最良実践ガイドラインがすでに改定されているところである。さらに、早くも来年には、ソーラーパネルの列が構内に設置される予定である。天候条件が晴れのときには、これらのパネルが、増え続ける多くの企業に対してすでにそうしているように、Matino 社の送電網依存を弱めることになる。

*問題16の挿入文の訳

15. 正解 **(B)**

訳
(A) 製品
(B) 公約
(C) 競争
(D) 全従業員

解説 ❶の1〜3行目は「Matino 産業社は、同社の-------のおかげで、同社のイメージを強化したところだ」というのが、文の中心の意味。空所の後ろの「同社の再生不能エネルギーの使用を5年以内に20パーセント未満に削減すること」は、空所に入る名詞の内容を示していると考えられるので、文意から(B) commitment「公約」が適切。

16. 正解 **(C)**

訳
(A) 全ての自社製品に対する割引が、Matino 社の顧客基盤を拡大してきた。
(B) 経営陣は、その企業買収は財務上の純利益をもたらすと予測している。
(C) この目標を達成するために同社は、自社のエネルギー効率を改善することから始める予定だ。
(D) 第1段階には、会社のロゴとスローガンを作り直すことが含まれる予定だ。

解説 空所の前の文では、Matino 産業社が同社の再生不能エネルギーの使用を5年以内に20パーセント未満に削減することが述べられている。この内容をthis goalで受けて、目標達成のために同社がこれから取り組むことを挙げている(C)が流れとして適切。

17. 正解 **(D)**

訳
(A) 〈be動詞の過去分詞＋現在分詞〉
(B) 現在完了形
(C) 動詞の三人称単数現在形
(D) to不定詞

解説 選択肢は全て動詞encourage「〜を推奨する」が変化した形。空所の前に〈主語＋動詞〉の形があり、andやorなどの接続詞もないことから、空所に動詞は入らない。空所には、to不定詞の(D) to encourageが適切。

18. 正解 **(A)**

訳
(A) 条件
(B) 指示
(C) 見解
(D) 報道

解説 空所を含む文の、文頭からカンマまでは「天候-------が晴れのときには」という意味。these panels以降では、その際にソーラーパネルがもたらす効果について述べられている。「天候条件が晴れのときには」とすると意味が通るため、(A) conditions「条件」が適切。

Directionsの訳

パート6

指示：以下の文書を読んでください。各文書の中で語や句、または文が部分的に抜けています。文書の下には各設問の選択肢が4つ与えられています。文書を完成させるのに最も適切な答えを選びます。そして解答用紙の (A)、(B)、(C)、または (D) にマークしてください。

Part 7 読解問題

いろいろな形式の、1つもしくは複数の文書に関する問題が出題されます。設問と4つの選択肢を読み、その中から最も適切なものを選ぶ問題です。実際のテストでは1つの文書に関する問題が29問、複数の文書に関する問題が25問出題されます。

PART 7

Directions: In this part you will read a selection of texts, such as magazine and newspaper articles, e-mails, and instant messages. Each text or set of texts is followed by several questions. Select the best answer for each question and mark the letter (A), (B), (C), or (D) on your answer sheet.

サンプル問題

Questions 19-20 refer to the following text-message chain.

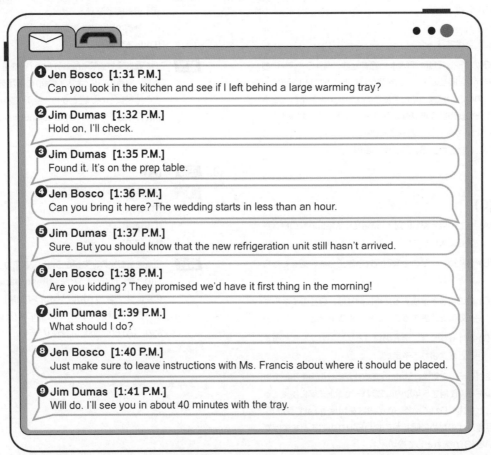

❶ **Jen Bosco** [1:31 P.M.]
Can you look in the kitchen and see if I left behind a large warming tray?

❷ **Jim Dumas** [1:32 P.M.]
Hold on, I'll check.

❸ **Jim Dumas** [1:35 P.M.]
Found it. It's on the prep table.

❹ **Jen Bosco** [1:36 P.M.]
Can you bring it here? The wedding starts in less than an hour.

❺ **Jim Dumas** [1:37 P.M.]
Sure. But you should know that the new refrigeration unit still hasn't arrived.

❻ **Jen Bosco** [1:38 P.M.]
Are you kidding? They promised we'd have it first thing in the morning!

❼ **Jim Dumas** [1:39 P.M.]
What should I do?

❽ **Jen Bosco** [1:40 P.M.]
Just make sure to leave instructions with Ms. Francis about where it should be placed.

❾ **Jim Dumas** [1:41 P.M.]
Will do. I'll see you in about 40 minutes with the tray.

---

19. For whom do the writers most likely work?

(A) A catering company
(B) A home-improvement store
(C) A kitchen-design company
(D) An appliance manufacturer

20. At 1:38 P.M., what does Ms. Bosco most likely mean when she writes, "Are you kidding"?

(A) She thinks Mr. Dumas is exaggerating.
(B) She knew she would have to wait a long time.
(C) She expects the refrigeration unit to arrive soon.
(D) She is upset that a delivery has not been made.

解答・解説

問題19-20は次のテキストメッセージのやり取りに関するものです。

Jen Bosco [午後 1 時 31 分]
調理場の中をのぞいて、私が大きな保温トレーを置き忘れたかどうかを確かめてくれるかしら。

Jim Dumas [午後 1 時 32 分]
待ってて、確認するよ。

Jim Dumas [午後 1 時 35 分]
見つけた。調理台の上にあるよ。

Jen Bosco [午後 1 時 36 分]
それをここに持ってきてくれる？ 結婚式が 1 時間足らずで始まるの。

Jim Dumas [午後 1 時 37 分]
もちろん。でも、新しい冷蔵装置がまだ届いていないことを知っておいた方がいいよ。

Jen Bosco [午後 1 時 38 分]
冗談でしょう？ 朝一番には私たちにそれを届けてくれると、彼らは約束したのよ。

Jim Dumas [午後 1 時 39 分]
僕はどうしたらいい？

Jen Bosco [午後 1 時 40 分]
とにかく、どこにそれを置けばいいか、Francis さんに必ず指示を残しておいて。

Jim Dumas [午後 1 時 41 分]
そうするよ。約 40 分後にトレーを持って君に会うね。

---

19. 正解 **(A)**

訳 書き手たちはどこに勤めていると考えられますか。

(A) ケータリング会社
(B) ホームセンター
(C) キッチン設計会社
(D) 電化製品メーカー

解説 ❶と❷のやり取りから、書き手たちの職場には調理場があることが分かる。また❹で、Bosco さんが Dumas さんに保温トレーを結婚式の場に持ってくるよう伝えていることから、書き手たちは料理を作り配達を行っていると考えられる。よって、(A)が適切。

20. 正解 **(D)**

訳 午後 1 時 38 分に Bosco さんは、"Are you kidding" という発言で、何を意味していると考えられますか。

(A) Dumas さんが誇張していると思っている。
(B) 長い間待たなくてはならないことを知っていた。
(C) 冷蔵装置がもうすぐ届くだろうと見込んでいる。
(D) 配達が行われていないことに動揺している。

解説 Dumas さんが❺「新しい冷蔵装置がまだ届いていないことを知っておいた方がいい」と伝えたのに対して、Bosco さんは「冗談でしょう？」と驚きを示し、「朝一番には私たちにそれを届けてくれると、彼らは約束した」と続けている。つまり、Bosco さんは配達が約束通りに行われていないことに動揺していると考えられる。

***Directions*の訳**

パート 7

指示：このパートでは、雑誌や新聞の記事、Eメールやインスタントメッセージなどのさまざまな文書を読みます。1 つの文書または複数の文書のセットにはそれぞれ、幾つかの設問が続いています。各設問について最も適切な答えを選び、解答用紙の (A)、(B)、(C)、または (D) にマークしてください。

Questions 21-24 refer to the following Web page.

---

http://straubuniversityschoolofmedicine.edu/vendors/rfp0023

❶ Straub University School of Medicine is currently seeking a vendor to provide surgical gloves, laboratory coats, and protective goggles. The university requires high-quality, hospital-grade equipment for its students and faculty and is especially interested in providers who currently work with local hospitals and clinics.

❷ You can download the complete Request for Proposal (RFP) instructions from our Web site. Below is a summary of the proposal requirements. — [1] —.

• A standard proposal form, which can be downloaded from our Web site
• A general description of the provider and its experience in the industry
• Product descriptions with a complete list of specifications and prices
• Contact information of three current or recent clients who are able to speak to the quality of the provider's products or services

❸ If you have any questions about the RFP, please submit them in writing to queries@straub.edu by July 20. — [2] —. Responses to questions will be posted publicly on the Straub University School of Medicine's Web page on August 4.

❹ Proposals must be received no later than August 15. — [3] —. All submissions will be thoroughly reviewed, and the winning proposal will be announced on September 10. A contract will be finalized with the strongest candidate that same month, and the agreement will take effect starting October 1. — [4] —.

---

21. Who are the instructions intended for?

(A) Sellers of medical supplies
(B) Applicants for hospital jobs
(C) Hospital administrators
(D) Medical students

22. What are candidates required to submit?

(A) Questions about the proposal
(B) Professional references
(C) An application fee
(D) Product samples

23. When will candidates learn if they have been selected?

(A) In July
(B) In August
(C) In September
(D) In October

24. In which of the positions marked [1], [2], [3], and [4] does the following sentence best belong?

"All documentation must arrive by this date in a sealed envelope addressed to the School of Medicine's Purchasing Department."

(A) [1]
(B) [2]
(C) [3]
(D) [4]

解答・解説

問題21-24は次のウェブページに関するものです。

http://straubuniversityschoolofmedicine.edu/vendors/rfp0023

Straub 大学医学部は現在、手術用手袋、白衣、保護用ゴーグルを供給してくれる業者を求めています。本学は、学生と教授陣向けの、高品質で病院仕様の備品を必要としており、特に、地元の病院や診療所と現在取引をしている販売会社に関心があります。

本学のウェブサイトから、提案依頼書（RFP）の指示一式をダウンロードすることができます。以下は提案要件の概略です。

・定型の提案書式。本学のウェブサイトからダウンロード可能
・販売会社の概要および業界における同社の経験
・仕様および価格の全一覧を付した、製品の説明
・販売会社の製品あるいはサービスの質について述べることのできる、現在もしくは最近の顧客 3 社の連絡先

RFP について何かご質問がございましたら、それらを文書で 7 月 20 日までに queries@straub.edu 宛てにご提出ください。ご質問に対する回答は、8 月 4 日に Straub 大学医学部のウェブページ上で公開されます。

提案書は 8 月 15 日必着です。*全ての書類は、封書でこの日付までに医学部の購買部宛てに到着しなければなりません。全ての提出物は入念に検討され、採用された提案書は 9 月 10 日に発表されます。契約書は最有力候補業者とその同月に最終的な形にされ、契約は10 月 1 日より発効します。

*問題 24 の挿入文の訳

---

21. 正解 **(A)**

訳 この指示は誰に向けられていますか。

(A) 医療用品の販売会社
(B) 病院の職への応募者
(C) 病院の管理者
(D) 医学生

解説 ❶1〜2行目に「Straub 大学医学部は現在、手術用手袋、白衣、保護用ゴーグルを供給する業者を求めている」とあり、❷では提案要件の概略について、❹では提出期日や選考過程などについて説明されている。よって、この指示は医療用品の販売会社に向けたものだと分かる。

22. 正解 **(B)**

訳 候補者は何を提出することを求められていますか。

(A) 提案書に関する質問
(B) 取引上の照会先
(C) 申込金
(D) 製品の見本

解説 ❷で提案要件の概略として挙げられている箇条書きの 4点目に、「販売会社の製品あるいはサービスの質について述べることのできる、現在もしくは最近の顧客 3 社の連絡先」とある。

23. 正解 **(C)**

訳 候補者はいつ、自分が選出されたかどうかを知りますか。

(A) 7 月
(B) 8 月
(C) 9 月
(D) 10 月

解説 ❹2行目に、the winning proposal will be announced on September 10「採用された提案書は 9 月 10 日に発表される」とある。

24. 正解 **(C)**

訳 [1]、[2]、[3]、[4]と記載された箇所のうち、次の文が入るのに最もふさわしいのはどれですか。

「全ての書類は、封書でこの日付までに医学部の購買部宛てに到着しなければなりません」

(A) [1]
(B) [2]
(C) [3]
(D) [4]

解説 挿入文は書類の提出方法と宛先を伝えている。(C) [3]に入れると、挿入文中のthis date「この日付」が❹1行目のAugust 15 を指し、提案書の提出期日に続けて提出方法と宛先を伝える自然な流れとなる。

Questions 25-29 refer to the following article, e-mail, and Web page.

❶ (November 6)—The Rudi's store at 47 Kask Highway in Glencoe Park will shut its doors next Saturday, adding another empty building to the local landscape. The shutdown is one of a rash of store closings in the greater Billington area and is a result of two major forces. First, Rudi's has changed its business plan, relying increasingly on online sales. Second, much of the traffic on Kask Highway has been rerouted to the recently completed bypass, resulting in fewer potential customers passing through Billington.

❷ Other Rudi's closings over the past two years include the store at 38 Quail Hill Road, the store at 21 Lowell Boulevard, and the downtown megastore at 59 Claremont Street on the banks of the Corks River. A Rudi's spokesperson stated that no further closures are expected.

To:	nathanpaugh@ioscodesign.com
From:	ccovey@tedesintl.com
Subject:	Tedes Building
Date:	January 25

Dear Mr. Paugh,

❶ The preliminary drawings you sent are right on target. I think your proposal to demolish most of the east wall and install floor-to-ceiling windows is terrific. If we were to leave everything as it now is, we would end up with a rather somber interior.

❷ Let's keep the current stairway where it is so that people can walk straight through the entrance and up to the second floor meeting rooms. We can configure the remaining area in the center of the first floor as open work space, with the executive offices off to the left side against the west wall. Including a large picture window at the entrance to the fitness center in the back of the first floor space is also a good idea.

❸ Please move forward with drawing up draft plans for our board's approval.

Thank you,

Cynthia Covey

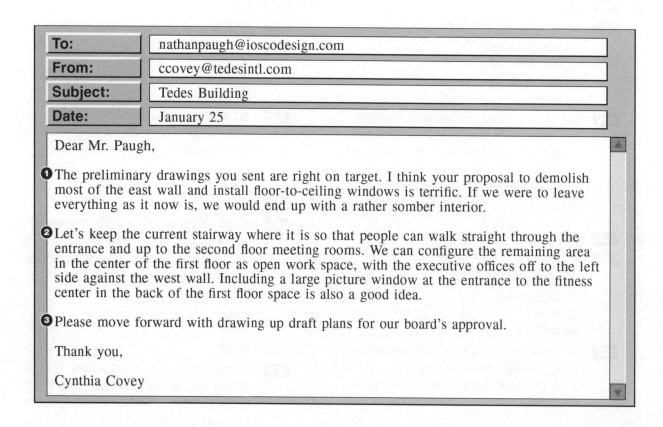

http://www.buildingmonthly.com/readersreviews

| HOME | LATEST ISSUE | **READERS' REVIEWS** | ADVERTISERS |

The new Tedes corporate building
Posted by Monty K.

❶ Tedes International has opened its corporate headquarters in a former Rudi's megastore building. In an area with many vacated retail buildings, one is now a workplace for over 400 Tedes employees. Corporations looking for prime real estate should take notice.

❷ The interior design of the Tedes Building is notable for its mixed use of open and closed space. The entrance is open and inviting and leads to a wide staircase up to the second floor, which houses offices for upper management. Large windows installed as one of the exterior walls create a bright atmosphere in the open work space and nearby meeting rooms, while boats glide by on the river right in front of them. On my visit, several employees were exercising on fitness bikes in full view at the rear of the first-floor space.

25. What is the purpose of the article?

(A) To notify readers of recent job openings
(B) To publicize an online sale
(C) To report on a store closing
(D) To alert motorists to changing traffic patterns

26. Who most likely is Mr. Paugh?

(A) An artist
(B) An architect
(C) A real estate agent
(D) A reporter

27. Which former Rudi's location did Tedes International choose for its headquarters?

(A) 47 Kask Highway
(B) 38 Quail Hill Road
(C) 21 Lowell Boulevard
(D) 59 Claremont Street

28. What aspect of the design suggested by Ms. Covey was ultimately rejected?

(A) The replacement of a wall with windows
(B) The layout of the entrance
(C) The inclusion of a fitness center
(D) The location of the offices

29. What is implied by the reviewer?

(A) Tedes International is planning to expand.
(B) Tedes International wants to sell its property.
(C) Vacant buildings have great potential.
(D) Local businesses may experience reduced profits.

問題25-29は次の記事、Eメール、ウェブページに関するものです。

1. 記事

（11月6日）――グレンコーパークのカスク街道47番地にあるRudi's社の店舗は、次の土曜日に扉を閉ざし、その地域の風景にもう1棟空きビルを加えることになる。この閉店は、ビリントン広域圏で頻発する店舗の閉鎖の1つであり、2つの大きな影響力によるものである。第1に、Rudi's社が事業計画を変更し、オンライン販売に一層依存するようになったこと。第2に、カスク街道の交通の大部分が、最近完成した迂回路の方へ流れ、ビリントンを通る潜在顧客が減少する結果となったことだ。

過去2年間のRudi's社の他の閉店には、クウェイルヒル通り38番地の店舗、ローウェル大通り21番地の店舗、そしてコークス川岸のクレアモント通り59番地にあった中心街の超大型店舗が含まれる。Rudi's社の広報担当者は、これ以上の閉店は一切予定されていないと明言した。

2. Eメール

受信者：nathanpaugh@ioscodesign.com
送信者：ccovey@tedesintl.com
件名：　Tedesビル
日付：　1月25日

Paugh様

お送りくださった仮の図面は、まさに期待通りのものです。東側の壁の大半を取り壊し、床から天井までの窓を設置するという貴殿のご提案は素晴らしいと思います。もし何もかも現状のままにしておいたとしたら、最終的にかなり陰気な内装になってしまうでしょう。

今の階段は、そのままの場所で残しましょう。そうすれば人々が入り口をまっすぐ通り抜け、2階の会議室に歩いて上がっていけます。1階の中央にある残りの区域は開放的な作業スペースとし、重役の執務室を左側へ、西の壁際に配置することができます。1階スペースの奥にあるフィットネスセンターへの入り口に大きな一枚ガラスの窓を入れることも良いアイデアです。

当社役員会の承認に向けて、設計図の草案の作成を進めてください。

よろしくお願いいたします。

Cynthia Covey

3. ウェブページ

http://www.buildingmonthly.com/readersreviews

| ホーム | 最新号 | 読者レビュー | 広告主 |

Tedes社の新しいビル
Monty K. 投稿

Tedesインターナショナル社は、かつてRudi's社の超大型店舗だった建物に本社を開設した。空き家となった小売店のビルが多数ある地域において、1棟は今や400名超のTedes社の従業員の職場である。優良な不動産を求めている企業は注目すべきである。

Tedesビルの内部設計は、開放的スペースと閉鎖的スペースを取り混ぜて使用していることで注目に値する。入り口は広々として、いざなうようであり、2階に至る広い階段に通じている。2階には、経営上層部のための執務室が入っている。外壁の一部として設置された大型の窓は、開放的な作業スペースと近くの会議室に明るい雰囲気を作り出し、他方で、すぐ目の前にある川をボートが滑るように進む。私の訪問時には、数名の従業員が1階スペースの奥で、よく見える所でフィットネスバイクで運動をしていた。

25. 正解 **(C)**

訳 記事の目的は何ですか。

(A) 読者に最近の求人を知らせること。
(B) オンラインのセールを宣伝すること。
(C) 店舗の閉鎖を報道すること。
(D) 車を運転する人に、交通パターンの変化について注意を喚起すること。

解説 **1**の記事の❶1〜3行目に、「グレンコーパークのカスク街道47番地にあるRudi's社の店舗は、次の土曜日に扉を閉ざす」とあり、その後も閉店の要因などが述べられている。よって、記事の目的はRudi's社の店舗の閉鎖を報道することだと分かる。

26. 正解 **(B)**

訳 Paughさんとは誰だと考えられますか。

(A) 芸術家
(B) 建築家
(C) 不動産仲介人
(D) 記者

解説 Paughさんは**2**のEメールの受信者。Eメールの本文では、❶1行目で「お送りくださった仮の図面は、まさに期待通りのものだ」と伝えられ、建物の設計についての話が続いている。さらに、❸で「設計図の草案の作成を進めてほしい」と依頼を受けていることから、Paughさんは建築家と考えられる。

27. 正解 **(D)**

訳 Tedesインターナショナル社は、かつてのRudi's社のどの場所を本社に選びましたか。

(A) カスク街道47番地
(B) クウェイルヒル通り38番地
(C) ローウェル大通り21番地
(D) クレアモント通り59番地

解説 **3**のウェブページの❶1〜2行目に、「Tedesインターナショナル社は、かつてRudi's社の超大型店舗だった建物に本社を開設した」とある。**1**の記事の❷3〜5行目に、閉店したRudi's社の店舗の1つとして、「コークス川岸のクレアモント通り59番地にあった中心街の超大型店舗」が挙げられているので、(D)が正解。

28. 正解 **(D)**

訳 Coveyさんによって示された設計のどの点が、最終的に不採用とされましたか。

(A) 壁を窓で置き換えること
(B) 入り口の配置
(C) フィットネスセンターを含めること
(D) 執務室の位置

解説 Coveyさんは**2**のEメールの送信者。仮の図面を作ったPaughさんに対して、❷2〜4行目で「1階の中央にある残りの区域は開放的な作業スペースとし、重役の執務室を左側へ、西の壁際に配置することができる」と述べている。一方、完成したビルの読者レビューを載せた**3**のウェブページには、❷2〜3行目に「入り口は広々として、いざなうようであり、2階に至る広い階段に通じている。2階には、経営上層部のための執務室が入っている」とあることから、重役の執務室はCoveyさんが提案した1階ではなく、2階に配置されたと分かる。

29. 正解 **(C)**

訳 レビュー投稿者によって何が示唆されていますか。

(A) Tedesインターナショナル社は拡大する予定である。
(B) Tedesインターナショナル社は同社の不動産を売却したいと思っている。
(C) 空きビルは大きな可能性を持っている。
(D) 地元の企業は減益を経験するかもしれない。

解説 **3**のウェブページの読者レビューの❶1〜3行目で、Tedesインターナショナル社がかつてRudi's社の超大型店舗だった建物に本社を開設したことで、空きビル1棟が今や多数の従業員の職場へと変化したことが述べられている。続けて「優良な不動産を求めている企業は注目すべきだ」とあることから、レビュー投稿者は空きビルに大きな可能性があることを示唆していると考えられる。

採点・結果について

TOEIC® Listening & Reading Test のテスト結果は合格・不合格ではなく、リスニングセクション 5〜495 点、リーディングセクション 5〜495 点、トータル 10〜990 点のスコアで、5 点刻みで表示されます。このスコアは、常に評価基準を一定に保つために統計処理が行われ、英語能力に変化がない限りスコアも一定に保たれる点が大きな特長です。

テスト結果は Official Score Certificate（公式認定証）として、試験日から 30 日以内に発送されます。また、インターネットからお申し込みいただく際、「テスト結果のインターネット表示」で「利用する」を選択すると、試験日から 17 日後にインターネットでスコアを確認することが可能です。（日米の祝日の影響により、遅れる場合がございます。）

Official Score Certificate（公式認定証）のサンプル

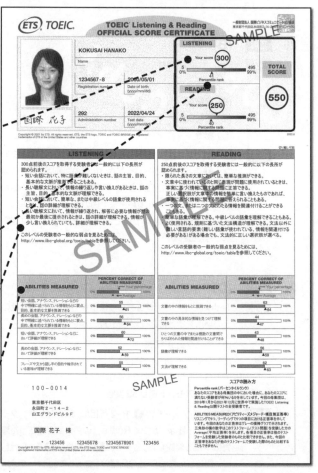

Your Score（スコア）:
今回取得したリスニング、リーディングの各セクションスコアです。右側にトータルスコアが記載されます。

Percentile Rank（パーセンタイルランク）:
あなたが取得したスコアに満たない受験者が全体でどのくらいを占めているかをパーセンテージで示しています。例えば、リスニングでスコア 300 点、パーセンタイルランクが 41% という場合には、リスニングスコア 300 点未満の受験者が全体の 41% いることを示します。つまり、リスニングスコア 300 点を取得した受験者は上位 59% に位置することになります。

Score Descriptors（スコアディスクリプターズ）:
レベル別評価です。今回取得したスコアをもとに、あなたの英語運用能力上の長所が書かれています。

Abilities Measured（アビリティーズメジャード）:
項目別正答率です。リスニング、リーディングの 5 つの項目における正答率を示しています。

TOEIC® Listening & Reading 公開テストのお申し込み

IIBC公式サイト **https://www.iibc-global.org** にてテスト日程、申込方法、注意事項をご確認の上、申込受付期間内にお申し込みください。試験の実施方法などに変更があった場合には IIBC 公式サイト等でご案内いたします。

お問い合わせ

一般財団法人 国際ビジネスコミュニケーション協会　IIBC 試験運営センター
〒 100-0014　東京都千代田区永田町 2-14-2　山王グランドビル
TEL：03-5521-6033（土・日・祝日・年末年始を除く 10:00 〜 17:00）

TEST 1

CD 1 11-92

LISTENING TEST　·························· p.30

READING TEST　·························· p.42

＊解答用紙は本誌 p.112 の後ろに綴じ込まれています。

実際のテストでは問題用紙の裏側に、以下のようなテスト全体についての指示が印刷されています。
この指示を念頭においてテストに取り組みましょう。

General Directions

This test is designed to measure your English language ability. The test is divided into two sections: Listening and Reading.

You must mark all of your answers on the separate answer sheet. For each question, you should select the best answer from the answer choices given. Then, on your answer sheet, you should find the number of the question and fill in the space that corresponds to the letter of the answer that you have selected. If you decide to change an answer, completely erase your old answer and then mark your new answer.

訳　　　　　　　　　　**全体についての指示**

このテストはあなたの英語言語能力を測定するよう設計されています。テストはリスニングとリーディングという 2 つのセクションに分けられています。

答えは全て別紙の解答用紙にマークしてください。それぞれの設問について、与えられた選択肢から最も適切な答えを選びます。そして解答用紙の該当する問題番号に、選択した答えを塗りつぶしてください。答えを修正する場合は、元の答えを完全に消してから新しい答えをマークしてください。

LISTENING TEST

In the Listening test, you will be asked to demonstrate how well you understand spoken English. The entire Listening test will last approximately 45 minutes. There are four parts, and directions are given for each part. You must mark your answers on the separate answer sheet. Do not write your answers in your test book.

PART 1

Directions: For each question in this part, you will hear four statements about a picture in your test book. When you hear the statements, you must select the one statement that best describes what you see in the picture. Then find the number of the question on your answer sheet and mark your answer. The statements will not be printed in your test book and will be spoken only one time.

Statement (C), "They're sitting at a table," is the best description of the picture, so you should select answer (C) and mark it on your answer sheet.

1.

2.

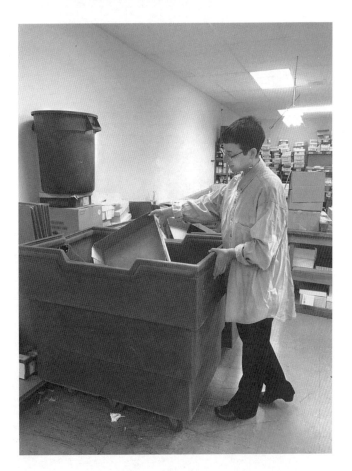

GO ON TO THE NEXT PAGE

3.

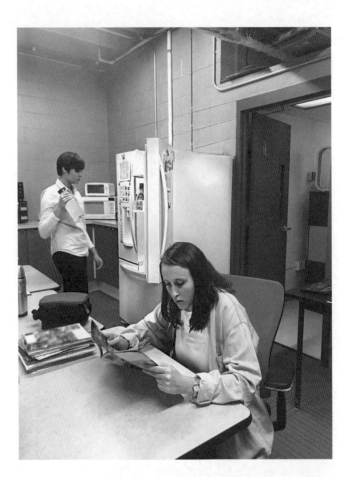

4.

5.

6.

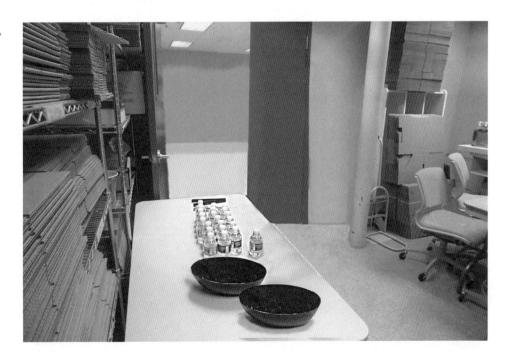

GO ON TO THE NEXT PAGE ➡

PART 2

Directions: You will hear a question or statement and three responses spoken in English. They will not be printed in your test book and will be spoken only one time. Select the best response to the question or statement and mark the letter (A), (B), or (C) on your answer sheet.

7. Mark your answer on your answer sheet.

8. Mark your answer on your answer sheet.

9. Mark your answer on your answer sheet.

10. Mark your answer on your answer sheet.

11. Mark your answer on your answer sheet.

12. Mark your answer on your answer sheet.

13. Mark your answer on your answer sheet.

14. Mark your answer on your answer sheet.

15. Mark your answer on your answer sheet.

16. Mark your answer on your answer sheet.

17. Mark your answer on your answer sheet.

18. Mark your answer on your answer sheet.

19. Mark your answer on your answer sheet.

20. Mark your answer on your answer sheet.

21. Mark your answer on your answer sheet.

22. Mark your answer on your answer sheet.

23. Mark your answer on your answer sheet.

24. Mark your answer on your answer sheet.

25. Mark your answer on your answer sheet.

26. Mark your answer on your answer sheet.

27. Mark your answer on your answer sheet.

28. Mark your answer on your answer sheet.

29. Mark your answer on your answer sheet.

30. Mark your answer on your answer sheet.

31. Mark your answer on your answer sheet.

PART 3

Directions: You will hear some conversations between two or more people. You will be asked to answer three questions about what the speakers say in each conversation. Select the best response to each question and mark the letter (A), (B), (C), or (D) on your answer sheet. The conversations will not be printed in your test book and will be spoken only one time.

32. Why is the woman planning to take Friday off?
(A) She has a doctor's appointment.
(B) She has family visiting from out of town.
(C) She will be attending a workshop.
(D) She will have work done at her house.

33. What does the man remind the woman about?
(A) A client meeting
(B) A product launch
(C) A project deadline
(D) A building inspection

34. What does the woman ask the man to do?
(A) Prepare some instructions
(B) E-mail some documents
(C) Set up a videoconference call
(D) Help another colleague

35. What does the man say will take place in London?
(A) An industry trade show
(B) A university graduation
(C) A job interview
(D) An international music festival

36. Who most likely is the woman?
(A) A newsstand vendor
(B) A security guard
(C) A baggage handler
(D) A ticket agent

37. Why does the woman correct the man?
(A) He paid an incorrect amount.
(B) He mispronounced a name.
(C) He was about to go in the wrong direction.
(D) He misunderstood a travel requirement.

38. What most likely is the man's job?
(A) Web site designer
(B) Interior decorator
(C) Accountant
(D) Journalist

39. What does the man ask the woman to do?
(A) Authorize a purchase
(B) Take some photographs
(C) Extend a deadline
(D) Send some information

40. What good news does the man give the woman?
(A) A hiring campaign was successful.
(B) Revisions are included in a contract.
(C) A project is being considered for an award.
(D) Employees will receive a cash bonus.

41. Who most likely are the speakers?
(A) Postal workers
(B) Warehouse managers
(C) Restaurant servers
(D) Bank tellers

42. What does the man say he will be doing this week?
(A) Taking inventory
(B) Repairing a vehicle
(C) Training a new employee
(D) Responding to customer complaints

43. What does the woman mean when she says, "my previous job was in landscaping"?
(A) She does not know the answer to a question.
(B) She is accustomed to working outside.
(C) She knows how to care for plants.
(D) She is ready to switch careers.

GO ON TO THE NEXT PAGE

44. What does the factory produce?

(A) Cars
(B) Airplanes
(C) Appliances
(D) Computers

45. Why has a shipment been delayed?

(A) Some roads are under construction.
(B) The weather has been poor.
(C) A computer system is undergoing maintenance.
(D) A company needs more drivers.

46. What will the man most likely do next?

(A) Rent a truck
(B) Pay an express delivery fee
(C) Contact a supplier
(D) Ask to extend a deadline

47. What did the woman's company recently do for Gilford Solutions?

(A) It cleaned some floors.
(B) It painted a building.
(C) It created some signs.
(D) It washed some windows.

48. Why is the man calling?

(A) To complain about the quality of some work
(B) To inquire about an additional service
(C) To reschedule a delivery time
(D) To request a discount on some products

49. What information does the woman say she needs?

(A) An address
(B) A phone number
(C) Some measurements
(D) Some dates

50. Why most likely are the women traveling?

(A) They are attending a family event.
(B) They are meeting with former classmates.
(C) They are on a business trip.
(D) They are on a vacation.

51. Why did the women receive a discount?

(A) They referred a friend.
(B) They are return customers.
(C) They applied a coupon.
(D) They booked in advance.

52. What does the man recommend?

(A) Taking some photos
(B) Using a different route
(C) Downloading a mobile app
(D) Stopping at a fuel station

53. Where do the speakers most likely work?

(A) At an amusement park
(B) At a children's bookstore
(C) At a dentist's office
(D) At a school

54. What does the man suggest doing?

(A) Changing the purpose of a room
(B) Providing a discount
(C) Assigning someone to clean a work space
(D) Booking a venue

55. What is the woman concerned about?

(A) How long some work will take
(B) How much a project might cost
(C) How many staff members are available
(D) How often inspections will be required

56. What is causing some traffic?

(A) A bus depot is being remodeled.
(B) A monument is being restored.
(C) A sports event is taking place.
(D) A holiday parade is being held.

57. What has the man been working on recently?

(A) Employee performance reviews
(B) A product redesign
(C) Staff training courses
(D) A department newsletter

58. Why does the woman say, "I've had this same problem before"?

(A) She wants a new assignment.
(B) She agrees with a manager's opinion.
(C) She is able to help the man.
(D) She is frustrated that her computer is old.

---

59. Where does the woman work?

(A) At a bank
(B) At a pharmacy
(C) At an auction house
(D) At a construction company

60. What does the man say he is doing in June?

(A) Starting a new business
(B) Exhibiting an art collection
(C) Beginning a certification course
(D) Moving to another country

61. What is the man surprised by?

(A) Some financial details
(B) Some government regulations
(C) The duration of a project
(D) The location of an office

Onion Prices	
$6	4 kilograms
$10	8 kilograms
$15	12 kilograms
$25	20 kilograms

62. Who most likely is the man?

(A) A food critic
(B) A chef
(C) A nutritionist
(D) An event planner

63. Look at the graphic. How much will the man pay on Wednesday?

(A) $6
(B) $10
(C) $15
(D) $25

64. What will the woman do before calling back?

(A) Write a review
(B) Advertise a job
(C) Check a quantity
(D) Reserve some rooms

TEST 1

GO ON TO THE NEXT PAGE

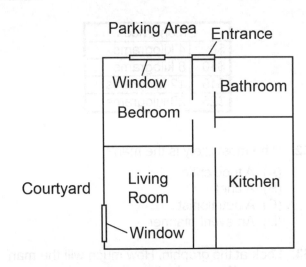

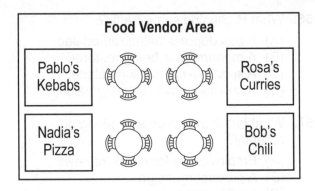

65. How did the woman hear about the apartment building?

(A) From an Internet advertisement
(B) From a television commercial
(C) From a billboard
(D) From a friend

66. Look at the graphic. Which room does the man refer to?

(A) The bedroom
(B) The bathroom
(C) The kitchen
(D) The living room

67. What will the woman most likely do next?

(A) Pay a deposit
(B) Fill out an application
(C) View a unit
(D) Measure some furniture

68. What event is the woman attending?

(A) A film festival
(B) A music festival
(C) A furniture show
(D) A car show

69. Look at the graphic. What kind of food does the man recommend?

(A) Kebabs
(B) Curries
(C) Pizza
(D) Chili

70. What does the man warn the woman about?

(A) She may have to wait.
(B) She will have to show her ticket.
(C) The prices are high.
(D) There is limited table space.

PART 4

Directions: You will hear some talks given by a single speaker. You will be asked to answer three questions about what the speaker says in each talk. Select the best response to each question and mark the letter (A), (B), (C), or (D) on your answer sheet. The talks will not be printed in your test book and will be spoken only one time.

71. What kind of event was held at the store last Saturday?

   (A) An end-of-season sale
   (B) A grand opening
   (C) A facility tour
   (D) A customer appreciation day

72. What does the store sell?

   (A) Plants
   (B) Clothing
   (C) Tea
   (D) Art supplies

73. What will the listeners receive?

   (A) A day off
   (B) A bonus
   (C) Free merchandise
   (D) Store discounts

74. Who is the speaker?

   (A) A hardware store clerk
   (B) A building inspector
   (C) A water service provider
   (D) A laboratory scientist

75. What is the speaker mainly discussing?

   (A) A maintenance concern
   (B) A city regulation
   (C) A price negotiation
   (D) A schedule delay

76. What does the speaker say he will send?

   (A) An article
   (B) A survey
   (C) A timeline
   (D) A report

77. What type of school is being advertised?

   (A) Cooking
   (B) Hospitality
   (C) Fashion design
   (D) Business management

78. According to the advertisement, what is guaranteed?

   (A) Small group classes
   (B) Flexible schedules
   (C) Job placement after graduation
   (D) Instruction by qualified teachers

79. What will happen on August 1?

   (A) A course will begin.
   (B) A payment will be due.
   (C) A course book will be available.
   (D) A special offer will expire.

80. What department does the speaker work in?

   (A) Human resources
   (B) Customer service
   (C) Research
   (D) Marketing

81. What does the speaker say he did yesterday?

   (A) He bought a gift.
   (B) He sent an invitation.
   (C) He contacted a caterer.
   (D) He spoke with a client.

82. What does the speaker imply when he says, "you've worked with her the most"?

   (A) The listener may be promoted.
   (B) A cost should be shared.
   (C) The listener should give a speech.
   (D) A staffing decision was unfair.

GO ON TO THE NEXT PAGE

83. According to the speaker, what problem is a company aware of?

    (A) An error in downloading
    (B) A delay in shipping
    (C) Some inaccurate instructions
    (D) Some damaged packaging

84. Why does the speaker direct the listeners to a Web site?

    (A) To submit a complaint
    (B) To read customer reviews
    (C) To enter a contest
    (D) To watch instructional videos

85. How can the listeners receive a discount?

    (A) By referring a friend
    (B) By posting a review
    (C) By purchasing many items
    (D) By paying in advance

___

86. What type of food is the speaker discussing?

    (A) Bread
    (B) Yogurt
    (C) Breakfast cereal
    (D) Fruit juice

87. What does the speaker imply when he says, "that remains a very popular brand"?

    (A) A new recipe has not affected sales.
    (B) A product package should not be changed.
    (C) The listeners should try a product.
    (D) A marketing campaign has been successful.

88. What does the speaker say he will do next?

    (A) Present some slides
    (B) Pass out some samples
    (C) Share a personal story
    (D) Invite a colleague to speak

89. Why did the speaker miss an episode last week?

    (A) She was on vacation.
    (B) She moved to a new city.
    (C) She attended a conference.
    (D) She had a project deadline.

90. Who is Isamu Sato?

    (A) A best-selling author
    (B) A university professor
    (C) A manager of an electronics store
    (D) An owner of a technology company

91. What does the speaker mean when she says, "we only have an hour"?

    (A) Not all questions will be answered.
    (B) A process is difficult to understand.
    (C) There is some confusion about a schedule.
    (D) A guest speaker has another appointment.

___

92. Why does the speaker congratulate Maria Ortiz?

    (A) She exceeded a sales goal.
    (B) She won an industry award.
    (C) She accepted a leadership role.
    (D) She recently wrote a book.

93. Where does the speaker work?

    (A) At a pharmaceutical company
    (B) At a publishing firm
    (C) At a film studio
    (D) At an employment agency

94. What will be announced at a press conference?

    (A) A business acquisition
    (B) A product release
    (C) A construction project
    (D) A charitable donation

Streki Tours
Palermo City Tour

Thursday, 23 November

Tour #: 1092

Bus #: 252

Group #: 4

Model	Number of Passengers	Flight Range
AT-01	2	5 kilometers
AT-02	1	12 kilometers
ZF-12	6	25 kilometers
PR-34	2	45 kilometers

TEST 1

98. Who most likely are the listeners?

(A) New employees at Nexflight Labs
(B) Board members for Nexflight Labs
(C) City council members at a public meeting
(D) Attendees at an industry conference

95. Why has a tour been delayed?

(A) A ticket reader is not working.
(B) A bus is being repaired.
(C) Some members of the group are late.
(D) Some bad weather is passing through.

96. What are the listeners asked to do?

(A) Show a confirmation e-mail
(B) Form a line
(C) Buy a ticket
(D) Choose a meal

97. Look at the graphic. Which number does the speaker refer to?

(A) 23
(B) 1092
(C) 252
(D) 4

99. What has the speaker's team been tasked with?

(A) Making a more lightweight vehicle
(B) Making a more comfortable vehicle
(C) Making a faster vehicle
(D) Making a quieter vehicle

100. Look at the graphic. According to the speaker, which model is Nexflight Labs most proud of?

(A) AT-01
(B) AT-02
(C) ZF-12
(D) PR-34

This is the end of the Listening test. Turn to Part 5 in your test book.

GO ON TO THE NEXT PAGE

READING TEST

In the Reading test, you will read a variety of texts and answer several different types of reading comprehension questions. The entire Reading test will last 75 minutes. There are three parts, and directions are given for each part. You are encouraged to answer as many questions as possible within the time allowed.

You must mark your answers on the separate answer sheet. Do not write your answers in your test book.

PART 5

Directions: A word or phrase is missing in each of the sentences below. Four answer choices are given below each sentence. Select the best answer to complete the sentence. Then mark the letter (A), (B), (C), or (D) on your answer sheet.

101. Please ------- your completed evaluation form on the table beside the door.

(A) write
(B) leave
(C) make
(D) consider

102. Arvid's latest game console, the Star 212, ------- resembles earlier models.

(A) closely
(B) closer
(C) closeness
(D) closest

103. Using the bank's app, customers can instantly pay bills through ------- transfer.

(A) various
(B) electronic
(C) patient
(D) eager

104. Remember to bring a laptop with you for today's software training ------- at the Alten Conference Center.

(A) meet
(B) met
(C) meets
(D) meeting

105. Pacetti Furnaces offers discounts on installations ------- the summer months.

(A) above
(B) during
(C) besides
(D) including

106. Agents from Research Excellence Ltd. will be touring ------- offices next week.

(A) us
(B) ourselves
(C) we
(D) our

107. When Mr. Awetimbi entered the conference room, he ------- that the audiovisual equipment had not been delivered.

(A) notices
(B) noticed
(C) noticing
(D) noticeable

108. Drivers must use parking area B while parking area A is undergoing -------.

(A) support
(B) traffic
(C) vehicles
(D) repairs

109. A newsletter is distributed to staff ------- to describe the company's accomplishments for that year.

(A) commonly
(B) broadly
(C) annually
(D) searchingly

110. Enable notifications and ------- updates by selecting your preferred device settings.
(A) automates
(B) automatically
(C) automation
(D) automatic

111. New employees of Lopez Construction must take several courses, ------- a power tool safety course.
(A) as if
(B) such as
(C) in case of
(D) even so

112. Some programmers remain at one company for several years, but ------- depart sooner for better-paying jobs at other firms.
(A) theirs
(B) either
(C) which
(D) many

113. According to *Travelers* magazine, people have grown increasingly interested in ------- their vacation time outdoors in recent years.
(A) visiting
(B) spending
(C) charging
(D) closing

114. After interviewing five candidates for the sales position, the manager ------- the most experienced one.
(A) choice
(B) chosen
(C) chose
(D) to choose

115. The City of Mayville's ------- job fair will feature representatives from a variety of local businesses.
(A) extreme
(B) specific
(C) upcoming
(D) prevailing

116. The Kopple Building was in very poor ------- before the renovation.
(A) condition
(B) conditioned
(C) conditioner
(D) conditional

117. ------- Mr. Khat has just been promoted to management, we now have an open sales-associate position.
(A) Upon
(B) Until
(C) Since
(D) Despite

118. Don's Café uses only local fruits and vegetables in its ------- prepared dishes.
(A) carefully
(B) careful
(C) caring
(D) cared

119. Sales of truck parts ------- approximately 45 percent to BTR Manufacturing's revenue last year.
(A) gave
(B) applied
(C) contributed
(D) donated

120. The ------- northbound Coastal Express train will be arriving on track 5.
(A) delay
(B) delays
(C) delayed
(D) delaying

121. The Shellville City Council acted ------- when it decided to convert an unused railway to a multipurpose trail.
(A) wisely
(B) entirely
(C) initially
(D) widely

122. Overall ------- of museum archivists and curators is expected to grow steadily over the next ten years.
(A) employee
(B) employment
(C) employed
(D) employable

GO ON TO THE NEXT PAGE

123. With her ------- experience in graphic design, Ms. Abebe appears to be a suitable candidate for the book designer position.
(A) vast
(B) plausible
(C) relieved
(D) conscious

124. ------- a Boskin electrical product is modified by the customer, the warranty is no longer valid.
(A) Except
(B) So
(C) That
(D) If

125. Retail sales of Kent Menswear collared dress shirts increase dramatically every October, ------- the brand's autumn sale.
(A) so that
(B) due to
(C) therefore
(D) whereas

126. For security purposes, only authorized personnel of Jeffers Mines Ltd. may proceed ------- this checkpoint.
(A) beyond
(B) without
(C) about
(D) between

127. Heron Stationers ------- new business cards by the end of the week.
(A) to order
(B) had been ordered
(C) will be ordering
(D) ordering

128. At Key Beach Fashions, customers can check the ------- of their orders online.
(A) reason
(B) agenda
(C) status
(D) intent

129. A prize will be awarded to ------- sells the most raffle tickets for the annual charity fund-raiser.
(A) anybody
(B) yourselves
(C) everyone
(D) whoever

130. The greenhouse temperature must remain ------- the specified range for plants to grow properly.
(A) within
(B) because of
(C) as long as
(D) after all

PART 6

Directions: Read the texts that follow. A word, phrase, or sentence is missing in parts of each text. Four answer choices for each question are given below the text. Select the best answer to complete the text. Then mark the letter (A), (B), (C), or (D) on your answer sheet.

Questions 131-134 refer to the following notice.

The Moon Township Development Authority ------- the search for two candidates for its board of
                                            131.

oversight. These candidates will fill existing ------- . Overseeing plans for the community's
                                                132.

business development will be ------- main responsibility. The new members will continue the
                              133.

process. If you are interested in volunteering your time to serve on the board, please apply at the

township clerk's office. ------- .
                          134.

131. (A) had begun
     (B) to begin
     (C) is beginning
     (D) will have begun

132. (A) issues
     (B) districts
     (C) locations
     (D) vacancies

133. (A) their
     (B) my
     (C) its
     (D) your

134. (A) Elections were held every two years.
     (B) The board of oversight consists of
         nine members.
     (C) The business district has been
         neglected for years.
     (D) Note that you must be a resident of
         Moon Township to serve.

GO ON TO THE NEXT PAGE

Estin Insurance Group Ltd.

1089 Centre Street, Brampton, Ontario L6P 2YA

14 October

Nobu Ito
231 Parkside Avenue
Burlington, Ontario L7L 3X4

Dear Mr. Ito,

On behalf of Estin Insurance Group Ltd., thank you for your ------- . I would be pleased to provide
135.
you with a quote for the personal auto insurance you requested. Simply contact me at
(905) 555-0172 when you are ready, and I will ------- you. To save time, please have your vehicle
136.
registration and driver's license in hand.

If you reach my voice mail, please leave a message. ------- . I am available Monday
137.
------- Friday from 9:00 A.M. to 5:00 P.M.
138.

Sincerely,

Theodore Reynolds, Insurance Agent

---

135. (A) cooperation
     (B) payment
     (C) inquiry
     (D) concern

136. (A) assisting
     (B) assisted
     (C) assists
     (D) assist

137. (A) I will return your call as soon as
         possible.
     (B) The discount expires on November 1.
     (C) Any difference will be credited toward
         your bill.
     (D) The contract for the new policy is in
         the mail.

138. (A) around
     (B) through
     (C) against
     (D) near

Questions 139-142 refer to the following e-mail.

To: All members of the Wincliff Tools Board of Directors
From: Althea Wilson, Corporate Planning
Date: December 1
Subject: Biannual meeting

A meeting of the Wincliff Tools Board of Directors ------- on Monday, January 11, at 1:00 P.M. in
                                                    139.
the conference room at the manufacturing plant in Brywood. ------- .
                                                            140.

We have arranged two events to follow the meeting. At 3:00 P.M., we invite you to take a guided

tour ------- the plant and hear from some employees. More important, you will have the
     141.
opportunity to see ------- in action. And at 6:00 P.M., you are invited to join us for dinner at
                   142.
Fairport Seafood Restaurant.

---

139. (A) will be held
     (B) was held
     (C) are held
     (D) to be held

140. (A) Our products are sold at hardware
         stores nationwide.
     (B) Please plan to have the plant fully
         staffed that month.
     (C) My assistant has a list of items
         available for purchase.
     (D) Please let me know this week if you
         plan to attend.

141. (A) along
     (B) of
     (C) for
     (D) with

142. (A) themselves
     (B) who
     (C) them
     (D) any

GO ON TO THE NEXT PAGE

Questions 143-146 refer to the following memo.

To: All Customer Service Specialists
From: Human Resources Director
Date: April 28
Subject: Performance Evaluations

Grantham Electronics' human resources department will begin annual performance evaluations for customer service specialists ------- June 1. These evaluations consist of three steps.
143.
------- . Completing this step should take you no more than 30 minutes. Next, supervisors will
144.
------- a meeting with each employee. These meetings are for you to discuss with your supervisor
145.
the results of the self-assessment and your professional goals for the coming year. Finally, both

parties will complete a questionnaire reflecting on the experience.

We look forward to working with each employee to foster an environment that encourages

continued ------- and innovation.
146.

143. (A) on
(B) for
(C) past
(D) throughout

144. (A) If you have any questions, please contact your supervisor.
(B) Please note that the procedure has changed.
(C) A self-assessment sets the process in motion.
(D) Our goal is the continued success of the company.

145. (A) address
(B) schedule
(C) include
(D) determine

146. (A) create
(B) created
(C) creative
(D) creativity

PART 7

Directions: In this part you will read a selection of texts, such as magazine and newspaper articles, e-mails, and instant messages. Each text or set of texts is followed by several questions. Select the best answer for each question and mark the letter (A), (B), (C), or (D) on your answer sheet.

Questions 147-148 refer to the following list of coupons.

Summer savings at Lathom's Laundry!
Open every day from 6:00 A.M. to 12:00 midnight
in Annandale, Walford, and Kellering.

- -

June
£10 OFF all drop-off orders over £25
Let us do the work for you!

- -

July
FREE dryer sheets and bottle of laundry detergent
(One coupon per household)

- -

August
Three loads of wash FREE
(One coupon per household)

- -

September
£200 laundry card raffle
Submit this coupon at any Lathom's Laundry
location to receive a raffle ticket. Raffle drawing
will be held on 30 September.

---

147. What is indicated about Lathom's Laundry?

(A) It is closed on weekends.
(B) It is open 24 hours a day.
(C) It offers self-service laundry only.
(D) It has more than one location.

148. When can a customer get free laundry supplies?

(A) In June
(B) In July
(C) In August
(D) In September

GO ON TO THE NEXT PAGE

Questions 149-150 refer to the following e-mail.

```
╔════════════════════════ *E-mail* ════════════════════════╗

   To:       Alexander Samuels <a.samuels@netmail.com>

   From:     Sales Team <sales@shineoutlights.co.uk>

   Date:     2 October

   Subject:  Thank you for your order
```

Dear Mr. Samuels,

Congratulations on taking advantage of our October Shine Out Lights online sale! By shopping during our promotion, you saved 15 percent on your purchase of our quality outdoor lighting.

Your order of six extra-bright ground lights, a motion-detector spotlight, and two slim over-door lights will arrive within three to five working days. If there are any problems, please call us at 0191 498 0512 and reference order number 1984226.

Sincerely,

The Shine Out Lights Sales Team

149. What is mentioned about the order?
    (A) The total price was reduced.
    (B) It was delivered later than expected.
    (C) The quality of the products is guaranteed.
    (D) One of the items is out of stock.

150. What is indicated about the spotlight?
    (A) It can be used indoors.
    (B) It is very lightweight.
    (C) It is activated by movement.
    (D) It can be mounted above a door.

Candace Fletcher (5:28 A.M.)
Good morning, Yun. We need to delay the start of the South Side road-paving project. We're supposed to have heavy rain all day today.

Yun Chen (5:31 A.M.)
OK. I'll have the crew work in the maintenance shop today.

Candace Fletcher (5:32 A.M.)
Great. There's plenty to do there.

Yun Chen (5:33 A.M.)
Will we start on Front Street tomorrow?

Candace Fletcher (5:34 A.M.)
It depends. Let's see what the weather forecast says.

Yun Chen (5:35 A.M.)
OK. Please text me when you've decided.

TEST 1

151. Why does Ms. Fletcher contact Mr. Chen?

(A) To send him a new schedule
(B) To alert him to a change in plans
(C) To add an item to his project list
(D) To ask for feedback about his crew

152. At 5:34 A.M., what does Ms. Fletcher imply when she writes, "It depends"?

(A) The maintenance shop may be closed.
(B) A supervisor may text her with a decision.
(C) Front Street may have been paved already.
(D) The paving project may be delayed by the rain.

GO ON TO THE NEXT PAGE

Questions 153-154 refer to the following notice.

Northern Regional Railways
NOTICE: March 2

Northern Regional Railways (NRR) invites all riders to take advantage of a special discount for early booking on local routes between Fairview and East City. Make your reservation online at least ten days in advance, and you can save 20 percent on any round-trip ticket. Simply enter promotion code 10302.

Restrictions: Tickets purchased under this discount program must be used by September 1. This offer does not apply to express routes. Riders cannot combine this offer with points earned in the NRR Frequent Rider Rewards program.

---

153. What is the main purpose of the notice?

(A) To promote the use of express train services

(B) To announce the opening of a new route

(C) To encourage participation in group tours

(D) To inform customers about a unique offer

154. What is indicated about Northern Regional Railways?

(A) It charges extra fees for checked baggage.

(B) It plans to expand weekend train services.

(C) It offers a customer loyalty program.

(D) It recently upgraded its Web site.

Questions 155-157 refer to the following Web page.

---

https://www.kelwynstorage.com.bm

| **Home** | Rates | Contact |

Kelwyn Storage
84 Montrose Street, Hamilton, HM 10

Are you relocating? Do you need a place to store your household goods or business items during the transition? Let Kelwyn Storage keep them safe for you. Our climate-controlled facility has 24-hour security, with a unique access code for each storage unit. We use backup generators to ensure that your belongings always remain safe and in good condition.

Our state-of-the-art facility in Hamilton is still under construction, but phase one construction is complete, and units in one of the buildings are ready for rental. We have three unit sizes to accommodate any storage need. Phase two will be complete on May 20, and more units will be available for monthly and longer-term rental. Reserve your space before May 20, and receive a free month of rent with any twelve-month contract.

If you want to have your items for storage picked up, our trained movers can help. The fee is determined by distance as well as the size and number of items to be moved. Visit our Contact page to request a free quote.

---

155. What is the purpose of the Web page?

(A) To announce a company's relocation
(B) To outline a shipping procedure
(C) To describe a company's services
(D) To explain an increase in rates

156. What is NOT true about the facility?

(A) It requires a code to access storage spaces.
(B) It is closed until May 20.
(C) It is climate-controlled.
(D) It has units of varying sizes.

157. According to the Web page, what is available for an additional fee?

(A) Pickup services
(B) The use of a generator
(C) A monthly contract
(D) Truck rentals

GO ON TO THE NEXT PAGE

Questions 158-160 refer to the following article.

Sydney Morning Times

City Culture Desk

(12 October)—Sydney native Lily Trevor is often asked two specific questions. How did she first come up with her idea to hold cooking classes at a public library, and how was she able to make her idea a reality? Ms. Trevor responds that she noticed the popularity of food shows on television but realised that some people seemed to lack even the most basic cooking skills. These observations provided Ms. Trevor's initial inspiration.

As to the second question, Ms. Trevor explains that it requires the dedication of library staff to provide the space and support. Generous financial contributions from city organisations and businesses have also helped, since the city's library system doesn't have a large operating budget. In addition, Ms. Trevor's project has received donations of cooking and baking equipment from grocery stores and restaurants.

"Two years ago I began with just one after-school cooking class for children at the library," Ms. Trevor said. "That expanded to adult classes and special programs featuring local chefs. Public interest has remained high, and it continues to be a rewarding project." What has evolved into the Culinary Centre of the Sydney Library now offers various programs each month, including special events and even online sessions.

158. What is the purpose of the article?

(A) To profile the success of an unusual program
(B) To promote upcoming events at a library
(C) To introduce a new library director
(D) To request donations for a community project

159. What is suggested about Ms. Trevor?

(A) She has hosted a world-famous chef at the Culinary Centre.
(B) She started to offer cooking classes at a library two years ago.
(C) She has been a guest on television shows.
(D) She writes reviews of local restaurants.

160. The word "interest" in paragraph 3, line 5, is closest in meaning to

(A) concern
(B) advantage
(C) share
(D) attention

Questions 161-163 refer to the following notice.

Celebration of Excellence

— [1] —. Congratulations to all our employees! Bharati Corporation has been named the top manufacturer in India by *Tober Business Review*! This magazine, as you might already know, is one of the most highly regarded magazines in the business world. We want to thank you for your hard work and diligence. — [2] —. Because of all of you, we have been recognized internationally as a world-leading company.

Please join us in your building's cafeteria on Friday, 8 November, for a corporate-wide Celebration of Excellence. We will be closing all factories and offices in India, the United Kingdom, and the United States for two hours, starting 12:00 noon local time for this event. — [3] —. One of our board members will be speaking at each of our locations. — [4] —. This will be followed by music and a complimentary buffet luncheon for all employees.

Thank you again for making this our best year ever. We look forward to celebrating with you.

TEST 1

161. What is the purpose of the notice?

(A) To announce the opening of a new factory in India

(B) To ask for nominations of staff members for an award

(C) To express gratitude to all company employees

(D) To promote the use of corporate cafeterias

162. What is indicated about Bharati Corporation?

(A) It was honored in a prestigious magazine.

(B) It has multiple locations in South America.

(C) It manufactures computer chips for vehicles.

(D) It closes two hours early every Friday.

163. In which of the positions marked [1], [2], [3], and [4] does the following sentence best belong?

"We truly appreciate this team effort."

(A) [1]
(B) [2]
(C) [3]
(D) [4]

Questions 164-167 refer to the following text-message chain.

Marie Truong (1:45 P.M.)
I was just forwarded a follow-up call from a customer in West Fordham. He said his power went out a few hours ago. He made a service request and was expecting a service crew earlier today. My records are incomplete for some reason. Do you have any similar reports in the dispatch record?

Brian Eighmy (1:46 P.M.)
What's the exact address?

Marie Truong (1:47 P.M.)
221 North James Street. The customer's name is Cameron Fellman.

Brian Eighmy (1:52 P.M.)
Nothing came up. However, I did dispatch a truck to 652 North James Street. It's probably unrelated.

Marie Truong (1:53 P.M.)
That's only a few blocks away. Could we have them stop by Mr. Fellman's house after they are done?

Brian Eighmy (1:54 P.M.)
Sure. Does he have any pets?

Marie Truong (1:55 P.M.)
Mr. Fellman? Pets are not indicated in the report.

Brian Eighmy (1:56 P.M.)
OK, I'll need you to confirm that before we send the truck over. The service team may need to go into the backyard.

Marie Truong (1:57 P.M.)
I'll ask Mr. Fellman and call you with details.

164. Why did Ms. Truong contact Mr. Eighmy?
(A) To confirm a customer's address
(B) To follow up on a request
(C) To ask how widespread a power outage was
(D) To question a recent decision

165. At 1:52 P.M., what does Mr. Eighmy mean when he writes, "Nothing came up"?
(A) He did not find a dispatch report.
(B) He could not locate the service crew.
(C) He could not open a document.
(D) He did not determine the cause of a power outage.

166. What information does Ms. Truong need to find out?
(A) If there have been similar issues in the area
(B) If all necessary paperwork is complete
(C) If the account in question has been paid in full
(D) If there are animals in a customer's yard

167. What is Ms. Truong most likely going to do next?
(A) Send an e-mail to Mr. Eighmy
(B) Check the service report
(C) Call Mr. Fellman
(D) Transfer a payment

Maritzburg to Welcome New Store

MARITZBURG (23 September)—Residents of Maritzburg will soon have a new place to buy their groceries. — [1] —. Webb's Market, which currently operates in Durban and last month celebrated five years of being in business, will open a Maritzburg branch on Monday, 4 October, making it the store's second location. The store has steadily made a name for itself.

Owned by longtime Durban residents Andrew and Marnie Webb, Webb's Market has made its mark by carrying products primarily grown and produced in the region. — [2] —. From its early days, it has been stocking milk, cheese, beef, chicken, juices, baked goods, and a host of other locally produced food items.

"Today's consumers want to know where their food comes from and how it is produced," Mr. Webb noted. "And they increasingly prefer to buy food that is produced closer to home. However, not many stores carry primarily locally made products."

Apparently, the Webbs heard similar sentiments from Maritzburg residents. "Our Durban store has been attracting a growing number of customers from Maritzburg," said Ms. Webb. "Some inquired whether we would consider opening a store there. — [3] —. So after careful review and extensive market research, we decided to do just that. If this expansion goes well, we hope to open other stores around the region."

— [4] —. Those interested in applying for a position at the new store location should visit www.webbsmarket.co.za.

168. What is mentioned about Webb's Market?

(A) It underwent a name change.
(B) It is currently under construction.
(C) It recently celebrated its anniversary.
(D) It will close its store in Durban.

169. What is indicated about Mr. and Ms. Webb?

(A) They own a farm.
(B) They live in Durban.
(C) They import most of their products.
(D) They regularly request customer feedback.

170. What is NOT mentioned as a product sold at Webb's Market?

(A) Dairy
(B) Meats
(C) Bread
(D) Flowers

171. In which of the positions marked [1], [2], [3], and [4] does the following sentence best belong?

"Hiring is now under way for the new location."

(A) [1]
(B) [2]
(C) [3]
(D) [4]

GO ON TO THE NEXT PAGE

```
╔══════════════════════════ *E-mail* ══════════════════════════╗
```

To:	Tsazo Bankers Association <info@tsazobankersassociation.co.za>
From:	Karabo Mphela <k.mphela@tsazobankersassociation.co.za>
Date:	15 June
Subject:	Community Banking Conference

Dear Conference Attendees,

The recent conference organized by Tsazo Bankers Association (TBA) was another success, boasting the largest attendance of all eighteen of our annual conferences so far. And you helped make that happen! We appreciate our presenters and attendees for sharing their knowledge and skills.

If you have not yet filled out a conference survey, please take a moment to do so at www.tsazobankersassociation.co.za/survey. We greatly value your feedback and make a point of putting it into practice. For example, we decided to lengthen this year's conference based on feedback from last year's survey. Extending the conference to three days made it possible for us to offer a more comprehensive programme.

Finally, you do not have to wait a whole year for more professional development opportunities. TBA offers learning activities year-round. In fact, our next event is coming up soon. Please join us on 5 July for our webinar, *Innovations in Online Banking*—and stay up-to-date on all future events by signing up for e-mail notifications at www.tsazobankersassociation.co.za/pd.

We look forward to seeing you again soon.

Karabo Mphela, Event Director
Tsazo Bankers Association

172. What is indicated about this year's Community Banking Conference?

   (A) It was a one-day event.
   (B) It was held in a new venue.
   (C) The keynote address was *Innovations in Online Banking*.
   (D) More people attended than in previous years.

173. The word "appreciate" in paragraph 1, line 3, is closest in meaning to

   (A) request
   (B) apologize
   (C) value
   (D) increase

174. What is one reason that Mr. Mphela e-mailed conference attendees?

   (A) To invite them to make a presentation
   (B) To request that they fill out a survey
   (C) To announce a schedule change
   (D) To solicit feedback on banking services

175. Why does Mr. Mphela suggest visiting a Web site?

   (A) To receive news about upcoming events
   (B) To search TBA's member directory
   (C) To schedule a career consultation
   (D) To update some contact information

TEST 1

GO ON TO THE NEXT PAGE

Bulk Items for Less

By Matilda Long

DILLSBORO (August 1)—Members of the public can now take advantage of a new way to get the products they want at a lower cost. There is no need to pay full retail price for products such as paper towels, as long as customers do not mind packaging that is slightly damaged. Greeberg Wholesalers, a company known for being the area's largest distributor to restaurants and catering companies, occasionally receives products in damaged packages. These products are difficult to resell even though the products themselves are in perfect condition. Therefore, Greeberg Wholesalers is now making these products available to the public at deep discounts.

For example, a case of paper towels may cost as little as $8.59. Greeberg Wholesalers offers these discounted prices for quality name-brand products in slightly damaged packages while supplies last. The warehouse is open to the public every Tuesday from 9:00 A.M. to 1:00 P.M.

Name-Brand Dry Goods at Incredibly Low Prices!

Greeberg Wholesalers

Now open to the public for special savings. Tuesdays 9:00 A.M. – 1:00 P.M.

You can get the quality products you need while saving money on packages that may have been slightly damaged. Products are based on availability.

Item	Item Number	Description	Cost
Paper Towels-Super	PT7	24 rolls	$11.99
Paper Towels-Regular	PT9	20 rolls	$ 8.59
Disposable Napkins	N11	1,000 count	$ 3.49
Plastic Utensils	BT8	30 pieces	$ 7.99
Paper Plates-Deluxe*	PP4	225 count	$ 8.27
Paper Plates	PP9	250 count	$ 8.19

*Sold out

176. What is the purpose of the article?

    (A) To promote restaurants in the Dillsboro area

    (B) To announce a new service from a local company

    (C) To complain about a company's business practices

    (D) To compare wholesale and retail prices

177. Why is Greeberg Wholesalers selling discounted products?

    (A) Because it always has a sale in August

    (B) Because it has extra products it wants to sell quickly

    (C) Because it is closing a store and needs to sell everything

    (D) Because its regular customers do not want damaged packaging

178. With whom does Greeberg Wholesalers mainly do business?

    (A) Food service businesses

    (B) Concert venues

    (C) Kitchen appliance manufacturers

    (D) Bulk-food clubs

179. What item is described in the article?

    (A) PT9

    (B) N11

    (C) PP4

    (D) PP9

180. In what way is item BT8 different from the other items in the notice?

    (A) Its packages are undamaged.

    (B) It is made out of plastic.

    (C) It is currently sold out.

    (D) It is available in different sizes.

GO ON TO THE NEXT PAGE

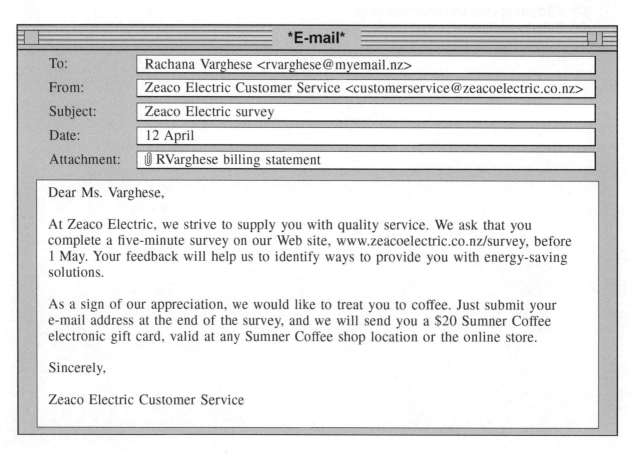

E-mail

To:	Mie Koruda <mkoruda@zeacoelectric.co.nz>
From:	Rawiri Wati <rwati@zeacoelectric.co.nz>
Subject:	Survey
Date:	2 April

Hello, Mie,

Feedback on our brochure about alternative power sources, which was sent to our small-business customers in March, has been positive. Unfortunately, we had to delay sending the power usage survey to our residential customers due to functionality issues. Our programmers fixed the broken links and are working on final verification that respondents will be able to access all the questions. Once we get their go-ahead, we can send the survey link to our residential customers with their regular electronic billing statements. We should be ready by Friday, 9 April, which keeps us on schedule to have the results in and analysed by 1 June.

Regards,

Rawiri

E-mail

To:	Rachana Varghese <rvarghese@myemail.nz>
From:	Zeaco Electric Customer Service <customerservice@zeacoelectric.co.nz>
Subject:	Zeaco Electric survey
Date:	12 April
Attachment:	⬙ RVarghese billing statement

Dear Ms. Varghese,

At Zeaco Electric, we strive to supply you with quality service. We ask that you complete a five-minute survey on our Web site, www.zeacoelectric.co.nz/survey, before 1 May. Your feedback will help us to identify ways to provide you with energy-saving solutions.

As a sign of our appreciation, we would like to treat you to coffee. Just submit your e-mail address at the end of the survey, and we will send you a $20 Sumner Coffee electronic gift card, valid at any Sumner Coffee shop location or the online store.

Sincerely,

Zeaco Electric Customer Service

181. Why most likely did Mr. Wati send the first e-mail?

(A) To report results from a survey
(B) To request technical assistance
(C) To ask for an extension on a task
(D) To provide an update on a project

182. What most likely is the survey about?

(A) Technical support
(B) Electricity usage
(C) Billing preferences
(D) Power outages

183. What is suggested about Ms. Varghese?

(A) She never responded to the survey.
(B) She requested a paper copy of her bill.
(C) She is a residential customer.
(D) She is a computer programmer.

184. What must Ms. Varghese do to receive a gift card?

(A) Submit her e-mail address
(B) Write a product description
(C) Visit a participating store
(D) Contact customer service

185. In the second e-mail, the word "sign" in paragraph 2, line 1, is closest in meaning to

(A) character
(B) gesture
(C) board
(D) name

GO ON TO THE NEXT PAGE

Questions 186-190 refer to the following advertisement and e-mails.

Job Change, Inc.
Part-Time Résumé Editors Needed

For three decades, Seattle-based Job Change, Inc., has coached thousands of people through the difficult process of applying for jobs—and we have an excellent track record. We are looking to hire several more part-time coaches/résumé editors who can work 20 hours per week providing clients with timely feedback and support.

The ideal candidate holds a bachelor's degree or higher in communications, human resources, or journalism and will have experience in career coaching, recruiting, or writing. Experience in tutoring, teaching, or editing is a plus. Must be able to start on August 1.

To be considered, send an e-mail and résumé to Aya Shimizu, a.shimizu@jci.com, briefly describing your professional history and why you are a good fit for the job.

E-mail

To:	Aya Shimizu <a.shimizu@jci.com>
From:	David Belmont <dbelmont@belmontcareerconsulting.com>
Subject:	Application
Date:	June 5
Attachment:	📎 Belmont résumé

Dear Ms. Shimizu,

Thank you for considering my application for the position of résumé editor with Job Change, Inc. I live just a few blocks from your office and could start immediately.

I graduated from State University with a master's degree in communications. I worked for twelve years at Western Placement Services. There, I gained extensive experience editing résumés and cover letters for clients seeking employment in a wide variety of industries. I also mentored and guided the applicants in their job searches. For the past year, I have been doing career coaching on a freelance basis, working out of my home. I am confident that I can provide your clients with prompt, effective guidance. If I am hired, my goal would be to prove to you that I am deserving of full-time work.

I look forward to hearing from you.

Sincerely,

David Belmont

To:	David Belmont <dbelmont@belmontcareerconsulting.com>
From:	Claire Ng <claireng@myemail.com>
Date:	July 13
Subject:	Thank you!

Dear David,

I'm delighted to report that, thanks to your help this past winter, I landed my dream job: landscape architect at Ari Builders in San Diego. Ari Builders' hiring manager said my résumé design—specifically the graphic elements you pulled from my portfolio—caught her eye. I start on August 20. You're the best job coach I've ever had!

As a token of my gratitude, I'd like to treat you and your wife to lunch before leaving town. Please let me know your availability, and we'll set something up.

Sincerely,

Claire Ng

186. What does the advertisement indicate about Job Change, Inc.?

(A) It has been in business for a long time.
(B) It reimburses tuition to staff who want to further their education.
(C) It is opening a branch office on August 1.
(D) It specializes in placing journalists in jobs.

187. According to the first e-mail, what is true about Mr. Belmont?

(A) He was a teacher at a local school.
(B) He has worked in a variety of industries.
(C) He worked from home for twelve years.
(D) He hopes to become a full-time employee.

188. What is suggested about Mr. Belmont?

(A) He needs to update his résumé.
(B) He is landscaping his home.
(C) He lives in Seattle.
(D) He has worked for Ms. Shimizu in the past.

189. What is most likely true about Ms. Ng?

(A) She did not accept a job offer.
(B) She prefers working at home.
(C) She received career advice from Mr. Belmont.
(D) She took a course in graphic design from Mr. Belmont.

190. According to the second e-mail, what does Ms. Ng want Mr. Belmont to do?

(A) E-mail her hiring manager
(B) Join her for a meal
(C) Review her updated portfolio
(D) Show her around his new office

GO ON TO THE NEXT PAGE

Questions 191-195 refer to the following article, order sheet, and report.

The Secret Behind Ravianos
By Nancy Horner

Fashion retailer Ravianos has stores in twelve cities across the country. While relatively new, Ravianos has become very popular with fashion-minded customers and is competing well against more established brands.

Instead of relying on traditional advertising methods, Ravianos pays close attention to market trends. Each month, Ravianos fills its stores' shelves with new clothing styles produced in small quantities and shipped in tiny sample batches of five pieces per size. As soon as sales data from the sample batches are in, decisions are made about which designs to move to full-scale production, which ones to redesign, and what new styles to implement in Ravianos' future offerings. This information is shared with in-house designers who meet by video to plan their next designs based on what sells best. The retailer then halts production of items with declining sales, and leftovers are sent back to the distribution center to be sold to online customers only.

Ravianos' designers are also interested in what customers have to say. Store personnel give customers special opinion forms in which they are asked to suggest what they would like to see in future Ravianos designs. Opinions gathered this way carry significant weight in the in-house design process.

Order #23623
Date: July 25
Ravianos Store, 290 Orchard Street,
Louisville, KY 40041

	Quantity		
	Small	Medium	Large
Tiaran dress	20	30	20
Vanonse blouse	15	30	20
Remessi shirt	20	30	20
Cromius T-shirt	5	5	5

Sales Figures for Jan Stawinski

This report shows the sales figures for items designed by you that moved beyond the sample stage. The numbers represent total purchases per product in all twelve Ravianos stores and online.

Name	Purchases	Change Relative to Previous Week
Oloaha skirt	367	+21%
Tiaran dress	511	+15%
Vanonse blouse	487	+12%
Yvonna blouse	342	+11%
Hygesse shirt	78	−20% (Production discontinued)

Note that these figures represent sales for the week of August 10–16. To view your figures for previous weeks, log in to your online account at ravianos.com/employee.

191. According to the article, what is discussed during video meetings?

(A) Customer preferences
(B) Pricing strategies
(C) Advertising methods
(D) Hiring needs

192. What does the article indicate about Ravianos?

(A) It has retail stores in multiple countries.
(B) It will soon merge with a competing fashion company.
(C) It is performing well within its market.
(D) It has purchased new shelves for its stores.

193. What article of Ravianos clothing in the July 25 order was sold as sample merchandise?

(A) The Tiaran dress
(B) The Vanonse blouse
(C) The Remessi shirt
(D) The Cromius T-shirt

194. What does the report suggest Mr. Stawinski can do through his account?

(A) View sales histories
(B) Find store locations
(C) Read customer reviews
(D) Receive work assignments

195. What is indicated about the Hygesse shirt?

(A) It will be sold at a 20 percent discount.
(B) It will be available to order online only.
(C) It became available on August 10.
(D) It was not released in all Ravianos stores.

GO ON TO THE NEXT PAGE

Questions 196-200 refer to the following policy, receipt, and credit card statement.

Tyche Bank Blue Business Card

Terms and Fees	
Rewards	Get 2% points on every purchase.
Payment Due Date	Monthly payment date is the fifth of the month unless cardholder requests a different due date.
Annual Percentage Rate (APR)	10% for purchases; 15% for other transactions
Annual Fee	$0
Late Payment Fee	$35; minimum monthly payment must be made by the due date in order to avoid a late fee.

If you wish to link your card to a Tyche Bank checking account, please contact inquiries@tychebank.com.

Hadley Office Supplies
33 Mossflower Road, Amherst, NH 03031

Customer: Francine Naar
Date: December 7

Product No.	Name	Amount
XM21	Table lamp, black	$54.12
DS13	Wall calendar—Autumn Trees	$11.39
OC02	Plushmax rolling office chair, dark green	$135.20
VB62	Letter-size printer paper (10-ream box)	$31.90
	Total	$232.61

Charged to Tyche Bank Blue Business Card
XXXXXXXXXXXX3245

Tyche Bank Blue Business Card

Francine Naar
320 Pelham St., Amherst, NH 03031
Account XXXXXXXXXXXX3245

ACCOUNT ACTIVITY
New balance: $287.87
Payment due date: February 20

Date of Transaction	Merchant Name	Amount
12/07	Hadley Office Supplies	$232.61
12/08	Downtown Donut Shack	$16.43
12/15	REFUND—Hadley Office Supplies	-$135.20
12/23	Maslin Dry Cleaning	$12.00
01/03	Callie's Carpet Corral	$86.57
01/04	Ogus Sportswear	$75.46

AUTOPAY ON. Your payment will be withdrawn from your Tyche Bank checking account on the due date.

Total points available: 1,996
Redeem your points at www.tychebank.com/rewards.

196. According to the policy, what is true about the Tyche Bank Blue Business Card?

(A) It charges a high annual fee.
(B) It offers points on selected purchases only.
(C) It charges the same rate for purchases and other transactions.
(D) It allows cardholders to pay automatically from a bank account.

197. Where did Ms. Naar make a purchase on January 3?

(A) At a restaurant
(B) At a dry cleaner
(C) At a carpet store
(D) At a clothing shop

198. According to the credit card statement, what can Ms. Naar do online?

(A) Enroll in a rewards program
(B) Redeem her points
(C) Purchase a gift card
(D) Apply for a lower interest rate

199. What is suggested about Ms. Naar?

(A) She asked for a new payment date.
(B) She works at an office supply store.
(C) She qualified to earn extra bonus points.
(D) She lives on Mossflower Road.

200. What purchase did Ms. Naar return for a refund?

(A) A table lamp
(B) A wall calendar
(C) A rolling chair
(D) A box of printer paper

Stop! This is the end of the test. If you finish before time is called, you may go back to Parts 5, 6, and 7 and check your work.

NO TEST MATERIAL ON THIS PAGE

TEST 2

＊解答用紙は本誌 p.112 の後ろに綴じ込まれています。

TEST 2

実際のテストでは問題用紙の裏側に、以下のようなテスト全体についての指示が印刷されています。
この指示を念頭においてテストに取り組みましょう。

General Directions

This test is designed to measure your English language ability. The test is divided into two sections: Listening and Reading.

You must mark all of your answers on the separate answer sheet. For each question, you should select the best answer from the answer choices given. Then, on your answer sheet, you should find the number of the question and fill in the space that corresponds to the letter of the answer that you have selected. If you decide to change an answer, completely erase your old answer and then mark your new answer.

訳　　　　　　　　　　　　　　**全体についての指示**

このテストはあなたの英語言語能力を測定するよう設計されています。テストはリスニングとリーディングという2つのセクションに分けられています。

答えは全て別紙の解答用紙にマークしてください。それぞれの設問について、与えられた選択肢から最も適切な答えを選びます。そして解答用紙の該当する問題番号に、選択した答えを塗りつぶしてください。答えを修正する場合は、元の答えを完全に消してから新しい答えをマークしてください。

LISTENING TEST

In the Listening test, you will be asked to demonstrate how well you understand spoken English. The entire Listening test will last approximately 45 minutes. There are four parts, and directions are given for each part. You must mark your answers on the separate answer sheet. Do not write your answers in your test book.

PART 1

Directions: For each question in this part, you will hear four statements about a picture in your test book. When you hear the statements, you must select the one statement that best describes what you see in the picture. Then find the number of the question on your answer sheet and mark your answer. The statements will not be printed in your test book and will be spoken only one time.

Statement (C), "They're sitting at a table," is the best description of the picture, so you should select answer (C) and mark it on your answer sheet.

1.

2.

GO ON TO THE NEXT PAGE ➡

3.

4.

5.

6.

GO ON TO THE NEXT PAGE ⟶

PART 2

Directions: You will hear a question or statement and three responses spoken in English. They will not be printed in your test book and will be spoken only one time. Select the best response to the question or statement and mark the letter (A), (B), or (C) on your answer sheet.

7. Mark your answer on your answer sheet.

8. Mark your answer on your answer sheet.

9. Mark your answer on your answer sheet.

10. Mark your answer on your answer sheet.

11. Mark your answer on your answer sheet.

12. Mark your answer on your answer sheet.

13. Mark your answer on your answer sheet.

14. Mark your answer on your answer sheet.

15. Mark your answer on your answer sheet.

16. Mark your answer on your answer sheet.

17. Mark your answer on your answer sheet.

18. Mark your answer on your answer sheet.

19. Mark your answer on your answer sheet.

20. Mark your answer on your answer sheet.

21. Mark your answer on your answer sheet.

22. Mark your answer on your answer sheet.

23. Mark your answer on your answer sheet.

24. Mark your answer on your answer sheet.

25. Mark your answer on your answer sheet.

26. Mark your answer on your answer sheet.

27. Mark your answer on your answer sheet.

28. Mark your answer on your answer sheet.

29. Mark your answer on your answer sheet.

30. Mark your answer on your answer sheet.

31. Mark your answer on your answer sheet.

PART 3

Directions: You will hear some conversations between two or more people. You will be asked to answer three questions about what the speakers say in each conversation. Select the best response to each question and mark the letter (A), (B), (C), or (D) on your answer sheet. The conversations will not be printed in your test book and will be spoken only one time.

32. What are the speakers preparing to do?

(A) Attend a convention
(B) Host an anniversary celebration
(C) Look for a new office space
(D) Update some software

33. Where do the speakers work?

(A) At an airline
(B) At a factory
(C) At a university
(D) At a hotel

34. What does the man say he is interested in doing?

(A) Joining the board of an association
(B) Meeting a company president
(C) Choosing some designs
(D) Learning about the history of an industry

35. What does the man say he likes about a job?

(A) It has opportunities for promotion.
(B) It is a full-time position.
(C) It has a high starting salary.
(D) It includes extensive training.

36. According to the woman, what do customers expect?

(A) Extended warranties
(B) Low prices
(C) Online assistance
(D) Quick delivery

37. What is the man concerned about?

(A) Providing his own tools
(B) Learning a software program
(C) Having a required license
(D) Processing customer payments

38. What are the speakers mainly discussing?

(A) A business merger
(B) A hiring event
(C) A training process
(D) A building renovation

39. What will Timvale's Stores most likely sell?

(A) Clothing
(B) Food
(C) Electronics
(D) Sporting goods

40. What does the man offer to do?

(A) Reserve a room
(B) Write a press release
(C) Contact a local official
(D) Design a logo

41. Where do the speakers most likely work?

(A) At an aquarium
(B) At a pet store
(C) At a botanical garden
(D) At a farm

42. What task does Alonso say he has never done before?

(A) Heater adjustments
(B) Plant fertilization
(C) Water testing
(D) Animal feeding

43. Why do the men need to finish their tasks by 1:00?

(A) They have a lunch break.
(B) They have to give some tours.
(C) They have to conduct an inspection.
(D) A facility is closing early.

GO ON TO THE NEXT PAGE

TEST 2

44. What has changed about an event?

(A) The date
(B) The location
(C) The time
(D) The cost

45. Where do the speakers most likely work?

(A) At a restaurant
(B) At a print shop
(C) At an art gallery
(D) At an event planning agency

46. What does the man mean when he says, "Linda's the only one scheduled to come in"?

(A) Linda is responsible for creating the schedule.
(B) Linda has been trained to do certain tasks.
(C) There is an error on the schedule.
(D) More workers are needed.

47. Which industry do the speakers most likely work in?

(A) Fashion
(B) Real estate
(C) Tourism
(D) Entertainment

48. What is the woman concerned about?

(A) The quality of a product
(B) The effect on the environment
(C) An increase in costs
(D) A delay in production

49. What does the man say he did?

(A) He bought some supplies.
(B) He tested some equipment.
(C) He scheduled a meeting.
(D) He read some reviews.

50. What does the woman confirm to the man?

(A) A job has been completed.
(B) Some workers have arrived.
(C) Some equipment is available.
(D) A vehicle has been repaired.

51. What type of business do the speakers most likely work for?

(A) A furniture factory
(B) A car dealership
(C) A home appliance store
(D) A moving company

52. What do the speakers disagree about?

(A) When to take a break
(B) How to arrange some items
(C) What price to charge
(D) How long a delivery will take

53. Why does the woman say, "I spent a lot of time putting together my advertising team"?

(A) To explain a success
(B) To express surprise
(C) To recommend a policy change
(D) To complain about a management decision

54. What problem does the man mention?

(A) Inaccurate inventory
(B) Material shortages
(C) Customer complaints
(D) A lack of qualified staff

55. What does the woman offer to do?

(A) Coordinate some shipments
(B) Contact a design specialist
(C) Look for a new vendor
(D) Organize some training sessions

56. What news does the man share?

(A) The company may be purchased.
(B) Research funding has been approved.
(C) A client wants to buy additional services.
(D) A new CEO was hired.

57. Why are the women concerned?

(A) A process is too complicated.
(B) A cost may increase.
(C) A location is inconvenient.
(D) An audit deadline is approaching.

58. What does the man want the women to do?

(A) Update a schedule
(B) Sign some documents
(C) Provide some feedback
(D) Check an industry requirement

---

59. Who most likely is the man?

(A) An engineer
(B) A forest ranger
(C) A restaurant owner
(D) A furniture maker

60. What does the man say is important about a product?

(A) That it is affordable
(B) That it is durable
(C) That it is environmentally friendly
(D) That it is easy to use

61. Why does the woman apologize?

(A) A delivery service is not offered.
(B) A storage area is far away.
(C) An item is unavailable.
(D) A price tag is incorrect.

Temperatures (°C)		
	High	**Low**
Monday	2°	-1°
Tuesday	2°	-1°
Wednesday	2°	-12°
Thursday	-1°	-3°
Friday	9°	2°

62. Look at the graphic. When does the man plan to go to the bank?

(A) Monday
(B) Tuesday
(C) Wednesday
(D) Thursday

63. What does the woman regret doing?

(A) Choosing a certain piece of equipment
(B) Planting some crops so early
(C) Cutting branches from a tree
(D) Not watering plants well enough

64. What does the man suggest doing?

(A) Gathering materials
(B) Making a new calendar
(C) Looking at different locations
(D) Harvesting everything possible

TEST 2

GO ON TO THE NEXT PAGE ➡

Price Per Square Meter

$43 $36

$25 $17

Agenda	
Introductions	2:05–2:20 P.M.
Live Reading	2:20–2:30 P.M.
Question-and-Answer Session	2:30–2:55 P.M.
Social Time and Refreshments	2:55–3:30 P.M.

65. Who is the woman?

(A) A painter
(B) A restaurant owner
(C) An interior designer
(D) A real estate agent

66. Why does the man recommend a product brand?

(A) It is discounted.
(B) It has bright colors.
(C) It is made from recycled materials.
(D) It is easy to clean.

67. Look at the graphic. What is the price of the pattern the woman prefers?

(A) $43
(B) $36
(C) $25
(D) $17

68. Where do the speakers work?

(A) At a bookstore
(B) At a café
(C) At a theater
(D) At a library

69. What does the woman say she will do after lunch?

(A) Send some invitations
(B) Hang up some posters
(C) Print some event tickets
(D) Unpack some boxes

70. Look at the graphic. What agenda item does the woman suggest extending?

(A) Introductions
(B) Live Reading
(C) Question-and-Answer Session
(D) Social Time and Refreshments

PART 4

Directions: You will hear some talks given by a single speaker. You will be asked to answer three questions about what the speaker says in each talk. Select the best response to each question and mark the letter (A), (B), (C), or (D) on your answer sheet. The talks will not be printed in your test book and will be spoken only one time.

71. Where is the speaker?

   (A) At an arena
   (B) At a museum
   (C) At a train station
   (D) At a community center

72. According to the speaker, why are people excited?

   (A) A famous musician will perform.
   (B) A championship game will be played.
   (C) A new exhibition will open.
   (D) A construction project will be completed.

73. What will the speaker do next?

   (A) Conduct some interviews
   (B) Walk around a building
   (C) Give away some tickets
   (D) Explain a contest

74. What did the company do last week?

   (A) It adopted a new inventory system.
   (B) It hosted a professional conference.
   (C) It signed an important contract.
   (D) It hired several employees.

75. According to the speaker, what does Diego have experience with?

   (A) Computer repair
   (B) Package design
   (C) Public speaking
   (D) Travel planning

76. What does the speaker ask the listeners to do?

   (A) Clean up their work areas
   (B) Place a supply order
   (C) Complete a registration form
   (D) Update their calendars

77. Where does the announcement most likely take place?

   (A) At a convention center
   (B) At a farmers market
   (C) At a kitchen supply store
   (D) At a cooking school

78. According to the speaker, what is unique about some cookware?

   (A) It is available in a variety of colors.
   (B) It was handcrafted by local artisans.
   (C) It is manufactured from recycled metal.
   (D) It was created for a famous chef.

79. What will happen in fifteen minutes?

   (A) An author will sign cookbooks.
   (B) A promotional sale will end.
   (C) A contest winner will be announced.
   (D) A product will be demonstrated.

80. What is the talk mostly about?

   (A) Filming a documentary
   (B) Photographing some artwork
   (C) Planning an advertising campaign
   (D) Organizing a nature tour

81. What does the speaker imply when she says, "we only have one chance to get this right"?

   (A) Several mistakes have already been made.
   (B) The listeners need to be prepared.
   (C) Previous tasks were less important.
   (D) Experienced staff should be in charge.

82. What does the speaker ask Claudine to do?

   (A) Repair a camera
   (B) Adjust the sound on a television
   (C) Get some equipment out of a vehicle
   (D) Review some documents

GO ON TO THE NEXT PAGE

TEST 2

83. What is the speaker mainly discussing?

    (A) The concerns of a client
    (B) The results of a survey
    (C) A work-space reorganization plan
    (D) An employee benefits package

84. What goal does the speaker mention?

    (A) Reducing operating expenses
    (B) Attracting more clients
    (C) Upgrading some technology
    (D) Improving a training program

85. What are the listeners expected to do before the next meeting?

    (A) Greet new employees
    (B) Provide some feedback
    (C) Finalize a supply order
    (D) Review an annual report

86. What most likely is the speaker's job?

    (A) Accountant
    (B) Building inspector
    (C) Insurance salesperson
    (D) Landscaper

87. What does the speaker advise the listener to be careful doing?

    (A) Registering a new car
    (B) Finding an architect
    (C) Putting up a fence
    (D) Reading some regulations

88. What does the speaker offer to help with?

    (A) Filing for a permit
    (B) Providing a meeting space
    (C) Painting a house
    (D) Setting up some computers

89. What area do the listeners most likely work in?

    (A) Law
    (B) Finance
    (C) Technology
    (D) Publishing

90. What will the listeners participate in?

    (A) A staff picnic
    (B) An intern orientation
    (C) A research experiment
    (D) A hiring selection

91. Why does the speaker say, "you can learn a lot from talking to someone"?

    (A) To recommend consulting an expert
    (B) To encourage attendance at a company party
    (C) To reject a suggestion about a process
    (D) To express surprise about a staff member's background

92. Where is the speaker?

    (A) At a library
    (B) At a community garden
    (C) At a town plaza
    (D) At a bookstore

93. What did the speaker do last year?

    (A) He traveled to another country.
    (B) He opened a restaurant.
    (C) He received an award.
    (D) He applied for a grant.

94. What does the speaker mean when he says, "I brought some of what we found this morning"?

    (A) The listeners should help him pack some materials.
    (B) The listeners should try a sample.
    (C) A problem is urgent.
    (D) A larger container is advised.

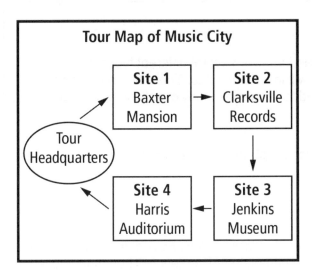

Tour Map of Music City

Site 1 — Baxter Mansion
Site 2 — Clarksville Records
Tour Headquarters
Site 4 — Harris Auditorium
Site 3 — Jenkins Museum

Dacey's Bakery

(1) Assorted Cookies: $18/dozen

(2) Assorted Muffins: $20/dozen

(3) Fruit Pies: $22/pie

(4) Layer Cakes: $18/cake

95. What problem does the speaker mention?

(A) A road is busy with traffic.
(B) A tire must be fixed.
(C) An item was left behind.
(D) A bus made a wrong turn.

96. Look at the graphic. Which site are the listeners going to now?

(A) Site 1
(B) Site 2
(C) Site 3
(D) Site 4

97. What fact does the speaker share about Music City?

(A) It is over two hundred years old.
(B) It is the birthplace of a famous singer.
(C) Public concerts are held there weekly.
(D) A large number of guitars are produced there.

98. Look at the graphic. Which line of the menu will be changed?

(A) Line 1
(B) Line 2
(C) Line 3
(D) Line 4

99. Why will Yuri not come to work tomorrow?

(A) He is feeling unwell.
(B) He has to take his car to an auto shop.
(C) He will be starting a new job.
(D) He will be attending a family event.

100. What does the speaker say about the back of the store?

(A) The door must be locked every night.
(B) The floor needs to be cleaned.
(C) Some boxes need to be unpacked.
(D) Some fans should be plugged in.

This is the end of the Listening test. Turn to Part 5 in your test book.

GO ON TO THE NEXT PAGE

READING TEST

In the Reading test, you will read a variety of texts and answer several different types of reading comprehension questions. The entire Reading test will last 75 minutes. There are three parts, and directions are given for each part. You are encouraged to answer as many questions as possible within the time allowed.

You must mark your answers on the separate answer sheet. Do not write your answers in your test book.

PART 5

Directions: A word or phrase is missing in each of the sentences below. Four answer choices are given below each sentence. Select the best answer to complete the sentence. Then mark the letter (A), (B), (C), or (D) on your answer sheet.

101. Please send a copy of ------- résumé to the hiring committee.

   (A) you
   (B) yours
   (C) yourself
   (D) your

102. Gnome Bicycle's employee turnover rate has been quite steady ------- the past year.

   (A) toward
   (B) over
   (C) rather
   (D) if

103. Mainer Soft, Inc., offers a selection of video games, which are only ------- through its Web site.

   (A) sale
   (B) sell
   (C) sold
   (D) sells

104. Changes to the travel reimbursement process will be explained at this month's staff -------.

   (A) level
   (B) schedule
   (C) proposal
   (D) meeting

105. Stillman Canning creates stews and soups using a ------- family recipe.

   (A) trust
   (B) trusted
   (C) trusts
   (D) trusting

106. In its first week ------- operation, Sabon Hairstyling Salon had about 150 customers.

   (A) of
   (B) to
   (C) as
   (D) by

107. Ekari Industries is proud to announce its ------- merger with Bogin Enterprises.

   (A) whole
   (B) external
   (C) upcoming
   (D) serious

108. All letters and packages are shipped in locked containers to ensure safe -------.

   (A) deliver
   (B) delivers
   (C) delivered
   (D) delivery

109. This year, ------- three million passengers across China boarded domestic flights the day before the holiday weekend.
 (A) almost
 (B) often
 (C) more
 (D) far

110. By the end of the workshop, participants will have a ------- understanding of how to request financial aid.
 (A) hard
 (B) full
 (C) best
 (D) busy

111. Removing personal items from the floor of your workstation will ------- facilitate tomorrow's carpet cleaning.
 (A) greatness
 (B) greats
 (C) great
 (D) greatly

112. Audience members are asked to resist looking at their phones because presenters find it -------.
 (A) distraction
 (B) distract
 (C) distractible
 (D) distracting

113. Hospital officials met with the architects ------- received an overview of the design of the new maternity center.
 (A) either
 (B) instead
 (C) or
 (D) and

114. Anyone planning to ------- for a pharmacy degree program should consider gaining laboratory work experience.
 (A) require
 (B) vote
 (C) apply
 (D) complete

115. Even first-time Pictafix subscribers can use the software to create photo collages nearly -------.
 (A) increasingly
 (B) effortlessly
 (C) recently
 (D) especially

116. The company's production issues were further ------- by an unexpected power outage.
 (A) complicate
 (B) complicated
 (C) complication
 (D) complicating

117. The board of directors at Ginishi Estate Investments is awaiting shareholder approval ------- acquiring more properties.
 (A) because
 (B) providing
 (C) before
 (D) though

118. ------- assistant will be in the office today, but they can be contacted by e-mail.
 (A) Many
 (B) Other
 (C) Neither
 (D) None

119. Brynextech now has manufacturing ------- on both the east and west coasts.
 (A) facilities
 (B) selections
 (C) performances
 (D) revisions

120. Cowan Company is usually filled with the sound of people talking ------- in its research library.
 (A) during
 (B) despite
 (C) among
 (D) except

GO ON TO THE NEXT PAGE

121. To predict erosion, geologists ------- the water absorption rate of soil near the mountain range.
(A) monitor
(B) practice
(C) surround
(D) occupy

122. Returns of merchandise with original tags and receipts are ------- accepted for up to 30 days after purchase.
(A) general
(B) generally
(C) generalize
(D) generalized

123. The visiting delegation will join the CEO for refreshments after they finish the factory -------.
(A) toured
(B) tourism
(C) tourist
(D) tour

124. Cost should not be the only factor taken into account ------- choosing a contractor for a renovation.
(A) back to
(B) when
(C) between
(D) in part

125. We could reserve the auditorium; -------, we could consider meeting in one of the larger conference rooms.
(A) alternatively
(B) immediately
(C) in particular
(D) such as

126. By requiring the ------- inspection of all assembly-line machines, the new policy will help improve workplace safety.
(A) periodic
(B) period
(C) periodically
(D) periods

127. The company, which Mr. Sato initially operated out of his own home, was ------- sold for several billion yen.
(A) tightly
(B) subsequently
(C) severely
(D) evenly

128. In the interest of -------, product designer Yu Cai will remain the team lead until the project is completed.
(A) continue
(B) continuity
(C) continuous
(D) continuously

129. Owing to their ------- of hot, dry climates, evergreens like the Arizona cypress grow well in drought-prone areas.
(A) tolerance
(B) abundance
(C) performance
(D) allowance

130. Alvin Parno's insightful column about the crisis in the international trade situation is very -------.
(A) attractive
(B) comfortable
(C) informative
(D) wealthy

Directions: Read the texts that follow. A word, phrase, or sentence is missing in parts of each text. Four answer choices for each question are given below the text. Select the best answer to complete the text. Then mark the letter (A), (B), (C), or (D) on your answer sheet.

Questions 131-134 refer to the following notice.

Lost and Found

If you think you may have lost an item in one of our ------- , we advise you to contact our Lost and
     131.
Found desk at 973-555-0147. Alternatively, you may send an e-mail to help@finnwayairport.com.

Include a description of your item and the date you lost it at the airport. We will ------- within
     132.

48 hours. Items are kept at Lost and Found for 90 days. ------- .
     133.

Note, however, that any inquiries involving either missing checked baggage or an item that you

------- on an aircraft should be directed to the airline you traveled with.
134.

TEST 2

131. (A) shopping carts
     (B) terminals
     (C) fitting rooms
     (D) taxis

132. (A) respond
     (B) depart
     (C) watch
     (D) begin

133. (A) They are renewed monthly.
     (B) During this time, they are discarded.
     (C) A claim may be submitted by each
          passenger.
     (D) After this time, most items are
          donated to local charities.

134. (A) must be leaving
     (B) were leaving
     (C) was left
     (D) may have left

GO ON TO THE NEXT PAGE

Questions 135-138 refer to the following e-mail.

To: All Employees
From: Holly Grimes
Subject: Dress Code
Date: 1 May

Dear Forestport Consulting Staff,

Beginning on 28 May, the Forestport Consulting Company ------- a new, more relaxed dress-code
                                                        135.
policy. Business-casual work attire will be allowed in the office except when meeting with clients.

------- , business-casual attire includes dress slacks and khaki trousers, skirts and dresses, and
  136.
blouses and collared shirts. ------- . Remember, this policy is intended to promote a comfortable
                               137.
but professional working environment to further support ------- productivity. If you have any
                                                         138.
questions, please consult Human Resources.

Thank you,

Holly Grimes
Chief Executive Officer

---

135. (A) will be instituting
     (B) will be instituted
     (C) to be instituting
     (D) had instituted

136. (A) For this reason
     (B) In the same fashion
     (C) For your reference
     (D) Now that

137. (A) Your new uniforms should be arriving
         next Tuesday or Wednesday.
     (B) Feedback about the updated policy
         should not be reviewed until next
         week.
     (C) All staff should be prepared to explain
         the new policy to clients.
     (D) Jeans, T-shirts, and sleeveless shirts
         are not appropriate.

138. (A) their
     (B) our
     (C) her
     (D) my

Dear Ms. Khan,

Thank you for enrolling in the back pain management sessions at Bend Physical Therapy. We are excited to partner with you on your journey back to health. In the next week, you will receive your health kit. ------- .
139.

Your personal trainer will be Coach Jenni. She will get in touch with you ------- . She will teach
140.
you exercises that hopefully will enable you ------- your back pain.
141.

Should you have any questions, please consult our Web site or give ------- a call at
142.
863-555-0122.

Sincerely,

Melissa Agarwal
Bend Physical Therapy

TEST 2

139. (A) It includes an exercise mat and a strength band for home use.
(B) Our clients often recommend our center to their colleagues.
(C) Please renew your payment option as soon as possible.
(D) Please submit this form by the due date, next Friday.

140. (A) temporarily
(B) shortly
(C) luckily
(D) similarly

141. (A) to eliminate
(B) is eliminating
(C) has eliminated
(D) the elimination of

142. (A) it
(B) us
(C) mine
(D) them

GO ON TO THE NEXT PAGE

FOR IMMEDIATE RELEASE

Media contact: Emiko Inoue, press officer <einoue@laurelhursttechnology.com>

SEATTLE (July 20)—Laurelhurst Technology announced today the upcoming launch of Fabulan, its new online streaming platform. ------- . Each segment is to be at most five minutes long and filmed
       143.
with smaller, handheld screen sizes in mind. Fabulan ------- will focus on home repairs, cooking
                                                        144.
tips, craft ideas, and other topics of common interest.

Content developers ------- to the challenge presented by the limited format specifications.
                    145.
"Personally, I'm excited to produce my first Fabulan segment," said producer Jared Holm. "This format requires thinking even more ------- about how we present a topic. I'm eager to see what
                                          146.
effect that has on my work."

---

143. (A) Its exclusive music-related audio channels are very popular.
     (B) The app is already installed on many top-rated smart televisions.
     (C) It will feature short content that is formatted for mobile phones.
     (D) Laurelhurst is known primarily for its child-friendly educational materials.

144. (A) signals
     (B) fashions
     (C) exhibits
     (D) videos

145. (A) will have risen
     (B) would be rising
     (C) are rising
     (D) to be risen

146. (A) created
     (B) creative
     (C) creativity
     (D) creatively

Directions: In this part you will read a selection of texts, such as magazine and newspaper articles, e-mails, and instant messages. Each text or set of texts is followed by several questions. Select the best answer for each question and mark the letter (A), (B), (C), or (D) on your answer sheet.

Questions 147-148 refer to the following roadside sign.

FIVE STATES BARBECUE

Turn left at the next traffic light.

Hot Sandwiches and Platters from $7

- Texas Beef Brisket
- Missouri Pork Ribs
- Kentucky Grilled Chicken
- Carolina Pulled Pork
- California Roasted Vegetables

Rated best restaurant 3 years in a row!

Open for lunch from 11:00 A.M. to 3:30 P.M.

CLOSED MONDAYS

147. What is suggested about Five States Barbecue?

(A) It offers breakfast.
(B) It has many locations.
(C) It is very popular.
(D) It is open on Mondays.

148. What is most likely true about the California menu item?

(A) It comes with a salad.
(B) It is served cold.
(C) It contains no meat.
(D) It is the most expensive item.

GO ON TO THE NEXT PAGE

Questions 149-150 refer to the following product usage instructions.

Drohol Lotion: For minor skin irritation, itching, or rash. Safe for use on adults and children over twelve years old.

Directions: Apply directly to the affected area twice a day for up to two weeks. Keep away from eyes and mouth. Store at room temperature (approximately 17–25 degrees Celsius). Protect lotion from freezing.

Net weight 16 grams
Produced by Dojing Pharmaceuticals, Singapore

---

149. What is the product intended to treat?

(A) The hair
(B) The eyes
(C) The mouth
(D) The skin

150. What are users instructed to do?

(A) Keep the product from getting too cold
(B) Apply the product once a day
(C) Administer the product on adults only
(D) Discard any of the product that is left
    after one year

Bike Pedal Recall

ABERDEEN (24 December)—Saorsa Mountain Bikes has recalled 5,000 bicycles sold in the United Kingdom between 9 October and 21 December. "This is a voluntary recall," said Jonathan Wakerman, spokesperson for Saorsa Mountain Bikes. "We have had a few cases where the plastic pedals cracked, and people could not complete their rides."

No consumer injuries in the field have been reported, but recent additional testing by the manufacturer has revealed that too high a percentage of pedals are failing with normal use. Consumers are urged to bring their Saorsa Mountain Bike model 700XFT bicycles with plastic pedals to any authorised retail dealer, where aluminium replacement pedals will be installed at no cost to the owner.

TEST 2

151. What is the purpose of the article?

(A) To introduce a new bicycle model
(B) To discuss biking accessories
(C) To issue a warning about a product
(D) To explain how bicycles are designed

152. What does the article indicate about the plastic pedals?

(A) They make riders more comfortable.
(B) They are usually less expensive.
(C) They are commonly available.
(D) They may break too easily.

153. What are some bicycle owners advised to do?

(A) Purchase replacement parts
(B) Take their bicycles to a dealership
(C) Read a bicycle repair manual
(D) Try out several bicycle models

GO ON TO THE NEXT PAGE

Nita Mittal (9:08 A.M.)
Hi, Mitch. I've boarded the plane, but the captain just announced that we're waiting for connecting passengers, so we'll be delayed. Can you let the car service know?

Mitch Richards (9:12 A.M.)
Of course. Tell me when you're about to take off. I'll adjust your pickup time as needed.

Nita Mittal (9:15 A.M.)
Thanks. And thanks also for e-mailing the safety handbook. Ned Grant needs to have copies printed by Friday.

Mitch Richards (9:17 A.M.)
No problem.

Nita Mittal (9:50 A.M.)
I'm still on the ground. I might not make my connection in Dallas.

Mitch Richards (9:55 A.M.)
Don't worry. We'll deal with it.

Nita Mittal (10:10 A.M.)
It looks like we'll be off in a few minutes. It will be close.

Mitch Richards (10:11 A.M.)
OK. I hope it works out!

154. At 10:10 A.M., what does Ms. Mittal most likely mean when she writes, "It will be close"?

(A) She might miss her next flight.
(B) She will receive a document just in time to meet a deadline.
(C) She thinks the airport in Dallas is conveniently located.
(D) She plans to send another message soon.

155. What will Mr. Richards probably do next?

(A) E-mail a safety handbook
(B) Ask Mr. Grant for copies of a document
(C) Make hotel reservations for Ms. Mittal
(D) Contact a car service

Questions 156-157 refer to the following instructions.

Caring for your Brewtime Supreme coffeemaker

Machine cleaning: Your Brewtime Supreme coffeemaker is designed to last many years, providing you with delicious coffee day after day. For optimal performance, clean your Brewtime Supreme on a monthly basis. While commercial cleaning solutions are available, a 50-50 mixture of white vinegar and water may also be used. First, pour the cleaning solution into the coffeemaker's reservoir, switch the coffeemaker on, and allow half of the solution to drip into the carafe. Then, switch the coffeemaker off and wait 30 minutes for it to cool. Next, refill the reservoir with more of the solution, and allow the brewing process to finish. Finally, with water only, repeat the brewing process so that any remaining residue is washed away. Perform this action twice if necessary.

---

156. For whom are the instructions most likely intended?

(A) Appliance retailers
(B) Product owners
(C) Product designers
(D) Repair technicians

157. According to the instructions, how often should cleaning be performed?

(A) Every day
(B) Every two weeks
(C) Once a month
(D) Twice a year

TEST 2

GO ON TO THE NEXT PAGE

To:	All Employees
From:	Ken Ishibashi
Date:	11 June
Subject:	New procedure

The Tech Help Desk tends to receive a high number of service requests between the hours of 8:00 A.M. and 10:00 A.M. Our staff has the capacity to handle all of these within a reasonable time frame, but to improve efficiency we need your help in implementing a new procedure.

Going forward, employees must designate a priority level when submitting service requests. "Critical priority" designations will be reserved for problems that directly jeopardize our ability to meet client obligations. These requests will be acted on immediately by Help Desk staff members. The "high priority" designation should be used for issues that are preventing employees from doing their work. These issues will be handled within three hours, if possible. However, 60% of the requests we typically receive are for less time-sensitive issues and should be marked "standard priority." We will respond to these requests within 24 hours of submission. Finally, "low priority" requests will be addressed within three business days. Requests for software enhancements, for example, would fall under this last category.

As usual, the status of your service requests will be updated on the Tech Help Desk's Web site.

Thank you.

158. What challenge is the Tech Help Desk experiencing?

(A) It has been affected by team-member retirements.
(B) Its expenses have unexpectedly increased.
(C) It has a higher volume of work at certain times.
(D) Its software needs to be upgraded.

159. According to the e-mail, how are service requests changing?

(A) They must be submitted during specific hours.
(B) They must be categorized by the employees making them.
(C) Their assigned priority level must be approved by a manager.
(D) Their status will be posted on a Web site.

160. Within what time frame are the "standard priority" requests addressed?

(A) One hour
(B) Three hours
(C) One day
(D) Three days

Questions 161-164 refer to the following notice.

Posted 12 March

Attention Dublin Transit riders:

Dublin Transit is pleased to launch a new and improved Web site and app. — [1] —. In addition to having the ability to view entire transit schedules, you can now receive live route updates and purchase same-day tickets online. As always, information is available in English, Spanish, and French.

If you have already purchased a ticket electronically and are ready to travel, simply print it out and bring it with you to the station or save the ticket to your mobile phone. — [2] —. Then scan the bar code that is on your ticket to open the gate at the entrance to your train platform. If you still need to purchase tickets, representatives at every station are available to serve you from 6:00 A.M. to 10:00 P.M. daily. — [3] —.

To save money, commuters are reminded to buy weekly or monthly passes in advance. Please note that beginning on 1 April, commuters who purchase weekly or monthly passes will see a 4 percent cost increase. — [4] —. However, the price for the transit passes will continue to represent a cost savings over a daily ticket purchase.

TEST 2

161. What is a new feature on the Web site and app?

(A) Seat assignment confirmation
(B) Updated weather conditions
(C) Real-time transit updates
(D) Frequent-traveler rewards

162. According to the notice, what is indicated about transit tickets?

(A) They must be stamped by a representative in the station office.
(B) They are scanned for entry to a train platform.
(C) They must be presented to a conductor upon boarding.
(D) They are intended for use by regular commuters only.

163. What is NOT mentioned in the notice?

(A) Transit information is available in several languages.
(B) Station offices are open daily.
(C) A new transit station will open soon.
(D) Transit passes will cost more starting in April.

164. In which of the positions marked [1], [2], [3], and [4] does the following sentence best belong?

"Innovative, user-friendly features have been added to both."

(A) [1]
(B) [2]
(C) [3]
(D) [4]

Questions 165-167 refer to the following Web page.

https://www.crowellclothingessentials.com/ps/01265

Collar stays are little strips of hard material that keep shirt collars looking crisp and sharp. Also called collar tabs or stiffeners, they are an essential accessory for any well-dressed professional.

Today, you can find collar stays in a variety of sizes and materials. While they are sometimes sewn or glued into shirts, our experts agree that nonremovable collar stays tend to become flimsy and ineffective over time. If you want to look your best, we advise choosing only removable collar stays, which will keep your shirts looking fresh and new.

For the past 30 years, Crowell Clothing Essentials has been selling high-quality collar stays to fit any size and budget. We offer assorted sizes of inexpensive plastic stays, and we also carry deluxe brass and stainless-steel stays that will last a lifetime. Even though people dress more casually nowadays, we believe that collar stays are here to stay!

Select the Online Store tab from our main page to browse our selection.

165. What is one purpose of the Web page?

(A) To describe how to clean a high-quality garment
(B) To announce a new price on a clothing accessory
(C) To explain how collar stays changed over time
(D) To persuade customers to purchase an item

166. What is suggested about Crowell Clothing Essentials?

(A) It manufactures casual shirts.
(B) It sells removable collar stays.
(C) It recently celebrated its grand opening.
(D) It offers brass and steel buttons in its online store.

167. The word "carry" in paragraph 3, line 3, is closest in meaning to

(A) lift
(B) sell
(C) wear
(D) take

Questions 168-171 refer to the following e-mail.

From:	Juan Romas
To:	All Staff; Conservancy Members
Sent:	Tuesday, April 21
Subject:	Questionnaire

Good morning,

A performance evaluation of Walkinson Conservancy's executive director has been initiated by the board of directors and is currently being conducted by my department. — [1] —. All Conservancy staff and current members will be receiving a hard-copy version of the questionnaire form in the mail this week. An online version is also available on our Web site at walkinsonconservancy.org/ed-questionnaire.

The questionnaire is anonymous unless you choose to include your name. — [2] —. There is room at the end of the form if you wish to expand on your answers with any additional thoughts.

Please be aware that submissions will be read by every member of the board. These forms will become part of the executive director's personnel file, with the same privacy protections and restricted access as any employee's personnel file. — [3] —.

The form must be submitted by 5 P.M. on Monday, May 10. — [4] —. If you are completing the paper version, please send it by mail, or put it in the interoffice mail in a sealed envelope marked: Executive Director Performance Evaluation, Human Resources.

Thank you in advance for your participation.

Sincerely,

Juan Romas, Director of Human Resources

168. Who started a performance-evaluation process at the organization?

(A) The board of directors
(B) The executive director
(C) The conservancy members
(D) The human resources department

169. What is true about the questionnaire?

(A) It should be completed and returned within a week.
(B) It can be completed on the Internet or on paper.
(C) It must be signed by the person submitting it.
(D) It will gather feedback on the organization's policies.

170. What is indicated about the personnel files of employees at the organization?

(A) They are updated annually.
(B) They are read by board members.
(C) They are used to determine promotions.
(D) They are kept private.

171. In which of the positions marked [1], [2], [3], and [4] does the following sentence best belong?

"As part of that process, a questionnaire has been prepared."

(A) [1]
(B) [2]
(C) [3]
(D) [4]

GO ON TO THE NEXT PAGE

Rita Carvallo (10:19 A.M.) Has Ms. Castelli decided on the type of wood she wants for her custom dining table and chairs?

Lawrence Bremen (10:21 A.M.) Not yet. She asked for samples and recommendations. I wanted to check with you first. Any suggestions?

Rita Carvallo (10:23 A.M.) It depends on her budget. She has to decide on either hardwood or softwood, and then if she wants the wood painted or stained.

Lawrence Bremen (10:25 A.M.) She wants a natural look, so not painted. Aren't softwoods too weak for tables and chairs?

Tom Ohrt (10:29 A.M.) They aren't, actually. Pine and cedar come from evergreen trees. They're naturally yellowish red, and our local suppliers always have them in stock.

Lawrence Bremen (10:31 A.M.) Good to know. What about hardwood?

Rita Carvallo (10:32 A.M.) Many clients love a hardwood's rich colors and textures. They look good with a dark stain or a natural finish.

Tom Ohrt (10:34 A.M.) Their grain patterns are beautiful, but they are more expensive because the trees grow slowly. Cherrywood might be a good choice because it resists scratches. It is also popular, so we have it in stock. There should be enough for Ms. Castelli's project if she chooses it.

Lawrence Bremen (10:36 A.M.) I'll run a sample by her. Thank you both!

172. What type of work do the writers do?

(A) They maintain gardens.
(B) They sell custom furniture.
(C) They are financial advisors.
(D) They work at a hardware store.

173. What is indicated about Ms. Castelli?

(A) She prefers a natural look.
(B) She is ordering cabinets.
(C) She is mostly concerned about price.
(D) She wants pinewood.

174. At 10:29 A.M., what does Mr. Ohrt most likely mean when he writes, "They aren't, actually"?

(A) He suggests a brighter color.
(B) He has no more samples left.
(C) He is not sure what wood to order.
(D) He believes that a softwood is suitable.

175. What is indicated about hardwood?

(A) It has lovely patterns.
(B) It is best used indoors.
(C) It is currently out of stock.
(D) It is difficult to carve.

GO ON TO THE NEXT PAGE

Questions 176-180 refer to the following e-mail and article.

To:	Althea Kim <a.kim@busselton.gov>
From:	Sam Thompson <s.thompson@gpecproductions.com>
Date:	January 12
Subject:	Summary of our recent discussion

Hello Ms. Kim,

Here are the notes from today's discussion regarding the upcoming film shoot at the Hastings Bridge. Please review them and let me know if there is anything that I may have overlooked.

• Two weeks before filming, notices will be placed at both ends of the bridge to keep drivers informed.
• During the week of filming, March 8–15, the road will be barricaded one block from both ends of the bridge. Security personnel will be stationed at the barricades to help direct traffic.
• I will contact Nadia Sonder, the owner of a piece of land near the bridge's east entrance, to see whether she will rent it to us as a parking area for our trucks and equipment.
• If Ms. Sonder is unwilling, I will make an alternative arrangement, which is likely to be the parking lot of a movie theater, a theme park, or a grocery store. We would only need a little space in the corner, as our crew can pack our vehicles in pretty tightly, and we won't have any trailers with us, as all of our actors will be staying in town.

With our deepest gratitude,
Sam Thompson, Location Manager, GPEC Productions

Busselton To Host Movie Shoot

BUSSELTON (January 23)—Hastings Bridge, which crosses the Lawrence River in Busselton, will be closed from 7:00 A.M. on March 8 to 7:00 P.M. on March 15 while a film production takes place. Those who routinely use the bridge are urged to plan alternate routes.

Motorists should also be aware of the potential for increased pedestrian traffic in the area and take precautions accordingly. For the duration of the shoot, the film studio's vehicles and equipment will be stationed in an undeveloped area near the east end of the bridge.

While residents may be frustrated by the inconveniences that accompany the film production's work in Busselton, Althea Kim, head of the city's Office of Tourism, points to the gains for local residents.

"I appreciate the public's concerns, but the film's cast and crew will stay in the city's hotels and visit local restaurants as well as purchase other necessities," said Ms. Kim.

Local officials estimate that the production could bring in as much as one million dollars to Busselton.

176. What is the date of the meeting that Mr. Thompson attended?

(A) January 11
(B) January 12
(C) March 8
(D) March 15

177. What does Mr. Thompson mention in the e-mail?

(A) The identity of actors involved in a film shoot
(B) The urgency of choosing a setting for a movie scene
(C) A plan for controlling traffic near a bridge
(D) A need to rent trucks and equipment

178. What type of property does Ms. Sonder most likely own?

(A) A movie theater
(B) An amusement park
(C) An undeveloped field
(D) A grocery store

179. In the article, the word "appreciate" in paragraph 4, line 1, is closest in meaning to

(A) acknowledge
(B) enjoy
(C) increase
(D) desire

180. What is suggested in the article about the city of Busselton?

(A) Its bridge has a walkway for use by people on foot.
(B) Its hotels are currently full.
(C) Its drinking water comes from the river.
(D) Its economy profits from the filming.

TEST 2

GO ON TO THE NEXT PAGE

Jardinar International
Rua da Nova 49
Funchal, 9000-720, Madeira, Portugal

Order and Shipping Date: 12 February
Order Status: Paid

Ship To: Emmy Kirsch
Kirsch Garden Center
8 Boulevard Leon
L-1623 Luxembourg

Item	Quantity
Autumn Beauty Marigold	24
Azorean Red Tomato (organic)	36
Classic Dill	12
Sweet Pea Mix	15
Blue Tarragon	15

Questions about your order?
Reach us at www.jardinarinternational.pt or call 351-291-555-017.

To:	ekirsch@kirschgardencenter.lu
From:	lenasilvia@jardinarinternational.pt
Sent:	21 February, 8:23 A.M.
Subject:	Seed packet misprint

Dear Ms. Kirsch:

I received the voice mail you left yesterday and checked into the matter. The seed packages you referred to did include a misprint. We had intended for the "organic" label to appear in the lower-right corner, but the printer inadvertently left it out. Unfortunately, we failed to spot the error before the packages were shipped.

We are sending you, by express mail, several sheets of stickers labeled "organic" that you can affix to the lower-right corner of the seed packets so customers in your shop can be certain that they are buying organic seeds. We are also putting a credit of 25 euros on your account to make up for any inconvenience.

Thank you for bringing the matter to our attention. Thank you, too, for your business over the years. We trust your customers will continue to be pleased with the seed varieties from Jardinar International.

Sincerely,

Lena Silvia, Customer Service Manager
Jardinar International

181. What is suggested about Jardinar International?

(A) It has a store in Luxembourg.
(B) It offers landscaping services.
(C) It sells its products to businesses.
(D) It provides gardening advice on its Web site.

182. Which item in the order was mislabeled?

(A) Azorean Red Tomato
(B) Classic Dill
(C) Sweet Pea Mix
(D) Blue Tarragon

183. How did Ms. Silvia solve Ms. Kirsch's problem?

(A) By sending Ms. Kirsch some stickers
(B) By advising Ms. Kirsch to purchase an alternative product
(C) By providing Ms. Kirsch with new seed packets
(D) By reimbursing Ms. Kirsch for the cost of an item

184. In the e-mail, the word "matter" in paragraph 3, line 1, is closest in meaning to

(A) idea
(B) issue
(C) amount
(D) material

185. What is indicated about Ms. Kirsch?

(A) She is a former employee of Jardinar International.
(B) She paid 25 euros for express shipping.
(C) She received a discount for ordering in bulk.
(D) She is a longtime customer of Jardinar International.

GO ON TO THE NEXT PAGE

TEST 2

Changes on Main Street

GORTON (4 August)—Shanitra Jones, director of the city's Small Business Coalition, welcomed two new businesses to Main Street during an outdoor ceremony last week. Both newcomers are occupying properties left vacant for over six months by previous businesses that closed down.

Great Customisables has moved into the old Walt's Jewellery Mart space at 65 Main Street. Great Customisables offers merchandise such as hats, shirts, and totes that can be personalised with names, designs, and company logos.

Fred Djirubal, the store's manager, said he looks forward to playing an active role in the Gorton community. "We love working with schools and charitable organisations by assisting with fund-raisers," he said.

Café Arepa, an eatery specialising in Venezuelan cuisine, now occupies the space formerly held by Pizza Kings at 14 Main Street. "The Small Business Coalition is delighted to have Café Arepa there," Ms. Jones said. "Having a fine restaurant right in the middle of the shopping district will draw people in."

Ms. Jones added that Hargrave Cleaning Services will be opening a branch office in downtown Gorton as soon as it can finalise the lease.

Hargrave Cleaning Services
Suite 220, Second Floor, 65 Main Street, Gorton

We clean commercial properties throughout the Gorton area. Whether you're looking for regular daily or weekly cleaning or for a one-time deep cleaning, we can do it! Let us know what you need. We can come up with a plan just for you.

October Deep Cleaning Special—20% off if scheduled before 31 October! For more information or to schedule an appointment, call 07 5550 6653.

```
┌──────────────────────────────────────────────────────────────┐
│                                                                │
│   ██ MEMO                                                      │
│                                                                │
│   To:     All employees of Ohanian Manufacturing              │
│   From:   Facilities department                               │
│   Date:   12 October                                          │
│   Re:     This weekend                                        │
│                                                                │
│   Hargrave Cleaning Services will be here this weekend, 17–18 │
│   October, to perform a deep cleaning of the entire facility, │
│   including the break room. Carpets will be shampooed. Please │
│   remove all personal items from the floor in your office or  │
│   cubicle and clear your desk. All food must be removed from  │
│   the break-room refrigerator, and anything left there will   │
│   be thrown away. Please make certain to complete these tasks │
│   before the end of the day on Friday, 16 October.            │
│                                                                │
└──────────────────────────────────────────────────────────────┘
```

TEST 2

186. According to the article, what is true about the building at 14 Main Street?

(A) It was owned by Mr. Djirubal.
(B) It is now a construction site.
(C) It houses the Small Business Coalition.
(D) It was empty for more than six months.

187. Why is Ms. Jones pleased about the opening of a restaurant?

(A) She enjoys Venezuelan cuisine.
(B) She plans to host special events there.
(C) She thinks it will attract shoppers to the area.
(D) She expects it will employ many people from the community.

188. What business is located in the same building as Hargrave Cleaning Services?

(A) Great Customisables
(B) Walt's Jewellery Mart
(C) Café Arepa
(D) Pizza Kings

189. What is suggested about Ohanian Manufacturing?

(A) It manufactures carpets.
(B) It received a discount on a service.
(C) Its facility was recently redecorated.
(D) Its employees will be given a day off from work.

190. What is the last day that employees of Ohanian Manufacturing can remove food from the refrigerator?

(A) October 12
(B) October 16
(C) October 17
(D) October 18

GO ON TO THE NEXT PAGE ▶

To:	Jim Bickman <jbickman@mtchalet.co.nz>
From:	Olga Danielova <odanielova@mtchalet.co.nz>
Date:	4 February
Subject:	Kids' menu
Attachment:	📎 article

Jim,

I want to address the weak sales figures for our kids' menu items. We are seating as many children as ever, but we are selling fewer kids' meals each month. It is time we took a hard look at the kids' menu.

I have attached a recent restaurant industry article that could be helpful. Please share it with the team and then put together some options for review. Pay particular attention to point number one regarding diners' preferences. The servers say that we often get requests like that.

Talk to you soon,

Olga Danielova
General Manager, Mountain Chalet Restaurant

Best Dining Magazine

Time to Update Your Children's Menu?

According to a recent *Best Dining Magazine* survey, restaurants need to make big changes to their children's menus if they want to appeal to young families. Diners preferred expanded kids' menu options in three main categories:

1. Seventy percent of respondents wanted menu options for children who are on special diets (e.g., vegetarian meals).

2. Eighty-seven percent of respondents requested options for healthier eating (e.g., fruits, vegetables, and grilled or baked poultry and fish).

3. Sixty-four percent of respondents said they would like to see more customizable kids' meals (e.g., choose-your-own toppings, sauces, and side items).

Interestingly, very few respondents (19 percent) requested lower prices.

> http://www.foodloveblog.co.nz ▼

Goodbye, Chicken Nuggets; Hello, Kale Salad!

Chef Jim Bickman at Mountain Chalet has made dining out with kids a lot healthier—and more enjoyable—by updating the restaurant's kids' menu. On a recent visit, the parents and children at our table all gave the new menu items an excellent review.

One young diner was thrilled that he could choose to top his kale salad with grilled chicken, tofu, or fish. Similarly, another child loved that she could choose from three sauces and multiple meats to create a pasta dish. Old favorites like grilled cheese sandwiches are also still available.

While we relaxed at our table, we enjoyed playing tabletop games that the restaurant had recently introduced. The atmosphere and the food made for a wonderful dining experience. I highly recommend Mountain Chalet to all food lovers with kids.

---

191. What most likely is Ms. Danielova's goal?

(A) To get better publicity for the restaurant
(B) To increase sales for a particular menu category
(C) To locate more suppliers of fresh food
(D) To resolve customer complaints more quickly

192. In the e-mail, what is Mr. Bickman asked to do?

(A) Look at sales figures
(B) Meet with Ms. Danielova
(C) Arrange for additional seating
(D) Share an article with employees

193. What change mentioned in the article would address the issue Ms. Danielova feels is most important?

(A) Adding vegetarian meals
(B) Offering fresh fruits
(C) Making meals customizable
(D) Decreasing prices

194. To whom did Ms. Danielova direct her concerns?

(A) A restaurant owner
(B) A general manager
(C) A chef
(D) A server

195. According to the Web page, what is newly available at Mountain Chalet?

(A) Chicken nuggets
(B) Outdoor seating
(C) Grilled cheese sandwiches
(D) Tabletop games

TEST 2

GO ON TO THE NEXT PAGE ▶

September 15

Edward Maunce, Operations Manager
Bronski Solutions, Inc.
21 Woerdens Road
Martindale, IN 46176

Dear Mr. Maunce,

Your company's monthly electricity charges fluctuated significantly over the past year. Many of our commercial customers with this kind of usage pattern have switched to Commercial SB billing. Under this plan, a company pays the same amount each month regardless of usage levels. This makes budgeting much easier. Contact me if your company is interested in Commercial SB billing.

Also, please note that next month all customers will be subject to a small 1% rate increase. The revenue generated from this increase will fund important repairs to our power delivery infrastructure.

Sincerely,

Patrice Tsui

Patrice Tsui
Commercial Accounts Representative
Oaklawn Electric Supply

E-mail	
To:	Sunita Colman, Vice President of Operations
From:	Edward Maunce, Operations Manager
Date:	September 30
Subject:	Electricity service
Attachment:	🖇 Service company letter - copy

Hello Sunita,

Please take a moment to read the attached copy of a letter I just received. I like Ms. Tsui's suggestion, and I believe we should move forward with it. Do you agree? Looking back at our recent records, I notice we experienced a major jump in costs starting in the exact month our temporary interns first arrived and began working on those short-term projects.

Thanks,

Ed
Operations Manager, Bronski Solutions, Inc.

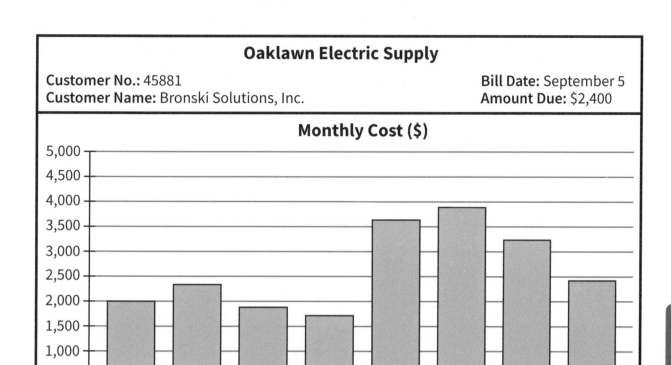

Oaklawn Electric Supply

Customer No.: 45881
Customer Name: Bronski Solutions, Inc.

Bill Date: September 5
Amount Due: $2,400

Monthly Cost ($)

196. What is one purpose of the letter?

(A) To apologize for a billing error
(B) To promote ideas for reducing energy usage
(C) To request payment for a past-due bill
(D) To explain a new way of paying for services

197. What does Ms. Tsui suggest is a common concern among commercial customers?

(A) Large variations in monthly bills
(B) Long wait times for customer service
(C) Frequent service disruptions
(D) Corporate restrictions on electricity usage

198. According to the letter, what will money from higher rates be used for?

(A) To increase technicians' wages
(B) To bid on new equipment
(C) To pay for maintenance
(D) To research alternative energy sources

199. What does Mr. Maunce think Bronski Solutions, Inc., should do?

(A) Choose Commercial SB billing
(B) Start an effort to reduce expenses
(C) Decrease the number of interns hired
(D) Stop being a client of Oaklawn Electric Supply

200. In what month were some temporary staff most likely hired?

(A) In May
(B) In June
(C) In July
(D) In August

Stop! This is the end of the test. If you finish before time is called, you may go back to Parts 5, 6, and 7 and check your work.

公式 TOEIC® Listening & Reading 問題集 9（音声 CD 2 枚付）

2022 年 10 月 19 日　第 1 版 第 1 刷発行
2024 年 4 月 25 日　第 1 版 第 5 刷発行

著者　　ETS

発行元　一般財団法人 国際ビジネスコミュニケーション協会

　　　　〒 100-0014
　　　　東京都千代田区永田町 2-14-2
　　　　山王グランドビル
　　　　電話　(03) 5521-5935

印刷　　TOPPAN株式会社

TEST 1

解答用紙

REGISTRATION No. 受験番号

フリガナ
NAME 氏名

LISTENING SECTION

Part 1

No.	ANSWER
	A B C D
1	A B C D
2	A B C D
3	A B C D
4	A B C D
5	A B C D
6	A B C D
7	A B C D
8	A B C D
9	A B C D
10	A B C D

Part 2

No.	ANSWER
	A B C
11	A B C
12	A B C
13	A B C
14	A B C
15	A B C
16	A B C
17	A B C
18	A B C
19	A B C
20	A B C
21	A B C
22	A B C
23	A B C
24	A B C
25	A B C
26	A B C
27	A B C
28	A B C
29	A B C
30	A B C

Part 3

No.	ANSWER
	A B C D
31	A B C
32	A B C D
33	A B C D
34	A B C D
35	A B C D
36	A B C D
37	A B C D
38	A B C D
39	A B C D
40	A B C D
41	A B C D
42	A B C D
43	A B C D
44	A B C D
45	A B C D
46	A B C D
47	A B C D
48	A B C D
49	A B C D
50	A B C D
51	A B C D
52	A B C D
53	A B C D
54	A B C D
55	A B C D
56	A B C D
57	A B C D
58	A B C D
59	A B C D
60	A B C D

Part 4

No.	ANSWER
	A B C D
61	A B C D
62	A B C D
63	A B C D
64	A B C D
65	A B C D
66	A B C D
67	A B C D
68	A B C D
69	A B C D
70	A B C D
71	A B C D
72	A B C D
73	A B C D
74	A B C D
75	A B C D
76	A B C D
77	A B C D
78	A B C D
79	A B C D
80	A B C D
81	A B C D
82	A B C D
83	A B C D
84	A B C D
85	A B C D
86	A B C D
87	A B C D
88	A B C D
89	A B C D
90	A B C D
91	A B C D
92	A B C D
93	A B C D
94	A B C D
95	A B C D
96	A B C D
97	A B C D
98	A B C D
99	A B C D
100	A B C D

READING SECTION

Part 5

No.	ANSWER
	A B C D
101	A B C D
102	A B C D
103	A B C D
104	A B C D
105	A B C D
106	A B C D
107	A B C D
108	A B C D
109	A B C D
110	A B C D
111	A B C D
112	A B C D
113	A B C D
114	A B C D
115	A B C D
116	A B C D
117	A B C D
118	A B C D
119	A B C D
120	A B C D
121	A B C D
122	A B C D
123	A B C D
124	A B C D
125	A B C D
126	A B C D
127	A B C D
128	A B C D
129	A B C D
130	A B C D

Part 6

No.	ANSWER
	A B C D
131	A B C D
132	A B C D
133	A B C D
134	A B C D
135	A B C D
136	A B C D
137	A B C D
138	A B C D
139	A B C D
140	A B C D

Part 7

No.	ANSWER
	A B C D
141	A B C D
142	A B C D
143	A B C D
144	A B C D
145	A B C D
146	A B C D
147	A B C D
148	A B C D
149	A B C D
150	A B C D
151	A B C D
152	A B C D
153	A B C D
154	A B C D
155	A B C D
156	A B C D
157	A B C D
158	A B C D
159	A B C D
160	A B C D
161	A B C D
162	A B C D
163	A B C D
164	A B C D
165	A B C D
166	A B C D
167	A B C D
168	A B C D
169	A B C D
170	A B C D
171	A B C D
172	A B C D
173	A B C D
174	A B C D
175	A B C D
176	A B C D
177	A B C D
178	A B C D
179	A B C D
180	A B C D
181	A B C D
182	A B C D
183	A B C D
184	A B C D
185	A B C D
186	A B C D
187	A B C D
188	A B C D
189	A B C D
190	A B C D
191	A B C D
192	A B C D
193	A B C D
194	A B C D
195	A B C D
196	A B C D
197	A B C D
198	A B C D
199	A B C D
200	A B C D

TEST 2

解答用紙

REGISTRATION No. 受験番号

フリガナ

NAME 氏名

LISTENING SECTION

Part 1

No.	ANSWER A B C D
1	Ⓐ Ⓑ Ⓒ Ⓓ
2	Ⓐ Ⓑ Ⓒ Ⓓ
3	Ⓐ Ⓑ Ⓒ Ⓓ
4	Ⓐ Ⓑ Ⓒ Ⓓ
5	Ⓐ Ⓑ Ⓒ Ⓓ
6	Ⓐ Ⓑ Ⓒ Ⓓ
7	Ⓐ Ⓑ Ⓒ Ⓓ
8	Ⓐ Ⓑ Ⓒ Ⓓ
9	Ⓐ Ⓑ Ⓒ Ⓓ
10	Ⓐ Ⓑ Ⓒ Ⓓ

Part 2

No.	ANSWER A B C
11	Ⓐ Ⓑ Ⓒ
12	Ⓐ Ⓑ Ⓒ
13	Ⓐ Ⓑ Ⓒ
14	Ⓐ Ⓑ Ⓒ
15	Ⓐ Ⓑ Ⓒ
16	Ⓐ Ⓑ Ⓒ
17	Ⓐ Ⓑ Ⓒ
18	Ⓐ Ⓑ Ⓒ
19	Ⓐ Ⓑ Ⓒ
20	Ⓐ Ⓑ Ⓒ

No.	ANSWER A B C
21	Ⓐ Ⓑ Ⓒ
22	Ⓐ Ⓑ Ⓒ
23	Ⓐ Ⓑ Ⓒ
24	Ⓐ Ⓑ Ⓒ
25	Ⓐ Ⓑ Ⓒ
26	Ⓐ Ⓑ Ⓒ
27	Ⓐ Ⓑ Ⓒ
28	Ⓐ Ⓑ Ⓒ
29	Ⓐ Ⓑ Ⓒ
30	Ⓐ Ⓑ Ⓒ

Part 3

No.	ANSWER A B C D
31	Ⓐ Ⓑ Ⓒ Ⓓ
32	Ⓐ Ⓑ Ⓒ Ⓓ
33	Ⓐ Ⓑ Ⓒ Ⓓ
34	Ⓐ Ⓑ Ⓒ Ⓓ
35	Ⓐ Ⓑ Ⓒ Ⓓ
36	Ⓐ Ⓑ Ⓒ Ⓓ
37	Ⓐ Ⓑ Ⓒ Ⓓ
38	Ⓐ Ⓑ Ⓒ Ⓓ
39	Ⓐ Ⓑ Ⓒ Ⓓ
40	Ⓐ Ⓑ Ⓒ Ⓓ

No.	ANSWER A B C D
41	Ⓐ Ⓑ Ⓒ Ⓓ
42	Ⓐ Ⓑ Ⓒ Ⓓ
43	Ⓐ Ⓑ Ⓒ Ⓓ
44	Ⓐ Ⓑ Ⓒ Ⓓ
45	Ⓐ Ⓑ Ⓒ Ⓓ
46	Ⓐ Ⓑ Ⓒ Ⓓ
47	Ⓐ Ⓑ Ⓒ Ⓓ
48	Ⓐ Ⓑ Ⓒ Ⓓ
49	Ⓐ Ⓑ Ⓒ Ⓓ
50	Ⓐ Ⓑ Ⓒ Ⓓ

No.	ANSWER A B C D
51	Ⓐ Ⓑ Ⓒ Ⓓ
52	Ⓐ Ⓑ Ⓒ Ⓓ
53	Ⓐ Ⓑ Ⓒ Ⓓ
54	Ⓐ Ⓑ Ⓒ Ⓓ
55	Ⓐ Ⓑ Ⓒ Ⓓ
56	Ⓐ Ⓑ Ⓒ Ⓓ
57	Ⓐ Ⓑ Ⓒ Ⓓ
58	Ⓐ Ⓑ Ⓒ Ⓓ
59	Ⓐ Ⓑ Ⓒ Ⓓ
60	Ⓐ Ⓑ Ⓒ Ⓓ

Part 4

No.	ANSWER A B C D
61	Ⓐ Ⓑ Ⓒ Ⓓ
62	Ⓐ Ⓑ Ⓒ Ⓓ
63	Ⓐ Ⓑ Ⓒ Ⓓ
64	Ⓐ Ⓑ Ⓒ Ⓓ
65	Ⓐ Ⓑ Ⓒ Ⓓ
66	Ⓐ Ⓑ Ⓒ Ⓓ
67	Ⓐ Ⓑ Ⓒ Ⓓ
68	Ⓐ Ⓑ Ⓒ Ⓓ
69	Ⓐ Ⓑ Ⓒ Ⓓ
70	Ⓐ Ⓑ Ⓒ Ⓓ

No.	ANSWER A B C D
71	Ⓐ Ⓑ Ⓒ Ⓓ
72	Ⓐ Ⓑ Ⓒ Ⓓ
73	Ⓐ Ⓑ Ⓒ Ⓓ
74	Ⓐ Ⓑ Ⓒ Ⓓ
75	Ⓐ Ⓑ Ⓒ Ⓓ
76	Ⓐ Ⓑ Ⓒ Ⓓ
77	Ⓐ Ⓑ Ⓒ Ⓓ
78	Ⓐ Ⓑ Ⓒ Ⓓ
79	Ⓐ Ⓑ Ⓒ Ⓓ
80	Ⓐ Ⓑ Ⓒ Ⓓ

No.	ANSWER A B C D
81	Ⓐ Ⓑ Ⓒ Ⓓ
82	Ⓐ Ⓑ Ⓒ Ⓓ
83	Ⓐ Ⓑ Ⓒ Ⓓ
84	Ⓐ Ⓑ Ⓒ Ⓓ
85	Ⓐ Ⓑ Ⓒ Ⓓ
86	Ⓐ Ⓑ Ⓒ Ⓓ
87	Ⓐ Ⓑ Ⓒ Ⓓ
88	Ⓐ Ⓑ Ⓒ Ⓓ
89	Ⓐ Ⓑ Ⓒ Ⓓ
90	Ⓐ Ⓑ Ⓒ Ⓓ

No.	ANSWER A B C D
91	Ⓐ Ⓑ Ⓒ Ⓓ
92	Ⓐ Ⓑ Ⓒ Ⓓ
93	Ⓐ Ⓑ Ⓒ Ⓓ
94	Ⓐ Ⓑ Ⓒ Ⓓ
95	Ⓐ Ⓑ Ⓒ Ⓓ
96	Ⓐ Ⓑ Ⓒ Ⓓ
97	Ⓐ Ⓑ Ⓒ Ⓓ
98	Ⓐ Ⓑ Ⓒ Ⓓ
99	Ⓐ Ⓑ Ⓒ Ⓓ
100	Ⓐ Ⓑ Ⓒ Ⓓ

READING SECTION

Part 5

No.	ANSWER A B C D
101	Ⓐ Ⓑ Ⓒ Ⓓ
102	Ⓐ Ⓑ Ⓒ Ⓓ
103	Ⓐ Ⓑ Ⓒ Ⓓ
104	Ⓐ Ⓑ Ⓒ Ⓓ
105	Ⓐ Ⓑ Ⓒ Ⓓ
106	Ⓐ Ⓑ Ⓒ Ⓓ
107	Ⓐ Ⓑ Ⓒ Ⓓ
108	Ⓐ Ⓑ Ⓒ Ⓓ
109	Ⓐ Ⓑ Ⓒ Ⓓ
110	Ⓐ Ⓑ Ⓒ Ⓓ

No.	ANSWER A B C D
111	Ⓐ Ⓑ Ⓒ Ⓓ
112	Ⓐ Ⓑ Ⓒ Ⓓ
113	Ⓐ Ⓑ Ⓒ Ⓓ
114	Ⓐ Ⓑ Ⓒ Ⓓ
115	Ⓐ Ⓑ Ⓒ Ⓓ
116	Ⓐ Ⓑ Ⓒ Ⓓ
117	Ⓐ Ⓑ Ⓒ Ⓓ
118	Ⓐ Ⓑ Ⓒ Ⓓ
119	Ⓐ Ⓑ Ⓒ Ⓓ
120	Ⓐ Ⓑ Ⓒ Ⓓ

No.	ANSWER A B C D
121	Ⓐ Ⓑ Ⓒ Ⓓ
122	Ⓐ Ⓑ Ⓒ Ⓓ
123	Ⓐ Ⓑ Ⓒ Ⓓ
124	Ⓐ Ⓑ Ⓒ Ⓓ
125	Ⓐ Ⓑ Ⓒ Ⓓ
126	Ⓐ Ⓑ Ⓒ Ⓓ
127	Ⓐ Ⓑ Ⓒ Ⓓ
128	Ⓐ Ⓑ Ⓒ Ⓓ
129	Ⓐ Ⓑ Ⓒ Ⓓ
130	Ⓐ Ⓑ Ⓒ Ⓓ

Part 6

No.	ANSWER A B C D
131	Ⓐ Ⓑ Ⓒ Ⓓ
132	Ⓐ Ⓑ Ⓒ Ⓓ
133	Ⓐ Ⓑ Ⓒ Ⓓ
134	Ⓐ Ⓑ Ⓒ Ⓓ
135	Ⓐ Ⓑ Ⓒ Ⓓ
136	Ⓐ Ⓑ Ⓒ Ⓓ
137	Ⓐ Ⓑ Ⓒ Ⓓ
138	Ⓐ Ⓑ Ⓒ Ⓓ
139	Ⓐ Ⓑ Ⓒ Ⓓ
140	Ⓐ Ⓑ Ⓒ Ⓓ

Part 7

No.	ANSWER A B C D
141	Ⓐ Ⓑ Ⓒ Ⓓ
142	Ⓐ Ⓑ Ⓒ Ⓓ
143	Ⓐ Ⓑ Ⓒ Ⓓ
144	Ⓐ Ⓑ Ⓒ Ⓓ
145	Ⓐ Ⓑ Ⓒ Ⓓ
146	Ⓐ Ⓑ Ⓒ Ⓓ
147	Ⓐ Ⓑ Ⓒ Ⓓ
148	Ⓐ Ⓑ Ⓒ Ⓓ
149	Ⓐ Ⓑ Ⓒ Ⓓ
150	Ⓐ Ⓑ Ⓒ Ⓓ

No.	ANSWER A B C D
151	Ⓐ Ⓑ Ⓒ Ⓓ
152	Ⓐ Ⓑ Ⓒ Ⓓ
153	Ⓐ Ⓑ Ⓒ Ⓓ
154	Ⓐ Ⓑ Ⓒ Ⓓ
155	Ⓐ Ⓑ Ⓒ Ⓓ
156	Ⓐ Ⓑ Ⓒ Ⓓ
157	Ⓐ Ⓑ Ⓒ Ⓓ
158	Ⓐ Ⓑ Ⓒ Ⓓ
159	Ⓐ Ⓑ Ⓒ Ⓓ
160	Ⓐ Ⓑ Ⓒ Ⓓ

No.	ANSWER A B C D
161	Ⓐ Ⓑ Ⓒ Ⓓ
162	Ⓐ Ⓑ Ⓒ Ⓓ
163	Ⓐ Ⓑ Ⓒ Ⓓ
164	Ⓐ Ⓑ Ⓒ Ⓓ
165	Ⓐ Ⓑ Ⓒ Ⓓ
166	Ⓐ Ⓑ Ⓒ Ⓓ
167	Ⓐ Ⓑ Ⓒ Ⓓ
168	Ⓐ Ⓑ Ⓒ Ⓓ
169	Ⓐ Ⓑ Ⓒ Ⓓ
170	Ⓐ Ⓑ Ⓒ Ⓓ

No.	ANSWER A B C D
171	Ⓐ Ⓑ Ⓒ Ⓓ
172	Ⓐ Ⓑ Ⓒ Ⓓ
173	Ⓐ Ⓑ Ⓒ Ⓓ
174	Ⓐ Ⓑ Ⓒ Ⓓ
175	Ⓐ Ⓑ Ⓒ Ⓓ
176	Ⓐ Ⓑ Ⓒ Ⓓ
177	Ⓐ Ⓑ Ⓒ Ⓓ
178	Ⓐ Ⓑ Ⓒ Ⓓ
179	Ⓐ Ⓑ Ⓒ Ⓓ
180	Ⓐ Ⓑ Ⓒ Ⓓ

No.	ANSWER A B C D
181	Ⓐ Ⓑ Ⓒ Ⓓ
182	Ⓐ Ⓑ Ⓒ Ⓓ
183	Ⓐ Ⓑ Ⓒ Ⓓ
184	Ⓐ Ⓑ Ⓒ Ⓓ
185	Ⓐ Ⓑ Ⓒ Ⓓ
186	Ⓐ Ⓑ Ⓒ Ⓓ
187	Ⓐ Ⓑ Ⓒ Ⓓ
188	Ⓐ Ⓑ Ⓒ Ⓓ
189	Ⓐ Ⓑ Ⓒ Ⓓ
190	Ⓐ Ⓑ Ⓒ Ⓓ

No.	ANSWER A B C D
191	Ⓐ Ⓑ Ⓒ Ⓓ
192	Ⓐ Ⓑ Ⓒ Ⓓ
193	Ⓐ Ⓑ Ⓒ Ⓓ
194	Ⓐ Ⓑ Ⓒ Ⓓ
195	Ⓐ Ⓑ Ⓒ Ⓓ
196	Ⓐ Ⓑ Ⓒ Ⓓ
197	Ⓐ Ⓑ Ⓒ Ⓓ
198	Ⓐ Ⓑ Ⓒ Ⓓ
199	Ⓐ Ⓑ Ⓒ Ⓓ
200	Ⓐ Ⓑ Ⓒ Ⓓ

公式 TOEIC®
Listening & Reading
問題集

9

別冊 『解答・解説』

目　次

解答・解説で使われている表記の説明

● **CDのトラック番号 (Part 1 ～ 4)** ⋯⋯⋯⋯⋯⋯⋯⋯⋯⋯⋯⋯⋯⋯⋯⋯⋯⋯⋯⋯⋯⋯⋯

会話の音声が **CD 1 のトラック番号 46** に、
問題の音声が **CD 1 のトラック番号 47** に入っていることを示しています。

● **スクリプトの前の記号 (Part 1 ～ 4)**

　🇺🇸 = 米国の発音
　🇬🇧 = 英国の発音
　🇨🇦 = カナダの発音
　🇦🇺 = オーストラリアの発音

　M = 男性 (Man)
　W = 女性 (Woman)

● **スクリプト中の ❶ ❷ 等の番号 (Part 3、4)**

解説の中で説明している箇所を示しています。

PART 3   ◎ | 会話 **CD 1 46** | | 問題 **CD 1 47** |

Questions 32 through 34 refer to the following conversation.

問題32-34は次の会話に関するものです。

🇺🇸 W Hi, Thomas. ❶I'm having new wood flooring installed at my home on Friday, so I'm planning to take the day off.

こんにちは、Thomas。金曜日に自宅に新しい木製の床材を設置してもらうことになっているので、私はその日に休みを取るつもりです。

🇨🇦 M Sure, that's fine. But ❷remember, we have a meeting with a new client at nine A.M. that day. ❸You're working on the advertising campaign, so it would be good for you to be there.

分かりました、大丈夫です。でも念のためお伝えしますが、その日の午前9時に新規顧客との会議があります。あなたは広告キャンペーンを手掛けているので、そこに同席してもらえるといいのですが。

🇺🇸 W Of course. ❹Can you make this a videoconference call then? And I can call in to the meeting?

そうでしたね。では、これをテレビ電話会議にしてもらえますか。そうすれば、私も会議に電話で参加できますよね？

🇨🇦 M Yes, definitely. It won't be a problem to have you join remotely.

はい、もちろんできます。あなたに遠隔で参加してもらっても問題ないでしょう。

---

32 Why is the woman planning to take Friday off?

(A) She has a doctor's appointment.
(B) She has family visiting from out of town.
(C) She will be attending a workshop.
(D) She will have work done at her house.

女性はなぜ、金曜日に休みを取るつもりなのですか。

(A) 彼女には医者の予約がある。
(B) 彼女には市外から訪ねて来る親族がいる。
(C) 彼女は講習会に出席する予定である。
(D) 彼女は自宅で作業をしてもらう予定である。

| 正解 **D** | 女性は男性にあいさつをした後、❶「金曜日に自宅に新しい木製の床材を設置してもらうことになっているので、私はその日に休みを取るつもりだ」と予定を伝えている。よって、新しい床材を設置してもらうことを have work done と表している(D)が正解。

(A) appointment「予約」。
(B) family「親族」、from out of town「市外から」。
(C) attend「～に出席する」、workshop「講習会」。

33 What does the man remind the woman about?

~~(A) A client meeting~~

| 正解 **A** | 女性が金曜日に休みを取るつもりだと聞

● **色の区別**

　青字：正答に関する解説や語句の意味
　黒字：誤答に関する解説や語句の意味

● 特典音声ファイルの番号（Part 5 〜 7）

「49-51」は特典音声のファイル番号を示しています。ダウンロード音声ファイルのタイトル名に、「特典 49」、「特典 50」、「特典 51」と表示されています。

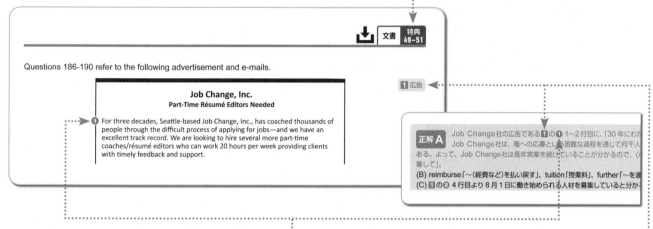

Questions 186-190 refer to the following advertisement and e-mails.

Job Change, Inc.
Part-Time Résumé Editors Needed

For three decades, Seattle-based Job Change, Inc., has coached thousands of people through the difficult process of applying for jobs—and we have an excellent track record. We are looking to hire several more part-time coaches/résumé editors who can work 20 hours per week providing clients with timely feedback and support.

● 文書中の ❶❷ 等の番号（Part 6、7）

解説の中で説明している文書中の段落番号等を示しています。解説文中の段落番号に続く行数は、英文中の各段落の何行目かを表しています。

● 文書を示す ❶ ❷ 等の番号（Part 7 複数の文書）

解説の中で説明している文書を示しています。

● Words & Phrases（Part 3、4、6、7）

会話やトーク、文書などに含まれる重要な語句と意味を紹介しています。Part 6、7 では、上記に示した ❶ ❷ や ❶❷ の番号により、本文で使われている場所が参照できます。

● Expressions（Part 6、7）

文書の中から、知っておくと便利な表現を例文とともに紹介しています。覚えて使えるようになると、大変便利です。

> **Expressions**
>
> apply for 〜　「〜に応募する、〜に申し込む」（❶ の❶ 2 行目）
> It is up to you to apply for the job with the publishing company.
> その出版社の仕事に応募するかどうかはあなた次第です。

---

*『公式 TOEIC® Listening & Reading 問題集 9』の特典として、ダウンロード音声の中には、TEST 1、2 のリーディングセクションの以下の音声が入っています。音声ダウンロードの手順は本誌 p. 3 をご参照ください。
　・正解が入った問題音声（Part 5、6）
　・文書の音声（Part 7）

参考スコア範囲の算出方法 ※ TEST 1、2 共通

1. 正解一覧（p.5、p.102）を参照し、リスニングセクションとリーディングセクションそれぞれの正答数を数えてください。各セクションの正答数がそれぞれの素点となります。
2. 下の参考スコア範囲の換算表であなたの素点に対応する換算点範囲を見つけます。
   例えばリスニングセクションの素点が45であれば、あなたの換算点範囲は「160点〜230点」です。
3. 各セクションの換算点範囲の合計が、あなたのトータルスコア（参考スコア範囲）となります。

参考スコア範囲の算出例

リスニングセクションの素点が 45 で、リーディングセクションの素点が 64 だった場合、
トータルスコアは① と② の合計である③ 415—570 の間ということになります。

	素点	換算点範囲	
リスニングセクション	45	160 — 230	①
リーディングセクション	64	255 — 340	②
トータルスコア（参考スコア範囲）		415 — 570	③（①＋②）

参考スコア範囲の換算表

リスニングセクション		リーディングセクション	
素点	換算点範囲	素点	換算点範囲
96 — 100	475 — 495	96 — 100	460 — 495
91 — 95	435 — 495	91 — 95	425 — 490
86 — 90	405 — 470	86 — 90	400 — 465
81 — 85	370 — 450	81 — 85	375 — 440
76 — 80	345 — 420	76 — 80	340 — 415
71 — 75	320 — 390	71 — 75	310 — 390
66 — 70	290 — 360	66 — 70	285 — 370
61 — 65	265 — 335	61 — 65	255 — 340 （算出例②）
56 — 60	240 — 310	56 — 60	230 — 310
51 — 55	215 — 280	51 — 55	200 — 275
46 — 50	190 — 255	46 — 50	170 — 245
41 — 45 （算出例①）	160 — 230	41 — 45	140 — 215
36 — 40	130 — 205	36 — 40	115 — 180
31 — 35	105 — 175	31 — 35	95 — 150
26 — 30	85 — 145	26 — 30	75 — 120
21 — 25	60 — 115	21 — 25	60 — 95
16 — 20	30 — 90	16 — 20	45 — 75
11 — 15	5 — 70	11 — 15	30 — 55
6 — 10	5 — 60	6 — 10	10 — 40
1 — 5	5 — 50	1 — 5	5 — 30
0	5 — 35	0	5 — 15

TEST 1 の正解一覧

リスニングセクション

問題番号	正解
Part 1	
1	A
2	C
3	D
4	D
5	B
6	C
Part 2	
7	B
8	B
9	C
10	A
11	B
12	A
13	A
14	C
15	B
16	B
17	B
18	A
19	B
20	A
21	A
22	A
23	B
24	C
25	C
26	A
27	A
28	B
29	B
30	A
31	B
Part 3	
32	D
33	A
34	C
35	B
36	D
37	C
38	A
39	D
40	B
41	A
42	C
43	B
44	D
45	D
46	C
47	D
48	B
49	C
50	C

問題番号	正解
51	D
52	B
53	C
54	A
55	B
56	B
57	A
58	C
59	C
60	D
61	A
62	B
63	C
64	C
65	D
66	D
67	C
68	D
69	B
70	A
Part 4	
71	D
72	A
73	B
74	B
75	A
76	D
77	A
78	C
79	D
80	D
81	A
82	C
83	A
84	D
85	C
86	C
87	B
88	A
89	A
90	D
91	A
92	C
93	B
94	A
95	C
96	B
97	D
98	D
99	A
100	C

リーディングセクション

問題番号	正解
Part 5	
101	B
102	A
103	B
104	D
105	B
106	D
107	B
108	D
109	C
110	D
111	B
112	D
113	B
114	C
115	C
116	A
117	C
118	A
119	C
120	C
121	A
122	B
123	A
124	D
125	B
126	A
127	C
128	C
129	D
130	A
Part 6	
131	C
132	D
133	A
134	D
135	C
136	D
137	A
138	B
139	A
140	D
141	B
142	C
143	A
144	C
145	B
146	D
Part 7	
147	D
148	B
149	A
150	C

問題番号	正解
151	B
152	D
153	D
154	C
155	C
156	B
157	A
158	A
159	B
160	D
161	C
162	A
163	B
164	B
165	A
166	D
167	C
168	C
169	B
170	D
171	D
172	D
173	C
174	B
175	A
176	B
177	D
178	A
179	A
180	B
181	D
182	B
183	C
184	A
185	B
186	A
187	D
188	C
189	C
190	B
191	A
192	C
193	D
194	A
195	B
196	D
197	C
198	B
199	A
200	C

PART 1

1 M

(A) She's crouching in front of a cabinet.
(B) She's watering some flowers.
(C) She's pulling some stools away from a countertop.
(D) She's rinsing some plates in a sink.

(A) 彼女は収納棚の前でしゃがんでいる。
(B) 彼女は花に水をやっている。
(C) 彼女はカウンターからスツールを引き出している。
(D) 彼女は流しで皿をすすぎ洗いしている。

正解 A 女性はcabinet「収納棚」の前でしゃがんでいるところである。crouch「しゃがむ」、in front of ～「～の前で」。
(B) 植物は写っているが、女性はそれに水をやっているところではない。water「～に水をやる」。
(C) 奥にstool「スツール、（カウンター用の）腰掛け」はあるが、女性はそれに触れていない。countertop「カウンター、調理台」。
(D) 皿は整理整頓された状態であり、sink「流し」にはない。rinse「～をすすぎ洗いする」。

2 W

(A) The woman is pushing a shopping cart.
(B) The woman is rolling up her shirtsleeves.
(C) The woman is putting an item into a bin.
(D) The woman is carrying a bucket out of the room.

(A) 女性はショッピングカートを押している。
(B) 女性は自分のシャツの袖をまくり上げているところである。
(C) 女性は大型容器に物を入れている。
(D) 女性は部屋からバケツを運び出している。

正解 C 女性がbin「大型容器、大箱」の中にitem「物、品物」を入れている。
(A) ショッピングカートは写っていない。
(B) 女性のシャツの袖はまくり上げられた状態であるが、まくり上げる動作をしているところではない。roll up ～「～をまくり上げる」、shirtsleeve「シャツの袖」。
(D) 壁際にbucket「バケツ」はあるが、女性はそれに触れていない。carry「～を運ぶ」。

3 W

(A) The people are standing next to each other.
(B) The people are arranging some magazines on a display.
(C) One of the people is cooking food in an oven.
(D) One of the people is looking at a refrigerator.

(A) 人々は隣り合わせに立っている。
(B) 人々は陳列されている雑誌を整えている。
(C) 人々の1人はオーブンで食べ物を調理している。
(D) 人々の1人は冷蔵庫を見ている。

正解 D 左側の人物はrefrigerator「冷蔵庫」の中を見ている。
(A) 左側の人物は立っているが、右側の人物は座っている。next to ～「～の隣に」、each other「互い（に）」。
(B) 雑誌類は机上にあるが、陳列されておらず、また2人はそれらを整えているところではない。arrange「～を整える」、display「陳列」。
(C) oven「オーブン」を使用して調理している人物はいない。

4

5

6

---

4 🍁 M

(A) The man is climbing up a flight of stairs.
(B) The man is examining a doorframe.
(C) The man is picking up some wood planks.
(D) The man is wiping a windowpane.

(A) 男性は階段を上っている。
(B) 男性はドアの枠を調べている。
(C) 男性は何枚かの木の板を持ち上げている。
(D) 男性は窓ガラスを拭いている。

正解 **D**　男性がwindowpane「窓ガラス」を拭いているところである。wipe「～を拭く」。
(A) 男性は木のはしごのようなものに片足を乗せているが、a flight of stairsは「ひと続きの階段、1階分の階段」を指す表現なので不適切。climb up ～「～を上る」。
(B) 男性が見ているのは窓であり、doorframe「ドアの枠」ではない。examine「～を調べる」。
(C) 複数の木の板は写っているが、壁に立て掛けられた状態であり、男性はそれらを持ち上げてはいない。pick up ～「～を持ち上げる」、plank「板」。

---

5 🇬🇧 W

(A) The surface of a lake is calm.
(B) Plants are growing along a riverbank.
(C) Some bridge railings are being replaced.
(D) Streetlights are being installed on a bridge.

(A) 湖面は穏やかである。
(B) 植物が川岸沿いに生えている。
(C) 橋の欄干が交換されているところである。
(D) 街灯が橋の上に設置されているところである。

正解 **B**　植物がriverbank「川岸」に生い茂っている。grow「生える」。
(A) 写っているのはlake「湖」ではなく川のように見え、水面も波立った状態である。surface「水面、表面」、calm「穏やかな」。
(C) 橋のrailings「欄干、手すり」は写っているが、それらは交換されているところではない。replace「～を交換する」。
(D) streetlight「街灯」は見当たらない。install「～を設置する」。

---

6 🇦🇺 M

(A) A bowl has been filled with bunches of grapes.
(B) Some chairs are occupied.
(C) Some flattened boxes are stacked on shelves.
(D) Some plastic bottles are being filled.

(A) ボウルが数房のブドウでいっぱいになっている。
(B) 椅子がふさがっている。
(C) 平らな状態の箱が棚に積み重ねられている。
(D) ペットボトルが満たされているところである。

正解 **C**　左側の棚に箱が平らな状態で積み重ねられている。shelvesはshelf「棚」の複数形。flatten「～を平らにする」、stack「～を積み重ねる」。
(A) bowl「ボウル、深鉢」は2個写っているが、どちらも空である。be filled with ～「～でいっぱいである、～で満たされている」、bunch「(果物の)房」。
(B) 椅子が2脚写っているが、どちらも使用されていない。occupied「(座席などが)ふさがっている、使用中の」。
(D) plastic bottle「ペットボトル」のようなものは写っているが、満たされているところではない。

PART 2

7 🇦🇺 M Who is supervising the front desk?
🇬🇧 W (A) The key for the back door.
　　(B) Susan is, I think.
　　(C) No, but I'll pay later.

誰が受付を管理していますか。
(A) 裏口の鍵です。
(B) Susanだと思います。
(C) いいえ、でも私が後で支払います。

正解 B　Who ～?で誰が受付を管理しているかと尋ねているのに対し、Susanという具体的な人物名を挙げて答えている(B)が正解。supervise「～を管理する、～を監督する」、front desk「受付」。
(A) 質問にあるfrontと関連するbackが含まれるが、応答になっていない。back door「裏口」。
(C) 人物が尋ねられているので、Yes/Noでは応答にならない。pay「支払う」。

8 🇦🇺 M Why is the computer network down?
🇺🇸 W (A) The networking event was fun.
　　(B) Because of the storm.
　　(C) I'm not sure which model I'll buy.

コンピューターネットワークは、なぜ停止しているのですか。
(A) 人脈づくりのイベントは楽しかったです。
(B) 嵐のせいです。
(C) 私はどちらのモデルを買うことにするか分かりません。

正解 B　Why ～?で、コンピューターネットワークが停止している原因を尋ねている。これに対し、Because of ～「～のせいで」を用いて、原因は嵐であると伝えている(B)が正解。network「ネットワーク」、down「停止した、作動していない」。storm「嵐」。
(A) 質問にあるnetworkと関連するnetworkingが含まれるが、ここでは「人脈づくり」という意味。
(C) コンピューターのmodel「モデル、型」は話題にされていない。

9 🇺🇸 W Which store is having a sale?
🇨🇦 M (A) For two weeks.
　　(B) OK, I can take that shift.
　　(C) The electronics store.

どの店がセールを行っていますか。
(A) 2週間です。
(B) 分かりました、私はそのシフトで勤務できます。
(C) 電子機器店です。

正解 C　Which ～?でどの店がセールを行っているかと尋ねているのに対し、「電子機器店だ」と特定の店を示している(C)が正解。have a sale「セールを行う」。electronics「電子機器」。
(A) 期間は尋ねられていない。
(B) 勤務シフトに関連することは尋ねられていない。shift「シフト」。

10 🇨🇦 M How are you traveling to New York?
🇬🇧 W (A) I'm taking the train.
　　(B) Tomorrow morning, thanks.
　　(C) Yes, on a business trip.

どうやってニューヨークへ行くのですか。
(A) 列車を使います。
(B) 明日の朝です、ありがとう。
(C) はい、出張で。

正解 A　How ～?でニューヨークへの移動手段を尋ねているのに対し、列車という交通手段を答えている(A)が正解。travel「移動する、旅行する」。
(B) 時は尋ねられていない。
(C) 質問にあるtravelingと関連するbusiness trip「出張」が含まれるが、手段が尋ねられているので、Yes/Noでは応答にならない。

11 🇦🇺 M When will the new chairs be delivered?
🇨🇦 M (A) The arms are adjustable.
　　(B) By three o'clock on Friday.
　　(C) The desks are very large.

新しい椅子はいつ配達される予定ですか。
(A) その肘掛けは調節可能です。
(B) 金曜日の3時までに。
(C) その机は非常に大きいです。

正解 B　When ～?で新しい椅子がいつ配達されるかと尋ねているのに対し、「金曜日の3時までに」と具体的な時を伝えている(B)が正解。deliver「～を配達する」。
(A) 質問にあるchairsと関連するarmsが含まれるが、応答になっていない。arm「(椅子などの)肘掛け」、adjustable「調節可能な」。
(C) 机については尋ねられていない。

12 🇨🇦 M　Is it going to rain tomorrow, or will it be sunny?

　　🇺🇸 W　(A) I think it's supposed to rain.
　　　　　(B) We arrived at four P.M.
　　　　　(C) What a beautiful sunset!

明日は雨が降りますか、それとも晴れそうですか。
　(A) 雨が降る見込みだと思います。
　(B) 私たちは午後4時に到着しました。
　(C) なんと美しい夕焼けでしょう!

正解 **A**　A or B?の形で、明日は雨が降るか、あるいは晴れそうかと尋ねている。これに対し、「雨が降る見込みだと思う」と伝えている(A)が正解。be supposed to do「～するはずである、～することになっている」。
(B) 到着した時刻は尋ねられていない。
(C) 天候についての質問と関連するsunset「夕焼け」が含まれるが、応答になっていない。

---

13 🇬🇧 W　Could you check the air pressure in my tires?

　　🇦🇺 M　(A) Of course, I'll do it now.
　　　　　(B) A retirement party.
　　　　　(C) I cashed the check.

私のタイヤの空気圧を確認していただけますか。
　(A) もちろんです、すぐに致します。
　(B) 退職パーティーです。
　(C) 私はその小切手を換金しました。

正解 **A**　Could you ～?でタイヤの空気圧の確認を依頼しているのに対し、Of courseと快諾し、I'll do it now (=I'll check the air pressure in your tires now)と付け加えている(A)が正解。check「～を確認する」、air pressure「空気圧」。
(B) 質問にあるtiresと似た音を含むretirement「退職」に注意。
(C) 質問にあるcheckが含まれるが、ここでは名詞「小切手」の意味で用いられており、応答になっていない。cash「～を現金に換える」。

---

14 🇨🇦 M　I'm glad our company's taking on more employees.

　　🇦🇺 M　(A) Sure, you can take it.
　　　　　(B) The customer service department.
　　　　　(C) Me, too—we need the help.

当社が追加の従業員を雇用することをうれしく思います。
　(A) はい、それを持っていっていいですよ。
　(B) 顧客サービス部です。
　(C) 私もです——私たちにはその助けが必要です。

正解 **C**　「当社が追加の従業員を雇用することをうれしく思う」という発言に対し、Me, too「私もだ」と賛同し、続けて自分たちには追加の従業員という助けが必要であると補足している(C)が正解。take on ～「～を雇う」、employee「従業員」。help「助力」。
(A) 発言にあるtakingの原形takeを含むが、itが何を指すか不明であり、応答になっていない。
(B) department「部署」は尋ねられていない。customer service「顧客サービス」。

---

15 🇨🇦 M　Where are the replacement windowpanes?

　　🇺🇸 W　(A) Yesterday, I believe.
　　　　　(B) They're stacked up in the lobby.
　　　　　(C) No, it's not painful at all.

交換用の窓ガラスはどこにありますか。
　(A) 昨日だと思います。
　(B) ロビーに積み重ねられています。
　(C) いいえ、それは全く痛くありません。

正解 **B**　Where ～?で交換用の窓ガラスがある場所を尋ねているのに対し、「ロビーに積み重ねられている」と置かれている場所を答えている(B)が正解。Theyは質問にあるthe replacement windowpanesを指す。replacement「交換、代わりの物」、windowpane「窓ガラス」。stack up ～「～を積み重ねる」。
(A) 時は尋ねられていない。
(C) 場所が尋ねられているので、Yes/Noでは応答にならない。質問にあるwindowpanesと似た音を含むpainful「痛みを伴う、困難な」に注意。

16 🇦🇺 M　Ms. Park sent a purchase order, right?

🇬🇧 W　(A) Sure, I can be there.
　　　(B) I'll forward you the e-mail.
　　　(C) Actually, they're not very expensive.

Parkさんは購入注文書を送付しましたよね？
(A) いいですよ、私はそこに行くことができます。
(B) あなたにそのEメールを転送しますね。
(C) 実は、それらはあまり高価ではありません。

正解 **B**　肯定文の文末に ～, right? を付けて、「～ですよね」と、Parkさんが購入注文書を送付したことを確認している。これに対し、そのEメールを転送すると返答して、Parkさんが購入注文書を送付済みだということを暗に伝えている(B)が正解。purchase order「購入注文書」。forward ～ …「～に…を転送する」。
(A) thereがどこを指すのか不明。
(C) theyが何を指すのか不明。expensive「高価な」。

---

17 🇬🇧 W　Why is the swimming pool closed early?

🇦🇺 M　(A) At the membership desk.
　　　(B) For routine cleaning.
　　　(C) Yes, the event starts at seven A.M.

水泳プールはなぜ、早く閉まっているのですか。
(A) 会員受付カウンターで。
(B) 定期清掃のためです。
(C) はい、そのイベントは午前7時に始まります。

正解 **B**　Why ～?で水泳プールが早く閉まっている理由を尋ねている。これに対し、前置詞for「～のために」を用いて、「定期清掃のためだ」と理由を答えている(B)が正解。closed「閉まって、休業して」。routine「定期的な」、cleaning「清掃」。
(A) 場所は尋ねられていない。membership「会員資格」。
(C) 理由が尋ねられているので、Yes/Noでは応答にならない。また、イベントについては尋ねられていない。

---

18 🇺🇸 W　Don't you want to schedule a press conference?

🇦🇺 M　(A) Yes, but the next few days will be busy.
　　　(B) Poor Internet service.
　　　(C) I just read a book review.

記者会見の予定を組まなくていいのですか。
(A) そうしたいですが、今後数日は忙しいのです。
(B) 貧弱なインターネットサービスです。
(C) 私はちょうど書評を読んだところです。

正解 **A**　Don't you want to do ～?は直訳すると「あなたは～したくはないか」という否定疑問文だが、ここでは「～しなくていいか」といった遠慮がちな提案と考えられる。これに対し、Yesで「そうしたい」と肯定しながらも、今後数日間の忙しさを伝えることで、すぐにはできないという状況を示唆している(A)が正解。schedule「～の予定を組む」、press conference「記者会見」。
(B) インターネットサービスに関連することには言及されていない。
(C) 質問にあるpressには「印刷、論評」の意味もあるが、応答になっていない。book review「書評」。

---

19 🇬🇧 W　I photocopied the travel reimbursement forms.

🇨🇦 M　(A) A hotel in the center of town.
　　　(B) Thanks for doing that.
　　　(C) Three more hours.

私は旅費精算書をコピーしました。
(A) 町の中心部にあるホテルです。
(B) そうしてくれてありがとう。
(C) さらに3時間です。

正解 **B**　「旅費精算書をコピーした」という発言に対し、Thanks for doing that.(=Thanks for photocopying the travel reimbursement forms.)と、コピーしたことに対してお礼を述べている(B)が正解。photocopy「～をコピーする」、reimbursement「払い戻し、返済」、form「用紙、書式」。
(A) 発言にあるtravelと関連するhotelを含むが、宿泊施設については述べられていない。
(C) 所要時間に関することには言及されていない。

20 M　Are you planning to lead the workshop on online marketing?

W　(A) Nadia has more experience in that area.
　　(B) Check down the hall.
　　(C) A significant increase in revenue.

あなたは、オンラインマーケティングに関する講習会で指導役をする予定ですか。
(A) Nadiaの方が、その分野での経験が豊富です。
(B) 廊下の先を確認してください。
(C) かなりの増収です。

正解 **A**　講習会で指導役をする予定かと尋ねているのに対し、「Nadiaの方が、その分野での経験が豊富だ」と、自分よりも適任な人物に言及し、自分は講習会で指導役をする予定はないことを暗に伝えている(A)が正解。plan to do「~する予定である」、lead「~を指導する、~を導く」、workshop「講習会」、marketing「マーケティング、販売促進活動」。
(B) 場所は尋ねられていない。hall「廊下」。
(C) significant「かなりの、相当数の」、increase「増加」、revenue「収益、収入」。

21 M　Where can I find the notes from yesterday's meeting?

W　(A) In the department's shared folder.
　　(B) At noon tomorrow.
　　(C) No, I wasn't at my desk.

昨日の会議記録はどこにありますか。
(A) 部の共有フォルダー内です。
(B) 明日の正午に。
(C) いいえ、私は自分のデスクにいませんでした。

正解 **A**　Where ～?で昨日の会議記録がどこにあるかと尋ねているのに対し、「部の共有フォルダー内だ」と、保管場所を伝えている(A)が正解。notes「(講義などの)記録、メモ」。department「部署」、shared「共有の」。
(B) 時は尋ねられていない。
(C) 場所が尋ねられているので、Yes/Noでは応答にならない。

22 W　Would you like to purchase a warranty for your new coffeemaker?

W　(A) No, I'd rather not.
　　(B) They made some earlier.
　　(C) I'll take tea instead.

新しいコーヒーメーカーの保証を購入されますか。
(A) いいえ、やめておきます。
(B) 彼らが前に幾つか作りました。
(C) 私は代わりに紅茶にします。

正解 **A**　Would you like to do ～?「~したいですか」は、丁寧に相手の意向を尋ねる表現。新しいコーヒーメーカーの保証を購入したいかと尋ねているのに対し、Noと否定し、I'd rather not (purchase a warranty)「(保証の購入を)やめておく」と断っている(A)が正解。I'dはI wouldの短縮形。would rather not (do)は「どちらかというと~したくない」という意味で、丁寧な断りの表現。purchase「~を購入する」、warranty「保証」。
(B) Theyやsomeが指す内容が不明。
(C) 商品保証の購入を希望するかと尋ねられているので、代わりに紅茶にするという発言は応答にならない。instead「その代わりに」。

23 M　When should we leave for the airport?

W　(A) Port Clearview has beautiful scenery.
　　(B) Traffic is quite heavy at the moment.
　　(C) My ticket was reasonably priced.

私たちはいつ空港に向けて出発すればいいですか。
(A) Clearview港からは美しい景色が望めます。
(B) 交通量は今、かなり多いです。
(C) 私のチケットは手頃な値段でした。

正解 **B**　When ～?で自分たちがいつ空港に向けて出発すべきかと尋ねているのに対し、「交通量は今、かなり多い」と道が混んでいることを述べ、出発すべき時刻を判断するための情報を伝えている(B)が正解。airport「空港」。traffic「交通量」、heavy「(交通量が)多い」、at the moment「現在のところ、目下」。
(A) port「港」、scenery「景色」。
(C) チケットやその価格は話題にされていない。reasonably priced「手頃な値段の」。

24 🇬🇧 w Why has the conference room been reserved all day?

🇨🇦 M (A) A table on the patio, please.
(B) No, but I have a pen you could borrow.
(C) Do you need a meeting space?

その会議室はなぜ終日予約されているのですか。
(A) テラス席のテーブルをお願いします。
(B) いいえ、でも、お貸しできるペンを持っています。
(C) 会議スペースが必要なのですか。

正解 C　Why ～? で会議室が終日予約されている理由を尋ねている。これに対し、その理由は答えていないが、会議スペースが必要なのかと尋ねて質問の意図を確認している(C)が正解。conference「会議」、reserve「～を予約する」、all day「終日」。space「スペース、空間」。
(A) patio「(食事用の)テラス、中庭」。
(B) 理由が尋ねられているので、Yes/Noでは応答にならない。

25 🇨🇦 M What time is the client lunch starting?

🇺🇸 w (A) At the Maryton Conference Center.
(B) Yes, he can type the memo this afternoon.
(C) The caterer hasn't even arrived yet.

顧客との昼食会は何時に始まりますか。
(A) Maryton会議場で。
(B) はい、彼は今日の午後そのメモをタイプすることができます。
(C) ケータリング業者はまだ到着すらしていません。

正解 C　What time ～? で顧客との昼食会が始まる時刻を尋ねているのに対し、「ケータリング業者はまだ到着すらしていない」と現況を伝え、昼食会の開始までにはまだ時間がかかりそうなことを示唆している(C)が正解。client「顧客」。caterer「ケータリング業者、料理の仕出し業者」。
(A) 場所は尋ねられていない。conference center「会議場」。
(B) heがthe clientを指すとしても、時刻が尋ねられているのでYes/Noでは応答にならない。type「～をタイプする、～をキーボード入力する」。

26 🇬🇧 w Is there soundproof insulation between the office spaces?

🇨🇦 M (A) I've never heard any noise through these walls.
(B) My desk chair is very comfortable, thanks.
(C) Isn't the view from the south window better?

執務スペース間には防音材がありますか。
(A) これらの壁越しにどんな物音も聞こえたことはありません。
(B) 私のデスクチェアは非常に座り心地がいいです、ありがとう。
(C) 南の窓からの眺めの方が良いのではありませんか。

正解 A　執務スペース間に防音材があるかと尋ねているのに対し、「これらの壁越しにどんな物音も聞こえたことはない」と述べ、執務スペース間の防音性が高いことを示唆している(A)が正解。soundproof「防音の」、insulation「防音材、絶縁体」。noise「物音、騒音」。
(B) デスクチェアの感想は尋ねられていない。comfortable「心地よい」。
(C) 比較対象が不明であり、またview「眺め」については話題にされていない。

27 🇨🇦 M How many air-conditioning units has your team assembled?

🇺🇸 w (A) We're still waiting for some parts.
(B) No, turn the heater on.
(C) You can get those glasses online.

あなたのチームは何台の空調装置を組み立てましたか。
(A) 私たちはまだ幾つかの部品の到着を待っているところです。
(B) いいえ、暖房装置の電源を入れてください。
(C) その眼鏡をオンラインで入手できますよ。

正解 A　How many ～? でチームが何台の空調装置を組み立てたかと尋ねているのに対し、「私たちはまだ幾つかの部品の到着を待っているところだ」と現況を述べ、組み立てができていないことを示唆している(A)が正解。air-conditioning unit「空調装置」、assemble「～を組み立てる」。part「部品」。
(B) 数が尋ねられているのでYes/Noでは応答にならず、続く内容も装置の組み立てと関連しない。質問にあるair-conditioning unitsと関連するheater「暖房装置」に注意。turn on ～「～の電源を入れる」。

28 🇺🇸 W Doesn't the building have a backup generator?

🇦🇺 M (A) Fifteen apartment buildings.
　　(B) It broke last year.
　　(C) OK, I'll meet you at the front.

その建物には予備の発電機がないのですか。
(A) 15棟のマンションです。
(B) それは昨年壊れました。
(C) 分かりました、正面でお会いしましょう。

正解 B　否定疑問文で、「その建物には予備の発電機がないのか」と尋ねているのに対し、「それは昨年壊れた」と述べ、現在使える予備の発電機はないことを示唆している(B)が正解。Itは質問にあるa backup generatorを指す。backup「予備の」、generator「発電機」。break「壊れる、故障する」。
(A) 質問にあるbuildingを含む点に注意。apartment building「マンション、集合住宅」。
(C) OKで何を了承しているか不明であり、続く内容も予備の発電機と関連しない。

29 🇬🇧 W Can the housekeeping staff start cleaning all the rooms by two o'clock?

🇨🇦 M (A) There's a house for sale on Taylor Street.
　　(B) Some hotel guests check out late.
　　(C) We offer morning and afternoon flights.

客室清掃係は2時までに全室の清掃を開始することができますか。
(A) テイラー通りに売り家があります。
(B) ホテルの宿泊客の中には遅くチェックアウトする方もいますよ。
(C) 当社は午前と午後のフライトを提供しています。

正解 B　客室清掃係は2時までに全室の清掃を開始することができるかと尋ねているのに対し、「ホテルの宿泊客の中には遅くチェックアウトする人もいる」と述べ、2時までに全室の清掃を開始するのは難しいことを暗に伝えている(B)が正解。housekeeping「(ホテルの)清掃部門」。guest「宿泊客」、check out「(ホテルを)チェックアウトする」。
(A) 質問にあるhousekeepingに含まれるhouseに注意。for sale「売りに出されて」。
(C) offer「～を提供する」、flight「フライト、(飛行機の)便」。

30 🇺🇸 W We have to enter through the side entrance at the office tomorrow.

🇦🇺 M (A) I'm working from home this week.
　　(B) There's another copy somewhere.
　　(C) We're not accepting new proposals.

私たちは明日、オフィスの脇の入り口から入る必要があります。
(A) 私は今週、在宅勤務をすることになっています。
(B) どこかにもう1部あります。
(C) 私たちは新しい提案を受け付けていません。

正解 A　「私たちは明日、オフィスの脇の入り口から入る必要がある」という発言に対し、「私は今週、在宅勤務をすることになっている」と予定を述べ、自分はオフィスの入り口を使う必要がないことを示唆している(A)が正解。enter「入る」、side「脇、側面」、entrance「入り口」。work from home「在宅勤務をする」。
(B) 出版物や紙などには言及されていない。copy「部、冊」。
(C) accept「～を受け入れる」、proposal「提案」。

31 🇦🇺 M Can you update the Web site with today's dinner specials?

🇬🇧 W (A) The café on Main Street.
　　(B) Did you get a list from Chef Makoto?
　　(C) It was a delicious dinner.

今日のディナーの特別料理に関してウェブサイトを更新してもらえますか。
(A) 大通りにあるカフェです。
(B) あなたはMakoto料理長からリストを受け取りましたか。
(C) それはとてもおいしいディナーでした。

正解 B　Can you ～?で今日のディナーの特別料理に関するウェブサイトの更新を依頼しているのに対し、「あなたはMakoto料理長からリストを受け取ったか」と聞き返し、ウェブサイトの更新に必要と思われる情報について尋ねている(B)が正解。update「～を更新する」、special「(レストランの)特別料理」。list「リスト」。
(A) 場所は尋ねられていない。
(C) 質問にあるdinnerを含むが、食事の感想は応答にならない。

PART 3

Questions 32 through 34 refer to the following conversation.

問題32-34は次の会話に関するものです。

W Hi, Thomas. ❶I'm having new wood flooring installed at my home on Friday, so I'm planning to take the day off.

こんにちは、Thomas。金曜日に自宅に新しい木製の床材を設置してもらうことになっているので、私はその日に休みを取るつもりです。

M Sure, that's fine. But ❷remember, we have a meeting with a new client at nine A.M. that day. ❸You're working on the advertising campaign, so it would be good for you to be there.

分かりました、大丈夫です。でも念のためお伝えしますが、その日の午前9時に新規顧客との会議があります。あなたは広告キャンペーンを手掛けているので、そこに同席してもらえるといいのですが。

W Of course. ❹Can you make this a videoconference call then? And I can call in to the meeting?

そうでしたね。では、これをテレビ電話会議にしてもらえますか。そうすれば、私も会議に電話で参加できますよね？

M Yes, definitely. It won't be a problem to have you join remotely.

はい、もちろんできます。あなたに遠隔で参加してもらっても問題ないでしょう。

32 Why is the woman planning to take Friday off?

(A) She has a doctor's appointment.
(B) She has family visiting from out of town.
(C) She will be attending a workshop.
(D) She will have work done at her house.

女性はなぜ、金曜日に休みを取るつもりなのですか。

(A) 彼女には医者の予約がある。
(B) 彼女には市外から訪ねて来る親族がいる。
(C) 彼女は講習会に出席する予定である。
(D) 彼女は自宅で作業をしてもらう予定である。

正解 D 女性は男性にあいさつをした後、❶「金曜日に自宅に新しい木製の床材を設置してもらうことになっているので、私はその日に休みを取るつもりだ」と予定を伝えている。よって、新しい床材を設置してもらうことをhave work doneと表している(D)が正解。
(A) appointment「予約」。
(B) family「親族」、from out of town「市外から」。
(C) attend「～に出席する」、workshop「講習会」。

33 What does the man remind the woman about?

(A) A client meeting
(B) A product launch
(C) A project deadline
(D) A building inspection

男性は何について女性に思い出させていますか。

(A) 顧客との会議
(B) 製品の発売開始
(C) プロジェクトの最終期限
(D) 建物の点検

正解 A 女性が金曜日に休みを取るつもりだと聞いた男性は、それを了承しつつも、❷「念のため伝えるが、その日の午前9時に新規顧客との会議がある」と女性に思い出させ、❸で、その会議への女性の同席を望んでいることを理由と共に伝えている。よって、(A)が正解。remind ~ about …「…について～に思い出させる」。
(B) product「製品」、launch「発売開始」。
(C) project「プロジェクト」、deadline「最終期限」。
(D) inspection「点検」。

34 What does the woman ask the man to do?

(A) Prepare some instructions
(B) E-mail some documents
(C) Set up a videoconference call
(D) Help another colleague

女性は男性に何をするよう頼んでいますか。

(A) 説明書を準備する
(B) 文書をEメールで送る
(C) テレビ電話会議を設定する
(D) 別の同僚を手伝う

正解 C 金曜日の会議への同席を打診された女性は、Of course.と了承してから、❹「では、これをテレビ電話会議にしてもらえるか」と頼んでいるので、(C)が正解。❹のthisは金曜日に予定されている顧客との会議を指す。set up ~「～を準備する」。
(A) 女性が男性に準備するよう頼んでいるのは、説明書ではなくテレビ電話会議。prepare「～を準備する」、instructions「説明書」。
(B) e-mail「～をEメールで送る」、document「文書、書類」。
(D) colleague「同僚」。

Words & Phrases

have ~ done　～を…してもらう　wood　木製の　flooring　床材　install　～を設置する
plan to do　～することを計画する　take a day off　1日休暇を取る　fine　差し支えない
remember　〈間投詞的に〉念のために言っておきますが　client　顧客　work on ~　～に取り組む　advertising　広告
campaign　キャンペーン　videoconference call　テレビ電話会議　call in to ~　～に電話で参加する
definitely　全くその通り　★強い肯定の返答　join　参加する　remotely　遠隔で

Questions 35 through 37 refer to the following conversation.　　問題35-37は次の会話に関するものです。

M ❶Are there any flights to London you can put me on? ❷I'm worried about making it there in time for my daughter's university graduation tomorrow.

私を乗せてもらえるロンドン行きの飛行機はありますか。明日の娘の大学の卒業式に間に合うよう現地に到着できるか心配です。

W ❸Yes, there's a flight to London that boards in 30 minutes. ❹I'll book that for you now.

はい、30分後に搭乗を開始するロンドン行きの便がございます。お客さまのためにそれをすぐご予約します。

M Perfect—thanks. Also, where's the closest place I can buy a newspaper in this airport?

完璧です——ありがとう。それと、この空港内で新聞を買える一番近い場所はどこですか。

W At Beacon Newsstand.

Beacon新聞雑誌店です。

M ❺Should I head out of this waiting area and turn right?

この待合エリアから出て右に曲ればいいですか。

W ❻No, if you make a left, you'll see it immediately.

いいえ、左に曲がればすぐに見えますよ。

---

35 What does the man say will take place in London?

(A) An industry trade show
(B) A university graduation
(C) A job interview
(D) An international music festival

男性はロンドンで何が行われると言っていますか。

(A) ある業界の展示会
(B) 大学の卒業式
(C) 就職面接
(D) 国際的な音楽祭

正解 B 男性は❶で、自分が乗ることのできるロンドン行きの飛行機があるかと尋ね、続けて❷「明日の娘の大学の卒業式に間に合うよう現地に到着できるか心配だ」と述べている。❷のthereはto Londonを表しているので、(B)が正解。take place「行われる」。
(A) industry「業界」、trade show「展示会」。
(C) job interview「就職面接」。
(D) international「国際的な」。

---

36 Who most likely is the woman?

(A) A newsstand vendor
(B) A security guard
(C) A baggage handler
(D) A ticket agent

女性は誰だと考えられますか。

(A) 新聞雑誌売り場の売り手
(B) 警備員
(C) 手荷物係員
(D) チケットの販売係

正解 D ロンドン行きの飛行機があるかと尋ねられた女性は、❸で、Yesと答えて30分後に搭乗開始する便があることを伝え、❹「お客さまのためにそれをすぐ予約する」と申し出ている。❹のthatは該当の便を指すので、女性は航空券の販売係だと考えられる。ticket agent「チケット販売係」。
(A) vendor「売る人」。
(B) security guard「警備員」。
(C) baggage handler「(空港の)手荷物係員」。

---

37 Why does the woman correct the man?

(A) He paid an incorrect amount.
(B) He mispronounced a name.
(C) He was about to go in the wrong direction.
(D) He misunderstood a travel requirement.

女性はなぜ、男性の誤りを訂正していますか。

(A) 彼は誤った金額を支払った。
(B) 彼は名前の発音を間違えた。
(C) 彼は間違った方向に向かおうとしていた。
(D) 彼は旅行の要件を誤解した。

正解 C 新聞を買える場所を聞いた男性は、❺「この待合エリアから出て右に曲ればいいか」と質問している。これに対し、女性は❻で、Noと否定して左に曲がればすぐにその売店が見えると教えている。よって、女性が誤りを訂正しているのは、男性が間違った方向に向かおうとしていたからだと分かる。correct「~の誤りを訂正する」。be about to do「今にも~しようとしている」、direction「方向」。
(A) pay「~を支払う」、incorrect「誤った」。
(B) mispronounce「~の発音を間違える」。
(D) misunderstand「~を誤解する」、requirement「要件」。

Words & Phrases

flight　飛行機の便、フライト　　put ~ on …　~を…に乗せる　　be worried about ~　~が心配である
make it　到着する、間に合う　　in time for ~　~に間に合って　　graduation　卒業式　　board　搭乗させる
book　~を予約する　　perfect　完璧な、素晴らしい　★満足を伝える返答としてよく使われる　　close　近い
newsstand　新聞雑誌売り場　　head　進む　　turn right　右に曲がる　　make a left　左に曲がる　　immediately　すぐに

Questions 38 through 40 refer to the following conversation.

W Hi, Pierre. ❶Everyone at the theater is pleased with the new Web site. ❷Thank you so much.

M ❸I'm glad you like it. ❹It was a fun project!

W There is one thing I wanted to ask about, though. We hired a new box office manager, and we'd like to include his biography in the "About Us" section.

M Sure, I have time to make that change this afternoon. ❺Could you e-mail me the biography?

W Of course. And how much will this update cost?

M ❻My standard contract includes five rounds of revisions, so you won't need to pay anything.

W Oh, ❼that's good news!

問題38-40は次の会話に関するものです。

こんにちは、Pierre。当劇場の皆が新しいウェブサイトに満足しています。本当にありがとうございます。

気に入っていただけてうれしいです。楽しいプロジェクトでした！

ですが、1点お尋ねしたかったことがあります。私たちは新しいチケット売り場責任者を雇用したので、彼の経歴を「当劇場について」のセクションに入れたいのです。

いいですよ、今日の午後、その変更を加える時間があります。経歴を私にEメールで送っていただけますか。

もちろんです。それから、この更新には幾らかかるでしょうか。

私の標準的な契約は5回分の修正を含んでいるので、何もお支払いいただく必要はありませんよ。

ああ、それは朗報です！

38 What most likely is the man's job?

(A) Web site designer
(B) Interior decorator
(C) Accountant
(D) Journalist

男性の仕事は何だと考えられますか。

(A) ウェブサイトのデザイナー
(B) 室内装飾家
(C) 会計士
(D) ジャーナリスト

正解 A 女性が❶「当劇場の皆が新しいウェブサイトに満足している」と言った後、❷で男性にお礼を述べているのに対し、男性は❸で気に入ってもらえてうれしいと伝え、続けて❹で楽しいプロジェクトだったと述べている。❸のitはthe new Web siteを指す。よって、男性はウェブサイトのデザイナーだと判断できる。designer「デザイナー、設計者」。
(B) interior decorator「室内装飾家」。
(C) accountant「会計士」。

39 What does the man ask the woman to do?

(A) Authorize a purchase
(B) Take some photographs
(C) Extend a deadline
(D) Send some information

男性は女性に何をするよう頼んでいますか。

(A) 購入を認可する
(B) 写真撮影をする
(C) 最終期限を延ばす
(D) 情報を送る

正解 D 劇場の新規雇用者の経歴をウェブサイトに加えたいと伝えた女性に対し、男性は快諾し、❺「経歴を私にEメールで送ってもらえるか」と頼んでいるので、(D)が正解。❺のthe biographyを(D)ではsome informationと表している。
(A) authorize「~を認可する」、purchase「購入」。
(B) take a photograph「写真を撮る」。
(C) extend「~を延ばす」、deadline「最終期限」。

40 What good news does the man give the woman?

(A) A hiring campaign was successful.
(B) Revisions are included in a contract.
(C) A project is being considered for an award.
(D) Employees will receive a cash bonus.

男性は女性にどんな朗報を伝えていますか。

(A) 雇用キャンペーンが成功裏に終わった。
(B) 修正作業が契約に含まれている。
(C) プロジェクトが賞の対象として選考されている。
(D) 従業員が現金賞与を受け取る予定である。

正解 B ❼で女性が「それは朗報だ」と述べているのは、追加更新の費用を尋ねたことに対して男性が❻「私の標準的な契約は5回分の修正を含んでいるので、何も支払う必要はない」と伝えたためである。よって、(B)が正解。
(A) hiring「雇用」、successful「成功した、好結果の」。
(C) consider ~ for …「~を…の対象として検討する」、award「賞」。
(D) cash「現金（払いの）」、bonus「賞与」。

Words & Phrases

theater 劇場　be pleased with ~ ~に満足している　fun 楽しい、楽しみを与えてくれる　project プロジェクト、計画　though でも　hire ~を雇用する　box office （劇場・映画館などの）チケット売り場　manager 責任者、管理者　include ~を含める　biography 経歴　section セクション、部分　make a change 変更する　e-mail ~ … ~に…をEメールで送る　update 更新　cost ~（金額）がかかる　standard 標準的な　contract 契約　round （一連のもののうちの）1回　revision 修正　pay ~を支払う

Questions 41 through 43 refer to the following conversation.

M Hello! I'm Bernard. ❶You must be Martina, our new postal carrier assistant. Welcome to your first day.

W Thank you! ❷I'm excited to start my mail route tomorrow.

M Excellent. ❸I'll be accompanying you this week to help you get used to your route. We'll leave at six A.M. You'll need to be at the loading dock by five thirty. ❹Make sure you bring a large water bottle. ❺It's going to be hot outside tomorrow.

W ❻Don't worry, my previous job was in landscaping.

問題41-43は次の会話に関するものです。

こんにちは! 私がBernardです。きっとあなたがうちの新しい郵便配達アシスタントのMartinaですね。初めての出勤を歓迎します。

ありがとうございます! 明日自分の郵便配達区域を開始するのが楽しみです。

素晴らしい。ご自分の配達区域に慣れてもらえるように、私が今週あなたに同行することになっています。私たちは午前6時に出発します。あなたは5時30分までに郵便物積み下ろし場に到着している必要があります。必ず、大きい水筒を持参してください。明日、屋外は暑くなりそうです。

ご心配なく、私の前職は造園業でしたから。

41 Who most likely are the speakers?

(A) Postal workers
(B) Warehouse managers
(C) Restaurant servers
(D) Bank tellers

話し手たちは誰だと考えられますか。

(A) 郵便局員
(B) 倉庫管理者
(C) レストランの給仕係
(D) 銀行の窓口係

正解 A 男性は❶「きっとあなたがうちの新しい郵便配達アシスタントのMartinaだね」と述べ、続けて女性の初出勤を歓迎している。これに対し、女性はお礼を言ってから、❷で、「自分の郵便配達区域を開始するのが楽しみだ」と伝えている。よって、2人は郵便局員だと判断できる。postal worker「郵便局員」。
(B) warehouse「倉庫」、manager「管理者」。
(C) server「給仕する人」。
(D) bank teller「銀行の窓口係」。

42 What does the man say he will be doing this week?

(A) Taking inventory
(B) Repairing a vehicle
(C) Training a new employee
(D) Responding to customer complaints

男性は今週、自分が何をすることになっていると言っていますか。

(A) 在庫目録を作成する
(B) 車両を修理する
(C) 新しい従業員を教育する
(D) 顧客の苦情に対応する

正解 C 男性は❸「自分の配達区域に慣れてもらえるように、私が今週あなたに同行することになっている」と述べ、続けて翌日の出勤時間や場所と持参すべき物を伝えている。女性をa new employeeと表し、業務に慣れさせることをtrain「～を教育する」と表現している(C)が正解。
(A) take inventory「在庫目録を作成する」。
(B) repair「～を修理する」、vehicle「車両」。
(D) respond to ～「～に応じる」、customer「顧客」、complaint「苦情」。

43 What does the woman mean when she says, "my previous job was in landscaping"?

(A) She does not know the answer to a question.
(B) She is accustomed to working outside.
(C) She knows how to care for plants.
(D) She is ready to switch careers.

"my previous job was in landscaping" という発言で、女性は何を意図していますか。

(A) 彼女は質問への答えが分からない。
(B) 彼女は屋外で働くことに慣れている。
(C) 彼女は植物の手入れの仕方を知っている。
(D) 彼女は転職する準備ができている。

正解 B 男性は❹で、大きい水筒を持参するよう女性に念を押し、❺「明日、屋外は暑くなりそうだ」と理由を述べている。これに対し女性は❻で心配は無用だと答え、続く下線部の発言で、前職は造園業だったと述べている。よって女性は、自分は屋外での仕事に慣れていることを伝えていると考えられる。be accustomed to doing「～することに慣れている」。
(C) care for ～「～の世話をする」、plant「植物」。
(D) be ready to do「～する準備ができている」、switch「～を切り替える」、career「キャリア、(生涯の)職業」。

Words & Phrases

postal carrier　郵便配達員　　assistant　アシスタント、補佐　　Welcome to ～.　～へようこそ。
be excited to do　～することにわくわくしている　　mail route　配達区域・経路　　excellent　素晴らしい　　accompany　～に同行する
get used to ～　～に慣れる　　loading dock　荷物の積み下ろし場　　make sure (that) ～　必ず～する、～であることを確実にする
water bottle　水筒　　previous　以前の　　in ～　～に従事して　　landscaping　造園

TEST1 PART 3

17

Questions 44 through 46 refer to the following conversation with three speakers.

問題44-46は3人の話し手による次の会話に関するものです。

M ①Has the shipment of circuit boards been delivered yet? ②We can't produce the laptop computers we need without those parts. We need them today.

プリント基板の発送品はもう届いていますか。あの部品なしでは、当社が必要とするノートパソコンを製造できません。私たちは今日それらが必要です。

W That shipment should've arrived yesterday. Elise, have you contacted the parts supplier?

あの荷物は昨日到着しているはずでした。Elise、部品の納入業者に連絡を取りましたか。

W I did. ③Our supplier is having some problems with hiring enough drivers. ④They're behind on all their orders this month.

取りました。納入業者は、十分な数のドライバーを雇用するのに問題を抱えています。同社は今月、全ての注文品に遅れが生じています。

M ⑤We need a new supplier, then, and fast. Wait, ⑥let me find the phone number of our old supplier.

それなら、当社は新しい納入業者が必要ですね、それも早急に。ちょっと待って、以前の納入業者の電話番号を探してみます。

---

44 What does the factory produce?

(A) Cars
(B) Airplanes
(C) Appliances
(D) Computers

工場は何を製造していますか。

(A) 自動車
(B) 飛行機
(C) 家電製品
(D) コンピューター

正解 D 男性は①で、プリント基板の発送品が到着しているか尋ねた後、②「あの部品なしでは、当社が必要とするノートパソコンを製造できない」と述べている。よって、この会話が行われている場所ではコンピューター機器を製造していると判断できるので、(D)が正解。factory「工場」。
(B) airplane「飛行機」。
(C) appliance「家庭用電化製品」。

---

45 Why has a shipment been delayed?

(A) Some roads are under construction.
(B) The weather has been poor.
(C) A computer system is undergoing maintenance.
(D) A company needs more drivers.

発送品はなぜ遅れているのですか。

(A) 複数の道路が工事中である。
(B) 天候がずっと不順である。
(C) コンピューターシステムがメンテナンス中である。
(D) 会社が追加のドライバーを必要としている。

正解 D 配送遅延について納入業者に連絡したかと尋ねられた女性は、③「納入業者は、十分な数のドライバーを雇用するのに問題を抱えている」と述べ、④で、その会社は全ての注文品に遅れが生じていると補足している。つまり、配送遅延の原因はドライバーが不足しているためと分かるので、(D)が正解。delay「～を遅らせる」。
(A) under construction「工事中で」。
(B) poor「(天気が)悪い」。
(C) system「システム」、undergo「～を受ける」、maintenance「メンテナンス、保守点検」。

---

46 What will the man most likely do next?

(A) Rent a truck
(B) Pay an express delivery fee
(C) Contact a supplier
(D) Ask to extend a deadline

男性は次に何をすると考えられますか。

(A) トラックをレンタルする
(B) 速達料金を支払う
(C) 納入業者に連絡する
(D) 最終期限を延ばすよう頼む

正解 C 納入業者からの配送が今月全て遅延していると知った男性は⑤で、新しい納入業者が早急に必要であると述べてから、⑥「以前の納入業者の電話番号を探してみる」と申し出ている。よって男性は、以前に部品を仕入れていた業者に連絡すると考えられるので、(C)が正解。
(A) rent「～をレンタルする、～を有料で借りる」。
(B) express delivery「速達便」、fee「料金」。
(D) ask to do「～するよう頼む」、extend「～を延ばす」、deadline「最終期限」。

Words & Phrases

shipment 発送品　circuit board　プリント基板　★電子機器の回路を作るのに必要な部品
produce　～を製造する　laptop computer　ノートパソコン　part 部品　supplier　納入業者、仕入れ先
have a problem with ～　～に関して問題がある　hire　～を雇用する　behind　遅れて　order　注文品　old　以前の

Questions 47 through 49 refer to the following conversation.　問題47-49は次の会話に関するものです。

M Hi, ❶this is Manuel Sanchez at Gilford Solutions.

もしもし、こちらはGilford Solutions社のManuel Sanchezです。

W Hello, Mr. Sanchez. ❷We just completed our monthly window washing of the Gilford headquarters. I hope everything was satisfactory.

こんにちは、Sanchezさん。当社はちょうど、月に1回のGilford本社の窓洗浄を終えたところです。万事ご満足いただけたことを願っています。

M Yes. The windows are spotless. Your company always does a great job. ❸That's why I'm calling. ❹We also need to have the exterior of our building power washed.

はい。窓には汚れ一つありませんね。御社は常々、素晴らしい仕事をしてくれていますね。実はそれでお電話しています。私たちは、当社の社屋の外壁も高圧洗浄してもらう必要があるのです。

W Sure, we can do that for you. Most of our clients have it done annually.

かしこまりました、当社で対応可能です。当社のお客さまの大半は、年に1回それを依頼されます。

M That's what we were imagining. ❺What kind of cost are we talking about?

それが私たちが思い描いていたものです。今話していることの費用はどのくらいでしょうか。

W Well, it depends on the total area. ❻Even though we're familiar with the Gilford building, I'll need some additional measurements to give you an accurate estimate.

そうですね、それは総面積によります。当社はGilford社の社屋のことはよく存じているとはいえ、正確な見積もりをお出しするには追加の測定値が必要になります。

---

47 What did the woman's company recently do for Gilford Solutions?
(A) It cleaned some floors.
(B) It painted a building.
(C) It created some signs.
(D) It washed some windows.

女性の会社は最近、Gilford Solutions社のために何をしましたか。
(A) フロアの清掃をした。
(B) 建物の塗装をした。
(C) 看板を製作した。
(D) 窓を洗浄した。

正解 D 男性が❶で、Gilford Solutions社のManuel Sanchezと名乗っているのに対し、女性は❷「当社はちょうど、月に1回のGilford本社の窓洗浄を終えたところだ」と述べている。よって、(D)が正解。recently「最近」。
(A) clean「～を清掃する」、floor「フロア、床」。
(B) paint「～を塗装する」。
(C) create「～を作る」、sign「看板、標識」。

48 Why is the man calling?
(A) To complain about the quality of some work
(B) To inquire about an additional service
(C) To reschedule a delivery time
(D) To request a discount on some products

男性はなぜ電話をしているのですか。
(A) 作業の質について苦情を言うため
(B) 追加の業務について尋ねるため
(C) 配達時間を変更するため
(D) 製品に対する割引を求めるため

正解 B 男性は、女性の会社による窓洗浄の質を称賛した後、❸で、それで電話しているのだと言ってから、❹「私たちは、当社の社屋の外壁も高圧洗浄してもらう必要がある」と用件を伝えている。また、❺ではその費用について質問している。よって、男性は追加の業務について問い合わせるために電話をしているのだと判断できる。inquire about ～「～について尋ねる」。
(A) 男性は仕事ぶりを称賛している。quality「質」。
(C) reschedule「～の日時を変更する」。

49 What information does the woman say she needs?
(A) An address
(B) A phone number
(C) Some measurements
(D) Some dates

女性は、どんな情報が必要だと言っていますか。
(A) 住所
(B) 電話番号
(C) 測定値
(D) 日付

正解 C 女性は、男性が尋ねている費用は総面積によると伝えた後、❻「当社はGilford社の社屋のことはよく知っているとはいえ、正確な見積もりを出すには追加の測定値が必要になる」と述べている。
(D) date「日付」。

Words & Phrases
solutions （顧客の要望に応じた）サービス、製品　washing 洗浄　headquarters 本社　satisfactory 満足のいく　spotless 汚れのない　exterior 外壁、外面　annually 年に1度　imagine ～を想像する　depend on ～ ～次第である　area 面積　even though ～ ～ではあるが　be familiar with ～ ～をよく知っている　additional 追加の　measurements 測定値　accurate 正確な　estimate 見積もり

Questions 50 through 52 refer to the following conversation with three speakers.

問題50-52は3人の話し手による次の会話に関するものです。

M Welcome to Speedy Car Rental.

Speedyレンタカー店へようこそ。

W I'm Jennifer Cho, and this is my work colleague, Claudine Wu. ❶We just came from the airport, and we're here to pick up a car we reserved. ❷It's under the corporate account for Eddington Services Limited.

私はJennifer Choで、こちらは職場の同僚のClaudine Wuです。私たちはたった今空港から来たところで、予約した車を受け取りに来ています。Eddington Services社の法人顧客名義のものです。

M Sure, let me pull up your info. OK, I have it here. ❸Since you made an advance reservation, you'll be receiving a discount on your rental today. Here are the keys.

かしこまりました、お客さまの情報をお出しします。はい、こちらにございますね。お客さまには事前予約をしていただいたので、本日はレンタル料の割引をお受けいただけます。こちらが車のキーです。

W Thanks. And ❹will Route 467 take us into town?

ありがとう。それから、467号線を進めば中心街に行きますか。

M ❺Yes, although there's some construction on it, ❻so you may want to take Denton Boulevard instead.

はい、とはいえその道路で工事が行われています。ですので、代わりにデントン大通りを通った方がいいかもしれません。

50 Why most likely are the women traveling?
(A) They are attending a family event.
(B) They are meeting with former classmates.
(C) They are on a business trip.
(D) They are on a vacation.

女性たちはなぜ旅行していると考えられますか。
(A) 彼女たちは家族の行事に出席する予定である。
(B) 彼女たちはかつての同級生たちと会う予定である。
(C) 彼女たちは出張中である。
(D) 彼女たちは休暇中である。

正解 C 1人目の女性は職場の同僚と来店したことを伝え、❶で、自分たちは空港から来たところであり、予約した車を受け取りに来たと述べている。続けて❷「Eddington Services社の法人顧客名義のものだ」と補足しているので、女性たちは社用で旅行していると判断できる。よって、(C)が正解。on a business trip「出張中で」。
(B) former「かつての」。
(D) on a vacation「休暇中で」。

51 Why did the women receive a discount?
(A) They referred a friend.
(B) They are return customers.
(C) They applied a coupon.
(D) They booked in advance.

女性たちはなぜ割引を受けたのですか。
(A) 彼女たちは友人を紹介した。
(B) 彼女たちは再来顧客である。
(C) 彼女たちはクーポンを適用した。
(D) 彼女たちは事前に予約した。

正解 D 女性たちの予約情報の確認が取れた男性は、❸で、事前予約がなされていたので今日はレンタル料の割引が受けられると2人に伝えている。よって、❸のmade an advance reservationを、book「予約する」とin advance「事前に、前もって」を用いて表した(D)が正解。
(A) refer「～を紹介する、～を差し向ける」。
(B) return customer「(主に2回目の)再来顧客」。
(C) apply「～を適用する」、coupon「クーポン」。

52 What does the man recommend?
(A) Taking some photos
(B) Using a different route
(C) Downloading a mobile app
(D) Stopping at a fuel station

男性は何を勧めていますか。
(A) 写真を撮ること
(B) 違う経路を利用すること
(C) 携帯用アプリをダウンロードすること
(D) 燃料補給所に立ち寄ること

正解 B 2人目の女性が❹で、467号線を進めば中心街に出られるかと尋ねているのに対し、男性は❺で、肯定しつつも工事に言及し、❻「そのため、代わりにデントン大通りを通った方がいいかもしれない」と別の道路の利用を勧めている。recommend「～を推奨する」。route「経路」。
(C) download「～をダウンロードする」、mobile「携帯用の」、app「アプリ(applicationの略)」。
(D) stop at ～「～に立ち寄る」、fuel「燃料」、station「特定のサービスを提供する施設」。

Words & Phrases
car rental レンタカー店　colleague 同僚　pick up ～ ～を受け取る　reserve ～を予約する　under ～という名で　corporate 法人の、企業の　account 顧客、口座　Limited (会社が)有限責任の　pull up ～ ～を引き上げる　info 情報 ★informationの略　make a reservation 予約する　advance 事前の　rental レンタル料　Route ～ ～号線 ★道路名　although とはいえ、～だけれども　construction 工事(作業)　～ Boulevard ～大通り ★道路名　instead 代わりに

Questions 53 through 55 refer to the following conversation.

🇺🇸 W ❶It's great that so many young children are coming here to have their teeth checked, but we're getting complaints from some of our other patients about how noisy and messy the waiting area is.

🇦🇺 M Right. ❷Maybe we could repurpose the first patient room to make a separate waiting area just for children. You know, renovate the space and add some books and toys for kids.

🇺🇸 W That might work. But ❸I'm a little worried about the price of renovations these days. ❹We'd better shop around for the right contractor.

問題53-55は次の会話に関するものです。

非常にたくさんの幼い子どもたちが歯の検査を受けにここへ来てくれるのは素晴らしいことですが、他の患者さんの一部から、待合室が非常に騒々しくて散らかっていると苦情を受けています。

そうですね。第1病室を子ども専用の別の待合室に転用してもいいかもしれませんよ。つまり、そのスペースを改修して子ども用の本や玩具を追加するのです。

それはうまくいくかもしれませんね。でも、私は近頃の改修作業の値段が少し心配です。適切な請負業者を比較検討した方がいいですね。

53 Where do the speakers most likely work?

(A) At an amusement park
(B) At a children's bookstore
(C) At a dentist's office
(D) At a school

話し手たちはどこで働いていると考えられますか。

(A) 遊園地
(B) 児童書専門店
(C) 歯科医院
(D) 学校

正解 **C** 女性は❶で、大勢の子どもたちが歯の検査を受けにここへ来てくれるのは素晴らしいと言っているので、2人は歯科医院で働いていると判断できる。また、男性が❷で病室を待合室に転用することに言及している点もヒントになる。dentist's office「歯科医院」。
(A) amusement park「遊園地」。
(B) 男性が児童書に言及しているのは子ども専用の待合室にそれらを置くことを提案するため。children's bookstore「児童書専門店」。

54 What does the man suggest doing?

(A) Changing the purpose of a room
(B) Providing a discount
(C) Assigning someone to clean a work space
(D) Booking a venue

男性は何をすることを提案していますか。

(A) 部屋の目的を変えること
(B) 割引を提供すること
(C) 誰かを仕事場の清掃業務に就かせること
(D) 会場を予約すること

正解 **A** 待合室の騒々しさや散らかり具合について苦情を受けていることを聞いた男性は、❷「第1病室を子ども専用の別の待合室に転用してもいいかもしれない」と提案している。よって、(A)が正解。purpose「目的」。
(B) provide「〜を提供する」、discount「割引」。
(C) 待合室の散らかり具合は指摘されているが、清掃業務には言及されていない。assign 〜 to do「〜を…する仕事に就かせる」。
(D) book「〜を予約する」、venue「会場」。

55 What is the woman concerned about?

(A) How long some work will take
(B) How much a project might cost
(C) How many staff members are available
(D) How often inspections will be required

女性は何について心配していますか。

(A) 作業にどのくらいの時間がかかるか
(B) 計画にどのくらいの費用がかかる可能性があるか
(C) 何人の職員が都合がつくか
(D) どのくらいの頻度で点検が必要になるか

正解 **B** 女性は男性の提案について、うまくいくかもしれないと言いながらも、❸「私は近頃の改修作業の値段が少し心配だ」と懸念点を伝え、続けて❹で、作業を依頼する請負業者の比較検討を提案している。よって、女性は部屋の改修という計画に費用がどの程度かかるのかを心配していると判断できる。be concerned about 〜「〜について心配している」。project「計画」、cost「〜（費用）がかかる」。
(A) take「〜（時間など）を要する」。
(C) staff member「職員」、available「都合がつく」。
(D) inspection「点検」、require「〜を必要とする」。

TEST1 PART 3

Words & Phrases

teeth 歯 ★toothの複数形　　check 〜を検査する　　complaint 苦情　　patient 患者
noisy 騒々しい　　messy 散らかった　　waiting area 待合室　　repurpose 〜を転用する、〜を他の目的で使用する
separate 別々の　　renovate 〜を改修する　　add 〜を加える　　work うまくいく　　renovation 改修作業
these days 近頃　　shop around for 〜 〜を比較検討する、〜を求めて幾つかの店を見て回る　　contractor 請負業者

Questions 56 through 58 refer to the following conversation.

M Sorry I'm late. ❶They're restoring the monument at Bennington Circle. All the workers and equipment are blocking a lane of Palmer Road.

W I know, ❷the traffic's been horrible during the restoration. I decided to take the train in to the office. Well, now that you're here, let's get started. ❸Did you get a chance to write the performance reviews for your team members?

M ❹I did. I wrote feedback on everyone's strengths and weaknesses. When I tried to access their individual sales results though, I kept getting an error message. ❺I was going to call the IT department.

W ❻No need. I've had this same problem before. ❼May I see your computer?

問題56-58は次の会話に関するものです。

遅れてすみません。Bennington円形広場にある記念碑の修復作業が行われているところでして。その作業員たちや機器などが、パーマー通りの1車線をふさいでいるのです。

知っています、修復作業期間中ずっと交通渋滞がひどいですよね。私は電車を利用して会社に来ることにしました。さて、あなたが到着したからには、始めましょう。ご自分のチームメンバーの業績評価を書く機会はありましたか。

ありました。皆の強みと弱みについての評価情報を書きました。ですが、個々の営業成績にアクセスを試みると、繰り返しエラーメッセージが出ました。私はIT部門に電話しようと思っていたのです。

その必要はありません。私も以前に、これと同じ問題を経験したことがあります。あなたのコンピューターを見てもいいですか。

56 What is causing some traffic?
(A) A bus depot is being remodeled.
(B) A monument is being restored.
(C) A sports event is taking place.
(D) A holiday parade is being held.

何が交通渋滞の原因となっていますか。
(A) バスターミナルが改築中である。
(B) 記念碑が修復中である。
(C) スポーツイベントが開催中である。
(D) 祝日のパレードが行われている。

正解 B 男性は遅刻を謝罪した後、❶で、円形広場の記念碑の修復作業が行われているためパーマー通りの1車線が利用できないことを伝えている。女性も❷「修復作業期間中はずっと交通渋滞がひどい」と述べているので、(B)が正解。cause「～の原因となる、～を引き起こす」。
(A) bus depot「バスターミナル」、remodel「～を改築する」。
(D) parade「パレード、行進」、hold「～を行う」。

57 What has the man been working on recently?
(A) Employee performance reviews
(B) A product redesign
(C) Staff training courses
(D) A department newsletter

男性は最近、何に取り組んできましたか。
(A) 従業員の業績評価
(B) 製品の再設計
(C) 従業員向けの研修講座
(D) 部内報

正解 A ❸「自分のチームメンバーの業績評価を書く機会はあったか」と尋ねる女性に対し、男性は❹で肯定し、皆の強みと弱みについての評価情報を書いたと補足している。よって、(A)が正解。
(B) product「製品」、redesign「再設計」。
(D) newsletter「会報、広報」。

58 Why does the woman say, "I've had this same problem before"?
(A) She wants a new assignment.
(B) She agrees with a manager's opinion.
(C) She is able to help the man.
(D) She is frustrated that her computer is old.

女性はなぜ "I've had this same problem before" と言っていますか。
(A) 彼女は新しい業務を望んでいる。
(B) 彼女は管理者の意見に同意している。
(C) 彼女は男性を手助けすることができる。
(D) 彼女は自分のコンピューターが古いということにいら立っている。

正解 C ❺で、IT部門に電話しようと思っていたと話す男性に対し、女性は❻「その必要はない」と言った後、下線部の発言で自分がその問題を経験済みであると述べている。直後に女性は❼で、男性のコンピューターを見ていいかと尋ねているので、女性は、自分が男性の問題を解決できることを伝えているのだと判断できる。よって、(C)が正解。be able to do「～することができる」。
(A) assignment「(割り当てられた)業務」。
(B) agree with ～「～に同意する」。
(D) frustrated that ～「～ということにいら立って」。

Words & Phrases
restore ～を修復する monument 記念碑 circle 円形広場、円形のもの equipment 機器 block ～をふさぐ lane 車線 traffic 交通渋滞、交通量 horrible ひどい restoration 修復 now that ～ 今や～なので get started 始める performance review 業績評価 feedback 評価情報、意見 strength 強み、長所 weakness 弱み、短所 try to do ～しようと試みる individual 個々の result 成績、結果 keep doing 繰り返し～する、～し続ける IT 情報通信技術 ★information technologyの略 need 必要性

Questions 59 through 61 refer to the following conversation.

🇬🇧 W Well, Mr. Alaoui, ❶you have several pieces of fine antique furniture that are in high demand among collectors. ❷My auction house should be able to attract a number of interested bidders.

🇨🇦 M I'm glad to hear that. ❸I'm moving overseas in June, and I'd rather not have to move so much heavy furniture. And it would be nice to have some extra money.

🇬🇧 W Of course. I'll have my appraiser come around next week to evaluate these pieces for auction. And ❹you understand that we keep 50 percent of the sale price as a commission, right?

🇨🇦 M Oh! ❺I'm surprised it's so much. I'll have to think about it a little more.

問題59-61は次の会話に関するものです。

さて、Alaouiさん、あなたは収集家の間で需要が高い素晴らしい骨董の家具を幾つもお持ちですね。うちの競売会社なら、多数の入札希望者を引き付けることができるはずですよ。

それを聞いてうれしいです。私は6月に海外へ引っ越す予定でして、これほどたくさんの重い家具を移動しなければならなくなるのは避けたいです。それに、多少の臨時収入を得られればうれしいでしし。

ごもっともです。来週うちの鑑定人に来てもらい、これらの品を競売に備えて査定してもらいましょう。それと、弊社が代理手数料として売却価格の50パーセントを頂いていることはご承知ですね?

えっ! そんなに高いとは驚きです。この件について、もう少し考える必要がありそうです。

TEST1 PART 3

59 Where does the woman work?
(A) At a bank
(B) At a pharmacy
(C) At an auction house
(D) At a construction company

女性はどこで働いていますか。
(A) 銀行
(B) 薬局
(C) 競売会社
(D) 建設会社

正解 C 女性は❶で、男性が需要の高い骨董の家具を幾つも所有していると述べた後、❷「うちの競売会社なら、多数の入札希望者を引き付けることができるはずだ」と見込みを伝えている。よって、(C)が正解。
(A) moneyやcommissionという語は登場するが、銀行に関する話題は出てこない。
(B) pharmacy「薬局」。
(D) construction「建設」。

60 What does the man say he is doing in June?
(A) Starting a new business
(B) Exhibiting an art collection
(C) Beginning a certification course
(D) Moving to another country

男性は6月に何をする予定だと言っていますか。
(A) 新しい事業を始める
(B) 美術収集品を展示する
(C) 資格認定講座を開始する
(D) 別の国に引っ越す

正解 D 男性は❸「私は6月に海外へ引っ越す予定だ」と伝えており、家具を売りたいと考える理由を続けている。よって、❸のoverseasをto another countryと表している(D)が正解。
(A) business「事業」。
(B) exhibit「〜を展示する」、art collection「美術収集品」。
(C) certification「(資格の)認定」、course「講座」。

61 What is the man surprised by?
(A) Some financial details
(B) Some government regulations
(C) The duration of a project
(D) The location of an office

男性は何に驚いていますか。
(A) 金銭的な詳細情報
(B) 政府の法令
(C) 計画の継続期間
(D) 会社の所在地

正解 A 女性は❹で、代理手数料として売却価格の50パーセントを取ることを承知しているかと男性に確認している。これに対し、男性はOh!と嘆声を漏らした後、❺「そんなに高いとは驚きだ」と述べている。❺のitはa commissionを指すので、それをsome financial detailsと表した(A)が正解。financial「金銭上の」、details「詳細情報」。
(B) government「政府」、regulations「法令、規則」。
(C) duration「継続期間」。

Words & Phrases

several 幾つもの、幾つかの a piece of 〜 1個の〜 ★不可算名詞を数えるときに用いる
fine 素晴らしい antique 骨董の furniture 家具 in demand 需要がある collector 収集家
auction house 競売会社 attract 〜を引き付ける a number of 〜 多数の〜 interested 関心を持った
bidder 入札者 be glad to do 〜してうれしく思う move 引っ越す、〜を動かす overseas 海外へ
would rather not do (どちらかというと)〜したくない extra 臨時の、余分の appraiser 鑑定人
come around やって来る evaluate 〜を査定する auction 競売、オークション commission 代理手数料

Questions 62 through 64 refer to the following conversation and price list.

W I'm calling to follow up on the vegetables you ordered from my farm. ❶How many kilograms of onions have you cooked with in the restaurant so far this week?

M ❷We're about halfway through the twenty-kilogram bag. I don't think we'll need as many next week.

W OK, ❸I can update your order to a twelve-kilogram bag. I'll bring it on Wednesday morning.

M ❹Perfect. Do you have any spinach available?

W I have mixed greens, if you like.

M No, thanks. ❺I need spinach for a special menu item I'm creating.

W ❻Let me check how much I have. ❼I'll call you back.

問題62-64は次の会話と価格表に関するものです。

お客さまが当農場にご注文くださった野菜に関して、追って確認するためお電話を差し上げております。今週これまでのところ、レストランで何キログラムのタマネギを料理にお使いになりましたか。

当店では、20キログラムの袋をおよそ半分ほど使い終わるところです。来週は同じだけの量は必要ないだろうと思います。

分かりました、ご注文の品を12キログラムの袋に変更できますよ。水曜日の朝それをお持ちしますね。

素晴らしいです。そちらにホウレンソウはありますか。

青野菜の詰め合わせがございます、もしよろしければ。

いえ、結構です。考案中の特別メニュー用にホウレンソウが必要なのです。

こちらにどれくらいの量があるか確認いたします。折り返しお電話差し上げますね。

Onion Prices	
$6	4 kilograms
$10	8 kilograms
$15	12 kilograms
$25	20 kilograms

タマネギの価格	
6ドル	4キログラム
10ドル	8キログラム
15ドル	12キログラム
25ドル	20キログラム

62 Who most likely is the man?

  (A) A food critic
  (B) A chef
  (C) A nutritionist
  (D) An event planner

男性は誰だと考えられますか。

  (A) 料理評論家
  (B) シェフ
  (C) 栄養士
  (D) イベントプランナー

63 Look at the graphic. How much will the man pay on Wednesday?

  (A) $6
  (B) $10
  (C) $15
  (D) $25

図を見てください。男性は水曜日に幾ら支払うでしょうか。

  (A) 6ドル
  (B) 10ドル
  (C) 15ドル
  (D) 25ドル

64 What will the woman do before calling back?

  (A) Write a review
  (B) Advertise a job
  (C) Check a quantity
  (D) Reserve some rooms

女性は、折り返し電話をかける前に何をするつもりですか。

  (A) レビューを書く
  (B) 求人広告を出す
  (C) 量を確認する
  (D) 部屋を予約する

TEST 1 PART 3

Words & Phrases			
follow up on ～	～に関して追って確認する	vegetables 野菜	farm 農場
kilogram キログラム	onion タマネギ	cook with ～ ～を使って料理する	so far これまでのところ
halfway 中間で、途中で	through ～を終えて	as many （すでに述べられた数と）同数の	update ～を最新のものにする
spinach ホウレンソウ	available 購入できる、利用可能な	mixed 混合の、雑多な	greens 青野菜
if you like もしよければ	item 品	create ～を考案する	call ～ back ～に折り返し電話する

Questions 65 through 67 refer to the following conversation and floor plan.

問題65-67は次の会話と間取り図に関するものです。

M ❶Welcome to Plaza Apartments. How can I help you?

Plazaマンションへようこそ。どのようなご用件でしょうか。

W Good morning. ❷A friend told me that this building was just completed, and I'm looking for somewhere to live in this area.

おはようございます。こちらの建物がちょうど完成したところだと友人が教えてくれたのですが、私はこの地域で住む場所を探しておりまして。

M Great! We have several units available. What size are you looking for?

いいですね! 入居可能なお部屋が幾つかございます。どのくらいの広さをお探しですか。

W I don't have much furniture, so a one-bedroom is fine. But I'd really like a unit with a nice view.

私はあまり家具を持っていないので、寝室が1部屋のもので十分です。でも、ぜひとも眺めの良い部屋がいいですね。

M Oh, well, ❸one of our available apartments has a room with a large window that overlooks our courtyard. Here's the floor plan.

ええと、そうですね。入居可能な住戸の一つに、建物の中庭を見渡せる大きな窓のある部屋がございます。こちらが間取り図です。

W Wonderful. That's just what I'm looking for.

素晴らしい。それこそまさに私が探しているものです。

M ❹Do you have some time right now? ❺I can show it to you.

今、お時間はおありですか。お客さまにそちらをお見せできますよ。

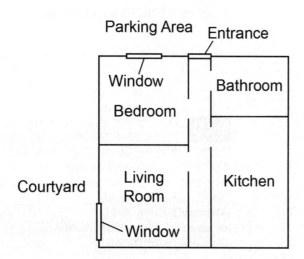

65 How did the woman hear about the apartment building?

    (A) From an Internet advertisement
    (B) From a television commercial
    (C) From a billboard
    (D) From a friend

女性はどのようにして、マンションの建物のことを聞きましたか。

    (A) インターネット広告から
    (B) テレビコマーシャルから
    (C) 掲示板から
    (D) 友人から

正解 D ❶でPlazaマンションへようこそと言ってから用件を尋ねる男性に対し、女性は❷「こちらの建物がちょうど完成したところだと友人が教えてくれた」と述べている。よって、(D)が正解。hear about ～「～について聞き知る」。
(A) Internet「インターネット」、advertisement「広告」。
(B) television「テレビ」、commercial「コマーシャル」。
(C) billboard「(屋外の大型)掲示板」。

---

66 Look at the graphic. Which room does the man refer to?

    (A) The bedroom
    (B) The bathroom
    (C) The kitchen
    (D) The living room

図を見てください。男性はどの部屋に言及していますか。

    (A) 寝室
    (B) バスルーム
    (C) 台所
    (D) 居間

正解 D 眺めの良い部屋を希望している女性に対し、男性は❸「入居可能な住戸の一つに、建物の中庭を見渡せる大きな窓のある部屋がある」と言ってから、その間取り図を見せている。図を確認すると、中庭に面した窓のある部屋は居間なので、(D)が正解。refer to ～「～に言及する」。
(A) 窓はあるが、窓から見えるのは中庭ではなく駐車場。
(B) (C) 中庭に面しておらず、窓もない部屋。

---

67 What will the woman most likely do next?

    (A) Pay a deposit
    (B) Fill out an application
    (C) View a unit
    (D) Measure some furniture

女性は次に何をすると考えられますか。

    (A) 手付金を支払う
    (B) 申込書に記入する
    (C) 住戸の内見をする
    (D) 家具の寸法を測る

正解 C 提案された住戸に関心を示す女性に対して、男性は、❹で時間があるか尋ねた後、❺「あなたにそれを見せられる」と申し出ている。❺のitは話題にされている住戸を指すので、女性はこれから、自分が気に入ったその住戸を見せてもらうと考えられる。view「～(不動産)を検分する」。
(A) pay「～を支払う」、deposit「手付金、内金」。
(B) fill out ～「～に記入する」、application「申込書」。
(D) 女性はあまり家具を持っていないと言っているだけ。measure「～の寸法を測る」。

Words & Phrases

floor plan 間取り図、フロアプラン　　apartment マンション・アパートの一区画、住戸
complete ～を完成させる　　look for ～ ～を探す、～を求める　　somewhere ある場所　　unit 1戸
available 利用可能な　　size 大きさ　　furniture 家具　　one-bedroom 寝室が1部屋の住戸　　fine 十分な、結構な
view 眺め　　overlook ～を見渡す　　courtyard 中庭　　here's ～ これが～です　　★here is ～の短縮形
right now ちょうど今

間取り図　parking area 駐車場　　entrance 玄関　　bathroom バスルーム　★浴室と化粧室を兼ねた部屋

Questions 68 through 70 refer to the following conversation and map.

🇬🇧 w Hello. ❶Are you a volunteer at this event?

🇦🇺 M Yes, I am. ❷Are you enjoying the car show?

🇬🇧 w Yes. ❸I've never seen so many antique cars in one place. But I'm starting to get hungry. Where are the food vendors set up?

🇦🇺 M Just on the other side of the main hall. ❹I recommend Rosa's. ❺Their food is delicious.

🇬🇧 w Rosa's? OK, I'll check it out.

🇦🇺 M ❻Just be warned that you may have to stand in line. It's the most popular booth every year.

問題68-70は次の会話と案内図に関するものです。

こんにちは。あなたはこのイベントのボランティアの方ですか。

はい、そうです。この自動車展示会を楽しんでいらっしゃいますか。

ええ。私はこれまで、こんなに多くのアンティークカーが一つの場所に集まっているのを見たことがありません。でも、おなかが空いてきたところです。食べ物の売店はどこに設置されていますか。

大ホールのちょうど反対側です。Rosa'sがお薦めです。あそこの料理はとてもおいしいですよ。

Rosa'sですか。分かりました、そこを見てみます。

列に並んで待つ必要があるかもしれないのでちょっとご注意ください。毎年、一番人気のある売店ですから。

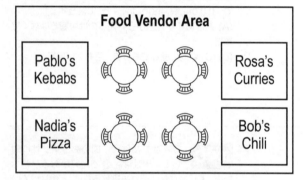

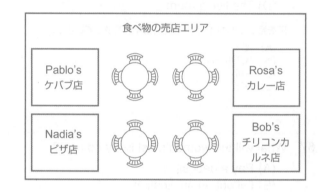

68 What event is the woman attending?

    (A) A film festival
    (B) A music festival
    (C) A furniture show
    (D) A car show

女性はどんなイベントに出席していますか。

    (A) 映画祭
    (B) 音楽祭
    (C) 家具展示会
    (D) 自動車展示会

正解 D ❶で、このイベントのボランティアかと尋ねる女性に対し、男性は肯定した後、❷「この自動車展示会を楽しんでいるか」と聞き返している。また、女性は❸「私はこれまで、こんなに多くのアンティークカーが一つの場所に集まっているのを見たことがない」と言っていることからも、女性は自動車展示会に出席していると分かる。attend「~に出席する」。
(A) film「映画」。
(C) furniture「家具」。

69 Look at the graphic. What kind of food does the man recommend?

    (A) Kebabs
    (B) Curries
    (C) Pizza
    (D) Chili

図を見てください。男性はどのような料理を薦めていますか。

    (A) ケバブ
    (B) カレー
    (C) ピザ
    (D) チリコンカルネ

正解 B 男性は、食べ物の売店の場所を女性に教えてから、❹「Rosa'sがお薦めだ」と述べた後、❺でそこの料理がおいしいと伝えている。案内図を見ると、右上にRosa's Curries「Rosa'sカレー店」という店名が記載されているので、男性が薦めている料理はカレーだと分かる。
(A) (C) (D) いずれの料理の売店にも言及がない。

70 What does the man warn the woman about?

    (A) She may have to wait.
    (B) She will have to show her ticket.
    (C) The prices are high.
    (D) There is limited table space.

男性は何について女性に警告していますか。

    (A) 彼女は待つ必要があるかもしれない。
    (B) 彼女は自分のチケットを提示する必要があるだろう。
    (C) 価格が高い。
    (D) テーブル席のスペースが限られている。

正解 A 男性が薦めた売店を見てみると伝える女性に対し、男性は❻「列に並んで待つ必要があるかもしれないので注意してくれ」と警告しているので(A)が正解。❻のstand in lineを(A)ではwaitと表している。warn ~ about …「…について~に警告する」。
(B) ticket「チケット、券」。
(C) price「価格、相場」。
(D) limited「限られた」、space「スペース、場所」。

Words & Phrases

map 案内図、地図　　volunteer ボランティア　　car show 自動車展示会
antique アンティークの、骨董の　　vendor 販売業者、物売り　　set up ~ ~を設置する　　hall ホール、大広間
recommend ~を推奨する　　delicious とてもおいしい　　check out ~ ~をよく見てみる
warn ~ that … ~に…だと警告する　　stand in line 列に並んで待つ　　booth 売店、ブース

案内図 kebabs ケバブ ★中東地域の串焼き料理　　curry カレー　　pizza ピザ
     chili チリコンカルネ ★chili con carneの略。チリトウガラシを用いたメキシコ料理

Questions 71 through 73 refer to the following excerpt from a meeting.

問題71-73は次の会議の抜粋に関するものです。

Good morning, staff. As you know, ❶this month we moved our customer appreciation day from Monday to last Saturday on the notion that the whole family would be able to visit. ❷I saw some of you at demonstration tables, showing our Super Green Leaf customers how to take care of the plants they purchase and how to repot them as they grow. Well, I just got our sales numbers—and guess what: we had record sales for the event! I'd like to congratulate you all on a job well done. And I'll go even further: ❸each one of you will receive a bonus this month. Enjoy!

おはようございます、従業員の皆さん。ご存じのように、一家そろってご来店いただけるようにするという考えから、今月、当店は顧客感謝デーを月曜日から先週の土曜日に動かしました。私は、皆さんの何名かが商品実演用のテーブルで、当Super Green Leafのお客さまに対して、ご購入いただく植物のお手入れ方法や、植物の成長に伴う別鉢への植え替え方法を説明する様子を目にしました。さて、ちょうど当店の売上高を入手したところなのですが——何が起こったと思いますか、私たちはあの催しで記録的な売上高を達成しました！見事な仕事ぶりについて、皆さん全員にお祝いを申し上げたく思います。そして、もっとありますよ。皆さんお一人お一人が、今月賞与を受け取ります。お楽しみに！

71 What kind of event was held at the store last Saturday?

(A) An end-of-season sale
(B) A grand opening
(C) A facility tour
(D) A customer appreciation day

先週の土曜日に、どんな種類の催しが店で開かれましたか。

(A) シーズン末の特売
(B) オープン記念イベント
(C) 施設の見学
(D) 顧客感謝デー

正解 D   話し手は、聞き手である従業員にあいさつした後、❶で、今月の顧客感謝デーが月曜日から先週の土曜日に日程変更されたことに言及しているので、(D)が正解。hold「～を開催する」。
(A) シーズンについての言及はない。end-of-season「シーズン末の」。
(B) grand opening「オープン記念イベント」。
(C) facility「施設」、tour「見学、ツアー」。

72 What does the store sell?

(A) Plants
(B) Clothing
(C) Tea
(D) Art supplies

店は何を販売していますか。

(A) 植物
(B) 衣料品
(C) お茶
(D) 美術用品

正解 A   話し手は❷「私は、皆さんの何名かが商品実演用のテーブルで、当Super Green Leafの顧客に対して、購入する植物の手入れ方法や、植物の成長に伴う別鉢への植え替え方法を説明する様子を目にした」と述べているので、この店は植物を販売していると判断できる。
(B) clothing「衣料品」。
(D) art「美術」、supplies「用品、備品」。

73 What will the listeners receive?

(A) A day off
(B) A bonus
(C) Free merchandise
(D) Store discounts

聞き手は何を受け取る予定ですか。

(A) 1日分の休暇
(B) 賞与
(C) 無料の商品
(D) 店内割引

正解 B   話し手は、聞き手である従業員たちの仕事ぶりを称賛した後、❸「皆さん一人一人が、今月賞与を受け取る」と知らせている。よって、(B)が正解。
(A) day off「休みの日」。
(C) free「無料の」、merchandise「商品」。
(D) discount「割引」。

Words & Phrases
excerpt 抜粋　appreciation 感謝　notion 考え　demonstration 商品の実演
green leaf 青葉　take care of ～　～の世話をする　repot ～を別の鉢に植え替える　as ～するにつれて
guess what 何か当ててみて、あのね ★話を切り出すときに注意を引く表現　record 記録的な
congratulate ～ on … …のことで～を祝う　well done 出来のよい、立派に遂行された　further さらに　bonus 賞与

Questions 74 through 76 refer to the following telephone message.

 M

Hi. This is Jung Soo Kim. ❶I've finished my inspection of the house, and it's in good shape, but I noticed something. ❷The rainwater's not draining properly. ❸When you move in, you'll need to have the rain gutters along the edge of the roof cleaned. They're filled with dead leaves, which prevents the water from flowing down the drainpipes and away from the house. ❹If it's not fixed, then, over time, water buildup could possibly damage the house's foundation. ❺I'm going to send you and the sellers my complete inspection report along with pictures, but I won't include repair estimates because those vary so widely.

問題74-76は次の電話のメッセージに関するものです。

こんにちは。こちらはJung Soo Kimです。私は例の住宅の点検を終え、それは良好な状態ですが、気付いた点があります。雨水が適切に排水されていないのです。ご入居の際、屋根の端に沿っている雨どいの掃除をしてもらう必要があるでしょう。雨どいに枯れ葉がぎっしり詰まっており、それが、水が排水管を伝って住宅から流れ去るのを妨げています。それが解決されないと、やがて、たまった水が、ことによると住宅の基礎部分に損傷を及ぼすかもしれません。あなたと販売業者に、私の点検報告書一式を写真と共にお送りしますが、修理の見積書は同封いたしません。そういったものは非常に大きく変動しますので。

74 Who is the speaker?

(A) A hardware store clerk
(B) A building inspector
(C) A water service provider
(D) A laboratory scientist

話し手は誰ですか。

(A) 工具店の店員
(B) 建物の検査官
(C) 水道供給事業者
(D) 研究所の科学者

正解 B 話し手は❶で自分が住宅の点検作業を完了したことを知らせ、それ以降では点検結果を詳しく説明しているので、建物の検査を行う仕事をしていると分かる。❺で、聞き手と販売業者に点検報告書を送ると述べていることもヒントになる。building「建物」、inspector「検査官」。
(A) hardware「金属製品（工具、刃物、金物など）」。
(C) 雨水の排水に言及しているが、水道については述べられていない。
(D) laboratory「研究所」、scientist「科学者」。

75 What is the speaker mainly discussing?

(A) A maintenance concern
(B) A city regulation
(C) A price negotiation
(D) A schedule delay

話し手は主に何について説明していますか。

(A) 維持管理上の懸念
(B) 市の条例
(C) 価格の交渉
(D) 予定の遅れ

正解 A 話し手は❷「雨水が適切に排水されていない」と、住宅の問題点を指摘し、続く❸で、雨どいの清掃の必要性とその理由を説明している。また❹では、それが解決されないとたまった水が住宅に損傷を与えかねないという懸念を伝えている。これらをa maintenance concernとまとめた(A)が正解。discuss「～を説明する」。maintenance「維持管理」、concern「懸念」。
(B) regulation「条例、規制」。
(C) negotiation「交渉」。

76 What does the speaker say he will send?

(A) An article
(B) A survey
(C) A timeline
(D) A report

話し手は何を送ると言っていますか。

(A) 記事
(B) アンケート
(C) 予定表
(D) 報告書

正解 D 住宅の点検結果を一通り説明し終えた話し手は、❺「あなたと販売業者に、私の点検報告書一式を写真と共に送る」と伝えている。
(A) article「記事」。
(B) survey「アンケート」。
(C) timeline「予定表」。

Words & Phrases

inspection 点検　in good shape 良好な状態で　notice ～に気が付く　rainwater 雨水　drain 排出する、流れ出る　properly 適切に　move in 入居する　rain gutter 雨どい　along ～に沿って　edge 端　be filled with ～ ～でいっぱいである　dead leaves 枯れ葉　prevent ～ from *doing* ～が…するのを妨げる　flow down ～ ～を伝って流れ落ちる　drainpipe 排水管　fix ～を解決する、～を修理する　over time やがて　buildup 蓄積　possibly ことによると　damage ～に損傷を及ぼす　foundation 基礎、土台　complete 完全な、漏れのない　along with ～ ～と一緒に　repair 修理　vary 変動する　widely 大きく、甚だしく

Questions 77 through 79 refer to the following advertisement.

問題77-79は次の広告に関するものです。

🍁 M

❶If you're interested in a career in cooking, then consider Estoff Culinary School! ❷From restaurants to catering businesses to food trucks, our program can help you achieve your goals. We emphasize healthy cooking, using only fresh ingredients. ❸At Estoff Culinary School, we guarantee job placement upon completion of the program. Our certificates are recognized by the top chefs in the city. And, ❹by enrolling now, the enrollment fee will be waived. However, ❺this offer ends on August first. Visit us online or call today!

料理の仕事にご関心をお持ちでしたら、Estoff調理学校をご検討ください！ レストランから仕出し業、キッチンカーに至るまで、当校のカリキュラムは皆さまがご自身の目標を達成するためにお役に立つことができます。当校は、新鮮な食材のみを使用した健康的な料理を重視しています。Estoff調理学校では、カリキュラム修了時の職業紹介を保証しています。当校の修了証書は、市内の一流シェフから高い評価を得ています。さらに、今入学することで入学金が免除となります。しかし、このサービスは8月1日に終了します。今すぐ、当校にオンラインでアクセスいただくかお電話ください！

77 What type of school is being advertised?

(A) Cooking
(B) Hospitality
(C) Fashion design
(D) Business management

どんな種類の学校が宣伝されていますか。

(A) 料理
(B) 接客
(C) ファッションデザイン
(D) 事業経営

正解 A 話し手は❶「料理の仕事に関心を持っているなら、Estoff調理学校を検討してください」と述べている。その後も❷で、レストランや仕出し業、キッチンカーといった料理関連の仕事を目標とすることに言及している。よって、料理学校の広告だと分かるので、(A)が正解。advertise「～を宣伝する」。
(B) hospitality「接客、もてなし」。
(D) management「経営」への言及はない。

78 According to the advertisement, what is guaranteed?

(A) Small group classes
(B) Flexible schedules
(C) Job placement after graduation
(D) Instruction by qualified teachers

広告によると、何が保証されていますか。

(A) 少人数制の授業
(B) 融通の利くスケジュール
(C) 卒業後の職業紹介
(D) 有資格の教師による指導

正解 C 話し手は、❸「Estoff調理学校では、カリキュラム修了時の職業紹介を保証している」と述べている。よって、❸のupon completion of the programをafter graduationと表し、職業紹介について述べている(C)が正解。graduation「卒業」。
(A) small group「少人数グループ」。
(B) flexible「融通の利く」。
(D) instruction「指導」、qualified「資格のある」。

79 What will happen on August 1?

(A) A course will begin.
(B) A payment will be due.
(C) A course book will be available.
(D) A special offer will expire.

8月1日に何が起こりますか。

(A) 講座が開始する。
(B) 支払い期日が来る。
(C) 講座用の教科書が入手可能になる。
(D) 特別サービスが終了する。

正解 D 話し手は❹で、今入学すれば入学金が免除となることを伝えた後、❺「このサービスは8月1日に終了する」と知らせている。よって、(D)が正解。expire「終了する、期限切れになる」。
(A) course「講座」。
(B) payment「支払い」、due「支払い期日になって、当然支払われるべき」。
(C) course book「講座用の教科書」、available「入手可能な」。

Words & Phrases

be interested in ～ ～に関心を持っている　career (生涯の)仕事、キャリア　consider ～を検討する　culinary 料理の　catering 仕出し(業)、ケータリング　food truck キッチンカー　program カリキュラム、学習課程　help ～ do ～が…するのに役立つ　achieve ～を達成する　emphasize ～を重視する、～を強調する　healthy 健康的な　ingredient 食材　guarantee ～を保証する　job placement 職業紹介　upon ～と同時に、～するとすぐに　completion 修了　certificate 修了証書　recognize ～を高く評価する　chef シェフ、料理人　enroll 入学する　enrollment fee 入学金　waive ～の適用を控える　offer サービス、提供

Questions 80 through 82 refer to the following telephone message.

問題80-82は次の電話のメッセージに関するものです。

🇦🇺 M

Hi, Li Na. This is Youssef. ❶I'm planning the luncheon to celebrate Nancy Baxter's retirement from our marketing department. ❷I went to the store yesterday to purchase her favorite chocolates for us to give to her at the luncheon. Now, ❸we need someone who can speak about some highlights of her career. ❹Of course, many people have worked with Nancy on successful ad campaigns over the years, but you've worked with her the most.

こんにちは、Li Na。こちらはYoussefです。私は、うちのマーケティング部のNancy Baxterの退職祝いの昼食会を計画中です。昨日店に行って、私たちが昼食会で渡すための、彼女の好きなチョコレートを購入しました。さて、彼女の経歴の重要な場面について話せる人が必要です。もちろん、大勢の人が長年にわたり、成功を収めた数々の広告キャンペーンでNancyと一緒に仕事をしてきましたが、あなたが一番たくさん彼女と一緒に仕事をしてきました。

---

80 What department does the speaker work in?

(A) Human resources
(B) Customer service
(C) Research
(D) Marketing

話し手はどんな部署で働いていますか。

(A) 人事
(B) 顧客サービス
(C) 研究
(D) マーケティング

正解 D 話し手は❶「私は、うちのマーケティング部のNancy Baxterの退職祝いの昼食会を計画中だ」と伝えているので、(D)が正解。また、話し手が❹で、同僚であるNancyが携わってきた仕事として広告キャンペーンに言及していることからも、マーケティング部で働いていると分かる。
(A) human resources「人事（部）」。
(B) customer service「顧客サービス（部）」。
(C) research「研究」。

---

81 What does the speaker say he did yesterday?

(A) He bought a gift.
(B) He sent an invitation.
(C) He contacted a caterer.
(D) He spoke with a client.

話し手は昨日何をしたと言っていますか。

(A) 彼は贈り物を購入した。
(B) 彼は招待状を発送した。
(C) 彼は仕出し業者に連絡した。
(D) 彼は顧客と話した。

正解 A 話し手は、同僚の退職祝いの昼食会を計画していると伝えた後、❷「昨日店に行って、私たちが昼食会で渡すための、彼女の好きなチョコレートを購入した」と知らせている。よって、その内容を言い換えた(A)が正解。gift「贈り物」。
(B) invitation「招待状」。
(C) contact「~に連絡する」、caterer「仕出し業者、ケータリング業者」。

---

82 What does the speaker imply when he says, "you've worked with her the most"?

(A) The listener may be promoted.
(B) A cost should be shared.
(C) The listener should give a speech.
(D) A staffing decision was unfair.

"you've worked with her the most" という発言で、話し手は何を示唆していますか。

(A) 聞き手は昇格する可能性がある。
(B) 費用は分担されるべきである。
(C) 聞き手はスピーチをすべきである。
(D) 人員配置に関する決定事項は不公平だった。

正解 C 話し手は❸で、Nancyの退職祝いの昼食会においてスピーチできる人が必要だと述べている。続けて❹で、大勢の人が彼女と共に仕事をしてきたと述べながらも、butに続けて下線部の発言で、一番たくさん彼女と一緒に仕事をしてきた人物は聞き手であると伝えている。よって話し手は、Nancyと共に働いた経験が最も多い聞き手こそがスピーチを行うべきだと示唆していると判断できる。give a speech「スピーチをする」。
(A) promote「~を昇格させる」。
(B) cost「費用」、share「~を分担する」。
(D) staffing「人員配置」、decision「決定事項」、unfair「不公平な」。

Words & Phrases		
plan ~の計画を立てる	luncheon 昼食会	celebrate ~を祝う	retirement 退職
department 部署	purchase ~を購入する	highlight 重要な場面、やま場	career 経歴、（生涯の）仕事
successful 成功した	ad 広告 ★advertisementの略	over the years 長年にわたり	

TEST 1 PART 4

Questions 83 through 85 refer to the following recorded message.

🇬🇧 w

問題83-85は次の録音メッセージに関するものです。

Thank you for calling the tech help hotline for DHJ Software, the makers of the Borata software program. ❶We are aware of an issue with the program. ❷Users are currently receiving error messages when attempting to download files. Our engineers are working to correct this, and an automatic program update should be available shortly. ❸If you are calling about program tutorials, you can find all training videos on our Web site. Don't forget, ❹we still have a discount for users buying 50 or more copies of the program, so be sure to indicate this when placing a purchase order. Thank you for choosing DHJ Software!

Borataソフトウエアプログラムの製造会社、DHJソフトウエア社の技術サポート電話相談窓口にお電話いただきありがとうございます。当社は、プログラムに発生している問題を認識しております。ユーザーの皆さまは現在、ファイルのダウンロードを試みる際にエラーメッセージをお受け取りになっています。当社のエンジニアがこの点を修正すべく取り組んでいるところで、プログラムの自動更新が間もなくご利用可能になる見込みです。プログラムのチュートリアルについてお電話いただいている場合は、当社のウェブサイト上にあらゆる教則動画がございます。忘れないでいただきたいのですが、当社は現在も、プログラムを50個以上ご購入いただいたユーザーの皆さまに割引をご用意していますので、購入注文の際に必ずこの点をお示しください。DHJソフトウエア社をお選びいただきありがとうございます。

---

83 According to the speaker, what problem is a company aware of?

(A) An error in downloading
(B) A delay in shipping
(C) Some inaccurate instructions
(D) Some damaged packaging

話し手によると、会社はどんな問題を認識していますか。

(A) ダウンロード時のエラー
(B) 発送の遅延
(C) 不正確な説明書
(D) 破損した梱包

正解 **A** 話し手は、会社の技術サポート電話相談窓口への連絡に対するお礼を述べた後、❶で、プログラムに発生中の問題を認識していることを伝えている。続けて❷「ユーザーの皆さんは現在、ファイルのダウンロードを試みる際にエラーメッセージを受け取っている」と、発生中の問題を説明している。よって、(A)が正解。
(B) delay「遅延」、shipping「発送」。
(C) inaccurate「不正確な」、instructions「説明書」。
(D) damaged「損傷を受けた」、packaging「梱包」。

---

84 Why does the speaker direct the listeners to a Web site?

(A) To submit a complaint
(B) To read customer reviews
(C) To enter a contest
(D) To watch instructional videos

話し手はなぜ、聞き手をウェブサイトに案内しているのですか。

(A) 苦情を提出するため
(B) 顧客レビューを読むため
(C) コンテストに参加申し込みをするため
(D) 教則動画を見るため

正解 **D** 話し手は❸「プログラムのチュートリアルについて電話している場合は、当社のウェブサイト上にあらゆる教則動画がある」と聞き手に伝えているので(D)が正解。❸のtraining videosを(D)ではinstructional videosと言い換えている。direct ～ to …「～を…に案内する」。instructional「教育の」。
(A) submit「～を提出する」、complaint「苦情」。
(C) enter「～に参加申し込みする」、contest「コンテスト、大会」。

---

85 How can the listeners receive a discount?

(A) By referring a friend
(B) By posting a review
(C) By purchasing many items
(D) By paying in advance

聞き手はどのようにして割引を受けることができますか。

(A) 友人を紹介することによって
(B) レビューを投稿することによって
(C) 多数の商品を購入することによって
(D) 前払いをすることによって

正解 **C** 話し手は、❹「当社は現在も、プログラムを50個以上購入してくれたユーザーの皆さんに割引を用意している」と述べているので(C)が正解。❹の50 or more copies of the programを(C)ではmany itemsと表している。purchase「～を購入する」、item「商品」。
(A) refer「～を紹介する、～を差し向ける」。
(B) post「～を投稿する、～を掲示する」。
(D) in advance「前もって」。

Words & Phrases

record　～を録音する　　tech　技術上の　★technicalの略
hotline　直通の電話相談サービス、ホットライン　　makers　製造業者　　be aware of ～　～を認識している　　issue　問題点
currently　現在　　attempt to do　～しようと試みる　　correct　～を正す　　automatic　自動の　　shortly　間もなく
tutorial　チュートリアル　★ソフトウエアなどの使用法を説明するプログラム　　a copy of ～　1点の～
be sure to do　必ず～する　★通例、命令文で使う　　indicate　～を示す　　place an order　注文する　　choose　～を選ぶ

Questions 86 through 88 refer to the following excerpt from a meeting.

問題86-88は次の会議の抜粋に関するものです。

M

❶Next on the management team agenda is a proposal to update the packaging for our breakfast cereals. ❷Some of our cereals have lost popularity in recent years and could definitely use a new look. But, as for Purple Berry Crunch, that remains a very popular brand. ❸It's still on the breakfast table of many homes across the country. So, I suggest we start by looking at our other cereal boxes one at a time. ❹I've prepared a few slides on each product. ❺I'll share those with the group now.

経営チームの議題として次に挙がっているのは、当社の朝食用シリアルの包装を新しくする提案です。近年、当社のシリアルの一部は人気が落ちており、ぜひとも新しい見た目が欲しいところです。しかし、Purple Berry Crunchについては、それは相変わらずとても人気の高い銘柄です。それは、今もなお全国の多くの家庭で朝食の食卓に上っています。そのため、私たちは、当社の他のシリアルの箱を一つずつ確認することから着手した方がいいと思います。私は、各製品に関するスライドを数枚用意しています。今からそれをこのグループと共有しましょう。

86 What type of food is the speaker discussing?

(A) Bread
(B) Yogurt
(C) Breakfast cereal
(D) Fruit juice

話し手はどんな種類の食品について話していますか。

(A) パン
(B) ヨーグルト
(C) 朝食用シリアル
(D) フルーツジュース

正解 **C** 話し手は❶「経営チームの議題として次に挙がっているのは、当社の朝食用シリアルの包装を新しくする提案だ」と述べ、それ以降でも、朝食用シリアルについての話を進めている。よって、(C)が正解。
(A)(B)(D) いずれも朝食用として出される傾向が高い飲食物だが、ここでは述べられていない。

87 What does the speaker imply when he says, "that remains a very popular brand"?

(A) A new recipe has not affected sales.
(B) A product package should not be changed.
(C) The listeners should try a product.
(D) A marketing campaign has been successful.

"that remains a very popular brand" という発言で、話し手は何を示唆していますか。

(A) 新しいレシピは売上高に影響を及ぼしていない。
(B) ある製品の包装は変更されるべきではない。
(C) 聞き手は、ある製品を試してみるべきである。
(D) マーケティングキャンペーンが成功を収めている。

正解 **B** 話し手は❷で、人気が落ちている製品の包装を新しくする必要性を述べ、その直後にBut「しかし」を続けて下線部を含む文でPurple Berry Crunchという製品が変わらず人気があることを伝えている。さらに❸でも同製品が今もよく食べられていることを述べている。よって、話し手は、同製品は他製品と異なり人気が高いままなので、現行の包装を変える必要はないということを示唆していると判断できる。
(A) recipe「レシピ」、affect「〜に影響を及ぼす」。
(D) successful「成功した」。

88 What does the speaker say he will do next?

(A) Present some slides
(B) Pass out some samples
(C) Share a personal story
(D) Invite a colleague to speak

話し手は次に何をすると言っていますか。

(A) スライドを提示する
(B) 商品見本を配る
(C) 個人的な話をする
(D) 同僚に話をしてもらう

正解 **A** 話し手は❹で、各製品に関するスライドを数枚用意していると述べた後、❺「今からそれをこのグループと共有する」と伝えている。❺のthoseはa few slidesを指しているので、(A)が正解。present「〜を提示する」。
(B) pass out 〜「〜を配る」、sample「商品見本」。
(C) share「〜(考えなど)を話す、〜を共有する」、personal「個人的な」。
(D) invite 〜 to do「〜に…するよう頼む」。

Words & Phrases

management 経営　　agenda 議題　　proposal 提案　　update 〜を新しくする
packaging 包装　　cereal シリアル ★主に朝食用の穀類加工食品　　lose 〜を失う　　popularity 人気
could use 〜 〜が欲しい、〜が必要である　　definitely 絶対に　　look 見た目、外見　　as for 〜 〜については
berry ベリー ★食用の小果実　　crunch かみ砕くこと・音　　remain 相変わらず〜である　　popular 人気の高い
brand 銘柄、ブランド　　across the country 国中の　　I suggest (that) 〜 〜ということを提案する
start by doing 〜することから始める　　one at a time 一度に一つずつ　　share 〜 with … 〜を…と共有する

TEST 1 PART 4

Questions 89 through 91 refer to the following podcast.

問題89-91は次のポッドキャストに関するものです。

 w

Thanks for listening to the podcast *Best in Business*. ❶I'm sorry there was no episode last week. ❷I took a relaxing trip to Italy with my family, and we had a wonderful time. But it's great to be back, and ❸I'd like to start by welcoming today's guest, Isamu Sato. ❹Isamu owns one of the country's largest technology companies, which he started just five years ago. ❺Before today's session, I asked you to submit questions for Isamu to answer. ❻I'm very happy that there's so much interest in this interview, but we only have an hour.

ポッドキャスト『事業の最適解』をお聞きいただきありがとうございます。先週は配信がなくて申し訳ありません。私は家族と一緒にイタリアへくつろぎの旅に出掛け、素晴らしいひとときを過ごしました。とはいえ、戻ってきてうれしいです。それでは、本日のゲストであるIsamu Satoをお迎えすることから始めたいと思います。Isamuは国内最大手のテクノロジー企業の一つを所有しており、わずか5年前にその会社を立ち上げました。本日の会の前に、私は、Isamuに答えてほしい質問を投稿するよう皆さんにお願いしました。このインタビューに大きな関心が寄せられているのは非常に喜ばしいですが、私たちには1時間しかありません。

---

89 Why did the speaker miss an episode last week?

(A) She was on vacation.
(B) She moved to a new city.
(C) She attended a conference.
(D) She had a project deadline.

話し手は先週、なぜ配信を休んだのですか。

(A) 彼女は休暇中だった。
(B) 彼女は新しい市へ引っ越した。
(C) 彼女は協議会に出席した。
(D) 彼女にはプロジェクトの締め切りがあった。

正解 A 話し手は❶で先週の配信がなかったことを謝罪し、❷「私は家族と一緒にイタリアへくつろぎの旅に出掛けた」と、番組を配信できなかった理由を伝えている。この内容をwas on vacation「休暇中だった」と表した(A)が正解。miss「~を抜かす、~をし損なう」。
(C) conference「協議会、会議」。
(D) deadline「締め切り」。

90 Who is Isamu Sato?

(A) A best-selling author
(B) A university professor
(C) A manager of an electronics store
(D) An owner of a technology company

Isamu Satoとは誰ですか。

(A) ベストセラー作家
(B) 大学教授
(C) 電子機器店の店長
(D) テクノロジー企業のオーナー

正解 D 話し手は❸で、Isamu Satoの名前を挙げた後、❹「Isamuは国内最大手のテクノロジー企業の一つを所有していて、わずか5年前にその会社を立ち上げた」と、人物紹介をしている。よって、(D)が正解。owner「オーナー、所有者」。
(A) best-selling「ベストセラーの」、author「作家」。
(B) university「大学」、professor「教授」。
(C) manager「管理者」、electronics「電子機器」。

91 What does the speaker mean when she says, "we only have an hour"?

(A) Not all questions will be answered.
(B) A process is difficult to understand.
(C) There is some confusion about a schedule.
(D) A guest speaker has another appointment.

"we only have an hour"という発言で、話し手は何を意図していますか。

(A) 全ての質問が回答されるわけではないだろう。
(B) 手順が理解しにくい。
(C) 予定について混乱が生じている。
(D) ゲストの話し手には別の約束がある。

正解 A 話し手は、❺で、ゲストに答えてほしい質問をあらかじめ募ったことを述べて、続く❻でインタビューに大きな関心が寄せられている事実を喜んでいる。その直後、逆接を示すbutに続けて「1時間しかない」という下線部の発言をしている。つまり話し手は、ゲストへの質問が多数寄せられているが、番組中に全ての質問に回答してもらう時間はないだろうと予想していると判断できる。よって、その内容を部分否定を用いて表した(A)が正解。
(B) process「手順」。
(C) confusion「混乱」。
(D) appointment「会う約束、取り決め」。

Words & Phrases

podcast ポッドキャスト ★オンライン上の音声・動画番組　business 事業
episode （番組などの）1回分　take a trip to ~ ~へ旅行に出掛ける　relaxing のんびりさせる
start by *doing* ~することから始める　welcome ~を歓迎する　own ~を所有する　technology テクノロジー、科学技術
session 会、討論　submit ~を投稿する、~を提出する　interest 関心

Questions 92 through 94 refer to the following excerpt from a meeting.

問題92-94は次の会議の抜粋に関するものです。

M

To begin, ❶I'd like to commend Maria Ortiz on her recent promotion to vice president of our legal department. ❷Maria's been a lawyer at our publishing house for nearly twenty years, and ❸we're thrilled she agreed to take on this role. ❹Congratulations, Maria! Next, I wanted to talk about some news that hasn't been made public yet: ❺we've bought one of our major competitors, Duckland Press. ❻This move nearly doubles the number of book titles we publish! But ❼please keep the news of the acquisition confidential until the press conference this Friday.

まず、当社法務部長への先日の昇進について、Maria Ortizに賛辞を贈りたいと思います。Mariaは20年近く当出版社の弁護士を務めており、私たちは、彼女がこの任務を引き受けることに同意してくれて感激しています。おめでとうございます、Maria! 次に、まだ公にされていない新情報についてお話ししたいと思っていました。当社は、主要な競合会社の一つであるDuckland出版社を買収しました。この展開により、当社が発行する書籍タイトルの数がほぼ倍増します! でも、今週金曜日の記者会見まで、買収の情報は内密にしておいてください。

92 Why does the speaker congratulate Maria Ortiz?

(A) She exceeded a sales goal.
(B) She won an industry award.
(C) She accepted a leadership role.
(D) She recently wrote a book.

話し手はなぜ、Maria Ortizに祝いの言葉を述べているのですか。

(A) 彼女は売上目標を突破した。
(B) 彼女は業界の賞を獲得した。
(C) 彼女は指導的役職を引き受けた。
(D) 彼女は最近、本を書いた。

正解 **C** 話し手は❶で、Maria Ortizの法務部長への昇進に賛辞を贈りたいと述べている。続けて彼女について簡単に紹介した後、❸「私たちは、彼女がこの任務を引き受けることに同意してくれて感激している」と言い、❹で祝いの言葉を述べている。よって(C)が正解。法務部長という役職を(C)ではa leadership role「指導的役職」と表している。congratulate「~に祝辞を述べる」。accept「~を受け入れる」。
(A) exceed「~を超える」、goal「目標」。
(D) 出版社での話だが、本の執筆への言及はない。

93 Where does the speaker work?

(A) At a pharmaceutical company
(B) At a publishing firm
(C) At a film studio
(D) At an employment agency

話し手はどこで働いていますか。

(A) 製薬会社
(B) 出版社
(C) 映画スタジオ
(D) 人材派遣会社

正解 **B** 話し手は、Maria Ortizについて述べる際に、❷「Mariaは20年近く当出版社の弁護士を務めている」と言っているので、(B)が正解。また、❺・❻で、話し手の会社が競合会社の出版社を買収したことや、それにより出版点数が増加する見込みであると述べられていることからも判断できる。publishing firm「出版社」。
(A) pharmaceutical company「製薬会社」。
(C) film studio「映画スタジオ」。
(D) employment agency「人材派遣会社」。

94 What will be announced at a press conference?

(A) A business acquisition
(B) A product release
(C) A construction project
(D) A charitable donation

記者会見では何が発表される予定ですか。

(A) 企業買収
(B) 製品発売
(C) 建設計画
(D) 慈善寄付

正解 **A** 話し手は、まだ公になっていない新情報について話したいと前置きした後、❺「当社は、主要な競合会社の一つであるDuckland出版社を買収した」と述べ、❼で、この企業買収の情報を記者会見まで内密にしておくよう聞き手に頼んでいる。よって、記者会見では企業買収について発表されると判断できる。announce「~を発表する」。
(B) release「発売」。
(C) construction「建設」。
(D) charitable「慈善の」、donation「寄付」。

TEST1 PART 4

Words & Phrases
to begin まず commend ~ on … …のことで~を称賛する promotion 昇進、昇格
vice president of ~ ~担当部長 legal department 法務部 lawyer 弁護士、法律家 publishing house 出版社
nearly ほぼ be thrilled (that) ~ ~ということに感激する agree to do ~することに同意する take on ~ ~を引き受ける
role 任務、役目 Congratulations! おめでとう! news 新情報 make ~ public ~を公表する competitor 競合会社
press 出版社、印刷所 move 展開、動き double ~を2倍にする publish ~を発行する
keep ~ … ~を…にしておく acquisition (企業)買収 confidential 内密の press conference 記者会見

Questions 95 through 97 refer to the following tour information and ticket.

🇺🇸 w

Good morning, everyone. ❶I'm sorry our tour's getting off to a late start. ❷We have some tour group members staying at hotels on the other side of town, and they'll be arriving at any moment. To help speed everything along, ❸please start lining up single file so we can board the bus as soon as everyone arrives. Oh, and ❹someone asked what the group number on the tickets means. ❺You can disregard that—it's part of an old system of ours.

問題95-97は次のツアー案内とチケットに関するものです。

おはようございます、皆さん。当ツアーの開始が遅れて申し訳ありません。町の反対側のホテルに宿泊しているこの団体ツアーのお客さまがいらっしゃいまして、その方々が今にも到着する予定です。全てを迅速に進めるために、全員が到着次第バスに乗車できるよう、縦一列に並び始めてください。ああ、それと、チケットに記載されている団体番号は何を表しているのかとどなたかが質問されました。それは無視していただいて構いません——当社の旧システムの一部なのです。

Streki Tours
Palermo City Tour

Thursday, 23 November

Tour #: 1092

Bus #: 252

Group #: 4

Streki ツアー社
パレルモ市ツアー

11月23日　木曜日

ツアー番号：1092

バス番号：252

団体番号：4

---

95 Why has a tour been delayed?

(A) A ticket reader is not working.
(B) A bus is being repaired.
(C) Some members of the group are late.
(D) Some bad weather is passing through.

ツアーはなぜ、遅れているのですか。

(A) チケットの読取機が作動していない。
(B) バスが修理中である。
(C) 団体の一部の客が遅れている。
(D) 荒天が通過中である。

正解 C 話し手は❶で、ツアー開始の遅れを謝罪した後、❷「町の反対側のホテルに宿泊しているこの団体ツアーの客がいて、彼らが今にも到着する予定だ」と遅延の原因を伝えている。よって、(C)が正解。delay「〜を遅らせる」。
(A) チケットについての言及はあるが、reader「読取機」については述べられていない。work「作動する」。
(B) repair「〜を修理する」。
(D) bad weather「悪天候」、pass through「通過する」。

96 What are the listeners asked to do?

(A) Show a confirmation e-mail
(B) Form a line
(C) Buy a ticket
(D) Choose a meal

聞き手は何をするよう頼まれていますか。

(A) 確認用Eメールを提示する
(B) 列を作る
(C) チケットを購入する
(D) 食事を選ぶ

正解 B 話し手は、遅れている客が間もなく到着する予定であると伝えてから、❸「全員が到着次第バスに乗車できるよう、縦一列に並び始めてください」と整列するよう聞き手に頼んでいる。よって、(B)が正解。form a line「列を作る」。
(A) confirmation「確認、確証」。
(C) 話し手が、チケットに記載されている内容について質問を受けたと言っているので、聞き手はすでにチケットを入手済みであると考えられる。
(D) choose「〜を選ぶ」、meal「(1回分の)食事」。

97 Look at the graphic. Which number does the speaker refer to?

(A) 23
(B) 1092
(C) 252
(D) 4

図を見てください。話し手はどの番号に言及していますか。

(A) 23
(B) 1092
(C) 252
(D) 4

正解 D 話し手は❹「チケットに記載されている団体番号は何を表しているのかと誰かが質問した」と述べ、❺で、その番号は古いシステムの一部であるため無視して構わないと伝えている。図を見ると、団体番号は4なので、(D)が正解。refer to 〜「〜に言及する」。
(A) (B) (C) それぞれ日付、ツアー番号、バス番号の数字であり、いずれについても言及はない。

Words & Phrases

tour ツアー、観光旅行　　get off to a 〜 start 〜なスタートを切る　　group 団体
at any moment 今にも　　help do 〜するのを促進する　　speed 〜のスピードを上げる　　along （どんどんと）先へ
line up 並ぶ　　single 一つの、単一の　　file 縦の列　　board 〜に乗り込む　　as soon as 〜 〜し次第、〜するとすぐに
mean 〜を表す　　disregard 〜を無視する　　part of 〜 〜の部分

Questions 98 through 100 refer to the following talk and table.

問題98-100は次の話と表に関するものです。

🇬🇧 w

I'm excited to give this presentation on behalf of Nexflight Labs. ❶I enjoy attending this conference every year, and this year, I get to lead a session! Today, I'll be sharing the research on flying vehicles that Nexflight has done. ❷My team ensures that the vehicles our company designs are as light as possible. ❸This is important because vehicles that weigh less require less energy to operate. Over the past decade, our company has developed four prototypes. ❹Of these, Nexflight is most proud of the model that can accommodate six passengers. ❺Granted, 25 kilometers isn't a long flight range, but it is a great start.

Nexflight研究所を代表してこのプレゼンテーションができることを喜ばしく思います。私は、毎年本協議会に出席するのを楽しんでおりますが、今年は会を主導する機会を得ました! 本日は、Nexflightが手掛けてきた航空機に関する研究についてお話しします。私のチームは、当社が設計する機体が可能な限り軽量であるようにしております。重量がより軽い機体は稼働のためのエネルギーがより少なくて済むため、この点は重要なのです。ここ10年にわたり、当社は4つの試作品を開発してきました。これらのうち、Nexflightは、6名の乗客を収容できるモデルを最も誇りに思っています。確かに25キロメートルというのは長い航続距離ではありませんが、これは優秀な滑り出しです。

Model	Number of Passengers	Flight Range
AT-01	2	5 kilometers
AT-02	1	12 kilometers
ZF-12	6	25 kilometers
PR-34	2	45 kilometers

モデル	乗客数	航続距離
AT-01	2	5キロメートル
AT-02	1	12キロメートル
ZF-12	6	25キロメートル
PR-34	2	45キロメートル

98 Who most likely are the listeners?

(A) New employees at Nexflight Labs
(B) Board members for Nexflight Labs
(C) City council members at a public meeting
(D) Attendees at an industry conference

聞き手は誰だと考えられますか。

(A) Nexflight研究所の新入社員
(B) Nexflight研究所の役員
(C) 公開会議に出席中の市議会議員
(D) ある業界の協議会への出席者

正解 D 話し手は、❶「私は、毎年本協議会に出席するのを楽しんでいるが、今年は会を主導する機会を得た」と述べ、以降では、Nexflight研究所がこれまでに開発してきた航空機について説明している。よって、聞き手は、航空機関連業界の協議会への出席者だと考えられる。attendee「出席者」、industry「業界」。
(A)(B) Nexflight研究所が手掛けた研究についての説明だが、協議会のセッションという状況なので、新入社員やboard member「役員、重役」といった社内メンバーへの話ではないと考えられる。
(C) city council member「市議会議員」、public meeting「公開会議」。

99 What has the speaker's team been tasked with?

(A) Making a more lightweight vehicle
(B) Making a more comfortable vehicle
(C) Making a faster vehicle
(D) Making a quieter vehicle

話し手のチームには、何の仕事が課せられてきましたか。

(A) より軽量な乗り物の製造
(B) より快適な乗り物の製造
(C) より高速な乗り物の製造
(D) より静かな乗り物の製造

正解 A 話し手は❷「私のチームは、当社が設計する機体が可能な限り軽量であるようにしている」と述べ、さらに❸で、軽量化の重要性について補足している。よって、(A)が正解。task ～ with … 「～に…(仕事)を課す」。lightweight「軽量の」。
(B)(C)(D) 快適さ、速度、静粛性については述べられていない。
(B) comfortable「快適な、心地よい」。
(D) quiet「静かな」。

100 Look at the graphic. According to the speaker, which model is Nexflight Labs most proud of?

(A) AT-01
(B) AT-02
(C) ZF-12
(D) PR-34

図を見てください。話し手によると、Nexflight研究所は、どのモデルを最も誇りに思っていますか。

(A) AT-01
(B) AT-02
(C) ZF-12
(D) PR-34

正解 C 話し手は、自分たちの会社が試作品を4つ開発してきたと伝えた後、❹「これらのうち、Nexflightは、6名の乗客を収容できるモデルを最も誇りに思っている」と述べ、❺で、25キロメートルというその航続距離に言及している。図を見ると、乗客数が6名で、かつ航続距離が25キロメートルなのはZF-12というモデルなので、(C)が正解。
(A)(B)(D) いずれのモデルも、乗客数が6名でなく、航続距離が25キロメートルでもない。

Words & Phrases

table 表　be excited to *do* ～することをうれしく思う
give a presentation プレゼンテーションをする　on behalf of ～ ～を代表して　lab 研究所 ★laboratoryの略
conference 協議会、会議　get to *do* ～する機会を得る　lead ～を主導する、～を主宰する　session 会、集まり
share ～(情報など)を伝える　research 研究　flying 飛行の　vehicle 乗り物、車両
ensure that ～ ～であることを確実にする　design ～を設計する　as ～ as possible できるだけ～　important 重要な
weigh ～ 重さが～である ★～は補語で、重量を表す語が入る　require ～を必要とする　operate 稼働する
past 〈完了時制で〉ここ～、今までの～　decade 10年間　develop ～を開発する　prototype 試作品
be proud of ～ ～を誇りに思う　accommodate ～を収容できる　passenger 乗客　granted ～, but … 確かに～だが…
kilometer キロメートル　flight range 航続距離 ★最大積載燃料で飛行可能な距離

PART 5

101 Please ------- your completed evaluation form on the table beside the door.

    (A) write
    (B) leave
    (C) make
    (D) consider

ご記入がお済みの評価表は、ドアの横のテーブルの上に置いていってください。

    (A) ～を書く
    (B) ～を置いていく
    (C) ～を作る
    (D) ～を熟考する

正解 **B** 　選択肢は全て動詞の原形であり、空所に入れると命令文になる。空所の後ろには目的語となるyour completed evaluation form「あなたの記入が済んだ評価表」とあり、さらにon the table beside the door「ドアの横のテーブルの上に」という副詞句が続くので、(B) leave「～を置いていく」を入れると意味が通る。completed「記入済みの、完成した」、evaluation「評価」、form「用紙」。

102 Arvid's latest game console, the Star 212, ------- resembles earlier models.

    (A) closely
    (B) closer
    (C) closeness
    (D) closest

Arvid社の最新のゲーム機であるStar 212は、以前のモデルに非常に似ています。

    (A) 密接に
    (B) より近い
    (C) 近いこと
    (D) 最も近い

正解 **A** 　Arvid's ...... Star 212 の部分が主語で、the Star 212 は Arvid's latest game consoleの同格の言い換え。resembles が述語動詞。空所に何も入れなくても文として成り立つので、空所には修飾語が入ると考えられる。動詞resembles「～に似ている」を修飾する副詞の(A) closely「密接に、細部まで」が適切。closely resembles で「非常に似ている」という意味になる。latest「最新の」、game console「ゲーム機」、earlier「以前の」、model「モデル、型」。
(B) 形容詞または副詞の比較級。副詞だとしても意味が通らない。
(C) 名詞。
(D) 形容詞または副詞の最上級。副詞だとしても意味が通らない。

103 Using the bank's app, customers can instantly pay bills through ------- transfer.

    (A) various
    (B) electronic
    (C) patient
    (D) eager

その銀行のアプリを使えば、顧客は電子振り込みによって即座に請求額を支払うことができます。

    (A) さまざまな
    (B) 電子的な
    (C) 辛抱強い
    (D) 熱心な

正解 **B** 　選択肢は全て形容詞の働きを持つ語。Using the bank's appは「その銀行のアプリを使えば」という意味で、条件を表す分詞構文。カンマの後ろは、「顧客は-------振り込みによって即座に請求額を支払える」という意味。(B) electronic「電子的な」を入れると、電子振り込みによって即座に支払いができることになり、意味が通る。app「アプリ（applicationの略）」、customer「顧客」、instantly「即座に」、bill「請求額、勘定書」、transfer「振り込み」。

104 Remember to bring a laptop with you for today's software training ------- at the Alten Conference Center.

(A) meet
(B) met
(C) meets
(D) meeting

Alten会議場で行われる本日のソフトウエア研修会には、ノートパソコンを忘れずに持ってきてください。

(A) 〜に会う
(B) 〜に会った
(C) 〜に会う
(D) 集会

正解 D remember to *do*「忘れずに〜する」を用いた命令文。空所の後ろは場所を示すatが導く副詞句であり、空所の前には前置詞forに続いてtoday's software trainingとある。trainingに続けて前置詞forの目的語になる(D) meeting「集会」が適切。laptop「ノートパソコン」、conference center「会議場」。
(A) (C) meetには名詞で「(スポーツなどの)大会」という意味もあるが、このような勉強会の意味では使わない。
(B) 動詞「〜に会う」の過去形または過去分詞。

105 Pacetti Furnaces offers discounts on installations ------- the summer months.

(A) above
(B) during
(C) besides
(D) including

Pacetti暖房炉社は夏の月の間、設置作業の値引きを行っています。

(A) 〜の上に
(B) 〜の間
(C) 〜に加えて
(D) 〜を含めて

正解 B 選択肢は全て前置詞の働きを持つ語。(B) during「〜の間」を入れると、during the summer monthsが「夏の月の間」を表し、暖房炉を扱うこの会社では夏季は設置料金の値引きを行う、という内容になって、意味が通る。furnace「暖房炉、ボイラー」、offer「〜を提供する」、discount「値引き」、installation「設置」。

106 Agents from Research Excellence Ltd. will be touring ------- offices next week.

(A) us
(B) ourselves
(C) we
(D) our

Research Excellence社の代理人の方々が来週、当社の営業所を視察する予定です。

(A) 私たちを
(B) 私たち自身
(C) 私たちは
(D) 私たちの

正解 D 選択肢は全て一人称複数の人称代名詞。主語はAgents from Research Excellence Ltd.「Research Excellence社の代理人たち」で、述語動詞はwill be touring「〜を視察するだろう」。空所に続けて名詞officesがあるので、これを修飾する所有格の(D) our「私たちの」が適切。our offices「当社の(複数の)営業所」が述語動詞の目的語となる。agent「代理人」、tour「〜を視察する、〜を巡回する」、office「営業所、事務所」。
(A) 目的格。
(B) 再帰代名詞。
(C) 主格。

TEST1 PART 5

43

107 When Mr. Awetimbi entered the conference room, he ------- that the audiovisual equipment had not been delivered.

(A) notices
(B) noticed
(C) noticing
(D) noticeable

会議室に入ったとき、Awetimbiさんは視聴覚機器が届いていないことに気付きました。

(A) 〜に気付く
(B) 〜に気付いた
(C) 〜に気付いて
(D) 人目を引く

> **正解 B** Whenからカンマまでは「Awetimbiさんが会議室に入ったとき」という意味で時を表す副詞節。カンマの後の主節の主語はheであり、that以降は「視聴覚機器が届いていないということ」という意味の名詞節。空所にはthat節を目的語とする述語動詞が必要。when節内が過去形であり、that節内が過去完了形なので、過去形の(B) noticedが適切。that節内は時制の一致で現在完了形が過去完了形になっていると考えられる。enter「〜に入る」、notice that 〜「〜ということに気付く」、audiovisual「視聴覚の」、equipment「機器」。
> (A) 三人称単数現在形。述語動詞にはなるが、過去について述べているので不適切。
> (C) 現在分詞または動名詞。述語動詞にならない。
> (D) 形容詞。

---

108 Drivers must use parking area B while parking area A is undergoing -------.

(A) support
(B) traffic
(C) vehicles
(D) repairs

駐車エリアAの補修工事中は、運転者は駐車エリアBを使用しなければなりません。

(A) 支持
(B) 交通
(C) 車両
(D) 補修

> **正解 D** 文頭からarea Bまでが主節であり、while以降は「駐車エリアAが-------を受けている間」という意味の副詞節。選択肢は全て名詞の働きを持つ語であり、空所にはundergo「〜（変化・検査・治療など）を受ける」の目的語となる語が入るので(D) repairs「補修（作業）」が適切。駐車エリアAが補修中で使用できないため、運転者は駐車エリアBを使わなければならない、という内容になり、意味が通る。
> (A) (B) (C) 意味の通る文にならない。

---

109 A newsletter is distributed to staff ------- to describe the company's accomplishments for that year.

(A) commonly
(B) broadly
(C) annually
(D) searchingly

その年の会社の業績を説明するため、スタッフには毎年社報が配布されます。

(A) 一般に
(B) 大まかに
(C) 毎年
(D) 鋭く

> **正解 C** 選択肢は全て副詞。空所の後の部分は、「その年の会社の業績を説明するために」という意味。(C) annually「毎年」を入れると、会社の業績を記載した社報がスタッフに毎年配布されるという内容になり、意味が通る。newsletter「社報、会報」、distribute「〜を配布する」、describe「〜を説明する、〜を描写する」、accomplishment「業績、成果」。

110 Enable notifications and ------- updates by selecting your preferred device settings.

(A) automates
(B) automatically
(C) automation
(D) automatic

端末の優先設定を選んで、通知と自動アップデートを有効にしてください。

(A) ～を自動化する
(B) 自動的に
(C) 自動化
(D) 自動的な

正解 D この文は命令文で、Enable notificationsは「通知を有効にしなさい」、by以降は「あなたの端末の優先設定を選ぶことによって」という意味。空所の後ろのupdatesをnotificationsと並ぶEnableの2つ目の目的語と考え、名詞updatesを修飾する形容詞の(D) automatic「自動的な」を入れるとautomatic updates「自動アップデート」となって意味が通る。enable「～を有効にする、～を動作可能にする」、notification「通知」、update「アップデート、更新」、preferred「優先の」、device「端末、デバイス」、setting「設定」。
(A) 原形のautomateなら命令形となり意味が通るが、三人称単数現在形は不適切。

111 New employees of Lopez Construction must take several courses, ------- a power tool safety course.

(A) as if
(B) such as
(C) in case of
(D) even so

Lopez建設社の新入社員は、例えば電動工具の安全講習などの幾つかの講習を受けなければなりません。

(A) あたかも～かのように
(B) 例えば～などの
(C) ～の場合には
(D) たとえそうでも

正解 B 文頭からカンマまでの部分は、「Lopez建設社の新入社員は、幾つかの講習を受けなければならない」という意味。これだけでも文として成り立つので、空所以降の部分は修飾語句と分かる。空所に続くのは名詞句のa power tool safety course「電動工具の安全講習」であり、受けなければならない講習の一例と考えられるので、空所には(B) such as「例えば～などの」が適切。course「講習、講座」、power tool「電動工具」、safety「安全」。
(A) (D) 節と節をつなぐ働きを持つので名詞句のみは続かない。
(C) 前置詞の働きを持ち名詞句を続けられるが、意味の通る文にならない。

112 Some programmers remain at one company for several years, but ------- depart sooner for better-paying jobs at other firms.

(A) theirs
(B) either
(C) which
(D) many

プログラマーの中には一つの会社に数年間とどまる人もいますが、多くは他の会社でのより高給の仕事を求めて、もっと早く会社を去ります。

(A) 彼らのもの
(B) どちらの～でも
(C) （物・事を先行詞とする主格の関係代名詞）
(D) 多くの人たち

正解 D カンマまでは、「プログラマーの中には一つの会社に数年間とどまる人もいる」という意味。butが続いているので、以降は逆接の内容になる。(D) many「多くの人たち」を入れると、some「一部の人たち」と対比され、同じ会社に数年間とどまる人もいるが多くの人はもっと早く別の会社に移る、となって意味が通る。remain「とどまる」、depart「(仕事・会社を)辞める」、better-paying「より賃金の高い」、firm「会社」。

TEST 1 PART 5

113 According to *Travelers* magazine, people have grown increasingly interested in ------- their vacation time outdoors in recent years.

(A) visiting
(B) spending
(C) charging
(D) closing

『トラベラーズ』誌によると、人々はここ何年かで休暇の時間を屋外で過ごすことにますます興味を持つようになりました。

(A) ～を訪れること
(B) ～を過ごすこと
(C) ～を充電すること
(D) ～を閉じること

正解 B 選択肢は全て動詞のing形であり、空所はinterested in ～「～に興味を持って」の前置詞inに続くため、空所の語は動名詞と考えられる。空所の直後のtheir vacation time「彼らの休暇の時間」は空所の動名詞の目的語なので、(B) spending「～を過ごすこと」を入れると「屋外で彼らの休暇の時間を過ごすことに興味を持って」という意味になり、自然な文になる。grow「次第に～の状態になる」、increasingly「ますます」、outdoors「屋外で」、in recent years「ここ何年かで」。
(A) (C) (D) 意味の通る文にならない。

114 After interviewing five candidates for the sales position, the manager ------- the most experienced one.

(A) choice
(B) chosen
(C) chose
(D) to choose

営業職の候補者5名を面接した後、部長は最も経験のある人を選びました。

(A) 選択
(B) 選ばれた
(C) ～を選んだ
(D) ～を選ぶための

正解 C 文頭からカンマまでは「営業職の候補者5名を面接した後で」という意味の副詞句。the managerがこの文の主語だが、述語動詞がないので空所には動詞が入る。述語動詞になる、過去形の(C) chose「～を選んだ」が適切。interview「～を面接する」、candidate「候補者」、position「職、仕事」、manager「部長、支配人」、experienced「経験を積んだ」。
(A) 名詞。
(B) 過去分詞、(D) to不定詞。いずれも単独では述語動詞にならない。

115 The City of Mayville's ------- job fair will feature representatives from a variety of local businesses.

(A) extreme
(B) specific
(C) upcoming
(D) prevailing

今度のMayville市の就職フェアは、さまざまな地元企業からの担当者の参加が目玉となります。

(A) 極度の
(B) 特定の
(C) 今度の
(D) 流行の

正解 C 選択肢は全て形容詞の働きを持つ語。文頭からfairまでが主語に当たり、空所には直後の名詞句job fair「就職フェア」を修飾する語が入る。will feature以降は、「さまざまな地元企業からの担当者が目玉となる」という意味。Mayville市の就職フェアを形容する語として適切なのは(C) upcoming「今度の、近づきつつある」。feature「～を目玉とする、～を特色とする」、representative「担当者、代表者」、a variety of ～「さまざまな～」、local「地元の」、business「企業」。
(A) (B) (D) 意味の通る文にならない。

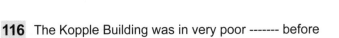

116 The Kopple Building was in very poor ------- before the renovation.

(A) condition
(B) conditioned
(C) conditioner
(D) conditional

改修前は、Koppleビルは非常に劣悪な状態でした。

(A) 状態
(B) 条件付けられた
(C) 調整剤
(D) 条件付きの

正解 **A** 　主語はThe Kopple Building。very poor ------- 「非常に劣悪な-------」が前置詞inの目的語になると考えられるので、空所には名詞が入る。be in ～ conditionで「～な状態である」という意味になるので、(A) condition「状態」が適切。renovation「改修」。
(B) 動詞condition「～を条件付ける」の過去形または過去分詞。
(C) 名詞だが「調整剤、調整者」という意味。文の意味が通らない。
(D) 形容詞。

117 ------- Mr. Khat has just been promoted to management, we now have an open sales-associate position.

(A) Upon
(B) Until
(C) Since
(D) Despite

ちょうどKhatさんが管理職に昇進したところなので、今、販売員の職に空きがあります。

(A) ～の上に
(B) ～まで
(C) ～なので
(D) ～にもかかわらず

正解 **C** 　カンマの前後ともに〈主語＋動詞〉の形があるので、空所に接続詞を入れてカンマまでを従属節にする必要がある。主節はカンマの後の部分で、「私たちには今、販売員の職に空きがある」という意味。従属節になるMr. Khatからカンマまでは、「Khatさんはちょうど管理職に昇進したところだ」という意味。2つの節の関係から、理由を表す接続詞(C) Since「～なので」が適切。promote ～ to …「～を…に昇進させる」、management「管理職、マネージメント」、open「空いた、空席の」、sales-associate「販売員の」、position「職」。
(A) (D) 前置詞。
(B) 前置詞または接続詞。接続詞だとしても意味の通る文にならない。

118 Don's Café uses only local fruits and vegetables in its ------- prepared dishes.

(A) carefully
(B) careful
(C) caring
(D) cared

Don'sカフェでは、同店の手の込んだ料理に地元の果物と野菜だけを使っています。

(A) 念入りに
(B) 念入りな
(C) 思いやりのある
(D) 気に掛けられた

正解 **A** 　選択肢は動詞care「～を気に掛ける」の変化した形や派生語。空所の前後のits ------- prepared dishesは「同店（＝Don'sカフェ）の-------調理された料理」という意味で、空所には直後の形容詞prepared「調理された」を修飾する副詞の(A) carefully「念入りに」が適切。carefully preparedで「念入りに調理された」、つまり「手の込んだ」といった意味になり、dishesを修飾する形となる。
(B) 形容詞、(C) 現在分詞、(D) 過去形または過去分詞。いずれも形容詞を修飾しない。

119 Sales of truck parts ------- approximately 45 percent to BTR Manufacturing's revenue last year.

(A) gave
(B) applied
(C) contributed
(D) donated

トラック用部品の売り上げは、昨年、BTR製造社の収益におよそ45パーセント寄与しました。

(A) 〜を与えた
(B) 〜を当てはめた
(C) 〜だけ寄与した
(D) 〜を寄付した

正解 **C** 選択肢は全て動詞の過去形。主語はSales of truck parts「トラック用部品の売り上げ」。空所に(C) contributedを入れると、contribute 〜 to …「〜(量・程度)だけ…に寄与する」の形となり、トラック用部品の売り上げがこの会社の収益の約45パーセントを占めたことになって、意味が通る。sales「売り上げ」、part「部品、パーツ」、approximately「およそ」、manufacturing「製造」、revenue「収益、収入」。
(A) (B) (D) 意味の通る文にならない。

120 The ------- northbound Coastal Express train will be arriving on track 5.

(A) delay
(B) delays
(C) delayed
(D) delaying

遅れている北行き沿岸急行列車は、5番線に到着する予定です。

(A) 〜を遅らせる
(B) 〜を遅らせる
(C) 遅れている
(D) 〜を遅らせて

正解 **C** 選択肢は動詞delay「〜を遅らせる」と、その変化した形。空所の前に定冠詞theがあり、後ろにはnorthbound Coastal Express train「北行き沿岸急行列車」という名詞句があるので、空所にはこの名詞句を修飾する語が入ると考えられる。過去分詞の(C) delayed「遅れている、遅延の」が適切。northbound「北行きの」、coastal「沿岸の」、express「急行」、track「プラットホーム、線路」。
(A) (B) 動詞または名詞、(D) 現在分詞。いずれも意味が通らない。

121 The Shellville City Council acted ------- when it decided to convert an unused railway to a multipurpose trail.

(A) wisely
(B) entirely
(C) initially
(D) widely

Shellville市議会が使用されていない鉄道線路を多目的道に転換すると決めたのは賢い行動でした。

(A) 賢く
(B) すっかり
(C) 初めに
(D) 幅広く

正解 **A** 選択肢は全て副詞であり、直前の動詞actedを適切に修飾するものを選ぶ。接続詞whenはこの場合、「〜であることを考えると」といった意味に捉えられ、whenの後ろは「Shellville市議会が使用されていない鉄道線路を多目的道に転換すると決めた」という意味。空所に(A) wisely「賢く」を入れると、同市議会の行動は賢明だったと述べる文になり、意味が通る。city council「市議会」、act「行動する」、convert 〜 to …「〜を…に転換する」、unused「使用されていない」、multipurpose「多目的の」、trail「道」。

122 Overall ------- of museum archivists and curators is expected to grow steadily over the next ten years.

(A) employee
(B) employment
(C) employed
(D) employable

博物館の文書局員や学芸員の全般的な雇用は、今後10年間にわたって着実に増加すると予想されています。

(A) 従業員
(B) 雇用
(C) 雇用された
(D) 雇用できる

正解 B 選択肢は動詞employ「〜を雇用する」の変化した形や派生語。Overall ------- of museum archivists and curators「博物館の文書局員と学芸員の全般的な-------」の部分が主語となり、空所にはoverall「全般的な、全体の」に修飾されて意味が通る名詞が入る。名詞の(B) employment「雇用」が適切。archivist「文書局員（収集・保存・管理などに携わる職員）」、curator「学芸員」。
(A) 名詞だが、意味が通らない。
(C) 過去分詞。
(D) 形容詞または名詞。名詞では「雇用対象者」という意味だが、文法的に不適切。

123 With her ------- experience in graphic design, Ms. Abebe appears to be a suitable candidate for the book designer position.

(A) vast
(B) plausible
(C) relieved
(D) conscious

グラフィックデザインにおいて極めて豊富な経験があるので、Abebeさんはそのブックデザイナーの職に適した候補者だと思われます。

(A) 膨大な
(B) もっともらしい
(C) ほっとした
(D) 意識のある

正解 A 選択肢は全て形容詞。カンマの後ろは、「Abebeさんはそのブックデザイナーの職に適した候補者だと思われる」という意味。文頭からカンマまでがその理由を表す副詞句になると考えられ、空所には続く名詞experienceを適切に修飾する語が入る。(A) vast「（数量や程度が）膨大な」を入れると、グラフィックデザインでの豊富な経験によりブックデザイナーの職に適した候補者であるとなり、意味が通る。appear to be 〜「〜のように思える」、suitable「適した」、candidate「候補者」、book designer「ブックデザイナー、装丁家」。

124 ------- a Boskin electrical product is modified by the customer, the warranty is no longer valid.

(A) Except
(B) So
(C) That
(D) If

Boskin社の電気製品が顧客によって改変されている場合、保証はもはや有効ではなくなります。

(A) 〜ということを除いて
(B) 〜できるように
(C) 〜ということ
(D) もし〜ならば

正解 D 選択肢は全て接続詞の働きを持つ語であり、カンマの前後の2つの節の内容からふさわしい語を選ぶ。カンマの前の節は「Boskin社の電気製品が顧客によって改変される」、カンマの後ろの主節は「保証はもはや有効ではない」という意味。空所に(D) If「もし〜ならば」を入れると、顧客が製品に手を加えた場合には保証は無効になる、となって意味が通る。electrical product「電気製品」、modify「〜を改変する」、warranty「保証」、no longer 〜「もはや〜でない」、valid「有効な」。
(A) (B) (C) いずれも接続詞の働きを持つが、意味が通らない。また、副詞節を導く接続詞としては通例文頭では用いない。

125 Retail sales of Kent Menswear collared dress shirts increase dramatically every October, ------- the brand's autumn sale.

(A) so that
(B) due to
(C) therefore
(D) whereas

Kent紳士服社のワイシャツの小売店での売り上げは、同ブランドの秋季セールのため、毎年10月に著しく増加します。

(A) ～できるように
(B) ～のため
(C) それゆえ
(D) ～であるのに対して

> **正解 B** カンマまでの部分は「Kent紳士服社のワイシャツの小売店での売り上げは、毎年10月に著しく増加する」という意味。これだけで文として成り立つので、カンマ以降は修飾語句になる。空所の後ろにはthe brand's autumn sale「同ブランドの秋季セール」という名詞句が続いているので、空所には前置詞に相当する語句が入る。(B) due to「～のため」が適切。retail「小売り」、sales「売り上げ」、collared「襟付きの」、dress shirt「ワイシャツ、礼服用シャツ」、dramatically「著しく、劇的に」、brand「ブランド、銘柄」。
> (A) (D) 接続詞（句）、(C) 副詞。いずれも名詞句のみは続かない。

126 For security purposes, only authorized personnel of Jeffers Mines Ltd. may proceed ------- this checkpoint.

(A) beyond
(B) without
(C) about
(D) between

保安上の目的により、権限を有するJeffers鉱山社職員のみが、この検問所より先に進むことを許可されています。

(A) ～を越えて
(B) ～なしで
(C) ～について
(D) ～の間に

> **正解 A** 選択肢は全て前置詞の働きを持つ語。空所の前までの部分は「保安上の目的により、権限を有するJeffers鉱山社職員のみが進んでよい」という意味であり、空所の後ろにはthis checkpoint「この検問所」と続く。(A) beyond「～を越えて」を入れると、限られた人のみが検問所を越えて進んでよい、となって意味が通る。security「安全確保」、purpose「目的」、authorized「権限を与えられた」、personnel「職員、人員」、mine「鉱山」、proceed「進む」、checkpoint「検問所」。

127 Heron Stationers ------- new business cards by the end of the week.

(A) to order
(B) had been ordered
(C) will be ordering
(D) ordering

Heron文房具社は今週末までに、新しい名刺を注文しているでしょう。

(A) ～を注文するための
(B) 注文されていた
(C) ～を注文しているだろう
(D) ～を注文して

> **正解 C** 動詞order「～を注文する」の適切な形を選ぶ。この文には述語動詞がないので、空所に必要。未来進行形の(C) will be orderingを入れると、「今週末までに新しい名刺を注文しているだろう」となって、意味が通る。stationer「文房具店、文房具商」、business card「名刺」。
> (A) to不定詞、(D) 現在分詞または動名詞。いずれも述語動詞にならない。
> (B) 過去完了の受動態。過去完了は、過去のある時点を基準にそれまでに起きたことを表す。述語動詞の役割は果たすが、ここでは基準となる時が「今週末」という未来なので不適切。

128 At Key Beach Fashions, customers can check the ------- of their orders online.

(A) reason
(B) agenda
(C) status
(D) intent

Key Beach Fashions社では、顧客は自分の注文品の状況をオンラインで確認できます。

(A) 理由
(B) 協議事項
(C) 状況
(D) 意図

正解 **C** 選択肢は全て名詞の働きを持つ語。空所には、動詞checkの目的語となり、続くof their ordersが説明する語が入る。onlineは「オンラインで、インターネット上で」という意味の副詞として用いられている。顧客が自分の注文品についてオンラインで確認できることとして適切なのは、(C) status「状況、状態」。check「〜を確認する」。

---

129 A prize will be awarded to ------- sells the most raffle tickets for the annual charity fund-raiser.

(A) anybody
(B) yourselves
(C) everyone
(D) whoever

毎年恒例の資金集めの慈善イベントに向けたラッフル券を一番たくさん売った人は、誰であれ賞が与えられます。

(A) 誰か
(B) あなたたち自身
(C) 皆
(D) 〜である人なら誰でも

正解 **D** 主語はA prize、述語動詞はwill be awarded。A prize will be awarded to -------は「-------に賞が与えられる」という意味であり、空所には前置詞toの目的語が入る。また、空所に続いて動詞sellsがあるので、空所にはsellsの主語となる語が必要。この両方を満たすのは先行詞を含む関係詞である複合関係代名詞の(D) whoever「〜である人なら誰でも」。prize「賞」、award「〜（賞など）を与える」、raffle ticket「ラッフル券（慈善事業のための宝くじ）」、annual「毎年の」、charity「慈善事業」、fund-raiser「資金集めのイベント」。
(A) 代名詞。anybody whoなら可。
(B) 再帰代名詞。
(C) 代名詞。

---

130 The greenhouse temperature must remain ------- the specified range for plants to grow properly.

(A) within
(B) because of
(C) as long as
(D) after all

植物が適切に育つよう、温室の温度は指定された範囲内に保たれなければなりません。

(A) 〜以内に
(B) 〜のせいで
(C) 〜もの間
(D) 結局

正解 **A** The greenhouse temperature must remainは「温室の温度はとどまっていなければならない」という意味。続く------- the specified rangeは「指定された範囲-------」という意味なので、(A) within「〜以内に」を入れて「指定された範囲内に」とすると、意味が通る。greenhouse「温室」、temperature「温度」、remain「とどまる」、specify「〜を指定する、〜を特定する」、range「範囲」、properly「適切に」。

Questions 131-134 refer to the following notice.

❶ The Moon Township Development Authority ------- the search for two candidates for its board of
131.
oversight. These candidates will fill existing ------- . Overseeing plans for the community's
132.
business development will be ------- main responsibility. The new members will continue the
133.
process. If you are interested in volunteering your time to serve on the board, please apply at the
township clerk's office. ------- .
134.

問題131-134は次のお知らせに関するものです。

ムーン郡区開発局では、2名の監視委員会候補者を探し始めます。これらの候補者は、現在出ている欠員を埋めることになります。地域
の事業開発計画を監視することが彼らの主要な責務となります。新しいメンバーはこの過程を引き続き進めることになります。この委員
会の一員としてご自身の時間を提供することにご興味のある方は、郡区書記官事務所でお申し込みください。*委員を務めるにはムーン
郡区の住民でなければならないことにご注意ください。

*問題134の挿入文の訳

Expressions

Note that ~.「~ということに注意しなさい」(❶5行目)
　Please note that there is an additional fee to enter Area C.
　Cエリアに入るためには追加料金がかかることにご注意ください。

131
(A) had begun
(B) to begin
(C) is beginning
(D) will have begun

＊選択肢の訳は省略

| 正解 **C** | 動詞begin「～を始める」の適切な形を選ぶ。空所を含む文は、The Moon Township Development Authority「ムーン郡区開発局」が主語、空所に続くthe search for two candidates for its board of oversight「2名の監視委員会候補者を探すこと」が目的語で、空所には述語動詞が入ると考えられる。後に続く3つの文がいずれも未来形になっていることから、候補者探しはこれから行われると考えて、近接した未来を表す現在進行形の(C) is beginningが適切。「候補者探しを始めようとしている」となり、自然なつながりになる。 |

(A) 過去完了形。
(B) to不定詞。述語動詞にならない。
(D) 未来完了形。未来を表すが、完了形と関連する未来の時点は示されていない。

132
(A) issues
(B) districts
(C) locations
(D) vacancies

(A) 問題点
(B) 地区
(C) 場所
(D) 欠員

| 正解 **D** | 選択肢は全て名詞。空所を含む文は、「これらの候補者たちは、現在存在している-------を埋めることになるだろう」という意味。文の主語はThese candidates「これらの候補者たち」、述語動詞はwill fill「～を埋めるだろう」であり、fillの目的語として意味が通るのは、(D) vacancies「欠員、空き」。「候補者たちが今出ている欠員を埋める」という内容になる。 |

(A) (B) (C) いずれも語のつながりが不適切で、文脈に合わない。

133
(A) their
(B) my
(C) its
(D) your

(A) 彼らの
(B) 私の
(C) それの
(D) あなたの

| 正解 **A** | 選択肢は全て代名詞の所有格であり、続く名詞句のmain responsibilityにかかる。空所を含む文は、「地域の事業開発計画を監視することが-------主要な責務となるだろう」という意味。(A) their「彼らの」を入れると、「彼ら」がthese candidates「これらの候補者たち」を指すことになり、適切。 |

134
(A) Elections were held every two years.
(B) The board of oversight consists of nine members.
(C) The business district has been neglected for years.
(D) Note that you must be a resident of Moon Township to serve.

(A) 選挙は2年ごとに行われました。
(B) 監視委員会は9名のメンバーで構成されています。
(C) その商業地区は、長年放置されてきました。
(D) 委員を務めるにはムーン郡区の住民でなければならないことにご注意ください。

| 正解 **D** | 空所の直前の文は、この監視委員会の仕事に興味を持った人に事務所で申し込むよう呼び掛ける内容。その直後なので、申し込む際の注意点を述べる(D)が適切。委員募集のお知らせの最後に付け加える内容として文脈に合う。resident「住民」。 |

(A) election「選挙」、hold「～を行う」、every two years「2年ごとに」。
(B) 監視委員会を説明する内容だが、募集のお知らせの最後に付け加える内容としては不自然。consist of ～「～で構成されている」。
(C) business district「商業地区、ビジネス街」、neglect「～を放置する、～を無視する」、for years「長年にわたって」。

Questions 135-138 refer to the following letter.

Estin Insurance Group Ltd.

1089 Centre Street, Brampton, Ontario L6P 2YA

14 October

Nobu Ito
231 Parkside Avenue
Burlington, Ontario L7L 3X4

Dear Mr. Ito,

① On behalf of Estin Insurance Group Ltd., thank you for your ------- . I would be pleased to provide
135.
you with a quote for the personal auto insurance you requested. Simply contact me at
(905) 555-0172 when you are ready, and I will ------- you. To save time, please have your vehicle
136.
registration and driver's license in hand.

② If you reach my voice mail, please leave a message. ------- . I am available Monday
137.
------- Friday from 9:00 A.M. to 5:00 P.M.
138.

Sincerely,

Theodore Reynolds, Insurance Agent

問題135-138は次の手紙に関するものです。

Estin保険グループ有限会社

センター通り1089番地、ブランプトン、オンタリオ州 L6P 2YA

10月14日

Nobu Ito 様
パークサイド大通り231番地
バーリントン, オンタリオ州 L7L 3X4

Ito 様

Estin保険グループ有限会社を代表して、お客さまのお問い合わせにお礼を申し上げます。ご依頼いただいた個人向け自動車保険のお見積もりを喜んで提供いたします。ご準備ができたときに、(905)555-0172まで私宛てにご連絡いただくだけで、私がお手伝いいたします。お時間を節約するため、お客さまの車両登録証と運転免許証をお手元にご用意ください。

私の留守番電話につながった場合は、ご伝言をお残しください。*できるだけ早く、折り返しお電話差し上げます。私は月曜日から金曜日の午前9時から午後5時まで対応可能です。

敬具

Theodore Reynolds、保険外交員

*問題137の挿入文の訳

135
(A) cooperation
(B) payment
(C) inquiry
(D) concern

(A) 協力
(B) 支払い
(C) 問い合わせ
(D) 心配

正解 **C**　選択肢は全て名詞の働きを持つ語。冒頭のレターヘッドと結びの署名から、この手紙を書いているのは保険会社の従業員であることが分かる。また、空所の直後の文に、「あなたが依頼した個人向け自動車保険の見積もりを喜んで提供する」とあることから、この手紙の宛先であるNobu Itoさんが自動車保険について問い合わせたと考えられる。よって、(C) inquiry「問い合わせ」が適切。保険会社の従業員が、問い合わせをした見込み客に対して謝意を述べる内容になり、文脈に合う。
(A) (B) (D) いずれも文脈に合わない。

136
(A) assisting
(B) assisted
(C) assists
(D) assist

＊選択肢の訳は省略

正解 **D**　動詞assist「～を手伝う」の適切な形を選ぶ。空所の前には主語のIと助動詞のwillがあるので、空所には動詞の原形が入る。よって、原形の(D) assistが適切。空所を含む文は、〈命令文, and …〉という形で「～しなさい。そうすれば…」という内容を表すので、「ただ(905)555-0172まで私に連絡してください。そうすれば、私はあなたを手伝う」という意味になる。
(A) 現在分詞または動名詞。
(B) 過去形または過去分詞。
(C) 三人称単数現在形。

137
(A) I will return your call as soon as possible.
(B) The discount expires on November 1.
(C) Any difference will be credited toward your bill.
(D) The contract for the new policy is in the mail.

(A) できるだけ早く、折り返しお電話差し上げます。
(B) 割引は、11月1日で終了します。
(C) 差額が生じたら、お客さまの請求書から差し引かれます。
(D) 新たな保険証券の契約書は、郵便物の中にあります。

正解 **A**　保険の問い合わせに対し、❶2～3行目で、「(905)555-0172まで私宛てに連絡してください」と述べ、空所の直前で「私の留守番電話につながった場合は、伝言を残してください」と、電話に応答できなかった場合について言及している。その場合にどのような対応を取るかを説明した(A)を入れると、自然な流れになる。return a call「折り返し電話する」、as soon as possible「できるだけ早く」。
(B) discount「割引」、expire「終了する、期限が切れる」。
(C) difference「差額」、credit「～(金額)を入金する、～(金額)を貸し方に記入する」、bill「請求書」。
(D) contract「契約(書)」、policy「保険証券」。

138
(A) around
(B) through
(C) against
(D) near

(A) ～頃に
(B) ～から…まで
(C) ～に対して
(D) ～の近くで

正解 **B**　選択肢は全て前置詞の働きを持つ語。空所を含む文は、「私は月曜日-------金曜日の午前9時から午後5時まで対応可能だ」という意味。❷1行目で、留守番電話につながった場合に言及していることから、自分の対応可能な日時を知らせていると考えられる。Monday through Fridayで「月曜日から金曜日まで」の意味になる(B) through「～から…まで」が適切。
(A) (C) (D) いずれも空所の前後のMonday、Fridayとつながらない。

Words & Phrases

insurance 保険　Ontario （カナダの）オンタリオ州　★アルファベットと数字の組み合わせ3文字＋3文字はカナダの郵便番号
❶ on behalf of ～　～を代表して　be pleased to do　喜んで～する、～できることをうれしく思う
provide ～ with …　～に…を提供する　quote 見積もり（価格）　personal 個人向けの　auto insurance 自動車保険
request ～を依頼する　simply ただ～のみ　contact ～と連絡を取る　save ～を節約する、～を省く
vehicle 車両、乗り物　registration 登録（証）　driver's license 運転免許証　❷ reach （電話などで）～と接触する
voice mail 留守番電話、ボイスメール　message 伝言　available 対応できる　agent 外交員、代理人

Expressions

have ～ in hand 「～を手元に用意しておく、～を手元に持っている」（❶3～4行目）
Please have your tickets in hand while waiting for your turn.
順番をお待ちの間にチケットをお手元にご用意ください。

Questions 139-142 refer to the following e-mail.

To: All members of the Wincliff Tools Board of Directors
From: Althea Wilson, Corporate Planning
Date: December 1
Subject: Biannual meeting

❶ A meeting of the Wincliff Tools Board of Directors ------- on Monday, January 11, at 1:00 P.M. in
139.
the conference room at the manufacturing plant in Brywood. ------- .
140.

❷ We have arranged two events to follow the meeting. At 3:00 P.M., we invite you to take a guided

tour ------- the plant and hear from some employees. More important, you will have the
141.

opportunity to see ------- in action. And at 6:00 P.M., you are invited to join us for dinner at
142.
Fairport Seafood Restaurant.

問題139-142は次のEメールに関するものです。

受信者：Wincliff工具社取締役会メンバー各位
送信者：Althea Wilson、経営企画部
日付：12月1日
件名：半年に1度の会議

Wincliff工具社取締役会の会議が、1月11日月曜日の午後1時にBrywoodの製造工場の会議室で開催されます。*出席される予定かどうかを今週中に私にお知らせください。

その会議の後に、2つのイベントを用意しました。午後3時、ぜひその工場のガイド付きツアーにご参加になり、何人かの従業員から話をお聞きください。さらに重要なのは、作業中の彼らを見る機会を得られるということです。そして午後6時、私たちと一緒にFairportシーフードレストランでの夕食会にぜひご参加ください。

*問題140の挿入文の訳

Words & Phrases

tool 工具   board of directors 取締役会   corporate planning 経営企画(部)
biannual 半年に1度の、年2回の ★biennial「2年ごとの」と混同しないよう注意 **❶** conference room 会議室
manufacturing 製造(の)   plant 工場 **❷** arrange ～を用意する、～の手配をする   follow ～の後に起こる
invite ～ to do ～に…するように依頼する・勧める   guided tour ガイド付きツアー、ガイド付き見学会
hear from ～ ～から意見を聞く
more important さらに重要なことに ★what is more importantのwhat isを省略した形で、文を修飾する
opportunity 機会、好機   in action 活動中の   join ～ for … ～と…を共にする

139 (A) will be held
(B) was held
(C) are held
(D) to be held

＊選択肢の訳は省略

正解 **A** 受動態 be held「開催される」の適切な形を選ぶ。メールの送信日が 12 月 1 日であり、空所の直後から会議が行われるのは 1 月 11 日と分かるので、未来形の(A)が適切。❷で、会議の後にガイド付きツアーと夕食会への参加を促していることからも、過去の話でなく未来の話だと判断できる。
(B) 過去形。
(C) 現在形。現在形で確定的未来を表すこともあるが、この場合は主語が単数形の a meeting なので、are は不適切。
(D) to 不定詞。述語動詞にならない。

140 (A) Our products are sold at hardware stores nationwide.
(B) Please plan to have the plant fully staffed that month.
(C) My assistant has a list of items available for purchase.
(D) Please let me know this week if you plan to attend.

(A) 当社の製品は、全国の工具店で販売されています。

(B) その月は、工場に従業員が十分に配置されているように計画してください。

(C) 私の助手は、購入可能な品目のリストを持っています。

(D) 出席される予定かどうかを今週中に私にお知らせください。

正解 **D** 件名から、このメールは半年ごとに行われる会議についてのものだと分かる。また、空所の直前の文では、会議の開催日時が述べられているので、出欠を尋ねる(D)を入れると、自然な流れになる。plan to do「～する予定である」、attend「出席する」。
(A) product「製品」、hardware store「工具店、ホームセンター」、nationwide「全国的に」。
(B) have ～ done「～を…させる」、fully「十分に、完全に」、staff「～に従業員を配置する」。
(C) assistant「助手、アシスタント」、item「品目」、available「入手可能な」、purchase「購入」。

141 (A) along
(B) of
(C) for
(D) with

(A) ～に沿って
(B) ～の
(C) ～のための
(D) ～と

正解 **B** 選択肢は全て前置詞の働きを持つ語。空所を含む we invite you to take a guided tour ------- the plant は、「私たちはあなたたちに、その工場-------ガイド付きツアーに参加するよう勧める」という意味。(B) of「～の」を入れると、a guided tour of the plant「その工場のガイド付きツアー」となって、意味が通る。
(A) (C) (D) いずれも意味が通らない。

142 (A) themselves
(B) who
(C) them
(D) any

(A) 彼ら自身
(B) ～する人
(C) 彼らを
(D) 誰でも

正解 **C** 空所を含む文は、「さらに重要なのは、あなたたちは作業中の-------を見る機会を得られるだろうということだ」という意味。空所には動詞 see「～を見る」の目的語で、in action「作業中の」に修飾される名詞が入る。前文の some employees を示す人称代名詞の(C) them「彼らを」を入れると文脈に合う。
(A) 再帰代名詞。文法的に不適切。
(B) 関係代名詞または疑問詞。文法的に不適切。
(D) 代名詞。何を指しているか不明で文脈に合わない。

Expressions

you are invited to do　「どうぞ～してください」（❷ 3～4行目）

You are invited to join this special workshop to learn *ikebana*.
生け花を学ぶこの特別研修会に、どうぞご参加ください。

Questions 143-146 refer to the following memo.

To: All Customer Service Specialists
From: Human Resources Director
Date: April 28
Subject: Performance Evaluations

❶ Grantham Electronics' human resources department will begin annual performance evaluations for customer service specialists ------- June 1. These evaluations consist of three steps.
                                                             143.
------- . Completing this step should take you no more than 30 minutes. Next, supervisors will
144.
------- a meeting with each employee. These meetings are for you to discuss with your supervisor
145.
the results of the self-assessment and your professional goals for the coming year. Finally, both parties will complete a questionnaire reflecting on the experience.

❷ We look forward to working with each employee to foster an environment that encourages continued ------- and innovation.
                      146.

問題143-146は次のメモに関するものです。

宛先：顧客サービス担当者各位
差出人：人事部長
日付：4月28日
件名：業績評価

Grantham電子機器社の人事部は、6月1日に顧客サービス担当者に対する年1回の業績評価を開始します。この評価は3つの段階から成ります。*自己評価が、その過程の始まりとなります。この段階を完了させるには、30分しかかからないはずです。次に、上司が各従業員との面談の予定を組みます。この面談は、自己評価の結果や来年度の職務上の目標について、あなたが上司と話し合うためのものです。最後に、両者がこの体験を振り返って調査票を完成させます。

私たちは、従業員の皆さんお一人お一人と共に力を合わせ、継続的な創造性と革新性を促進する環境を育んでいくことを楽しみにしています。

*問題144の挿入文の訳

143
(A) on
(B) for
(C) past
(D) throughout

(A) ～に
(B) ～のために
(C) ～を過ぎて
(D) ～を通して

正解 **A** 選択肢は全て前置詞の働きを持つ語。空所にはJune 1と日付が続いており、文全体は、「Grantham電子機器社の人事部は、6月1日-------顧客サービス担当者に対する年1回の業績評価を開始する」という意味。6月1日は業績評価を開始する日付と考えられるので、「～(日付)に」を示す前置詞(A) onが適切。
(D) 6月1日丸一日かけて業績評価を開始するという意味になり、動詞beginで起点を示す文の内容と合わない。

144
(A) If you have any questions, please contact your supervisor.
(B) Please note that the procedure has changed.
(C) A self-assessment sets the process in motion.
(D) Our goal is the continued success of the company.

(A) もし何か質問があれば、あなたの上司に連絡してください。
(B) 手続きが変更になったことに注意してください。
(C) 自己評価が、その過程の始まりとなります。
(D) 私たちの目標は、会社の継続的な成功です。

正解 **C** 空所直前の文で「この(業績)評価は3つの段階から成る」と述べられている。空所の直後にCompleting this step should take you no more than 30 minutes.「この段階を完了させるには、30分しかかからないはずだ」とあるので、空所には段階の1つを説明する文が入ると考えられる。空所に(C)を入れると、自己評価によって評価の過程が始まることを述べる流れになり、適切。続く❶ 3～5行目のNext, ... for the coming year. が2つ目の段階を、同5～6行目のFinally, ... on the experience. が3つ目の段階を表している。set ～ in motion「～を始める」、process「過程、プロセス」。
(A) (B) (D) いずれも具体的な手順を示す2つの文の間に入る文としては不自然。
(A) contact「～に連絡する」。
(B) note that ～「～ということに注意する」、procedure「手続き」。

145
(A) address
(B) schedule
(C) include
(D) determine

(A) ～を述べる
(B) ～の予定を立てる
(C) ～を含む
(D) ～を決心する

正解 **B** 選択肢は全て他動詞の働きを持つ語。空所を含む文はNext「(1つ目の段階である自己評価の)次に」から始まり、業績評価の3つの段階のうちの2つ目を説明していると考えられる。空所に入る他動詞の目的語はa meeting with each employee「各従業員との面談」なので、(B) schedule「～の予定を立てる」が適切。上司が各従業員との面談の予定を組むという自然な流れとなる。
(A) (C) (D) いずれも文脈に合わない。

146
(A) create
(B) created
(C) creative
(D) creativity

(A) ～を作り出す
(B) 作り出された
(C) 創造的な
(D) 創造性

正解 **D** 空所の前には動詞encourages「～を促進する」と形容詞continued「継続的な」がある。動詞encouragesの主語はan environmentを先行詞とする関係代名詞のthatで、continued ------- and innovationが目的語になると考えられる。よって空所には、continuedに修飾され、innovationと並列される名詞が入るので、(D) creativity「創造性」が適切。
(A) 動詞の原形。
(B) 動詞の過去形または過去分詞。
(C) 形容詞。

Expressions

no more than ～ 「～しか、わずか～」(❶ 3行目)
Our office is no more than a five-minute walk from County Hall Bus Stop.
当社のオフィスは郡庁舎バス停から徒歩わずか5分です。

Questions 147-148 refer to the following list of coupons.

① Summer savings at Lathom's Laundry!
Open every day from 6:00 A.M. to 12:00 midnight
in Annandale, Walford, and Kellering.

- -

② June
£10 OFF all drop-off orders over £25
Let us do the work for you!

- ✂

③ July
FREE dryer sheets and bottle of laundry detergent
(One coupon per household)

- -

④ August
Three loads of wash FREE
(One coupon per household)

- -

⑤ September
£200 laundry card raffle
Submit this coupon at any Lathom's Laundry
location to receive a raffle ticket. Raffle drawing
will be held on 30 September.

問題147-148は次のクーポンのリストに関するものです。

Lathom'sクリーニング店で夏の割引!
毎日午前6時から深夜12時まで
アナンデール、ウォルフォード、ケラーリングにて営業。

6月
25ポンドを超える全ての持ち込みのご注文が10ポンド引き
私たちに作業をお任せください!

7月
無料の乾燥機用シート型柔軟剤と洗濯洗剤1本
(1家族当たり1クーポン)

8月
3回分の洗濯が無料
(1家族当たり1クーポン)

9月
200ポンドのクリーニング・カードくじ
Lathom'sクリーニング店のいずれかの店舗で、このクーポンを出してくじ引き券をお受け取りください。くじの抽選は9月30日に行われます。

147 What is indicated about Lathom's Laundry?　　Lathom'sクリーニング店について何が示されていますか。

    (A) It is closed on weekends.　　　　　　　　(A) 週末は閉まっている。

    (B) It is open 24 hours a day.　　　　　　　　(B) 24時間営業である。

    (C) It offers self-service laundry only.　　　　(C) セルフサービスの洗濯のみ提供している。

    (D) It has more than one location.　　　　　　(D) 2店舗以上ある。

> **正解 D**　❶1行目からこれはLathom'sクリーニング店のクーポンと考えられ、同2行目には店の営業時間、同3行目には所在地と考えられる地名が記されている。所在地は、in Annandale, Walford, and Kellering「アナンデール、ウォルフォード、ケラーリングにて」と3カ所示されていることから、(D)が正解。more than ~は「~より多い」と、続く数詞を超える数を示すので、more than one locationは「2店舗以上」という意味になる。
> (A) ❶2行目より、週末も営業していると分かる。
> (B) ❶2行目より、営業時間は午前6時から深夜12時までと分かる。
> (C) ❷3行目より、Lathom'sクリーニング店が洗濯の作業をすると考えられる。self-service「セルフサービスの」。

148 When can a customer get free laundry supplies?　　顧客はいつ無料の洗濯用品をもらえますか。

    (A) In June　　　　　　(A) 6月

    (B) In July　　　　　　(B) 7月

    (C) In August　　　　(C) 8月

    (D) In September　　(D) 9月

> **正解 B**　7月のクーポンの内容を記した❸2行目に、FREE dryer sheets and bottle of laundry detergent「無料の乾燥機用シート型柔軟剤と洗濯洗剤1本」とある。よって、(B)が正解。supplies「用品、備品」。
> (C) ❹2行目より、無料になるのは3回分の洗濯であり、洗濯用品ではない。

Words & Phrases

coupon　クーポン　❶ saving　割引、節約　laundry　クリーニング店、洗濯　12:00 midnight　深夜12時
❷ £（pound）　ポンド　★英国の通貨単位　drop-off　(荷物などの)引き渡し　order　注文(品)　over　~を超えて
❸ dryer sheet　乾燥機用シート型柔軟剤　detergent　洗剤　per　~につき　household　家族、世帯
❹ load　1回分の量、荷物　wash　洗濯(物)　❺ raffle　くじ、ラッフル　submit　~を提出する　location　店舗、所在地
drawing　抽選、くじ引き

Expressions

be held　「(式などが)行われる、(会などが)開かれる」(❺5行目)

The annual meeting is expected to be held in Tokyo in April.
年次総会は4月に東京で開かれる予定です。

Questions 149-150 refer to the following e-mail.

```
*E-mail*

To:       Alexander Samuels <a.samuels@netmail.com>

From:     Sales Team <sales@shineoutlights.co.uk>

Date:     2 October

Subject:  Thank you for your order
```

Dear Mr. Samuels,

① Congratulations on taking advantage of our October Shine Out Lights online sale! By shopping during our promotion, you saved 15 percent on your purchase of our quality outdoor lighting.

② Your order of six extra-bright ground lights, a motion-detector spotlight, and two slim over-door lights will arrive within three to five working days. If there are any problems, please call us at 0191 498 0512 and reference order number 1984226.

Sincerely,

The Shine Out Lights Sales Team

問題149-150は次のEメールに関するものです。

受信者：Alexander Samuels <a.samuels@netmail.com>
送信者：販売チーム <sales@shineoutlights.co.uk>
日付：10月2日
件名：ご注文ありがとうございます

Samuels様

10月Shine Out照明社オンラインセールをご利用いただき、ありがとうございます。キャンペーン期間中にお買い物をしていただいたので、当社の上質な屋外照明のご購入が15パーセント引きとなりました。

お客さまご注文の、高輝度地上灯6台、動作感知スポットライト1台、細型の扉上照明2台は、3～5営業日以内にお届けする予定です。何か問題がございましたら、当社まで0191 498 0512にお電話いただき、注文番号1984226をお伝えください。

敬具

Shine Out 照明社 販売チーム

149 What is mentioned about the order?

注文について何が述べられていますか。

(A) The total price was reduced.
(B) It was delivered later than expected.
(C) The quality of the products is guaranteed.
(D) One of the items is out of stock.

(A) 総額が値引きされた。
(B) それは予想よりも遅く配達された。
(C) 製品の品質は保証されている。
(D) 品物の一つは在庫がない。

正解 A 件名から、注文に対するお礼のEメールと考えられる。❶ 1～3行目で、By shopping during our promotion, you saved 15 percent on your purchase of our quality outdoor lighting.「キャンペーン期間中に買い物されたので、当社の上質な屋外照明の購入が15パーセント引きとなった」とSamuelsさんの注文について値引きされたことが述べられているので、(A)が正解。mention「～のことを述べる」。total price「総額」、reduce「～を減らす」。
(B) ❷ 1～2行目に配達予定の日程への言及があり、注文品はこれから配達されると分かる。deliver「～を配達する」、expect「～を予想する」。
(C) ❶ 2～3行目にquality outdoor lighting「上質な屋外照明」とあるが、製品の品質が保証されているという記述はない。guarantee「～を保証する」。
(D) out of stock「在庫のない」。

---

150 What is indicated about the spotlight?

スポットライトについて何が示されていますか。

(A) It can be used indoors.
(B) It is very lightweight.
(C) It is activated by movement.
(D) It can be mounted above a door.

(A) 屋内で使用することができる。
(B) 非常に軽量である。
(C) 動きによって起動する。
(D) ドアの上に取り付けることができる。

正解 C スポットライトについては注文した照明を列記した❷ 1行目に、a motion-detector spotlight「動作感知スポットライト1台」とある。よって、It is activated by movement.「それ（＝スポットライト）は動きによって起動する」と表している(C)が正解。activate「～を起動する」、movement「動き」。
(A) ❶ 2～3行目にyour purchase of our quality outdoor lighting「当社の上質な屋外照明の購入」とあり、スポットライトも屋外用だと分かる。indoors「屋内で」。
(B) 重量に関する記述はない。lightweight「軽量の」。
(D) ❷ 1～2行目に、two slim over-door lights「細型の扉上照明2台」とあるが、スポットライトについての記述ではない。mount「～を取り付ける」。

Words & Phrases

sales team 販売チーム   order 注文   ❶ Congratulations on ～   ～おめでとう   online sale オンラインセール
shop 買い物をする   promotion （販売促進の）キャンペーン   save ～ on … …について～を節約する   purchase 購入
quality 上質な   outdoor 屋外の   lighting 照明   ❷ extra-bright 特別に明るい   ground light 地上灯
motion-detector 動作感知(型)の   spotlight スポットライト   slim 細身の、ほっそりした   over-door light 扉上照明
within ～以内に   working day 営業日   reference ～に言及する   order number 注文番号

Expressions

take advantage of ～ 「～を利用する」（❶ 1行目）

I'd like to take advantage of this opportunity to promote our products.
当社の製品を宣伝するためにこの機会を利用したいと思います。

Questions 151-152 refer to the following text-message chain.

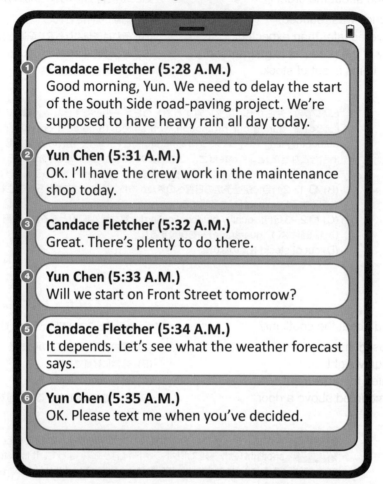

Candace Fletcher (5:28 A.M.)
Good morning, Yun. We need to delay the start of the South Side road-paving project. We're supposed to have heavy rain all day today.

Yun Chen (5:31 A.M.)
OK. I'll have the crew work in the maintenance shop today.

Candace Fletcher (5:32 A.M.)
Great. There's plenty to do there.

Yun Chen (5:33 A.M.)
Will we start on Front Street tomorrow?

Candace Fletcher (5:34 A.M.)
It depends. Let's see what the weather forecast says.

Yun Chen (5:35 A.M.)
OK. Please text me when you've decided.

問題151-152は次のテキストメッセージのやりとりに関するものです。

Candace Fletcher（午前5時28分）	おはようございます、Yun。私たちはサウスサイド道路舗装プロジェクトの開始を遅らせる必要があります。今日は一日中、大雨が降るようです。
Yun Chen（午前5時31分）	分かりました。作業班には、今日は整備工場で作業してもらいます。
Candace Fletcher（午前5時32分）	いいですね。あちらではやることがたくさんありますから。
Yun Chen（午前5時33分）	明日はフロント通りに着手しますか。
Candace Fletcher（午前5時34分）	状況次第ですね。天気予報が何と言っているか確かめましょう。
Yun Chen（午前5時35分）	分かりました。決めたら私にテキストメッセージを送ってください。

151 Why does Ms. Fletcher contact Mr. Chen?

(A) To send him a new schedule
(B) To alert him to a change in plans
(C) To add an item to his project list
(D) To ask for feedback about his crew

FletcherさんはなぜChenさんに連絡を取っていますか。

(A) 彼に新しい予定表を送るため
(B) 彼に計画の変更に対する注意喚起をするため
(C) 1つの項目を彼の計画表に加えるため
(D) 彼の作業班についての意見を求めるため

> **正解 B** Fletcherさんは❶で、We need to delay the start of the South Side road-paving project. We're supposed to have heavy rain all day today.「私たちはサウスサイド道路舗装プロジェクトの開始を遅らせる必要がある。今日は一日中、大雨が降るようだ」と伝えており、Chenさんは❷で了承している。FletcherさんはChenさんに雨による計画の変更を知らせるために連絡したと判断できるので、(B)が正解。alert ~ to …「~に…に対して注意喚起する」。
> (A) Fletcherさんは予定変更の必要性を伝えているが、新しい予定表を送っているわけではない。
> (C) add ~ to …「~を…に加える」。
> (D) ask for ~「~を求める」、feedback「意見」。

152 At 5:34 A.M., what does Ms. Fletcher imply when she writes, "It depends"?

(A) The maintenance shop may be closed.
(B) A supervisor may text her with a decision.

(C) Front Street may have been paved already.
(D) The paving project may be delayed by the rain.

午前5時34分に、"It depends"という発言で、Fletcherさんは何を示唆していますか。

(A) 整備工場が閉まっているかもしれない。
(B) 上司が決定事項を彼女にテキストメッセージで送るかもしれない。
(C) フロント通りはすでに舗装されたかもしれない。
(D) 舗装プロジェクトは雨によって遅れるかもしれない。

> **正解 D** Chenさんは❹で、Will we start on Front Street tomorrow?「明日はフロント通りに着手するか」と尋ねており、話の流れから、Front Streetとは❶で言及されている道路舗装プロジェクトに関連する道路を指すと考えられる。Fletcherさんの下線部の発言はこの質問に応答するもの。その後Fletcherさんは、Let's see what the weather forecast says.「天気予報が何と言っているか確かめよう」と続けているので、「状況次第」という発言は、舗装プロジェクトが雨によって遅れる可能性があることを示唆していると判断できる。よって、(D)が正解。
> (B) supervisor「上司」、decision「決断」。
> (C) may have done「~したかもしれない」、pave「~を舗装する」。

Words & Phrases

text-message　テキストメッセージの　　chain　一続き　　❶ delay　~を遅らせる　　road-paving　道路舗装の
project　プロジェクト、計画　　all day　一日中　　❷ crew　（一緒に仕事をする）班、一団　　maintenance shop　整備工場
❸ plenty　たくさん、十分　　❹ start on ~　~に着手する　　❺ It depends.　それは状況次第である。
weather forecast　天気予報　　❻ text　~にテキストメッセージを送る

Expressions

be supposed to *do*　「~することになっている」（❶3～4行目）
The delivery day was supposed to be March 7, but we haven't received the products yet.
配達日は3月7日のはずでしたが、私たちはまだ製品を受け取っていません。

Questions 153-154 refer to the following notice.

Northern Regional Railways
NOTICE: March 2

❶ Northern Regional Railways (NRR) invites all riders to take advantage of a special discount for early booking on local routes between Fairview and East City. Make your reservation online at least ten days in advance, and you can save 20 percent on any round-trip ticket. Simply enter promotion code 10302.

❷ Restrictions: Tickets purchased under this discount program must be used by September 1. This offer does not apply to express routes. Riders cannot combine this offer with points earned in the NRR Frequent Rider Rewards program.

問題153-154は次のお知らせに関するものです。

北部地域鉄道
お知らせ：3月2日

北部地域鉄道（NRR）は全ての乗客の皆さまに、Fairview駅とEast City駅間の普通列車路線の早期予約特別割引をぜひご利用くださるようご案内します。10日前までにオンラインで予約をされると、全ての往復切符が20パーセント引きになります。販売促進コード10302を入力するだけです。

制限条件：本割引プログラムで購入された切符は、9月1日までに使用しなければなりません。このサービスは急行列車路線には適用されません。乗客はこのサービスをNRRお得意さま特典プログラムで得たポイントと組み合わせることはできません。

Words & Phrases

notice お知らせ、告知　northern 北部の、北の　regional 地域の　railway 鉄道（会社）
❶ invite ～ to do ～に…するように勧める　rider 乗客　take advantage of ～ ～を利用する　booking 予約
local 普通列車の、各駅停車の　route 路線、経路　between A and B AとBの間の　make one's reservation 予約する
online オンラインで、インターネット経由で　at least 少なくとも　in advance 前もって
save ～ on … …について～を節約する　round-trip ticket 往復切符　simply ただ～のみ、単に　enter ～を入力する
promotion code 販売促進コード　❷ restrictions 制限条件　purchase ～を購入する　offer サービス、提供
express 急行の　combine ～ with … ～を…と組み合わせる　earn ～を得る　frequent 頻繁な
rewards program 特典プログラム　★継続利用した顧客に特典を提供する施策

153 What is the main purpose of the notice?

    (A) To promote the use of express train services

    (B) To announce the opening of a new route

    (C) To encourage participation in group tours

    (D) To inform customers about a unique offer

お知らせの主な目的は何ですか。

    (A) 急行列車便の利用を促すこと

    (B) 新路線の開設を告知すること

    (C) 団体ツアーへの参加を勧めること

    (D) 顧客に独自のサービスについて知らせること

正解 D ❶1〜2行目に、Northern Regional Railways (NRR) invites all riders to take advantage of a special discount for early booking on local routes between Fairview and East City.「北部地域鉄道(NRR)は全ての乗客に、Fairview駅とEast City駅間の普通列車路線の早期予約特別割引を利用するよう案内する」とある。そして、続く同2〜4行目で、Make your reservation online at least ten days in advance, and you can save 20 percent on any round-trip ticket.「10日前までにオンラインで予約すると、全ての往復切符が20パーセント引きになる」と述べられているので、北部地域鉄道が顧客である乗客に対して独自のサービスについて知らせることが主な目的だと分かる。よって、(D)が正解。inform 〜 about …「〜に…について知らせる」、customer「顧客」、unique「独自の、独特な」。

(A) ❷2行目に、割引は急行列車路線には適用されないとあり、急行列車の利用を促してはいない。promote「〜を促す、〜を促進する」。

(B) announce「〜を告知する、〜を発表する」。

(C) encourage「〜を勧める、〜を促す」、participation「参加」。

---

154 What is indicated about Northern Regional Railways?

    (A) It charges extra fees for checked baggage.

    (B) It plans to expand weekend train services.

    (C) It offers a customer loyalty program.

    (D) It recently upgraded its Web site.

北部地域鉄道について何が示されていますか。

    (A) 預入手荷物に追加料金を請求する。

    (B) 週末の列車の便を増やす予定である。

    (C) 優良顧客向けプログラムを提供している。

    (D) 最近ウェブサイトを改良した。

正解 C ❷2〜3行目に、Riders cannot combine this offer with points earned in the NRR Frequent Rider Rewards program.「乗客はこのサービスをNRRお得意さま特典プログラムで得たポイントと組み合わせることはできない」とあるので、北部地域鉄道がお得意さま特典プログラムを提供していることが分かる。そのサービスをa customer loyalty program「優良顧客向けプログラム(ポイント制度など、顧客をつなぎとめるための施策)」と表している(C)が正解。customer loyaltyは「顧客忠誠心」という意味。

(A) charge「〜を請求する」、checked baggage「預入手荷物」。

(B) expand「〜を拡大する」。

(D) upgrade「〜を改良する」。

Expressions

apply to 〜 「〜に適用される」(❷2行目)

The same rule applies to part-time workers.
同じ規則がパートタイム従業員に適用されます。

Questions 155-157 refer to the following Web page.

---

https://www.kelwynstorage.com.bm

| **Home** | Rates | Contact |

Kelwyn Storage
84 Montrose Street, Hamilton, HM 10

❶ Are you relocating? Do you need a place to store your household goods or business items during the transition? Let Kelwyn Storage keep them safe for you. Our climate-controlled facility has 24-hour security, with a unique access code for each storage unit. We use backup generators to ensure that your belongings always remain safe and in good condition.

❷ Our state-of-the-art facility in Hamilton is still under construction, but phase one construction is complete, and units in one of the buildings are ready for rental. We have three unit sizes to accommodate any storage need. Phase two will be complete on May 20, and more units will be available for monthly and longer-term rental. Reserve your space before May 20, and receive a free month of rent with any twelve-month contract.

❸ If you want to have your items for storage picked up, our trained movers can help. The fee is determined by distance as well as the size and number of items to be moved. Visit our Contact page to request a free quote.

問題155-157は次のウェブページに関するものです。

https://www.kelwynstorage.com.bm

ホーム　　　料金　　　問い合わせ

Kelwyn 保管社
モントローズ通り84番地、ハミルトン、HM 10

移転をご予定ですか？ 移行期間に家財道具や業務用品を保管する場所が必要ですか？ Kelwyn 保管社が皆さまのために安全にそれらを保管いたします。当社の温湿度が管理された施設は、保管区画ごとに個別のアクセスコードがあり、24 時間の警備体制が整っています。当社は、皆さまの所有物が常に安全で良好な状態に確実に保たれるよう、予備発電機を使用しています。

当社のハミルトンの最新鋭施設はまだ建設中ですが、建設の第 1 段階が完了しており、建物の一つにある区画はレンタルのご用意ができています。どんな保管のご要望にも応えられるよう 3 つの区画サイズがあります。第 2 段階は 5 月 20 日に完了する予定で、より多くの区画が月単位そしてより長期のレンタルでご利用可能となります。5 月 20 日までにご自身のスペースをご予約いただくと、12 カ月契約 1 件につき 1 カ月分のレンタル料が無料となります。

もし保管される物品の集荷をご希望なら、当社の訓練を受けた運送員がお手伝いできます。料金は距離および運ぶ物品のサイズや個数によって決まります。当社の問い合わせページにアクセスして無料のお見積もりをご依頼ください。

Words & Phrases

rate 料金　　storage 保管　❶ relocate 移転する　　store ～を保管する　　household goods 家財道具
item 用品、品物　　transition 移行　　climate-controlled 温度と湿度が管理された　　facility 施設、設備　　security 警備
unique 唯一の、独自の　　access code アクセスコード　　unit 区画、ユニット　　backup 予備(の)　　generator 発電機
ensure that ～ 確実に～であるようにする　　belongings 所有物　　remain ～ ～のままでいる
in good condition 良い状態で　❷ state-of-the-art 最新鋭の　　under construction 建設中で　　phase 段階
be ready for ～ ～の準備ができている　　rental レンタル、賃借　　accommodate ～(要求など)に応じる　　need 要求
monthly 月単位の　　long-term 長期の　　reserve ～を予約する　　rent 賃料　　contract 契約
❸ pick up ～ ～を引き取る　　trained 訓練された　　mover 運送員　　fee 料金　　determine ～を決定する
distance 距離　　A as well as B　BだけでなくAも　　request ～を依頼する　　quote 見積もり

155 What is the purpose of the Web page?

    (A) To announce a company's relocation

    (B) To outline a shipping procedure

    (C) To describe a company's services

    (D) To explain an increase in rates

ウェブページの目的は何ですか。

    (A) 会社の移転を発表すること

    (B) 配送手続きの概要を説明すること

    (C) 会社のサービスを説明すること

    (D) 料金の値上げを説明すること

> **正解 C** ❶1～2行目に、「移行期間に家財道具や業務用品を保管する場所が必要ですか？ Kelwyn保管社が皆さまのために安全にそれらを保管する」とあるので、会社が物品の保管場所を提供するサービスについて述べていると考えられる。続く同2～5行目では、温度と湿度が管理されていること、24時間の警備体制、予備発電機の使用など、保管施設の特徴が述べられ、さらに、❷・❸では、保管施設のレンタルに関連する情報が紹介されている。以上より、Kelwyn保管社のサービスについて説明されていると分かるので、(C)が正解。describe「～を説明する」。
> (A) ❶1行目でrelocation「移転」に言及されているのは読み手である顧客の移転についてであり、会社の移転は発表していない。
> (B) outline「～の概要を説明する」、shipping「配送、運送」、procedure「手続き」。

156 What is NOT true about the facility?

    (A) It requires a code to access storage spaces.

    (B) It is closed until May 20.

    (C) It is climate-controlled.

    (D) It has units of varying sizes.

施設について正しくないことは何ですか。

    (A) 保管スペースに入るにはコードを必要とする。

    (B) 5月20日まで閉まっている。

    (C) 温度と湿度が管理されている。

    (D) さまざまな大きさの区画がある。

> **正解 B** ❷3～4行目に、Phase two will be complete on May 20, and more units will be available for monthly and longer-term rental.「第2段階は5月20日に完了する予定で、より多くの区画が月単位そしてより長期のレンタルで利用可能となる」とある。また、同1～2行目に、「当社のハミルトンの最新鋭施設はまだ建設中だが、建設の第1段階が完了しており、建物の一つにある区画はレンタルの用意ができている」とあるので、第1段階完了時から施設の一部は利用でき、第2段階が完了する5月20日以降はさらに多くの区画が利用可能となることが分かる。つまり、5月20日より前にも施設は部分的に利用できるので、(B)が正解。
> (A) ❶2～4行目より、施設には、保管区画ごとにアクセスコードがあると分かる。require「～を必要とする」、code「コード、暗号」、access「～に入る」。
> (C) ❶2～3行目に、温度と湿度が管理されているとある。
> (D) ❷2～3行目より、3つの区画サイズがあることが分かる。varying「さまざまな」。

157 According to the Web page, what is available for an additional fee?

    (A) Pickup services

    (B) The use of a generator

    (C) A monthly contract

    (D) Truck rentals

ウェブページによると、追加料金で何が利用できますか。

    (A) 集荷サービス

    (B) 発電機の使用

    (C) 1カ月単位の契約

    (D) トラックのレンタル

> **正解 A** ❸1～3行目に、「もし保管する物品の集荷を希望するなら、当社の訓練を受けた運送員が手伝える。料金は距離および運ぶ物品のサイズや個数によって決まる」とある。よって、集荷サービスは距離やサイズ、個数によって料金が決まる有料のサービスと分かるので、(A)が正解。additional fee「追加料金」。pickup「集荷」。
> (B) ❶4～5行目に予備発電機への言及はあるが、発電機の有料使用については述べられていない。
> (C) ❷3～4行目に1カ月単位の契約への言及はあるが、追加料金が必要とは述べられていない。

Expressions

have ～ done 「～を…してもらう、～を…される」(❸1行目)

I would like to have the following items checked by 2 o'clock today.
私は今日2時までに次の項目を確認してもらいたいと思っています。

Questions 158-160 refer to the following article.

Sydney Morning Times

City Culture Desk

❶ (12 October)—Sydney native Lily Trevor is often asked two specific questions. How did she first come up with her idea to hold cooking classes at a public library, and how was she able to make her idea a reality? Ms. Trevor responds that she noticed the popularity of food shows on television but realised that some people seemed to lack even the most basic cooking skills. These observations provided Ms. Trevor's initial inspiration.

❷ As to the second question, Ms. Trevor explains that it requires the dedication of library staff to provide the space and support. Generous financial contributions from city organisations and businesses have also helped, since the city's library system doesn't have a large operating budget. In addition, Ms. Trevor's project has received donations of cooking and baking equipment from grocery stores and restaurants.

❸ "Two years ago I began with just one after-school cooking class for children at the library," Ms. Trevor said. "That expanded to adult classes and special programs featuring local chefs. Public <u>interest</u> has remained high, and it continues to be a rewarding project." What has evolved into the Culinary Centre of the Sydney Library now offers various programs each month, including special events and even online sessions.

問題158-160は次の記事に関するものです。

シドニー・モーニング・タイムズ

市の文化部

(10月12日)——シドニー出身のLily Trevorは2つの特定の質問をしばしば尋ねられる。彼女は最初どのようにして公立図書館で料理教室を開くというアイデアを思い付いたのか、そしてどのようにしてそのアイデアを実現することができたのか。Trevorさんは、テレビの料理番組の人気に気付いたが、一部の人は最も基本的な料理技術さえ持っていないようだと分かったのだと答える。これらの所見がTrevorさんに最初のひらめきを与えた。

2つ目の質問については、Trevorさんは場所と支援を提供してくれる図書館員の献身が必要だと説明する。市の図書館システムには多額の運営予算はないので、市の団体や企業からの寛大な財政支援もまた助けになっている。さらに、Trevorさんのプロジェクトは食料雑貨店やレストランから調理器具やパン焼き器具の寄付を受けている。

「2年前、私は図書館で放課後の子ども向け料理教室のたった1クラスから始めました」とTrevorさんは述べた。「それが大人向けクラスや地元のシェフを招く特別プログラムにまで広がりました。一般の関心は依然高く、やりがいのあるプロジェクトであり続けています」。シドニー図書館料理センターへと発展したこのプロジェクトは、今では特別なイベントやさらにはオンラインセッションも含むさまざまなプログラムを毎月提供している。

Words & Phrases

article 記事　culture desk （新聞社などの）文化部　❶ ~ native ~出身の人　specific 特定の
come up with ~ ~を思い付く　public 公の、一般大衆の　make ~ a reality ~を実現する
respond that ~ ~であると答える　notice ~に気付く　popularity 人気　show 番組
realise that ~ ~ということが分かる　★realiseの米国表記はrealize　seem to do ~するように思われる
lack ~を欠いている　basic 基本的な　skill 技術　observations （観察して得た）所見・情報
provide ~を与える、~をもたらす　initial 最初の　inspiration ひらめき　❷ explain that ~ ~ということを説明する
require ~を必要とする　dedication 献身　generous 寛大な、たっぷりの　financial 財政の
contribution 支援、寄付　organisation 団体　★米国表記はorganization　business 企業　operating 運営上の
budget 予算　in addition さらに、その上　donation 寄付　baking （パン・菓子などを）焼くこと　equipment 器具
grocery store 食料雑貨店　❸ begin with ~ ~から始める　after-school 放課後の　expand to ~ ~に拡大する
feature ~を目玉とする　chef シェフ　remain ~ ~のままである　continue to do ~し続ける
rewarding やりがいのある　evolve into ~ ~に発展する　culinary 料理の　centre センター　★米国表記はcenter
offer ~を提供する　various さまざまな　including ~を含めて

158 What is the purpose of the article?

   (A) To profile the success of an unusual program
   (B) To promote upcoming events at a library
   (C) To introduce a new library director
   (D) To request donations for a community project

記事の目的は何ですか。

   (A) 独特なプログラムの成功を紹介すること
   (B) 図書館で近々開催されるイベントを宣伝すること
   (C) 新しい図書館長を紹介すること
   (D) 地域プロジェクトに対する寄付を要請すること

正解 A ❶ 1～5行目で、Trevorさんがよく尋ねられる2つの質問を記載することでTrevorさんの始めたプログラムを紹介している。2つの質問とは、同2～4行目の「彼女は最初どのようにして公立図書館で料理教室を開くというアイデアを思い付いたのか」と、同4～5行目の「どのようにしてそのアイデアを実現することができたのか」であり、同6～11行目で1つ目の質問に関して、❷で2つ目の質問に関して説明されている。続く❸では、2年前のプログラム開始時の内容と、現在の発展した姿が述べられている。よって、記事はTrevorさんの始めた独特な

プログラムの成功について紹介する内容と言えるので、(A)が正解。profile「～の紹介を書く」、unusual「独特な、珍しい」。
(B) 図書館でのイベントへの言及はあるが、それを宣伝することが記事の目的ではない。promote「～を宣伝する」、upcoming「近く起こる」。
(C) introduce「～を紹介する」、director「館長、責任者」。
(D) ❷ 4～6行目で地域の団体や企業からの寄付が助けになっていることは述べられているが、寄付の要請はこの記事の目的ではない。request「～を要請する」、community「地域社会」。

---

159 What is suggested about Ms. Trevor?

   (A) She has hosted a world-famous chef at the Culinary Centre.
   (B) She started to offer cooking classes at a library two years ago.
   (C) She has been a guest on television shows.
   (D) She writes reviews of local restaurants.

Trevorさんについて何が分かりますか。

   (A) 彼女は料理センターで世界的に有名なシェフを接待したことがある。
   (B) 彼女は2年前に図書館で料理教室の提供を始めた。
   (C) 彼女はテレビ番組にゲスト出演している。
   (D) 彼女は地元のレストランのレビューを書いている。

正解 B ❸ 1～3行目に "Two years ago I began with just one after-school cooking class for children at the library," Ms. Trevor said.「『2年前、私は図書館で放課後の子ども向け料理教室のたった1クラスから始めた』とTrevorさんは述べた」と書かれている。よって、(B)が正解。
(A) ❸ 3～5行目で「地元のシェフを招く特別プログラム」に言及

されているが、世界的に有名なシェフを接待したとは書かれていない。host「～を接待する」。
(C) ❶ 6～9行目にテレビ番組への言及はあるが、Trevorさんはテレビ番組から気付きを得たのであり、出演したとは述べられていない。guest「ゲスト」。
(D) review「レビュー、批評」。

---

160 The word "interest" in paragraph 3, line 5, is closest in meaning to

   (A) concern
   (B) advantage
   (C) share
   (D) attention

第3段落・5行目にある "interest" に最も意味が近いのは

   (A) 心配
   (B) 利点
   (C) 共有
   (D) 関心

正解 D Trevorさんは、❸ 1～5行目で、自身の料理教室がこの2年で拡大してきたことを述べている。続く同5～7行目の該当の語を含む文は、「一般の-------は依然高く、やりがいのあるプロジェクトであり続けている」という意味。さらに同7～10行目に、現在ではシドニー図書館料理センターへと発展し、

特別なイベントなどのさまざまなプログラムを毎月提供していることが述べられているので、一般の関心が高い状態が続いていると考えられる。よって、(D) attention「関心、注目」が正解。
(A)「関心事」という語義もあるが、個人的に影響のあることや深刻さを含むニュアンスの語であるため、ここでは不適切。

Expressions

as to ～「～について言えば、～に関しては」(❷ 1行目)
As to this year's budget, labor costs were reduced drastically.
今年の予算については、人件費が大幅に削減されました。

Questions 161-163 refer to the following notice.

Celebration of Excellence

❶ — [1] —. Congratulations to all our employees! Bharati Corporation has been named the top manufacturer in India by *Tober Business Review*! This magazine, as you might already know, is one of the most highly regarded magazines in the business world. We want to thank you for your hard work and diligence. — [2] —. Because of all of you, we have been recognized internationally as a world-leading company.

❷ Please join us in your building's cafeteria on Friday, 8 November, for a corporate-wide Celebration of Excellence. We will be closing all factories and offices in India, the United Kingdom, and the United States for two hours, starting 12:00 noon local time for this event. — [3] —. One of our board members will be speaking at each of our locations. — [4] —. This will be followed by music and a complimentary buffet luncheon for all employees.

❸ Thank you again for making this our best year ever. We look forward to celebrating with you.

問題161-163は次のお知らせに関するものです。

優秀祝賀会

当社従業員の皆さん、おめでとうございます! Bharati社は『Toberビジネスレビュー』誌においてインドのトップメーカーに選出されました。すでにご存じかもしれませんが、同誌はビジネス界で最も高く評価されている雑誌の一つです。私たちは皆さんの努力と勤勉さに感謝したいと思います。*私たちはこの全社一丸となった努力に心から感謝しています。皆さん全員のおかげで、当社は世界の主要企業として国際的に認められました。

11月8日金曜日に、全社規模の優秀祝賀会のためにご自分のオフィスビルのカフェテリアにお集まりください。インド、英国、そしてアメリカ合衆国の全ての工場とオフィスをこのイベントのために現地時間の正午から2時間休業とします。当社の取締役の一人がそれぞれの場所でスピーチをする予定です。この後、全従業員のために、音楽と無料のビュッフェ形式の昼食会が行われます。

当社にとってこれまでで最高の年にしてくださったことに感謝いたします。皆さんと共に祝うことを楽しみにしています。

*問題163の挿入文の訳

Words & Phrases

celebration 祝賀会　excellence 優秀さ　❶ Congratulations to ～! ～、おめでとう!　corporation 企業、株式会社
name ～ … ～を…(賞など)に選ぶ　top 最上位の　manufacturer メーカー、製造業者　highly regarded 高く評価された
business world ビジネス界　thank ～ for … …に対して～に感謝する　diligence 勤勉
because of ～ ～のために、～のせいで　recognize ～ as … ～を…として認める　internationally 国際的に
world-leading 世界の主要な、世界をリードする　❷ join ～ for … ～と…を共にする
cafeteria カフェテリア、セルフサービスの食堂　corporate-wide 全社規模の　the United Kingdom 英国
12:00 noon 正午　local time 現地時間　board member 取締役　speak スピーチをする　location 場所、店舗
be followed by ～ ～が続く　complimentary 無料の　buffet ビュッフェ形式　luncheon 昼食会
❸ look forward to *doing* ～することを心待ちにする　celebrate 祝う

Expressions

as you might already know 「すでにご存じかもしれませんが」(❶2～3行目)
As you might already know, it has been 100 years since our company was established.
すでにご存じかもしれませんが、当社は創業して100年になります。

161 What is the purpose of the notice?

    (A) To announce the opening of a new factory in India

    (B) To ask for nominations of staff members for an award

    (C) To express gratitude to all company employees

    (D) To promote the use of corporate cafeterias

お知らせの目的は何ですか。

    (A) インドでの新しい工場の開業を発表すること

    (B) 賞の候補となるスタッフの推薦を求めること

    (C) 会社の全従業員に謝意を示すこと

    (D) 社員食堂の利用を促すこと

> **正解 C** お知らせは、❶1行目のCongratulations to all our employees!「当社従業員の皆さん、おめでとうございます」で始まり、同1～2行目に、「Bharati社は『Toberビジネスレビュー』誌においてインドのトップメーカーに選出された」と書かれている。そして、同3～4行目で、We want to thank you for your hard work and diligence.「私たちは皆さんの努力と勤勉さに感謝したいと思う」と述べられている。また、❷では優秀祝賀会を行うことが書かれており、お知らせの最後のまとめとなる❸1行目では、Thank you again for making this our best year ever.「当社にとってこれまでで最高の年にしてくれたことに感謝する」と、再び従業員に謝意が示されている。以上より(C)が正解。express「～を示す」、gratitude「感謝」。
> (B) nomination「候補者、推薦」、award「賞」。
> (D) corporate cafeteria「社員食堂」。

162 What is indicated about Bharati Corporation?

    (A) It was honored in a prestigious magazine.

    (B) It has multiple locations in South America.

    (C) It manufactures computer chips for vehicles.

    (D) It closes two hours early every Friday.

Bharati社について何が示されていますか。

    (A) 一流の雑誌で称賛された。

    (B) 南米に複数の拠点を持つ。

    (C) 乗り物用のコンピューターチップを製造している。

    (D) 毎週金曜日は2時間早く閉まる。

> **正解 A** ❶1～2行目に、Bharati Corporation has been named the top manufacturer in India by *Tober Business Review*!「Bharati社は『Toberビジネスレビュー』誌においてインドのトップメーカーに選出された」と書かれている。『Toberビジネスレビュー』誌については、続く同2～3行目に、This magazine ...... is one of the most highly regarded magazines in the business world.「同誌はビジネス界で最も高く評価されている雑誌の一つだ」とある。よって、Bharati社は一流の業界誌である『Toberビジネスレビュー』誌で称賛されたと分かるので、(A)が正解。honor「～を称賛する」、prestigious「一流の」。
> (B) ❷2～3行目から、インド、英国、アメリカ合衆国で操業していることが分かるが、南米については言及されていない。multiple「複数の」。
> (C) Bharati社が何を製造しているかについては言及がない。manufacture「～を製造する」、computer chip「コンピューターチップ」、vehicle「乗り物」。

163 In which of the positions marked [1], [2], [3], and [4] does the following sentence best belong?

"We truly appreciate this team effort."

    (A) [1]   (C) [3]

    (B) [2]   (D) [4]

[1]、[2]、[3]、[4]と記載された箇所のうち、次の文が入るのに最もふさわしいのはどれですか。

「私たちはこの全社一丸となった努力に心から感謝しています」

> **正解 B** 挿入文では謝意が述べられている。❶3～4行目にWe want to thank you for your hard work and diligence.「私たちは皆さんの努力と勤勉さに感謝したいと思う」とあり、挿入文と同じくWeという主語で謝意を表している。この直後の(B) [2]に挿入文を入れると、this team effort「この全社一丸となった努力」が直前の文のyour hard work and diligenceを言い換える形となる。そして前文に続いてBharati社が認められたことに対して従業員への感謝を述べる内容が続くことになり、流れとして適切。truly「心から、本当に」、appreciate「～に感謝する」、team effort「一丸となっての努力、協力してする仕事」。

Questions 164-167 refer to the following text-message chain.

1 Marie Truong (1:45 P.M.)
I was just forwarded a follow-up call from a customer in West Fordham. He said his power went out a few hours ago. He made a service request and was expecting a service crew earlier today. My records are incomplete for some reason. Do you have any similar reports in the dispatch record?

2 Brian Eighmy (1:46 P.M.)
What's the exact address?

3 Marie Truong (1:47 P.M.)
221 North James Street. The customer's name is Cameron Fellman.

4 Brian Eighmy (1:52 P.M.)
Nothing came up. However, I did dispatch a truck to 652 North James Street. It's probably unrelated.

5 Marie Truong (1:53 P.M.)
That's only a few blocks away. Could we have them stop by Mr. Fellman's house after they are done?

6 Brian Eighmy (1:54 P.M.)
Sure. Does he have any pets?

7 Marie Truong (1:55 P.M.)
Mr. Fellman? Pets are not indicated in the report.

8 Brian Eighmy (1:56 P.M.)
OK, I'll need you to confirm that before we send the truck over. The service team may need to go into the backyard.

9 Marie Truong (1:57 P.M.)
I'll ask Mr. Fellman and call you with details.

問題164-167は次のテキストメッセージのやりとりに関するものです。

Marie Truong（午後1時45分） たった今ウェストフォーダムの顧客から追って確認の電話が転送されてきました。数時間前に停電になったとのことでした。彼は作業を依頼し、作業班が今日もっと早くに来るのを待っていました。私の記録はどういう訳か不完全なのです。同様の報告が派遣記録にありますか。
Brian Eighmy（午後1時46分） 正確な住所はどこですか。
Marie Truong（午後1時47分） ノースジェームズ通り221番地です。顧客の名前はCameron Fellmanです。
Brian Eighmy（午後1時52分） 何も出てきません。しかし、私はノースジェームズ通り652番地にはトラックを派遣しました。それはおそらく無関係でしょう。
Marie Truong（午後1時53分） そこはほんの数ブロックの距離です。作業が終わったら、彼らにFellmanさんの家に立ち寄ってもらうことはできるでしょうか。
Brian Eighmy（午後1時54分） もちろんです。彼は何かペットを飼っていますか。
Marie Truong（午後1時55分） Fellmanさんがですか。報告にペットについては示されていません。
Brian Eighmy（午後1時56分） そうですか。トラックを送る前に、あなたにその点を確認してもらう必要があります。作業班は裏庭に入る必要があるかもしれませんから。
Marie Truong（午後1時57分） Fellmanさんに聞いて、あなたに詳細を電話しますね。

Expressions

for some reason 「どういう訳か、何らかの理由で」（❶5行目）
One of our candidates didn't come up to the interview for some reason.
当社の応募者の一人は、どういう訳か面接に現れませんでした。

164 Why did Ms. Truong contact Mr. Eighmy?
- (A) To confirm a customer's address
- (B) To follow up on a request
- (C) To ask how widespread a power outage was
- (D) To question a recent decision

TruongさんはなぜEighmyさんに連絡を取りましたか。
- (A) 顧客の住所を確認するため
- (B) 依頼を追跡調査するため
- (C) 停電がどのくらい広がっているのか尋ねるため
- (D) 最近の決定に異議を唱えるため

正解 B Truongさんは❶で、数時間前に停電になった顧客が作業依頼をし、作業班が今日もっと早くに来るのを待っていたと伝えている。続けて、自分の記録が不完全なため、同様の報告が派遣記録にあるかと尋ねている。よって、Truongさんは顧客の依頼について詳細を調査するためにEighmyさんに連絡していると判断できるので、(B)が正解。follow up on ～「～を追跡する、～を追及する」。
(C) widespread「広範囲に及ぶ」、power outage「停電」。
(D) question「～に異議を唱える、～を疑問視する」、decision「決定」。

165 At 1:52 P.M., what does Mr. Eighmy mean when he writes, "Nothing came up"?
- (A) He did not find a dispatch report.
- (B) He could not locate the service crew.
- (C) He could not open a document.
- (D) He did not determine the cause of a power outage.

午後1時52分に、"Nothing came up"という発言で、Eighmyさんは何を意図していますか。
- (A) 彼は派遣の報告を見つけられなかった。
- (B) 彼は作業班のいる場所を見つけられなかった。
- (C) 彼は文書ファイルを開けられなかった。
- (D) 彼は停電の原因を特定しなかった。

正解 A ❶で、Truongさんは顧客からの依頼について自分の記録が不完全だと伝えた後、同様の報告が派遣記録にあるかと尋ねている。それに対し、Eighmyさんは❷で、正確な住所を聞き返し、Truongさんは❸で、顧客の住所と氏名を伝えている。続く午後1時52分のEighmyさんの「何も出てこなかった」という発言は、派遣記録を探したが報告は見つからなかったと伝えていると考えられる。よって、(A)が正解。
(B) locate「～の場所を見つける」。
(C) document「文書ファイル、書類」。
(D) determine「～を特定する」、cause「原因」。

166 What information does Ms. Truong need to find out?
- (A) If there have been similar issues in the area
- (B) If all necessary paperwork is complete
- (C) If the account in question has been paid in full
- (D) If there are animals in a customer's yard

Truongさんはどんな情報を見つける必要がありますか。
- (A) そのエリアに似たような問題があったかどうか
- (B) 全ての必要な書類事務が完了しているかどうか
- (C) 問題になっている口座に全額支払われたかどうか
- (D) 顧客の庭に動物がいるかどうか

正解 D 別の場所に派遣されたトラックをFellmanさんの家に立ち寄らせるという提案に、Eighmyさんは❻で賛成して「彼は何かペットを飼っているか」と尋ねている。❼で、ペットについては報告にないと答えるTruongさんに対し、Eighmyさんは❽でトラックを送る前にその点を確認してもらう必要があると述べ、作業班が裏庭に入るかもしれないと理由を伝えている。よって、TruongさんはFellmanさんの庭にペットがいるかを確かめる必要があると分かるので、(D)が正解。
(A) issue「問題」。
(B) necessary「必要な」、paperwork「書類事務」。
(C) account「口座」、in question「問題になっている」。

167 What is Ms. Truong most likely going to do next?
- (A) Send an e-mail to Mr. Eighmy
- (B) Check the service report
- (C) Call Mr. Fellman
- (D) Transfer a payment

Truongさんは次に何をすると考えられますか。
- (A) EighmyさんにEメールを送る
- (B) 作業報告書を確認する
- (C) Fellmanさんに電話する
- (D) 支払いを送金する

正解 C Fellmanさんがペットを飼っているか確認するよう言われたTruongさんは、❾で「Fellmanさんに聞いて、あなたに詳細を電話する」と答えている。よって、Truongさんはその確認のためFellmanさんに連絡すると考えられるので、(C)が正解。
(D) transfer「～を送金する」、payment「支払い」。

Words & Phrases
❶ forward ～ … 　～に…を転送する　　follow-up　追跡確認の　　power　電力　　go out　(明かりが)消える
service request　作業依頼　　expect　～が来るのを待つ　　crew　班、一団　　incomplete　不完全な　　dispatch　派遣
❷ exact　正確な　　❹ come up　(情報が画面に)現れる、出る　　dispatch　～を派遣する　　unrelated　関係がない
❺ stop by ～　～に立ち寄る　　be done　終わる、済む　　❽ confirm　～を確認する　、　backyard　裏庭

Questions 168-171 refer to the following article.

Maritzburg to Welcome New Store

① MARITZBURG (23 September)—Residents of Maritzburg will soon have a new place to buy their groceries. — [1] —. Webb's Market, which currently operates in Durban and last month celebrated five years of being in business, will open a Maritzburg branch on Monday, 4 October, making it the store's second location. The store has steadily made a name for itself.

② Owned by longtime Durban residents Andrew and Marnie Webb, Webb's Market has made its mark by carrying products primarily grown and produced in the region. — [2] —. From its early days, it has been stocking milk, cheese, beef, chicken, juices, baked goods, and a host of other locally produced food items.

③ "Today's consumers want to know where their food comes from and how it is produced," Mr. Webb noted. "And they increasingly prefer to buy food that is produced closer to home. However, not many stores carry primarily locally made products."

④ Apparently, the Webbs heard similar sentiments from Maritzburg residents. "Our Durban store has been attracting a growing number of customers from Maritzburg," said Ms. Webb. "Some inquired whether we would consider opening a store there. — [3] —. So after careful review and extensive market research, we decided to do just that. If this expansion goes well, we hope to open other stores around the region."

⑤ — [4] —. Those interested in applying for a position at the new store location should visit www.webbsmarket.co.za.

問題 168-171 は次の記事に関するものです。

新店舗を歓迎するマリッツバーグ

マリッツバーグ（9 月 23 日）──マリッツバーグの住民はまもなく食料雑貨品を買う新しい場所を得るだろう。Webb's 商店は、現在ダーバンで営業しており、先月創業 5 周年を祝ったが、10 月 4 日月曜日にマリッツバーグ支店を開業し、同店の 2 番目の店舗とする予定である。同店は着実に名を上げてきた。

Webb's 商店は、長年ダーバンに住んでいる Andrew Webb と Marnie Webb が所有しており、主に地域内で栽培・製造された製品を取り扱うことによって成功してきた。同店は初期から、牛乳、チーズ、牛肉、鶏肉、ジュース類、パン・焼き菓子類、その他多くの地元産の食品を扱っている。

「今日の消費者は、自分の食べる物の産地やそれがどのように生産されているのかを知りたいと思っています」と Andrew Webb 氏は述べた。「そしてますます、より身近な場所で生産された食べ物を買いたいと考えています。しかし、地元で生産された製品を第一に扱う店は多くありません」。

どうやら Webb 両氏はマリッツバーグ住民から同様の意見を聞いたようだ。「私どものダーバンの店は、マリッツバーグからますます多くのお客さまを引き付けています」と Marnie Webb 氏は言った。「中には私たちが同地で店を開く考えはあるかと尋ねる方もいました。そこで慎重な検討と広範囲の市場調査の後、そうすることに決めました。もしこの拡大がうまくいけば、私たちは地域のあちこちに他の店舗を開きたいと思います」。

*新しい店舗のために、雇用が現在進行中である。新店舗での仕事への応募に興味がある方は www.webbsmarket.co.za にアクセスのこと。

*問題 171 の挿入文の訳

Words & Phrases

welcome ～を歓迎する **①** resident 住民　groceries 食料雑貨類　market 食料品店、市場　currently 現在　operate 営業をする　celebrate ～を祝う　be in business 商売をしている　branch 支店　location 店舗、所在地　steadily 着実に　make a name for *oneself* 名を上げる、有名になる　**②** own ～を所有する　longtime 長年の　make *one's* mark 成功する、有名になる　carry ～（商品）を取り扱う　primarily 主に、第一に　grow ～を栽培する　produce ～を製造する、～を生産する　region 地域　stock ～を在庫として持つ　baked goods パン・焼き菓子類　a host of ～ 多くの～　locally 地元で　**③** consumer 消費者　come from ～ ～産である、～からとれる　note ～と述べる　increasingly ますます　prefer to *do* ～する方を好む　close to home 身近で　**④** apparently どうやら～らしい　sentiments 意見、感想　attract ～を引き寄せる　a growing number of ～ ますます多くの～　inquire whether ～ ～かどうか尋ねる　consider *doing* ～することを検討する　review 精査、吟味　extensive 広範囲にわたる　market research 市場調査　expansion 拡大　go well うまくいく　**⑤** apply for ～ ～に応募する　position 仕事、職

168 What is mentioned about Webb's Market?

(A) It underwent a name change.
(B) It is currently under construction.
(C) It recently celebrated its anniversary.
(D) It will close its store in Durban.

Webb's商店について何が述べられていますか。

(A) 名称の変更があった。
(B) 現在建設中である。
(C) 最近周年祭を祝った。
(D) ダーバンの店舗を閉める予定である。

正解 C	❶ 3〜6行目に、Webb's Market, which currently operates in Durban and last month celebrated five years of being in business「Webb's商店は、現在ダーバンで営業しており、先月創業5周年を祝った」とあるので、(C)が	正解。anniversary「周年祭、記念日」。 (A) undergo「〜(変化など)を経験する」。 (B) 新店舗が話題にされているが、建設中とは述べられていない。under construction「建設中で」。

169 What is indicated about Mr. and Ms. Webb?

(A) They own a farm.
(B) They live in Durban.
(C) They import most of their products.
(D) They regularly request customer feedback.

Webb両氏について何が示されていますか。

(A) 彼らは農場を所有している。
(B) 彼らはダーバンに住んでいる。
(C) 彼らは製品のほとんどを輸入している。
(D) 彼らは定期的に顧客の意見を求めている。

正解 B	Webb's商店の特徴を述べる文の❷ 1〜2行目に Owned by longtime Durban residents Andrew and Marnie Webb「長年ダーバンに住んでいるAndrew WebbとMarnie Webbが所有しており」とある。Durban residentsをlive in Durbanと表している(B)が正解。	(C) ❷・❸より、地元産の製品を第一に扱っていると分かる。import「〜を輸入する」。 (D) ❹ 1〜2行目に、「マリッツバーグ住民から同様の意見を聞いたようだ」とあるが、定期的に顧客の意見を求めているという記述はない。regularly「定期的に」、feedback「意見」。

170 What is NOT mentioned as a product sold at Webb's Market?

(A) Dairy
(B) Meats
(C) Bread
(D) Flowers

Webb's商店で売られている製品として述べられていないものは何ですか。

(A) 乳製品
(B) 肉
(C) パン
(D) 花

正解 D	Webb's商店で売られている製品について、❷ 5〜8行目にit has been stocking milk, cheese, beef, chicken, juices, baked goods, and a host of other locally produced food items「牛乳、チーズ、牛肉、鶏肉、ジュース類、	パン・焼き菓子類、その他多くの地元産の食品を扱っている」とある。(D)の花は含まれていないので、正解は(D)。 (A) milk、cheeseはdairy「乳製品」。 (C) bread「パン」はbaked goodsの一つ。

171 In which of the positions marked [1], [2], [3], and [4] does the following sentence best belong?

"Hiring is now under way for the new location."

(A) [1]   (C) [3]
(B) [2]   (D) [4]

[1]、[2]、[3]、[4]と記載された箇所のうち、次の文が入るのに最もふさわしいのはどれですか。

「新しい店舗のために、雇用が現在進行中である」

正解 D	挿入文は新店舗のための雇用が進行中であることを述べたもの。記事の❶〜❹には、雇用に関する記述はない。❺の最初の(D) [4]に挿入文を入れると、直後のThose interested in applying for a position at the new store location should visit ......「新店舗での仕事への応募に興味がある方は......にアクセスのこと」という応募方法を案内する文に自然につながるので、適切。hiring「雇用、採用」、under way「進行中で」。

Expressions

those interested in 〜 「〜に興味のある人々」(❺ 1行目)

Our Web site is beneficial to those interested in starting their own businesses.
当ウェブサイトは起業することに興味のある方々にとって有益です。

Questions 172-175 refer to the following e-mail.

E-mail

To:	Tsazo Bankers Association <info@tsazobankersassociation.co.za>
From:	Karabo Mphela <k.mphela@tsazobankersassociation.co.za>
Date:	15 June
Subject:	Community Banking Conference

Dear Conference Attendees,

1 The recent conference organized by Tsazo Bankers Association (TBA) was another success, boasting the largest attendance of all eighteen of our annual conferences so far. And you helped make that happen! We <u>appreciate</u> our presenters and attendees for sharing their knowledge and skills.

2 If you have not yet filled out a conference survey, please take a moment to do so at www.tsazobankersassociation.co.za/survey. We greatly value your feedback and make a point of putting it into practice. For example, we decided to lengthen this year's conference based on feedback from last year's survey. Extending the conference to three days made it possible for us to offer a more comprehensive programme.

3 Finally, you do not have to wait a whole year for more professional development opportunities. TBA offers learning activities year-round. In fact, our next event is coming up soon. Please join us on 5 July for our webinar, *Innovations in Online Banking*—and stay up-to-date on all future events by signing up for e-mail notifications at www.tsazobankersassociation.co.za/pd.

4 We look forward to seeing you again soon.

Karabo Mphela, Event Director
Tsazo Bankers Association

問題 172-175 は次の E メールに関するものです。

受信者：Tsazo 銀行家協会 <info@tsazobankersassociation.co.za>
送信者：Karabo Mphela <k.mphela@tsazobankersassociation.co.za>
日付：6月15日
件名：地域銀行業協議会

協議会参加者各位

Tsazo 銀行家協会(TBA)による最近の協議会はこの度も成功で、これまでの全 18 回の当協会年次会議のうちで最多の出席者数を誇りました。そして、皆さんはその実現に手を貸してくださいました！ 当協会は発表者と参加者が知識と技能を共有してくださったことを高く評価しております。

もしまだ協議会のアンケートにご記入されていなければ、どうぞお時間を少し取って www.tsazobankersassociation.co.za/survey にてご記入ください。当協会は皆さんのご意見を非常に尊重しており、必ずそれを実行するようにしています。例えば、昨年のアンケートのご意見に基づいて今年の協議会を延長することにしました。協議会を 3 日間に延ばすことによって、当協会はより包括的なプログラムを提供することができました。

最後に、皆さんはさらなる専門的能力開発の機会を丸 1 年間お待ちになる必要はありません。TBA は一年中、学びの活動を提供しています。実際、当協会の次のイベントが間近に控えています。7 月 5 日のオンラインセミナー『オンラインバンキングにおける新機軸』にご参加ください――そして、www.tsazobankersassociation.co.za/pd で E メール通知をお申し込みいただくことで、今後の全てのイベントの最新情報を随時ご入手ください。

皆さんと間もなく再会できることを心待ちにしております。

イベント責任者　Karabo Mphela
Tsazo 銀行家協会

172 What is indicated about this year's Community Banking Conference?

(A) It was a one-day event.
(B) It was held in a new venue.
(C) The keynote address was *Innovations in Online Banking*.
(D) More people attended than in previous years.

今年の地域銀行業協議会について何が示されていますか。

(A) 1日のイベントだった。
(B) 新しい会場で開かれた。
(C) 基調演説は『オンラインバンキングにおける新機軸』だった。
(D) これまでの年よりも、多くの人たちが出席した。

> **正解 D** 件名と冒頭の名宛人より、このEメールは地域銀行業協議会についての内容で、会の参加者に宛てたものと分かる。❶1～2行目に、The recent conference organized by Tsazo Bankers Association (TBA) was another success, boasting the largest attendance of all eighteen of our annual conferences so far.「Tsazo銀行家協会(TBA)による最近の協議会はこの度も成功で、これまでの全18回の当協会年次会議のうちで最多の出席者数を誇った」と書かれている。よって、(D)が正解。previous「前の」。
> (A) ❷4～5行目より、今年の協議会は3日間開催されたと分かる。
> (B) venue「開催地」。
> (C) keynote address「基調演説」。

173 The word "appreciate" in paragraph 1, line 3, is closest in meaning to

(A) request
(B) apologize
(C) value
(D) increase

第1段落・3行目にある "appreciate" に最も意味が近いのは

(A) ～を求める
(B) 謝る
(C) ～を高く評価する
(D) ～を増やす

> **正解 C** Eメールの送信者であるMphelaさんは、❶1～2行目で、協議会参加者に向けてTsazo銀行家協会の最近の協議会の成功を報告し、続く同3行目で、And you helped make that happen「そして、皆さんはその実現に手を貸してくれた」と書いている。同3～4行目の該当の語を含む文は、「当協会は発表者と参加者が知識と技能を共有してくれたこと------」という意味。それまでの文の流れから、発表者と参加者の尽力が貴重なものだと思っているということを述べていると考えられる。よって、(C) value「～を高く評価する、～を尊重する」が正解。

Words & Phrases

banker 銀行家　association 協会　community 地域社会、コミュニティー　banking 銀行業
conference 協議会、会議　attendee 参加者　❶ organize ～を催す　success 成功　boast ～(業績)を誇りにする
attendance 出席者数　annual 年次の、年1回の　so far 今までのところ　help *do* ～する助けとなる
appreciate ～を高く評価する、～の価値を認める　presenter 発表者　share ～を共有する　knowledge 知識
skill 技能　❷ fill out ～ ～に全て記入する　survey アンケート、調査票　take a moment to *do* 時間を取って～する
greatly 非常に　value ～を尊重する　feedback 意見　put ～ into practice ～を実行する　lengthen ～を延長する
based on ～ ～に基づいて　extend ～を延ばす、～を延長する　offer ～を提供する　comprehensive 包括的な
programme プログラム　★米国表記は program　❸ finally 最後に　whole 丸～、全体の
professional 専門的な、職業上の　development 開発　opportunity 機会　activity 活動　year-round 一年中
in fact 実際　come up 近づく　webinar オンラインセミナー　★Web上で開催されるセミナー(seminar)
innovation 新機軸、革新　stay up-to-date on ～ ～の最新情報を把握している、～について遅れないようにする
sign up for ～ ～に申し込む　notification 通知　❹ look forward to *doing* ～することを心待ちにする
event director イベント責任者

174 What is one reason that Mr. Mphela e-mailed conference attendees?

    (A) To invite them to make a presentation
    (B) To request that they fill out a survey
    (C) To announce a schedule change
    (D) To solicit feedback on banking services

Mphelaさんが協議会の参加者にEメールを送った一つの理由は何ですか。

    (A) 彼らに発表するよう依頼するため
    (B) 彼らがアンケートに記入するよう依頼するため
    (C) 予定の変更を知らせるため
    (D) 銀行業務に関する意見を求めるため

> **正解 B** ❷ 1～2行目に、If you have not yet filled out a conference survey, please take a moment to do so at www.tsazobankersassociation.co.za/survey.「もしまだ協議会のアンケートに記入していなければ、時間を少し取ってwww.tsazobankersassociation.co.za/surveyにて記入してください」とあり、協議会の参加者にアンケートに記入することを求めている。よって、(B)が正解。e-mail「～にEメールを送る」。
> (A) invite ～ to *do*「～に…するように依頼する」、presentation「発表」。
> (C) ❸で、同協会が提供する学習活動の直近の予定を知らせているが、予定の変更については言及されていない。announce「～を知らせる」。
> (D) ❷より、求めているのは協議会についての意見であり、銀行業務についての意見ではない。solicit「～を求める、～を請う」、banking services「銀行業務」。

175 Why does Mr. Mphela suggest visiting a Web site?

    (A) To receive news about upcoming events
    (B) To search TBA's member directory
    (C) To schedule a career consultation
    (D) To update some contact information

Mphelaさんはなぜウェブサイトにアクセスすることを勧めていますか。

    (A) 今後のイベントについて、知らせを受け取るため
    (B) TBAの会員名簿を検索するため
    (C) 職業相談の予定を立てるため
    (D) 連絡先情報を更新するため

> **正解 A** ❸ 1～4行目で、TBAは一年中学習活動を提供しており、次のイベントが7月5日に行われることが述べられている。続く同4～5行目に、stay up-to-date on all future events by signing up for e-mail notifications at www.tsazobankersassociation.co.za/pd「www.tsazobankersassociation.co.za/pdでEメール通知を申し込むことで、今後の全てのイベントの最新情報を随時入手してください」と書かれている。ウェブサイトにアクセスし、今後のイベントの知らせを受け取る登録をするよう勧めているので、(A)が正解。upcoming「近く起こる」。
> (B) search「～を検索する」、directory「名簿」。
> (C) schedule「～の予定を立てる」、career「職業」、consultation「相談」。
> (D) update「～を更新する」、contact information「連絡先情報」。

Expressions

make a point of *doing* 「必ず～するようにする、決まって～する」（❷2～3行目）
I make a point of replying to e-mails from my clients as soon as possible.
私はお客さまからのEメールにできるだけ早く返信するようにしています。

Questions 176-180 refer to the following article and notice.

Bulk Items for Less

By Matilda Long

① DILLSBORO (August 1)—Members of the public can now take advantage of a new way to get the products they want at a lower cost. There is no need to pay full retail price for products such as paper towels, as long as customers do not mind packaging that is slightly damaged. Greeberg Wholesalers, a company known for being the area's largest distributor to restaurants and catering companies, occasionally receives products in damaged packages. These products are difficult to resell even though the products themselves are in perfect condition. Therefore, Greeberg Wholesalers is now making these products available to the public at deep discounts.

② For example, a case of paper towels may cost as little as $8.59. Greeberg Wholesalers offers these discounted prices for quality name-brand products in slightly damaged packages while supplies last. The warehouse is open to the public every Tuesday from 9:00 A.M. to 1:00 P.M.

Name-Brand Dry Goods at Incredibly Low Prices!

Greeberg Wholesalers

Now open to the public for special savings. Tuesdays 9:00 A.M. – 1:00 P.M.

① You can get the quality products you need while saving money on packages that may have been slightly damaged. Products are based on availability.

Item	Item Number	Description	Cost
Paper Towels-Super	PT7	24 rolls	$11.99
Paper Towels-Regular	PT9	20 rolls	$ 8.59
Disposable Napkins	N11	1,000 count	$ 3.49
Plastic Utensils	BT8	30 pieces	$ 7.99
Paper Plates-Deluxe*	PP4	225 count	$ 8.27
Paper Plates	PP9	250 count	$ 8.19

*Sold out

82

問題176-180は次の記事とお知らせに関するものです。

大容量の品をより安い価格で

Matilda Long記

ディルズボロ（8月1日）—— 一般の人々はいまや、欲しい製品をより低価格で入手するための新たな方法を利用できるようになった。顧客がわずかに破損した包装を気にしない限り、ペーパータオルなどの製品に定価を満額支払う必要はない。レストランやケータリング会社向けの地域最大の卸売業者として知られる会社、Greeberg卸売販売社は、時に破損した包装の製品を受け取る。これらの製品は、製品自体が完全な状態であっても卸すのが難しい。それゆえ、Greeberg卸売販売社は今、これらの製品を一般の人々が大幅割引で入手できるようにしている。

例えば、ペーパータオル1箱はたった8.59ドルしかかからない場合がある。在庫品がある限り、Greeberg卸売販売社は包装がわずかに破損した上質な有名ブランドの製品にこれらの割引価格をつけている。同卸売店は毎週火曜日午前9時から午後1時まで一般向けにオープンしている。

有名ブランドの日用雑貨を驚きの低価格で！
Greeberg卸売販売社
現在、特別割引価格で一般向けにオープン。毎週火曜日午前9時〜午後1時

わずかに破損した可能性のある包装でお金を節約しながら、あなたが必要とする上質な製品を手に入れることができます。製品は在庫の有無によります。

品物	商品番号	明細	価格
ペーパータオル・スーパー	PT7	24ロール	11.99ドル
ペーパータオル・レギュラー	PT9	20ロール	8.59ドル
使い捨てナプキン	N11	1,000枚入り	3.49ドル
プラスチック製什器	BT8	30個	7.99ドル
紙皿・デラックス*	PP4	225枚入り	8.27ドル
紙皿	PP9	250枚入り	8.19ドル

*売り切れ

176 What is the purpose of the article?

    (A) To promote restaurants in the Dillsboro area

    (B) To announce a new service from a local company

    (C) To complain about a company's business practices

    (D) To compare wholesale and retail prices

記事の目的は何ですか。

    (A) ディルズボロ地域のレストランを宣伝すること

    (B) 地元の会社の新しいサービスを知らせること

    (C) 会社の商慣行について不満を述べること

    (D) 卸売価格と小売価格を比較すること

> **正解 B** 記事❶の❶1～3行目に、「一般の人々はいまや、欲しい製品をより低価格で入手するための新たな方法を利用できるようになった」とある。同8～9行目でthe area's largest distributor「地域最大の卸売業者」と紹介されているGreeberg卸売販売社のサービスとして、同11～16行目で包装が破損した製品を一般消費者向けに大幅割引で提供するようになったことが述べられている。また、同❷には、Greeberg卸売販売社の割引商品の一例と販売日時が書かれている。以上より、記事は、地元の会社であるGreeberg卸売販売社による、包装が破損した製品を安く売るという新しいサービスを知らせる内容と分かるので、(B)が正解。announce「～を知らせる」。
> (A) promote「～を宣伝する」。
> (C) complain about ～「～について不満を述べる」、business practice「商慣行」。
> (D) compare A and B「AとBを比較する」、wholesale「卸売りの」。

177 Why is Greeberg Wholesalers selling discounted products?

    (A) Because it always has a sale in August

    (B) Because it has extra products it wants to sell quickly

    (C) Because it is closing a store and needs to sell everything

    (D) Because its regular customers do not want damaged packaging

Greeberg卸売販売社はなぜ割引商品を販売していますか。

    (A) いつも8月にセールをするから

    (B) すぐに販売したい余った製品があるから

    (C) 店じまいをするので全てのものを販売する必要があるから

    (D) 同社の通常の顧客が破損した包装を望まないから

> **正解 D** Greeberg卸売販売社について、記事❶の❶7～13行目に、「レストランやケータリング会社向けの地域最大の卸売業者として知られる会社、Greeberg卸売販売社は、時に破損した包装の製品を受け取る。これらの製品は、製品自体が完全な状態であっても卸すのが難しい」とあり、続けて、そのため同社はそういった製品を一般向けに大幅な割引価格で販売していると述べられている。つまり、同社の通常の顧客はレストランやケータリング会社であるが、それらの顧客は破損した包装を望まないと分かるので、(D)が正解。
> (B) extra「余分の」。

178 With whom does Greeberg Wholesalers mainly do business?

    (A) Food service businesses

    (B) Concert venues

    (C) Kitchen appliance manufacturers

    (D) Bulk-food clubs

Greeberg卸売販売社は主にどこと取引していますか。

    (A) 食品サービス会社

    (B) コンサート会場

    (C) 台所家電メーカー

    (D) バルク食品購入会

> **正解 A** 記事❶の❶7～10行目に、「レストランやケータリング会社向けの地域最大の卸売業者として知られる会社、Greeberg卸売販売社」とある。主な取引先であるrestaurants and catering companiesをfood service businessesと言い換えた(A)が正解。mainly「主に」、do business with ～「～と取引する」。
> (B) venue「開催地」。
> (C) appliance「電化製品」、manufacturer「メーカー、製造会社」。
> (D) bulk foodとは、大量ロットで販売・購入される食品のこと。

179 What item is described in the article?

(A) PT9
(B) N11
(C) PP4
(D) PP9

どの品物が記事で述べられていますか。

(A) PT9
(B) N11
(C) PP4
(D) PP9

> **正解 A** 記事 **1** の **❷** 1〜2行目に、一般消費者向けに販売する製品の例として、For example, a case of paper towels may cost as little as $8.59.「例えば、ペーパータオル1箱はたった 8.59ドルしかかからない場合がある」と述べられている。8.59ドルのペーパータオルとは、お知らせ **2** の **❷** の表の中で、上から2つ目にあるPT9のこと。よって、(A)が正解。

---

180 In what way is item BT8 different from the other items in the notice?

(A) Its packages are undamaged.
(B) It is made out of plastic.
(C) It is currently sold out.
(D) It is available in different sizes.

BT8という品物は、お知らせにおける他の品物とどのように異なりますか。

(A) 包装が破損していない。
(B) プラスチック製である。
(C) 現在売り切れている。
(D) さまざまなサイズで売られている。

> **正解 B** BT8とは、お知らせ **2** の **❷** の表の中で、上から4つ目にあるPlastic Utensils「プラスチック製什器」のこと。他の品物は、使い捨てナプキンであるN11を含め全て紙製品だと考えられるが、商品BT8だけがプラスチック製である。よって、(B)が正解。be made out of 〜「〜から作られている」。
> (A) **2** の **❶** より、お知らせにある全ての品物は包装が破損している可能性があると考えられる。undamaged「破損していない」。
> (C) **2** の **❷** の表の注釈より、売り切れているのは「紙皿・デラックス」のPP4。
> (D) BT8という品物のサイズの種類は述べられていない。

Words & Phrases

1 記事
bulk 大量(の)　item 品物　❶ the public 一般の人々　take advantage of 〜 〜を利用する
full 満額の、完全な　retail price 小売価格　such as 〜 例えば〜などの　paper towel ペーパータオル
mind 〜を気にする　packaging 包装(材料)、梱包(材料)　slightly わずかに　damaged 破損した
wholesaler 卸売業者　(be) known for 〜 〜で知られて(いる)　distributor 卸売業者
catering ケータリング、仕出し業　occasionally 時に　package 包装、(商品の)パッケージ
resell 〜を再販売する　even though 〜 〜であっても、〜にもかかわらず　in perfect condition 完全な状態で
therefore それゆえ　available 入手できる　at deep discounts 大幅な値引きで　❷ cost 〜(費用)がかかる
as little as 〜 たった〜、わずか〜　offer 〜を提示する　discounted 割引された　quality 上質な
name-brand 有名ブランドの　while 〜する限り、〜する間に　supplies 在庫品、供給品
last 足りる、存続する　warehouse 卸売店、倉庫

2 お知らせ
dry goods （食料品・金物類などと区別して)日用雑貨、繊維製品　incredibly 信じられないほど、非常に
saving 割引、節約　❶ save 〜を節約する　may have done 〜したかもしれない
be based on 〜 〜に基づいている　availability 入手・利用できるもの、入手・利用の可能性
❷ description 明細、説明　disposable napkin 使い捨てナプキン　count 総数　utensil 用具、用品
piece 個　paper plate 紙皿　deluxe 豪華な、デラックスな　sold out 売り切れで

Expressions

as long as 〜 「〜である限りは、〜でありさえすれば」（**1** の **❶** 4〜7行目）

Sophia says that she can work anywhere as long as she has access to the Internet.
Sophiaはインターネットにアクセスできさえすればどこでも仕事ができると言います。

Questions 181-185 refer to the following e-mails.

E-mail 1 1通目のEメール

To:	Mie Koruda <mkoruda@zeacoelectric.co.nz>
From:	Rawiri Wati <rwati@zeacoelectric.co.nz>
Subject:	Survey
Date:	2 April

Hello, Mie,

Feedback on our brochure about alternative power sources, which was sent to our small-business customers in March, has been positive. Unfortunately, we had to delay sending the power usage survey to our residential customers due to functionality issues. Our programmers fixed the broken links and are working on final verification that respondents will be able to access all the questions. Once we get their go-ahead, we can send the survey link to our residential customers with their regular electronic billing statements. We should be ready by Friday, 9 April, which keeps us on schedule to have the results in and analysed by 1 June.

Regards,

Rawiri

E-mail 2 2通目のEメール

To:	Rachana Varghese <rvarghese@myemail.nz>
From:	Zeaco Electric Customer Service <customerservice@zeacoelectric.co.nz>
Subject:	Zeaco Electric survey
Date:	12 April
Attachment:	🔗 RVarghese billing statement

Dear Ms. Varghese,

At Zeaco Electric, we strive to supply you with quality service. We ask that you complete a five-minute survey on our Web site, www.zeacoelectric.co.nz/survey, before 1 May. Your feedback will help us to identify ways to provide you with energy-saving solutions.

As a sign of our appreciation, we would like to treat you to coffee. Just submit your e-mail address at the end of the survey, and we will send you a $20 Sumner Coffee electronic gift card, valid at any Sumner Coffee shop location or the online store.

Sincerely,

Zeaco Electric Customer Service

問題181-185は次の2通のEメールに関するものです。

受信者：Mie Koruda <mkoruda@zeacoelectric.co.nz>
送信者：Rawiri Wati <rwati@zeacoelectric.co.nz>
件名：アンケート
日付：4月2日

Mieさん

3月に中小企業顧客に送った代替エネルギー源に関する当社のパンフレットへの意見は、好意的なものでした。あいにく、機能性の問題のため、住宅顧客への電力使用アンケートの送付を延期しなければなりませんでした。当社のプログラマーは壊れたリンクを修正し終え、回答者が全ての質問にアクセスできるということの最終確認に取り組んでいます。彼らの進行許可を得たらすぐに、アンケートのリンクを通常の電子請求明細書と共に住宅顧客に送付することができます。4月9日金曜日までに準備が整うはずで、そうすれば6月1日までに結果を回収して分析するという予定通りに進められます。

よろしくお願いします。

Rawiri

受信者：Rachana Varghese <rvarghese@myemail.nz>
送信者：Zeaco電力会社 顧客サービス <customerservice@zeacoelectric.co.nz>
件名：Zeaco電力会社アンケート
日付：4月12日
添付ファイル：RVarghese請求明細書

Varghese様

Zeaco電力会社では、皆さまに良質なサービスを提供するよう努めております。お客さまには5月1日までに、当社ウェブサイトwww.zeacoelectric.co.nz/survey上での5分間のアンケートにご回答くださるようお願いいたします。お客さまのご意見は、当社が省エネの対応策をお客さまにご提供する方法を特定する助けになります。

当社の感謝の印として、お客さまにコーヒーをごちそういたします。アンケートの最後でEメールアドレスをご提出くださるだけで、Sumnerコーヒー全店舗またはオンラインストアで有効な、20ドルのSumnerコーヒー電子ギフトカードをお送りいたします。

敬具

Zeaco電力会社 顧客サービス

181 Why most likely did Mr. Wati send the first e-mail?

(A) To report results from a survey
(B) To request technical assistance
(C) To ask for an extension on a task
(D) To provide an update on a project

Watiさんはなぜ1通目のEメールを送ったと考えられますか。

(A) アンケートの結果を報告するため
(B) 技術的な支援を要請するため
(C) 仕事について延長を求めるため
(D) 計画に関する最新情報を提供するため

> **正解 D** Watiさんは1通目のEメール**1**の❶1～2行目で、パンフレットに対する中小企業顧客の意見が好意的なものだったと書いている。続く同2～7行目で、住宅顧客に送付するアンケートに関する作業の進行状況を説明している。さらに、同7～8行目では、アンケートの送付から結果分析までの今後の見通しを述べている。つまり、Watiさんは顧客へのアンケートの実施計画に関する最新情報を提供するためにEメールを書いたと判断できるので、(D)が正解。update「最新情報」。
> (A) **1**の❶7～8行目にアンケート結果の分析への言及があるのは今後のスケジュールの見通しを伝えるためであり、結果を報告するためではない。report「～を報告する」。
> (B) **1**の❷2～3行目に機能性の問題への言及はあるが、プログラマーがすでに対応していることが述べられており、支援の要請はしていない。technical「技術的な」、assistance「支援」。
> (C) extension「延長」、task「(課された)仕事」。

182 What most likely is the survey about?

(A) Technical support
(B) Electricity usage
(C) Billing preferences
(D) Power outages

アンケートは何についてだと考えられますか。

(A) 技術的な支援
(B) 電力使用
(C) 請求方法の希望
(D) 停電

> **正解 B** 1通目のEメールである**1**の❷2～3行目に、Unfortunately, we had to delay sending the power usage survey to our residential customers due to functionality issues.「あいにく、機能性の問題のため、住宅顧客への電力使用アンケートの送付を延期しなければならなかった」と書かれているので、アンケートは電力使用についてと分かる。よって、(B)が正解。electricity「電力、電気」。
> (A) support「支援」。
> (C) preference「好み、選択」。
> (D) 電力に関して述べられているが、停電への言及はない。power outage「停電」。

183 What is suggested about Ms. Varghese?

(A) She never responded to the survey.
(B) She requested a paper copy of her bill.
(C) She is a residential customer.
(D) She is a computer programmer.

Vargheseさんについて何が分かりますか。

(A) 彼女はアンケートに答えなかった。
(B) 彼女は紙面の請求書を依頼した。
(C) 彼女は住宅顧客である。
(D) 彼女はコンピュータープログラマーである。

> **正解 C** Vargheseさんとは、2通目のEメールの受信者。2通目のEメール**2**には、請求明細書が添付されており、同❶1～3行目でリンクを介したアンケートへの回答が依頼されている。1通目のEメール**1**の❶5～7行目で、「アンケートのリンクを通常の電子請求明細書と共に住宅顧客に送付できる」と述べられているので、Vargheseさんが受け取ったEメールにあるアンケートとは、1通目のEメール**1**で書かれている住宅顧客に対するものだと考えられる。よって、Vargheseさんは住宅顧客の一人であると判断できるので、(C)が正解。
> (A) respond to ～「～に答える」。
> (B) bill「請求書」。

184 What must Ms. Varghese do to receive a gift card?

 (A) Submit her e-mail address
 (B) Write a product description
 (C) Visit a participating store
 (D) Contact customer service

Vargheseさんはギフトカードを受け取るには何をしなければなりませんか。

 (A) Eメールアドレスを提出する
 (B) 製品の説明を書く
 (C) 加盟店を訪れる
 (D) 顧客サービスに連絡する

> **正解 A** Vargheseさんが受信したEメールである**2**の**❷**1行目で、アンケート協力の謝礼としてコーヒーをごちそうすると述べられており、同1〜3行目にJust submit your e-mail address at the end of the survey, and we will send you a $20 Sumner Coffee electronic gift card「アンケートの最後でEメールアドレスを提出するだけで、20ドルのSumnerコーヒー電子ギフトカードを送る」とある。よって、Vargheseさんがギフトカードを受け取るにはEメールアドレスを提出すればよいと分かるので、(A)が正解。
> (B) description「説明」。
> (C) participating store「加盟店、協賛店」。

185 In the second e-mail, the word "sign" in paragraph 2, line 1, is closest in meaning to

 (A) character
 (B) gesture
 (C) board
 (D) name

2通目のEメールの第2段落・1行目にある "sign" に最も意味が近いのは

 (A) 特徴
 (B) 意思表示
 (C) 掲示板
 (D) 名前

> **正解 B** 2通目のEメール**2**の**❶**で、Zeaco電力会社顧客サービスはVargheseさんにアンケートへの回答を依頼している。続く**❷**の1行目の該当の語を含む文は、「当社の感謝の------として、あなたにコーヒーをごちそうする」という意味。続く同1〜3行目の文では、アンケートの最後でEメールアドレスを提出すればコーヒーのギフトカードを送ると述べられている。Zeaco電力会社はアンケート協力に対する感謝の意を示すためにギフトカードを送ると考えられるので、(B) gesture「意思表示」が正解。

Words & Phrases

1 Eメール ❶ brochure パンフレット alternative 代替の power source エネルギー源
small-business 中小企業の positive 好意的な unfortunately あいにく、残念ながら
delay *doing* 〜することを遅らせる power usage 電力使用(量)
residential customer 住宅顧客 ★電気などを住宅で使う個人顧客。法人顧客に対して用いられる
functionality (コンピューターなどの)機能性 issue 問題 programmer プログラマー fix 〜を修理する
work on 〜 〜に取り組む verification (正しいことの)確認 respondent 回答者
access 〜にアクセスする once 〜するとすぐに go-ahead 開始の許可 electronic 電子の
billing statement 請求明細書 on schedule 予定通りに in 提出されて、到着して
analyse 〜を分析する ★米国表記はanalyze

2 Eメール electric 電気、電力 customer service 顧客サービス ❶ strive to *do* 〜しようと努力する
supply 〜 with … 〜に…を提供する quality 上質な service サービス、(電力などの)供給
ask that 〜 〜ということを依頼する help 〜 to *do* 〜が…するのに役立つ identify 〜を特定する
provide 〜 with … 〜に…を提供する energy-saving 省エネの solution 対応策、解決策
❷ appreciation 感謝 treat 〜 to … 〜に…をおごる valid 有効な

Expressions

due to 〜 「〜のため、〜のせいで」(**1**の**❶**3行目)
Due to the large demand for fabrics used in face masks, we have increased our production.
マスク用の布地への高い需要のため、当社は生産を増加しました。

Questions 186-190 refer to the following advertisement and e-mails.

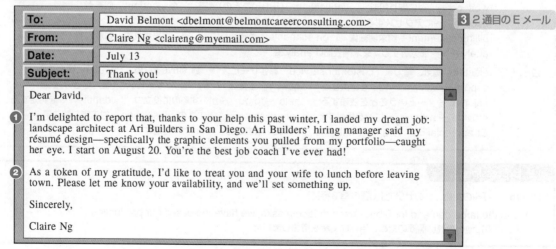

Job Change, Inc.
Part-Time Résumé Editors Needed

❶ For three decades, Seattle-based Job Change, Inc., has coached thousands of people through the difficult process of applying for jobs—and we have an excellent track record. We are looking to hire several more part-time coaches/résumé editors who can work 20 hours per week providing clients with timely feedback and support.

❷ The ideal candidate holds a bachelor's degree or higher in communications, human resources, or journalism and will have experience in career coaching, recruiting, or writing. Experience in tutoring, teaching, or editing is a plus. Must be able to start on August 1.

❸ To be considered, send an e-mail and résumé to Aya Shimizu, a.shimizu@jci.com, briefly describing your professional history and why you are a good fit for the job.

E-mail

To: Aya Shimizu <a.shimizu@jci.com>
From: David Belmont <dbelmont@belmontcareerconsulting.com>
Subject: Application
Date: June 5
Attachment: 📎 Belmont résumé

Dear Ms. Shimizu,

❶ Thank you for considering my application for the position of résumé editor with Job Change, Inc. I live just a few blocks from your office and could start immediately.

❷ I graduated from State University with a master's degree in communications. I worked for twelve years at Western Placement Services. There, I gained extensive experience editing résumés and cover letters for clients seeking employment in a wide variety of industries. I also mentored and guided the applicants in their job searches. For the past year, I have been doing career coaching on a freelance basis, working out of my home. I am confident that I can provide your clients with prompt, effective guidance. If I am hired, my goal would be to prove to you that I am deserving of full-time work.

❸ I look forward to hearing from you.

Sincerely,

David Belmont

To: David Belmont <dbelmont@belmontcareerconsulting.com>
From: Claire Ng <claireng@myemail.com>
Date: July 13
Subject: Thank you!

Dear David,

❶ I'm delighted to report that, thanks to your help this past winter, I landed my dream job: landscape architect at Ari Builders in San Diego. Ari Builders' hiring manager said my résumé design—specifically the graphic elements you pulled from my portfolio—caught her eye. I start on August 20. You're the best job coach I've ever had!

❷ As a token of my gratitude, I'd like to treat you and your wife to lunch before leaving town. Please let me know your availability, and we'll set something up.

Sincerely,

Claire Ng

問題186-190は次の広告と2通のEメールに関するものです。

Job Change社
パートタイムの履歴書編集者募集

30年にわたり、シアトルを本拠とするJob Change社は、職への応募という困難な過程を通じて何千人もの人々を指導してきました——そして当社には素晴らしい実績があります。当社は、依頼主に適時に意見や支援を提供しつつ週20時間勤務できるパートタイムの指導員／履歴書編集者を、追加で数名採用する予定です。

理想的な候補者は、コミュニケーション学、人的資源管理学、またはジャーナリズム学で学士号以上を保持していて、職業指導、採用活動、またはライティングの経験をお持ちの方です。個人指導、教職、または編集の経験があればなお可。8月1日に働き始めることが可能でなければなりません。

選考を受けるには、職歴と、なぜご自分がこの仕事に適任であるのかを簡潔にご記載の上、Aya Shimizu宛てにa.shimizu@jci.comまでEメールと履歴書をお送りください。

受信者：Aya Shimizu <a.shimizu@jci.com>
送信者：David Belmont <dbelmont@belmontcareerconsulting.com>
件名：応募
日付：6月5日
添付ファイル：Belmont履歴書

Shimizu様

Job Change社の履歴書編集者の職に応募いたしますので、ご検討をよろしくお願いいたします。私は貴社からほんの数ブロックの所に住んでおり、今すぐにでも働き始めることができます。

私はコミュニケーション学の修士号を取得して州立大学を卒業しました。12年間、Western Placement Services社に勤めました。そこでは、多種多様な業界で職を求める依頼者のために、履歴書やカバーレターを編集する幅広い経験を積みました。また、求職者の就職活動の際には、彼らに助言を与えて指導しました。この1年は、フリーランスとして自宅から職業指導を行ってきました。私は、貴社のご依頼人に迅速で効果的な指導をすることができると確信しています。もし私が採用されましたら、私の目標は、自分がフルタイムの仕事にふさわしい人材であると貴社に証明するというものになるでしょう。

ご連絡を心待ちにしております。

敬具

David Belmont

受信者：David Belmont <dbelmont@belmontcareerconsulting.com>
送信者：Claire Ng <claireng@myemail.com>
日付：7月13日
件名：ありがとうございました！

David様

この冬のあなたのご助力のおかげで私が夢の仕事に就いたということを、大喜びでご報告します。サンディエゴのAri Builders社の景観設計士です。Ari Builders社の雇用責任者は、私の履歴書のデザイン——特にあなたが私の作品集から引き出してくれたグラフィック要素——が目を引いたと言っていました。私は8月20日に働き始めます。あなたは今まで私がお世話になった中で一番素晴らしい職業指導者です！

感謝の印として、町を出る前にあなたと奥さまに昼食をごちそうしたいと思っています。ご都合をお知らせください。そして何か機会を持ちましょう。

敬具

Claire Ng

186 What does the advertisement indicate about Job Change, Inc.?

(A) It has been in business for a long time.
(B) It reimburses tuition to staff who want to further their education.
(C) It is opening a branch office on August 1.
(D) It specializes in placing journalists in jobs.

広告は Job Change 社について何を示していますか。

(A) 長期間営業している。
(B) 教育の継続を希望する従業員に授業料を払い戻す。
(C) 8月1日に支社を開く予定である。
(D) ジャーナリストに職を斡旋することを専門にしている。

> **正解 A** Job Change 社の広告である **1** の **1** 1～2 行目に、「30 年にわたり、シアトルを本拠とする Job Change 社は、職への応募という困難な過程を通じて何千人もの人々を指導してきた」とある。よって、Job Change 社は長年営業を続けていることが分かるので、(A)が正解。in business「営業して」。
> (B) reimburse「～(経費など)を払い戻す」、tuition「授業料」、further「～を進める」、education「教育」。
> (C) **1** の **2** 4 行目より 8 月 1 日に働き始められる人材を募集していると分かるが、branch office「支社」を開くとは述べられていない。
> (D) specialize in ～「～を専門にする」、place ～ in …「～を…(仕事など)に就かせる」。

187 According to the first e-mail, what is true about Mr. Belmont?

(A) He was a teacher at a local school.
(B) He has worked in a variety of industries.
(C) He worked from home for twelve years.
(D) He hopes to become a full-time employee.

1 通目の E メールによると、Belmont さんについて正しいことは何ですか。

(A) 彼は地元の学校の教師だった。
(B) 彼はさまざまな業界で働いてきた。
(C) 彼は 12 年間在宅で仕事をしていた。
(D) 彼はフルタイムの社員になることを希望している。

> **正解 D** 1 通目の E メール **2** は受信者と件名より、広告 **1** の **3** の採用連絡先に Belmont さんが応募して送ったものと考えられる。Belmont さんは、**2** の **1** と **2** 1～6 行目で自身について述べた後、同 **2** 6～7 行目で、「もし私が採用されれば、私の目標は、自分がフルタイムの仕事にふさわしい人材であると貴社に証明するというものになるだろう」と書いている。つまり、Belmont さんはフルタイムの社員になることを希望していると判断できるので、(D)が正解。
> (B) **2** の **2** 2～4 行目に、多種多様な業界で職を求める依頼者に対応したとあるが、Belmont さんが多種多様な業界で働いてきたとは述べられていない。
> (C) **2** の **2** 4～5 行目より、在宅で仕事をしているのはこの 1 年間。work from home「在宅勤務をする」。

188 What is suggested about Mr. Belmont?

(A) He needs to update his résumé.
(B) He is landscaping his home.
(C) He lives in Seattle.
(D) He has worked for Ms. Shimizu in the past.

Belmont さんについて何が分かりますか。

(A) 彼は自分の履歴書を更新する必要がある。
(B) 彼は自分の家の景観整備をしている。
(C) 彼はシアトルに住んでいる。
(D) 彼はこれまで Shimizu さんの下で働いてきた。

> **正解 C** Belmont さんは 1 通目の E メール **2** の **1** 2 行目で、I live just a few blocks from your office「私は貴社からほんの数ブロックの所に住んでいる」と書いている。your office とは、Shimizu さんの働く Job Change 社のこと。広告 **1** の **1** 1 行目に、Seattle-based Job Change, Inc.「シアトルを本拠とする Job Change 社」とあるので、Belmont さんはシアトルに住んでいることが分かる。よって、(C)が正解。
> (B) landscape「(造園により)～の景観整備をする」。
> (D) in the past「これまで」。

Expressions

apply for ～ 「～に応募する、～に申し込む」(**1** の **1** 2 行目)

It is up to you to apply for the job with the publishing company.
その出版社の仕事に応募するかどうかはあなた次第です。

189 What is most likely true about Ms. Ng?

(A) She did not accept a job offer.
(B) She prefers working at home.
(C) She received career advice from Mr. Belmont.
(D) She took a course in graphic design from Mr. Belmont.

Ngさんについて正しいと考えられることは何ですか。

(A) 彼女は仕事の申し出を受けなかった。
(B) 彼女は在宅勤務する方を好む。
(C) 彼女はBelmontさんから職業に関するアドバイスを受けた。
(D) 彼女はBelmontさんによるグラフィックデザインの講座を受講した。

> **正解 C** Ngさんとは、2通目のEメール**3**の送信者。NgさんはBelmontさん宛てのEメールである**3**の**1** 1～2行目で、あなたのおかげで希望する職に就くことができたと報告している。続く同2～4行目で、BelmontさんがNgさんの履歴書作成に関わったことが書かれており、同4行目に、「あなたは今まで私がお世話になった中で一番素晴らしい職業指導者だ」とあることから、NgさんはBelmontさんから職業に関するアドバイスを受けたことが分かる。よって、(C)が正解。
> (A) accept「～を引き受ける」、offer「申し出、提供」。
> (D) course「講座」。

190 According to the second e-mail, what does Ms. Ng want Mr. Belmont to do?

(A) E-mail her hiring manager
(B) Join her for a meal
(C) Review her updated portfolio
(D) Show her around his new office

2通目のEメールによると、NgさんはBelmontさんに何をしてほしいと思っていますか。

(A) 彼女の雇用責任者にEメールを送る
(B) 彼女と一緒に食事をする
(C) 彼女の更新した作品集を見直す
(D) 彼女に彼の新しいオフィスを案内する

> **正解 B** NgさんはBelmontさん宛てのEメール**3**の**2** 1～2行目で、As a token of my gratitude, I'd like to treat you and your wife to lunch before leaving town.「感謝の印として、町を出る前にあなたと奥さんに昼食をごちそうしたいと思っている」と書いており、NgさんはBelmontさんに一緒に食事をしてほしいと思っていると分かるので、(B)が正解。
> (C) review「～を見直す」。
> (D) show ～ around …「～に…を案内する」。

Words & Phrases

1 広告
～, Inc. ～社 ★incorporatedの略　résumé 履歴書　editor 編集者　**1** decade 10年間　-based ～を本拠にした　coach ～を指導する　thousands of ～ 何千もの～　process 過程　excellent 素晴らしい　track record 実績　be looking to do ～するつもりである　hire ～を雇用する　per ～につき　provide ～ with … ～に…を提供する　client 依頼人、顧客　timely 適時の、折りよい　support 支援　**2** ideal 理想的な　hold ～（学位など）を保有する　bachelor's degree 学士号　human resources 人的資源　career coaching 職業指導　recruiting 採用活動　tutoring 個人指導　editing 編集　plus 利点、好条件　**3** consider ～を検討する　briefly 簡潔に　describe ～を述べる　professional 職業上の　history 経歴　good fit for ～ ～にぴったり合う人・状態

2 Eメール
application 応募　**1** immediately 今すぐ、即座に　**2** graduate from ～ ～を卒業する　master's degree 修士号　placement 職業紹介　gain ～を獲得する、～を得る　extensive 広範囲にわたる　edit ～を編集する　cover letter カバーレター、添え状　seek ～を求める　employment 職、雇用　a wide variety of ～ 多種多様な～　industry 業界　mentor ～に助言する、～の助言者となる　guide ～を指導する　applicant 志願者　job search 就職活動　past これまでの、過去の　on a ～ basis ～制で、～の基準で　freelance フリーランスの、自由契約の　work out of one's home 自宅で仕事をする　be confident that ～ ～ということを確信している　prompt 迅速な　effective 効果的な　guidance 指導　prove that ～ ～ということを証明する　deserving of ～ ～に値する

3 Eメール　**1** be delighted to do ～して非常にうれしい　report that ～ ～ということを報告する　land ～（仕事など）を獲得する　dream job 理想の仕事　landscape 景観　architect 設計士、建築家　hiring manager 雇用責任者　specifically 特に　element 要素　portfolio 作品のサンプル集、ポートフォリオ　★自分の実績を示すためのもの　catch one's eye ～の目を引く　**2** token 印　gratitude 感謝　treat ～ to … ～に…をごちそうする　availability 都合のよい日時、都合がつくこと

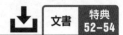

Questions 191-195 refer to the following article, order sheet, and report.

The Secret Behind Ravianos
By Nancy Horner

❶ Fashion retailer Ravianos has stores in twelve cities across the country. While relatively new, Ravianos has become very popular with fashion-minded customers and is competing well against more established brands.

❷ Instead of relying on traditional advertising methods, Ravianos pays close attention to market trends. Each month, Ravianos fills its stores' shelves with new clothing styles produced in small quantities and shipped in tiny sample batches of five pieces per size. As soon as sales data from the sample batches are in, decisions are made about which designs to move to full-scale production, which ones to redesign, and what new styles to implement in Ravianos' future offerings. This information is shared with in-house designers who meet by video to plan their next designs based on what sells best. The retailer then halts production of items with declining sales, and leftovers are sent back to the distribution center to be sold to online customers only.

❸ Ravianos' designers are also interested in what customers have to say. Store personnel give customers special opinion forms in which they are asked to suggest what they would like to see in future Ravianos designs. Opinions gathered this way carry significant weight in the in-house design process.

1 記事

2 注文書

Order #23623
Date: July 25
Ravianos Store, 290 Orchard Street,
Louisville, KY 40041

	Quantity		
	Small	Medium	Large
❶ Tiaran dress	20	30	20
Vanonse blouse	15	30	20
Remessi shirt	20	30	20
Cromius T-shirt	5	5	5

3 報告書

Sales Figures for Jan Stawinski

❶ This report shows the sales figures for items designed by you that moved beyond the sample stage. The numbers represent total purchases per product in all twelve Ravianos stores and online.

❷
Name	Purchases	Change Relative to Previous Week
Oloaha skirt	367	+21%
Tiaran dress	511	+15%
Vanonse blouse	487	+12%
Yvonna blouse	342	+11%
Hygesse shirt	78	−20% (Production discontinued)

❸ Note that these figures represent sales for the week of August 10–16. To view your figures for previous weeks, log in to your online account at ravianos.com/employee.

問題191-195は次の記事、注文書、報告書に関するものです。

Ravianos社の隠れた秘密
Nancy Horner記

ファッション小売業者のRavianos社は国内12の都市に店舗を持つ。比較的新顔であるが、Ravianos社はファッション志向の顧客に大いに人気を博しており、より老舗の有名ブランドと十分に競合している。

　従来の広告手法に依存するのではなく、Ravianos社は市場動向を注視している。毎月、Ravianos社は、少量生産されて1サイズにつきわずか5点のサンプル群として出荷される新しいスタイルの衣服で店舗の棚を埋める。そのサンプル群からの販売データが届くとすぐに、どのデザインを本格的な規模の生産に移すべきか、どれをデザインし直すべきか、そしてRavianos社の今後の製品にどんな新しいスタイルを取り入れるべきかについて決定がなされる。この情報は、売れ行きが一番良いものに基づいて次のデザインを計画するために、ビデオ会議で社内デザイナーと共有される。そして同社は売り上げの減少している商品の生産を停止し、売れ残りの商品は流通センターに返送されてオンライン顧客のみに販売される。

　Ravianos社のデザイナーは顧客の意見にも耳を傾ける。店員は顧客に、今後のRavianos社のデザインでどんなものが欲しいかの提案を求める特別な意見フォームを渡す。このようにして集められた意見は社内のデザイン過程で大きな重要性を持つ。

注文番号 23623
日付：7月25日
Ravianos店舗、オーチャード通り290番地、
ルイビル、KY 40041

	数量		
	Sサイズ	Mサイズ	Lサイズ
Tiaran ドレス	20	30	20
Vanonse ブラウス	15	30	20
Remessi シャツ	20	30	20
Cromius Tシャツ	5	5	5

Jan Stawinskiさんの販売数値

この報告書は、あなたによってデザインされた、サンプル過程を通過した品物の販売数値を示しています。数字は、Ravianos社の全12店舗およびオンライン上での製品別の購入総数を表しています。

商品名	購入数	対前週比での変化
Oloaha スカート	367	+21%
Tiaran ドレス	511	+15%
Vanonse ブラウス	487	+12%
Yvonna ブラウス	342	+11%
Hygesse シャツ	78	−20%（生産中止）

これらの数字は8月10日〜16日の週の売り上げを示していることにご留意ください。それ以前の週の数字を見るには、ravianos.com/employeeでご自身のオンラインアカウントにログインしてください。

191 According to the article, what is discussed during video meetings?

(A) Customer preferences
(B) Pricing strategies
(C) Advertising methods
(D) Hiring needs

記事によると、ビデオ会議中に何が話し合われますか。

(A) 顧客の好み
(B) 値付け戦略
(C) 広告手法
(D) 雇用の必要性

> **正解 A** 記事❶の❷ 12〜15 行目に、This information is shared with in-house designers who meet by video to plan their next designs based on what sells best. 「この情報は、売れ行きが一番良いものに基づいて次のデザインを計画するために、ビデオ会議で社内デザイナーと共有される」とある。「この情報」とは、前文で述べられている、販売データを含む今後の方向性に関する情報であり、その中で「売れ行きが一番良いもの」に基づいて、ビデオ会議で次のデザイン計画が話し合われると分かる。売れ行きが一番良いものとは「顧客の好み」を反映していることになるので、(A)が正解。
> (B) pricing「価格設定」、strategy「戦略」。
> (C) ❶の❷ 1〜3 行目で、従来の広告手法には依存しないと述べられているだけ。

192 What does the article indicate about Ravianos?

(A) It has retail stores in multiple countries.
(B) It will soon merge with a competing fashion company.
(C) It is performing well within its market.
(D) It has purchased new shelves for its stores.

記事は Ravianos 社について何を示していますか。

(A) 複数の国に小売店を持つ。
(B) 競合するファッション会社と間もなく合併する。
(C) 業界の市場において、良い業績を上げている。
(D) 店舗向けに新しい棚を購入した。

> **正解 C** 記事❶の❶ 2〜6 行目に、While relatively new, Ravianos has become very popular with fashion-minded customers and is competing well against more established brands.「比較的新顔であるが、Ravianos 社はファッション志向の顧客に大いに人気を博しており、より老舗の有名ブランドと十分に競合している」とある。よって、同社は人気を獲得し、より認知度の高い他社とも競合するほど市場で良い業績を上げていると判断できるので、(C)が正解。perform well「良い成績を収める、うまくいく」。
> (A) ❶の❶ 1〜2 行目に「国内 12 の都市に店舗を持つ」とあるだけで、複数の国に小売店があるとは述べられていない。multiple「複数の」。
> (B) merge with 〜「〜と合併する」、competing「競合する」。

193 What article of Ravianos clothing in the July 25 order was sold as sample merchandise?

(A) The Tiaran dress
(B) The Vanonse blouse
(C) The Remessi shirt
(D) The Cromius T-shirt

7 月 25 日の注文で、Ravianos 社の衣料品のうちどの品物が商品見本として販売されましたか。

(A) Tiaran ドレス
(B) Vanonse ブラウス
(C) Remessi シャツ
(D) Cromius T シャツ

> **正解 D** 記事❶の❷ 3〜7 行目に、Each month, Ravianos fills its stores' shelves with new clothing styles produced in small quantities and shipped in tiny sample batches of five pieces per size.「毎月、Ravianos 社は、少量生産されて 1 サイズにつきわずか 5 点のサンプル群として出荷される新しいスタイルの衣服で店舗の棚を埋める」と書かれている。日付が 7 月 25 日となっている注文書❷の❶の表を見ると、Cromius T シャツが全サイズ 5 点ずつになっている。つまり、これが商品見本として販売されたと考えられる。よって、(D)が正解。article「品物」、merchandise「商品」。

Expressions

instead of 〜 「〜しないで、〜の代わりに」（❶の❷ 1〜2 行目）

Instead of complaining about what you don't have, why don't you make the most of what you do have?
持っていないものについて不満を言うのではなく、持っているものを最大限に活用したらどうですか。

194 What does the report suggest Mr. Stawinski can do through his account?

(A) View sales histories
(B) Find store locations
(C) Read customer reviews
(D) Receive work assignments

報告書は、Stawinskiさんが自分のアカウントを通して何をすることができると示唆していますか。

(A) 販売履歴を見る
(B) 店舗の場所を見つける
(C) 顧客レビューを読む
(D) 割り当てられた仕事を受け取る

> **正解 A** 報告書 **3** の見出しと **1** 1～2行目より、これは Jan Stawinski さんがデザインした衣服の販売数値に関する報告書と分かる。同 **2** に、販売実績などが記され、同 **3** 1行目には、これらの数字は8月10日～16日の週のものだと書かれている。続く同 **3** 1～2行目で、「それ以前の週の数字を見るには、自身のオンラインアカウントにログインしてください」とある。よって、Stawinskiさんは自分のアカウントを通して過去の販売数を見ることができると分かるので、(A)が正解。sales history「販売履歴」。
> (C) review「レビュー、批評」。
> (D) work assignment「仕事の割り当て、担当業務」。

195 What is indicated about the Hygesse shirt?

(A) It will be sold at a 20 percent discount.
(B) It will be available to order online only.
(C) It became available on August 10.
(D) It was not released in all Ravianos stores.

Hygesse シャツについて何が示されていますか。

(A) 20パーセント引きで販売される予定である。
(B) オンラインでのみ注文できるようになる。
(C) 8月10日に入手可能になった。
(D) Ravianos社の全店舗で発売されたわけではなかった。

> **正解 B** Hygesse シャツは、報告書 **3** の **2** の最後の欄の商品である。前週と比較して販売数が20パーセント減、かっこ内に Production discontinued「生産中止」と記されている。記事 **1** の **2** 15～18行目に、「同社は売り上げの減少している商品の生産を停止し、売れ残りの商品は流通センターに返送されてオンライン顧客のみに販売される」とあるので、売り上げが減少し、生産中止となった Hygesse シャツは、注文できるのがオンラインのみになると考えられる。よって、(B)が正解。
> (A) **3** の **2** の Hygesse シャツの欄に－20%とあるのは販売数の前週比であり、価格の割引を示しているのではない。at a ～ percent discount「～パーセント引きで」。
> (C) **3** の **2** の数字は8月10日～16日の週のものであり、販売数の前週比が示されていることから、8月10日より前から販売されていたと考えられる。
> (D) **3** の **1** 2～3行目に、「数字は、Ravianos社の全12店舗およびオンライン上での製品別の購入総数を表す」とあるので、全店舗で発売されていたと判断できる。release「～を発売する」。

Words & Phrases

1 記事 secret 秘密　behind ～に隠れた、～の裏にある　**1** retailer 小売業者　across ～の至る所に
while ～だけれども　relatively 比較的　popular with ～ ～に人気がある　-minded ～に関心を持った
compete against ～ ～と競う　established 広く認められた、定評のある　**2** rely on ～ ～に依存する
traditional 従来通りの、伝統的な　method 手法、方法　pay close attention to ～ ～を注視する
market trend 市場動向　fill ～ with … ～を…で埋める　shelves 棚　★shelfの複数形　clothing 衣類
produce ～を生産する　in small quantities 少量で　tiny ごくわずかの　batch 一度分、ひとまとまり
piece 1つ、1個　per ～につき　as soon as ～ ～するとすぐに　in 到着して、提出されて
make a decision 決定する　move ～ to … ～を…に移す　full-scale 本格的な、完全な
redesign ～をデザインし直す　implement ～を実行する　offering 売り物　share ～ with … ～を…と共有する
in-house 社内の　meet by video ビデオ会議をする　based on ～ ～に基づいて　halt ～を停止させる
decline 減少する、低下する　leftovers 残り物　send back ～ to … ～を…に送り返す
distribution center 流通センター　**3** store personnel 店員　suggest ～を提案する　gather ～を集める
carry weight 重要性を持つ　significant かなりの、重大な　process 過程

2 注文書 quantity 数量　**1** blouse ブラウス

3 報告書 figure 数値、金額　**1** beyond ～を越えて　stage 段階　represent ～を表す
2 relative to ～ ～と比較して　previous 前の　discontinue ～を中止する
3 note that ～ ～であることに留意する　view ～を見る　log in to ～ ～にログインする

Questions 196-200 refer to the following policy, receipt, and credit card statement.

Tyche Bank Blue Business Card

Terms and Fees	
Rewards	Get 2% points on every purchase.
Payment Due Date	Monthly payment date is the fifth of the month unless cardholder requests a different due date.
Annual Percentage Rate (APR)	10% for purchases; 15% for other transactions
Annual Fee	$0
Late Payment Fee	$35; minimum monthly payment must be made by the due date in order to avoid a late fee.

If you wish to link your card to a Tyche Bank checking account, please contact inquiries@tychebank.com.

Hadley Office Supplies
33 Mossflower Road, Amherst, NH 03031

Customer: Francine Naar
Date: December 7

Product No.	Name	Amount
XM21	Table lamp, black	$54.12
DS13	Wall calendar—Autumn Trees	$11.39
OC02	Plushmax rolling office chair, dark green	$135.20
VB62	Letter-size printer paper (10-ream box)	$31.90
	Total	$232.61

Charged to Tyche Bank Blue Business Card
XXXXXXXXXXXX3245

Tyche Bank Blue Business Card

Francine Naar
320 Pelham St., Amherst, NH 03031
Account XXXXXXXXXXXX3245

ACCOUNT ACTIVITY
New balance: $287.87
Payment due date: February 20

Date of Transaction	Merchant Name	Amount
12/07	Hadley Office Supplies	$232.61
12/08	Downtown Donut Shack	$16.43
12/15	REFUND—Hadley Office Supplies	-$135.20
12/23	Maslin Dry Cleaning	$12.00
01/03	Callie's Carpet Corral	$86.57
01/04	Ogus Sportswear	$75.46

AUTOPAY ON. Your payment will be withdrawn from your Tyche Bank checking account on the due date.

Total points available: 1,996
Redeem your points at www.tychebank.com/rewards.

問題196-200は次の基本方針、領収書、クレジットカード明細書に関するものです。

Tyche銀行ブルービジネスカード

条件と料金	
報奨	全ての購入1件ごとに2パーセントのポイントを獲得する。
支払期日	カード保有者が異なる支払日を希望しない限り、毎月の支払日は5日である。
年率（APR）	購入には10パーセント；他の取引には15パーセント
年会費	0ドル
延滞金	35ドル；延滞金の発生を避けるために、毎月の最低支払額が支払期日までに支払われなければならない。

ご自身のカードをTyche銀行当座預金口座と連結することをご希望の場合、inquiries@tychebank.comにご連絡ください。

Hadleyオフィス用品店
モスフラワー通り33番地、アマースト、NH 03031

顧客：Francine Naar様
日付：12月7日

商品番号	商品名	金額
XM21	卓上電気スタンド、黒色	54.12ドル
DS13	壁掛けカレンダー ──秋の木々	11.39ドル
OC02	Plushmaxキャスター付きオフィスチェアー、深緑色	135.20ドル
VB62	レターサイズの印刷用紙（10連入りボックス）	31.90ドル
	合計	232.61ドル

Tyche銀行ブルービジネスカードによるお支払い
XXXXXXXXXXXX3245

Tyche銀行ブルービジネスカード

Francine Naar様
ペラム通り320番地、アマースト、NH 03031
口座 XXXXXXXXXXXX3245

口座入出金
新残高：287.87ドル
支払期日：2月20日

取引日	業者名	金額
12月7日	Hadleyオフィス用品店	232.61ドル
12月8日	Downtownドーナツ店	16.43ドル
12月15日	返金──Hadleyオフィス用品店	−135.20ドル
12月23日	Maslinドライクリーニング店	12.00ドル
1月3日	Callie'sカーペット店	86.57ドル
1月4日	Ogusスポーツウエア店	75.46ドル

自動支払有効。支払金額は支払期日にお客さまのTyche銀行当座預金口座から引き落とされます。

利用可能な合計ポイント：1,996
ポイントは www.tychebank.com/rewards でお引き換えください。

196 According to the policy, what is true about the Tyche Bank Blue Business Card?

    (A) It charges a high annual fee.

    (B) It offers points on selected purchases only.

    (C) It charges the same rate for purchases and other transactions.

    (D) It allows cardholders to pay automatically from a bank account.

基本方針によると、Tyche銀行ブルービジネスカードについて正しいことは何ですか。

    (A) 高い年会費を請求する。

    (B) 選ばれた購入にだけポイントを付与する。

    (C) 購入と他の取引に同じ金利を課す。

    (D) カード保有者は銀行口座から自動的に支払うことができる。

> **正解 D** Tyche銀行ブルービジネスカードの基本方針 **1** の **❷** に、If you wish to link your card to a Tyche Bank checking account, please contact inquiries@tychebank.com.「ご自身のカードをTyche銀行当座預金口座と連結することを希望する場合、inquiries@tychebank.comに連絡してください」とあるので、連絡すれば、カードに銀行口座を紐付けて自動的に支払うようにできると判断できる。よって、(D)が正解。allow ～ to do「～が…できるようにする」、automatically「自動的に」。
> (A) **1** の **❶** 「年会費」の欄に0ドルとあり、年会費は無料。
> (B) **1** の **❶** 「報奨」の欄より、全ての購入にポイントが付与されると分かる。selected「選ばれた」。
> (C) **1** の **❶** 「年率」の欄に、購入は10パーセント、他の取引は15パーセントとあるので金利が異なると分かる。

197 Where did Ms. Naar make a purchase on January 3?

    (A) At a restaurant

    (B) At a dry cleaner

    (C) At a carpet store

    (D) At a clothing shop

1月3日にNaarさんはどこで買い物をしましたか。

    (A) レストラン

    (B) ドライクリーニング店

    (C) カーペット店

    (D) 衣料品店

> **正解 C** Naarさん宛てのクレジットカード明細書 **3** の **❷** で、取引日が1月3日の業者名の欄に、「Callie's カーペット店」とある。よって、Naarさんは1月3日にカーペット店で買い物をしたと分かるので、(C)が正解。
> (B) **3** の **❷** より、ドライクリーニング店で支払いをしたのは12月23日。
> (D) **3** の **❷** より、衣料品店で買い物をしたのは1月4日。clothing shop「衣料品店」。

198 According to the credit card statement, what can Ms. Naar do online?

    (A) Enroll in a rewards program

    (B) Redeem her points

    (C) Purchase a gift card

    (D) Apply for a lower interest rate

クレジットカード明細書によると、Naarさんはオンラインで何をすることができますか。

    (A) 報奨プログラムに入会する

    (B) ポイントを引き換える

    (C) ギフトカードを購入する

    (D) より低い金利を申し込む

> **正解 B** クレジットカード明細書 **3** の **❹** 2行目に、Redeem your points at www.tychebank.com/rewards.「ポイントはwww.tychebank.com/rewardsで引き換えてください」と記されているので、(B)が正解。
> (A) enroll in ～「～に入会する」、rewards program「報奨プログラム（優良顧客に特典を提供する施策）」。
> (D) apply for ～「～を申し込む」、interest rate「金利」。

Expressions

unless 「～でない限り、もし～しなければ」（**1** の **❶**）

The financial conditions will get worse unless the board changes its strategy.
取締役会が戦略を変えない限り、財務状況は悪化するでしょう。

199 What is suggested about Ms. Naar?

(A) She asked for a new payment date.
(B) She works at an office supply store.
(C) She qualified to earn extra bonus points.
(D) She lives on Mossflower Road.

Naarさんについて何が分かりますか。

(A) 彼女は新たな支払期日を求めた。
(B) 彼女はオフィス用品店で働いている。
(C) 彼女は追加のボーナスポイントを獲得する資格を得た。
(D) 彼女はモスフラワー通りに住んでいる。

正解 A クレジットカード明細書❸の❶ 6行目より、Naarさんの支払期日は「2月20日」であることが分かる。基本方針❶の❶のPayment Due Date「支払期日」の欄に、Monthly payment date is the fifth of the month unless cardholder requests a different due date.「カード保有者が異なる支払期日を希望しない限り、毎月の支払日は5日である」と書かれている。よって、Naarさんは20日という新たな支払期日を希望したと判断できるので、(A)が正解。ask for ~「~を求める」。
(B) オフィス用品店の領収書である❷の「顧客」の欄にNaarさんの名前があるので、Naarさんはオフィス用品店で働いているのではなく、顧客として利用したと分かる。
(C) qualify to do「~する資格を得る」、earn「~を獲得する」、extra「追加の」。
(D) ❸の❶より、Naarさんが住んでいるのはペラム通りと分かる。❷のヘッダーの住所にあるモスフラワー通りはHadleyオフィス用品店の所在地。

200 What purchase did Ms. Naar return for a refund?

(A) A table lamp
(B) A wall calendar
(C) A rolling chair
(D) A box of printer paper

Naarさんはどの購入品を返品して代金を払い戻してもらいましたか。

(A) 卓上電気スタンド
(B) 壁掛けカレンダー
(C) キャスター付きチェアー
(D) 印刷用紙1箱

正解 C クレジットカード明細書❸の❷で、REFUND「返金」と書かれているのは、12月15日のHadleyオフィス用品店における135.20ドルの支払いに対するもの。Hadleyオフィス用品店での買い物の領収書である❷の❶の表で、135.20ドルとあるのは商品番号OC02のPlushmax rolling office chair, dark green「Plushmaxキャスター付きオフィスチェアー、深緑色」。よって、Naarさんが返品して払い戻してもらったのは、このキャスター付きオフィスチェアーだと判断できるので、(C)が正解。

Words & Phrases

❶ 基本方針

policy 方針、ポリシー　　receipt 領収書　　credit card statement クレジットカード明細書

❶ terms 条件　　fee 料金　　reward 報奨、報酬　　due date 支払期日、締切日
cardholder （クレジット）カード保有者　　request ~を求める
annual percentage rate 年率　★買い物をして支払期日までに全額支払わなかった場合やキャッシングをした際に課される金利　　transaction 取引　　minimum 最低限の　　in order to do ~するために
avoid ~を避ける　　❷ wish to do ~したいと思う　　link ~ to … ~を…に結び付ける
checking account 当座預金口座

❷ 領収書

office supplies オフィス用品　　❶ amount 金額　　table lamp 卓上電気スタンド
rolling chair キャスター付きチェアー
letter-size レターサイズの　★米国の一般的な用紙サイズで、A4よりやや小さい
ream 連　★用紙を数える単位で、《米》500枚、《英》480枚
❷ charge ~ to … ~を…（クレジットカード）で支払う

❸ クレジットカード明細書

❶ account activity 口座の入出金　　balance 残高　　❷ merchant 業者、商人　　shack 小屋
refund 返金　　dry cleaning ドライクリーニング
corral （家畜などの）囲い　★広い店舗を持つ店の店名に使われることがある　　❸ auto- 自動の~
withdraw ~を引き落とす　　❹ redeem ~を引き換える

TEST 2 の正解一覧

リスニングセクション

問題番号	正解
Part 1	
1	C
2	B
3	B
4	D
5	B
6	D
Part 2	
7	A
8	A
9	A
10	B
11	B
12	C
13	B
14	A
15	B
16	C
17	B
18	C
19	A
20	A
21	B
22	A
23	A
24	B
25	C
26	A
27	A
28	C
29	C
30	C
31	B
Part 3	
32	A
33	B
34	D
35	B
36	D
37	C
38	A
39	B
40	D
41	A
42	C
43	B
44	A
45	B
46	D
47	D
48	D
49	C
50	A

問題番号	正解
51	D
52	B
53	A
54	C
55	A
56	A
57	C
58	C
59	D
60	C
61	C
62	C
63	B
64	A
65	B
66	D
67	B
68	A
69	D
70	B
Part 4	
71	A
72	B
73	A
74	C
75	B
76	D
77	C
78	D
79	D
80	A
81	B
82	C
83	B
84	D
85	D
86	B
87	B
88	A
89	C
90	D
91	C
92	D
93	A
94	B
95	B
96	C
97	D
98	D
99	A
100	B

リーディングセクション

問題番号	正解
Part 5	
101	D
102	B
103	C
104	D
105	B
106	A
107	C
108	D
109	A
110	B
111	D
112	D
113	D
114	C
115	B
116	B
117	C
118	C
119	A
120	D
121	A
122	B
123	D
124	B
125	A
126	A
127	B
128	B
129	A
130	C
Part 6	
131	B
132	A
133	D
134	D
135	A
136	C
137	D
138	B
139	A
140	B
141	A
142	B
143	C
144	D
145	C
146	D
Part 7	
147	C
148	C
149	D
150	A

問題番号	正解
151	C
152	D
153	B
154	A
155	D
156	B
157	C
158	C
159	B
160	C
161	C
162	B
163	C
164	A
165	D
166	B
167	B
168	A
169	B
170	D
171	A
172	B
173	A
174	D
175	A
176	B
177	C
178	C
179	A
180	D
181	C
182	A
183	A
184	B
185	D
186	D
187	C
188	A
189	B
190	B
191	B
192	D
193	A
194	C
195	D
196	D
197	A
198	C
199	A
200	A

PART 1

1

2

3

---

1 🍁 M

(A) The woman is assembling some chairs.
(B) The woman is sweeping the floor.
(C) The woman is working in a seating area.
(D) The woman is leaning over a tray of food.

(A) 女性は椅子を組み立てている。
(B) 女性は床を掃いている。
(C) 女性は座席エリアで作業している。
(D) 女性は食べ物が載ったトレーの上に身を乗り出している。

正解 C 女性は座席エリアでテーブルを拭く作業をしている。seating「座席」。
(A) 椅子は写っているが、女性は椅子を組み立てているところではない。assemble「～を組み立てる」。
(B) 女性はfloor「床」を掃いているところではない。sweep「～を掃く」。
(D) 女性が身を乗り出しているテーブルの上には何も置かれていない。lean over ～「～の上に身を乗り出す」、tray「トレー、盆」。

---

2 🇬🇧 W

(A) A bus is pulling into a garage.
(B) A bus is passing by a building.
(C) A bus is parked on a bridge.
(D) A bus is driving through a tunnel.

(A) バスは車庫に入っていくところである。
(B) バスは建物のそばを通っている。
(C) バスは橋の上に駐車されている。
(D) バスはトンネルの中を進んでいる。

正解 B 1台のバスが建物のそばを通っている。pass by ～「～のそばを通る」。
(A) garage「車庫」は写っていない。pull into ～「(車などが)～に入る」。
(C) 橋は写っていない。park「～を駐車する」。
(D) tunnel「トンネル」は写っていない。drive「(車などが)進む」。

---

3 🍁 M

(A) Some of the women are pointing to a poster.
(B) Some of the women are greeting each other.
(C) One of the women is ordering a beverage at a café.
(D) One of the women is drinking from a water bottle.

(A) 女性の何人かがポスターを指さしている。
(B) 女性の何人かが互いにあいさつしている。
(C) 女性の1人がカフェで飲み物を注文している。
(D) 女性の1人が水筒から飲んでいる。

正解 B 中央の女性と右側の女性がお互いに向き合い、握手を交わしている。greet「～にあいさつする」。
(A) ポスターらしき物は写っているが、それを指さしている女性はいない。point to ～「～を指さす」。
(C) order「～を注文する」、beverage「飲み物」。
(D) 左側の女性はwater bottle「水筒」のようなものを手に持っているが、それから飲んではいない。

4

5

6

---

4 M

(A) They're swimming in a pool.
(B) They're diving into the ocean.
(C) One of the men is releasing a net into the ocean.
(D) One of the men is riding a personal watercraft.

(A) 彼らはプールで泳いでいる。
(B) 彼らは海に飛び込んでいる。
(C) 男性の1人が海中に網を放っている。
(D) 男性の1人が水上バイクに乗っている。

正解 D　水上で、1人の男性が乗り物にまたがっている。personal watercraft「水上バイク（1人用のモーターボート）」。
(A) 写っているのはプールではなく海と思われ、また人々も泳いではいない。
(B) ocean「海」は写っているが、人々はそこに飛び込んではいない。dive into 〜「〜に飛び込む」。
(C) net「網」を放っている男性はいない。release「〜を放つ」。

---

5 W

(A) One of the people is shoveling some snow.
(B) One of the people is standing between some railings.
(C) One of the people is putting on a jacket.
(D) One of the people is climbing a tree.

(A) 人々の1人が雪かきをしている。
(B) 人々の1人が欄干と欄干の間に立っている。
(C) 人々の1人が上着を身に着けているところである。
(D) 人々の1人が木に登っているところである。

正解 B　手前に写っている人物が橋の左右の欄干の間に立っている。railings「欄干、手すり」。
(A) 雪は写っているが、雪かきをしている人物はいない。shovel「〜をシャベルですくう」。
(C) 人物はjacket「上着」を着用しているが、身に着ける動作の途中ではない。put on 〜 は「〜を身に着ける」という動作を表す。
(D) 木々は写っているが、木に登っている人物はいない。climb「〜に登る」。

---

6 W

(A) One of the women is filling a container.
(B) One of the women is walking through a doorway.
(C) One of the women is rolling a suitcase down a hall.
(D) One of the women is arranging boxes beside a wall.

(A) 女性の1人が容器を満たしている。
(B) 女性の1人が出入口を歩いて通り抜けている。
(C) 女性の1人がスーツケースを転がして廊下の先へ進んでいる。
(D) 女性の1人が壁のそばで箱を並べている。

正解 D　右側の女性が、壁のそばで複数の箱を並べているところである。arrange「〜を並べる」、beside「〜のそばで」。
(A) 左側の女性は大型容器を前にしているが、ふたは閉じてあり、それを満たしているところではない。fill「〜を満たす」、container「容器」。
(B) doorway「出入口」を通っている人物はいない。walk through 〜「〜を歩いて通り抜ける」。
(C) suitcase「スーツケース」は写っていない。roll「〜を転がす、〜を転がして運ぶ」、hall「廊下」。

PART 2

CD 2 10-14

7 🇺🇸 W Would you like to meet the clients?

🇦🇺 M (A) Sure, I'd love to meet them.
(B) This is a well-written business plan.
(C) Twenty centimeters.

その顧客の方々にお会いになりたいですか。
(A) はい、ぜひお会いしたいです。
(B) これはしっかりと書かれた事業計画ですね。
(C) 20センチメートルです。

| 正解 A | Would you like to do ～?「～したいですか」は、丁寧に相手の意向を尋ねる表現。顧客に会いたいかと尋ねているのに対し、Sure と肯定し、「ぜひ会いたい」と希望を伝えている(A)が正解。themは質問にあるthe clientsを指す。I'dはI wouldの短縮形。would love to do「ぜひ～したい」。(B) well-written「うまく書かれた」、business「事業」。 |

---

8 🇦🇺 M When can I pick up the antique table from your shop?

🇺🇸 W (A) Any time after five P.M.
(B) Sure, I'll take care of it.
(C) On Maple Avenue.

私はいつ、そちらのお店から骨董のテーブルを受け取ることができますか。
(A) 午後5時以降であればいつでも。
(B) もちろんです、私がそれを引き受けましょう。
(C) メープル大通りに。

| 正解 A | When ～?でいつ店から骨董のテーブルを受け取ることができるかと尋ねているのに対し、「午後5時以降であればいつでも(よい)」と受け取り可能な時間帯を伝えている(A)が正解。pick up ～「～を受け取る」、antique「骨董の」。(B) itがthe antique tableを指すとしても、Sureで何を肯定しているか不明であり、応答にならない。take care of ～「～を引き受ける」。(C) 場所は尋ねられていない。 |

---

9 🇨🇦 M Do you think we should take the train or fly to the conference?

🇺🇸 W (A) We should fly.
(B) Don't worry, you'll do great.
(C) We've spent a long time preparing.

私たちは協議会まで電車で行くのがいいと思いますか、それとも飛行機で行くのがいいと思いますか。
(A) 飛行機で行くのがいいでしょう。
(B) 心配しないでください、あなたはうまくやるでしょう。
(C) 私たちは準備に長い時間を費やしてきました。

| 正解 A | A or B?の形で、電車と飛行機のどちらで協議会に行くのがいいと思うかと尋ねている。これに対し、「飛行機で行くのがいいだろう」と、後者の移動手段を勧めている(A)が正解。fly「飛行機で行く」、conference「協議会」。(B) 移動手段が尋ねられているので、相手を励ます発言は応答にならない。(C) spend ～ doing「…するのに～(時間)を費やす」、prepare「準備する」。 |

---

10 🇺🇸 W Your office is moving to a new location, isn't it?

🇦🇺 M (A) A local supply company.
(B) Yes, we've been packing all week.
(C) Somewhere in the storage room.

あなたの事務所は新しい場所に移転するのですよね?
(A) 地元の供給業者です。
(B) はい、私たちは1週間ずっと荷造りをしています。
(C) 貯蔵室内のどこかに。

| 正解 B | 肯定文の文末に ～, isn't it?を付けて「～ですよね」と、事務所が新しい場所に移転することを確認している。これに対し、Yesと肯定し、移転に向けた準備をしていることを伝えている(B)が正解。location「場所」。pack「荷造りをする」、all week「1週間ずっと」。(A) local「地元の」、supply「供給」。(C) 場所について述べているが、事務所移転の話題と合わない。storage room「貯蔵室」。 |

---

11 🇬🇧 W Did you send Mr. Yang his contract?

🇨🇦 M (A) Please form a line here.
(B) No, not yet.
(C) A new e-mail contact.

Yangさんに彼の契約書を送付しましたか。
(A) こちらで列を作ってください。
(B) いいえ、まだです。
(C) 新しいEメールの連絡先です。

| 正解 B | 契約書を送付したかと尋ねているのに対し、Noと答え、not yet「まだだ」と、送っていないことを伝えている(B)が正解。contract「契約書」。(A) form a line「列を作る」。(C) 質問にあるcontractと似た音のcontact「連絡」に注意。 |

12 [M] Where can I get new lightbulbs for the office?

[W] (A) Open weekdays until six P.M.
(B) That'll be eleven dollars.
(C) Check with someone in maintenance.

私はどこで事務所用の新しい電球を入手できますか。
(A) 平日午後6時まで開いています。
(B) 11ドルになります。
(C) 保守管理部の人に確認してください。

正解 C Where ～?で事務所用の新しい電球をどこで入手できるかと尋ねているのに対し、場所を答える代わりに、保守管理部の人に確認するよう促している(C)が正解。lightbulb「電球」。check with ～「～に確認する」、maintenance「保守管理」。
(A) 開いている日時は尋ねられていない。weekdays「平日に」。
(B) That'll be ～ に金額を続けるのは、店員が客に金額を伝える表現。

13 [M] Why did our team switch project managers?

[W] (A) July fifteenth, I think.
(B) Because Dolores has more experience.
(C) I'll make a note of that.

私たちのチームはなぜ、プロジェクトマネージャーを替えたのですか。
(A) 7月15日だと思います。
(B) Doloresの方が経験を積んでいるからです。
(C) 私がそれを書き留めましょう。

正解 B Why ～?でチームがプロジェクトマネージャーを替えた理由を尋ねている。これに対し、理由を示すBecause ～ を用いて、「Doloresの方が経験を積んでいるからだ」と、別の人物がより適任であることを伝えている(B)が正解。switch「～を取り替える」。experience「経験」。
(A) 日程は尋ねられていない。
(C) make a note of ～「～を書き留める」。

14 [M] Who recommended that meal plan to you?

[M] (A) My nutrition consultant.
(B) At my favorite restaurant.
(C) Mainly fruits and vegetables.

誰がその献立をあなたに薦めたのですか。
(A) 私の栄養コンサルタントです。
(B) 私のお気に入りのレストランで。
(C) 主に果物と野菜です。

正解 A Who ～?で誰がその献立を薦めたのかと尋ねているのに対し、「私の栄養コンサルタントだ」と推薦者を答えている(A)が正解。recommend「～を推薦する」、meal plan「献立」。nutrition「栄養」、consultant「コンサルタント」。
(B) 場所は尋ねられていない。
(C) 献立の内容は尋ねられていない。

15 [W] Don't you have a gym membership?

[M] (A) The locker room is over there.
(B) No, I just canceled it.
(C) Let's order a dozen.

あなたはジムの会員資格を持っていないのですか。
(A) ロッカールームはあちらです。
(B) 持っていません、ちょうどそれを解約しました。
(C) 1ダース注文しましょう。

正解 B 否定疑問文で、「ジムの会員資格を持っていないのか」と尋ねているのに対し、Noで持っていないことを伝え、ちょうど解約したばかりであると補足している(B)が正解。itは質問にあるa gym membershipを指す。membership「会員資格」。cancel「～を解約する」。
(A) ロッカールームの位置は尋ねられていない。
(C) order「～を注文する」、dozen「1ダース」。

16 [W] Which contractor did you use for your kitchen renovation?

[M] (A) Sure, you can borrow it.
(B) Two months long.
(C) I hired the Martino Brothers.

台所の改装にどの請負業者を利用したのですか。
(A) はい、それを借りていいですよ。
(B) 2カ月間です。
(C) Martino Brothers社に依頼しました。

正解 C Which ～?で台所の改装にどの請負業者を利用したかと尋ねているのに対し、「Martino Brothers社に依頼した」と具体的な業者名を答えている(C)が正解。contractor「請負業者」、renovation「改装、修繕」。hire「～を雇う」。
(A) Sureで何を肯定しているか不明であり、続く内容も請負業者を尋ねる質問に合わない。
(B) 期間は尋ねられていない。～ long「～の長さで」。

17 🇨🇦 M When will the lights in the parking area be turned on?

🇬🇧 W (A) No, I didn't put them off.

(B) They're on an automatic timer.

(C) Yes, that's right.

駐車場の照明はいつ点灯するのでしょうか。

(A) いいえ、私はそれらを消しませんでした。

(B) それらは自動タイマーにつながっています。

(C) はい、その通りです。

正解 **B** When ～?で照明がいつ点灯するかと尋ねているのに対し、照明は自動タイマーにつながっていると答えている(B)が正解。Theyは質問にあるthe lightsを指す。parking area「駐車場」、turn on ～「～（明かりなど）をつける」。automatic「自動の」、timer「タイマー」。
(A) 質問にあるturned onと関連するput off ～「～（明かりなど）を消す」に注意。
(C) 時が尋ねられているので、Yes/Noでは応答にならない。

18 🇬🇧 W Who's on vacation this week?

🇨🇦 M (A) Job application forms.

(B) Yes, it went well.

(C) There's an online calendar.

誰が今週休暇を取っていますか。

(A) 就職の申し用紙です。

(B) はい、それはうまくいきました。

(C) オンラインの予定表があります。

正解 **C** Who ～?で誰が今週休暇を取っているかと尋ねているのに対し、特定の人物を答える代わりに「オンラインの予定表がある」と述べ、休暇を取っている人物をオンライン上で確認するよう促している(C)が正解。There'sはThere isの短縮形。on vacation「休暇中で」。calendar「予定表」。
(A) 質問にあるvacationと語尾が共通しているapplication「申し込み」に注意。form「用紙、書式」。
(B) go well「（物事が）うまくいく、順調に運ぶ」。

19 🇬🇧 W Why do we have to finish the sales report today?

🇦🇺 M (A) The deadline was moved up.

(B) I've already sold them all.

(C) Yes, she reports the business news.

私たちはなぜ、今日、販売報告書を仕上げる必要があるのですか。

(A) 締め切りが早まりました。

(B) 私はすでにそれらを全て販売しました。

(C) はい、彼女はビジネスニュースを報道しています。

正解 **A** Why ～?で販売報告書を今日仕上げなくてはならない理由を尋ねている。これに対し、「締め切りが早まった」と、理由を答えている(A)が正解。sales report「販売報告書」。deadline「締め切り」、move up ～「～（時期など）を早める」。
(B) 質問にあるsalesと関連するsell「～を販売する」の過去分詞soldを含むが、応答になっていない。
(C) 質問にあるreportを含むが、ここでは動詞で「～を報道する」の意味。

20 🇺🇸 W Excuse me, we ordered over 30 minutes ago.

🇬🇧 W (A) I'll check with the chef.

(B) That's an excellent choice.

(C) A half-hour train ride.

すみません、私たちは30分以上前に注文したのですが。

(A) 料理長に確認いたします。

(B) それは素晴らしい選択ですね。

(C) 30分の電車移動です。

正解 **A** Excuse meと呼び掛けて「私たちは30分以上前に注文した」と伝えているので、レストランなどで注文した品の提供が遅れている状況と考えられる。それに対し、確認を申し出ている(A)が正解。check with ～「～に確認する」、chef「料理長、シェフ」。
(B) choice「選択」については言及されていない。excellent「素晴らしい」。
(C) かかる時間や移動手段は尋ねられていない。ride「乗っている時間、乗車すること」。

21 🇬🇧 W Have the laboratory coats come back from the laundry service?

🇦🇺 M (A) Try folding it this way.

(B) Yes, they arrived this morning.

(C) I haven't used that machine.

実験用白衣は洗濯サービスから戻ってきましたか。

(A) こうやってそれを畳んでみてください。

(B) はい、今朝届きました。

(C) 私はその機械を使ったことがありません。

正解 **B** 実験用白衣が洗濯サービスから戻ってきたかと尋ねているのに対し、Yesと肯定し、the laboratory coatsをtheyで受けて今朝届いたと補足している(B)が正解。laboratory coat「実験用白衣、実験着」、laundry「洗濯（物）」。
(A) 畳み方を指示する発言は応答にならない。try doing「試しに～してみる」、fold「～を畳む」。
(C) machine「機械」については尋ねられていない。

22 M Wasn't that actress in another show recently?

W (A) I don't watch much television.
(B) No, it's two hours long.
(C) He'll show you how.

その女優は最近、別の番組に出演していませんでしたか。
(A) 私はあまりテレビを見ません。
(B) いいえ、それは2時間です。
(C) 彼があなたにやり方を教えます。

正解 A 否定疑問文で、「その女優は最近、別の番組に出演していなかったか」と尋ねているのに対し、「私はあまりテレビを見ない」と述べ、質問に答えられないということを暗に伝えている(A)が正解。actress「女優」、show「(テレビ・ラジオの)番組」、recently「最近」。television「テレビ」。
(B) itがanother showを指すとしても、時間の長さに関する発言は応答にならない。
(C) 質問にあるshowを含むがここでは動詞であり、show ~ …「~に…を教える」という意味。

---

23 M Where can I get a copy of the conference schedule?

M (A) At the registration table.
(B) Thanks, I don't need a receipt.
(C) Would you like an appointment?

どこで協議会の日程表をもらえますか。
(A) 受付で。
(B) ありがとう、領収書は不要です。
(C) 予約をご希望ですか。

正解 A Where ~?で協議会の日程表をどこでもらえるかと尋ねているのに対し、「受付で」と言って場所を教えている(A)が正解。a copy of ~「1部の~」、conference「協議会」、schedule「日程表」。registration「登録、記名」。
(B) receipt「領収書」が必要かどうかは尋ねられていない。
(C) 日程表をもらえる場所が尋ねられているので、appointment「予約」について尋ねる発言は応答にならない。

---

24 W Could you listen to my sales pitch?

M (A) That's on the tenth floor.
(B) I have a few minutes on Monday.
(C) Yes, I bought it on sale.

私のセールストークを聞いていただけますか。
(A) それは10階にあります。
(B) 私は月曜日に何分か時間があります。
(C) はい、私は特価でそれを購入しました。

正解 B Could you ~?で自分のセールストークを聞いてほしいと依頼しているのに対し、「私は月曜日に何分か時間がある」と述べ、対応できる日を伝えている(B)が正解。sales pitch「セールストーク、売り込みの口上」。
(A) Thatが何を指すか不明。floor「階、床」。
(C) 質問にあるsalesの単数形saleを含むが、itが何を指すか不明で応答にならない。on sale「特価で」。

---

25 M How are we going to meet Thursday's production quota?

W (A) That's good to hear.
(B) On top of the file cabinet.
(C) By working overtime.

私たちはどのようにして、木曜日の生産ノルマを達成する予定なのですか。
(A) それを聞いてうれしく思います。
(B) 書類整理棚の上に。
(C) 残業することによってです。

正解 C How ~?でどのように生産ノルマを達成する予定かと尋ねているのに対し、「残業することによって」と、その手段を答えている(C)が正解。meet「~を満たす」、production「生産」、quota「ノルマ、割当量」。work overtime「残業する」。
(A) 質問にあるgoing toと似た音のgood toに注意。
(B) 場所は尋ねられていない。on top of ~「~の一番上に」、file cabinet「書類整理棚」。

---

26 W What decisions were made at the board meeting yesterday?

M (A) I had to leave at noon.
(B) Does he prefer meat or fish?
(C) Yes, I have some charts.

昨日の取締役会議ではどんな決定が下されましたか。
(A) 私は正午に退席しなければなりませんでした。
(B) 彼は肉の方が好きですか、それとも魚ですか。
(C) はい、私は幾つか図表を持っています。

正解 A What ~?で昨日の取締役会議でどんな決定が下されたのかと尋ねているのに対し、「私は正午に退席しなければならなかった」と述べ、会議の場を離れたため決定された内容を知らないということを示唆している(A)が正解。make a decision「決定を下す」、board「取締役会、役員会」。
(B) heが誰を指すか不明。質問にあるmeetingと似た音のmeat「肉」に注意。prefer「~の方を好む」。
(C) chart「図表」。

27 🇬🇧 W I'd like to go somewhere with live music.

🇨🇦 M (A) My cousin's band is performing this weekend.
(B) Where's the pasta sauce?
(C) Yes, it was a good improvement.

どこか生演奏の音楽が聴ける所に行きたいです。

(A) 私のいとこのバンドが今週末演奏する予定です。
(B) パスタのソースはどこにありますか。
(C) はい、それは優れた改良点でした。

正解 A　生演奏の音楽が聴ける場所に行きたいという発言に対し、「いとこのバンドが今週末演奏する予定だ」と希望に合いそうな情報を伝えている(A)が正解。I'dはI wouldの短縮形。somewhere「どこかに」、live「生演奏の、ライブの」。cousin「いとこ」、perform「演奏する」。
(B) pasta「パスタ」、sauce「ソース」。
(C) itが何を指すのか不明であり、応答にならない。improvement「改良点」。

28 🇦🇺 M This train stops at Jefferson Street, doesn't it?

🇨🇦 M (A) The new employee training.
(B) Just press the start button on the side.
(C) You'll need to transfer at Central Station.

この電車はジェファソン通り駅に止まりますよね?

(A) 新しい従業員の研修です。
(B) 側面にあるスタートボタンを押すだけです。
(C) セントラル駅で乗り換える必要があります。

正解 C　肯定文の文末に ～, doesn't it?を付けて「～ですよね」と、この電車がジェファソン通り駅に停車することを確認しているのに対し、ジェファソン通り駅に行くにはセントラル駅での乗り換えが必要であると教えている(C)が正解。stop「止まる」。transfer「乗り換える」。
(A) 質問にあるtrainと似たtraining「研修」に注意。
(B) press「～を押す」、button「ボタン」、side「側面」。

29 🇬🇧 W You can use your credit card to withdraw money from most banks in Germany.

🇦🇺 M (A) The train is convenient.
(B) Please sign the receipt.
(C) Are there any service fees?

ドイツのほとんどの銀行からお金を下ろすのに、クレジットカードが使えますよ。

(A) その電車は便利です。
(B) 領収書に署名してください。
(C) 手数料はかかりますか。

正解 C　ドイツのほとんどの銀行からお金を下ろすのにクレジットカードが使えると教える発言に対し、手数料が発生するかと尋ねている(C)が正解。credit card「クレジットカード」、withdraw「～(預金)を引き出す」。service fee「手数料」。
(A) convenient「便利な」。
(B) クレジットカードの使用に関する発言に対し、領収書への署名を求める発言は応答にならない。sign「～に署名する」、receipt「領収書」。

30 🇨🇦 M Does your team want to have food delivered or to go out for lunch?

🇬🇧 W (A) An empty office on Water Street.
(B) I enjoyed that meal, too.
(C) There's a buffet at the company cafeteria.

あなたのチームは、昼食に料理を届けてもらいたいですか、それとも外へ行きたいですか。

(A) ウォーター通りの空き事務所です。
(B) 私もその食事を楽しみました。
(C) 社員食堂にビュッフェがあります。

正解 C　A or B?の形で、昼食に出前を取るのと外に出るのとではどちらが希望か尋ねている。これに対し、どちらかを答える代わりに、「社員食堂にビュッフェがある」と別の選択肢を挙げている(C)が正解。have ～ done「～を…してもらう」、deliver「～を配達する」。buffet「ビュッフェ、セルフサービス式の食事」、company cafeteria「社員食堂」。
(A) 場所は尋ねられていない。empty「空いている」。
(B) 食事の感想は尋ねられていない。

31 🇬🇧 W How long will the electricity be out?

🇦🇺 M (A) Probably ten months ago.
(B) The storm only just started.
(C) Of course, near the closet.

どのくらいの間、停電するのでしょうか。

(A) おそらく10カ月前です。
(B) 嵐はまだ始まったばかりです。
(C) もちろんです、収納室の近くです。

正解 B　How long ～?でどのくらいの間停電するだろうかと尋ねているのに対し、「嵐はまだ始まったばかりだ」と述べ、停電はまだしばらく続く可能性があることを暗に伝えている(B)が正解。electricity「電気」、out「機能しなくなって、消えて」。storm「嵐」。
(A) 過去の時期は尋ねられていない。
(C) Of courseで何を肯定しているか不明。また、場所は尋ねられていない。closet「収納室」。

PART 3

会話 CD 2 36　問題 CD 2 37

Questions 32 through 34 refer to the following conversation.

🏴 M Hi, Luisa. ❶Are you ready to travel to the manufacturing convention tomorrow?

🇺🇸 W ❷Yes, I am. I'm glad we're participating this year. ❸There's a lot of new technology for factories like ours, and we'll get a first-hand glimpse during the demonstrations.

🏴 M That'll be great. ❹I'm also interested in attending the lecture on Friday—the one about the history of manufacturing. ❺I'd like to know more about how production has changed over time.

問題32-34は次の会話に関するものです。

こんにちは、Luisa。明日の製造業協議会へ行く準備はできていますか。

はい、できています。私たちが今年参加できてうれしいです。うちのような工場向けの新技術がたくさんあり、実演中にじかに垣間見ることができるでしょうね。

それは素晴らしいことですよね。私は金曜日の講演にも出席したいと思っています——製造業の歴史に関するものです。製造が時とともにどのように変化してきたかということについてもっと知りたいのです。

---

32 What are the speakers preparing to do?

(A) Attend a convention
(B) Host an anniversary celebration
(C) Look for a new office space
(D) Update some software

話し手たちは何をする準備を行っていますか。

(A) 協議会に出席する
(B) 記念式典を主催する
(C) 新しい事務所用のスペースを探す
(D) ソフトウエアを更新する

正解 A 男性は女性に対して、❶「明日の製造業協議会へ行く準備はできているか」と尋ね、女性は❷でそれを肯定している。その後も 2 人はその協議会について話し合っているので、(A)が正解。prepare to do「～する準備を行う」。
(B) host「～を主催する」、anniversary「記念日、記念行事」、celebration「式典」。
(C) look for ～「～を探す」、office「事務所」、space「スペース、場所」。
(D) update「～を更新する」。

---

33 Where do the speakers work?

(A) At an airline
(B) At a factory
(C) At a university
(D) At a hotel

話し手たちはどこで働いていますか。

(A) 航空会社
(B) 工場
(C) 大学
(D) ホテル

正解 B 女性は自分たちが参加予定の協議会について、❸「うちのような工場向けの新技術がたくさんある」と言及している。❸の所有代名詞oursはour factoryを表しているので、話し手たちは工場で働いていると判断できる。
(A) airline「航空会社」。
(C) university「大学」。

---

34 What does the man say he is interested in doing?

(A) Joining the board of an association
(B) Meeting a company president
(C) Choosing some designs
(D) Learning about the history of an industry

男性は何をしたいと言っていますか。

(A) 協会の委員会に参加すること
(B) 会社の社長と会うこと
(C) デザインを選択すること
(D) 産業の歴史について学ぶこと

正解 D 男性は❹「私は金曜日の講演にも出席したいと思っている——製造業の歴史に関するものだ」と述べ、続けて❺「製造が時とともにどのように変化してきたかということについてもっと知りたい」と言っている。よって、(D)が正解。製造業のことを(D)ではan industryと表している。industry「産業、業界」。
(A) join「～に参加する」、board「委員会、重役会」、association「協会」。
(B) president「社長」。
(C) choose「～を選択する」。

Words & Phrases

be ready to do　～する準備ができている　　travel to ～　～へ行く　　manufacturing　製造業
convention　協議会　　participate　参加する　　technology　科学技術、テクノロジー　　get a glimpse　垣間見る
first-hand　じかの　　demonstration　実演　　be interested in doing　～したいと思っている、～することに関心を抱いている
lecture　講演　　production　製造　　over time　時がたつにつれて

Questions 35 through 37 refer to the following conversation.

W Thanks for coming today, Jerome. ❶Can you tell me why you're interested in the job delivering auto parts for us?

M Well, ❷I like the fact that it's full-time. That's what I'm looking for.

W Good! ❸We need people full-time to keep up with customer expectations. ❹Fast service is really important to them. We can usually deliver parts within two hours of ordering.

M I see. Now, ❺I'm not certified as a commercial driver. Is that a problem?

W No, a regular driver's license is all you need.

問題35-37は次の会話に関するものです。

今日は来てくれてありがとう、Jerome。あなたがなぜ当社の自動車部品の配達の仕事に関心があるのか教えてもらえますか。

そうですね、私は常勤だという事実を好ましく思っています。それが、私が探しているものなんです。

よかったです！当社では、顧客の期待に応え続けるために常勤の人材を必要としています。顧客にとっては迅速なサービスが極めて重要なのです。当社は通常、注文2時間以内に部品を配達することが可能です。

なるほど。ところで、私は商業用ドライバーの免許を持っていません。それは問題ですか。

いいえ、必要なのは通常の運転免許証のみです。

35 What does the man say he likes about a job?

(A) It has opportunities for promotion.
(B) It is a full-time position.
(C) It has a high starting salary.
(D) It includes extensive training.

男性は、職について何を気に入っていると言っていますか。

(A) 昇進の機会がある。
(B) 常勤の職である。
(C) 初任給が高い。
(D) 広範な研修を含んでいる。

正解 B 女性が❶で、男性が配達の仕事に関心を持つ理由を尋ねているのに対し、男性は❷「私は常勤だという事実を好ましく思っている」と答え、続けてそれが自分が探しているものだと補足している。よって、(B)が正解。position「職」。
(A) opportunity「機会」、promotion「昇進」。
(C) starting salary「初任給」。
(D) include「～を含む」、extensive「広範な」、training「研修」。

36 According to the woman, what do customers expect?

(A) Extended warranties
(B) Low prices
(C) Online assistance
(D) Quick delivery

女性によると、顧客は何を期待していますか。

(A) 長期保証
(B) 低価格
(C) オンラインサポート
(D) 迅速な配達

正解 D 女性は❸で、顧客の期待に応え続けるために常勤の人材が必要だと伝え、❹「彼らにとっては迅速なサービスが極めて重要だ。当社は通常、注文2時間以内に部品を配達することが可能だ」と補足している。❹のthemは顧客を示している。よって、(D)が正解。expect「～を期待する」。
(A) extended「長期にわたる」、warranty「保証」。
(C) assistance「援助、支援」。

37 What is the man concerned about?

(A) Providing his own tools
(B) Learning a software program
(C) Having a required license
(D) Processing customer payments

男性は何について心配していますか。

(A) 自前の道具を用意すること
(B) ソフトウエアプログラムの知識を身に付けること
(C) 必須の免許を有していること
(D) 顧客の支払いを処理すること

正解 C 男性はNow「ところで」と話題を転換してから、❺「私は商業用ドライバーの免許を持っていない。それは問題か」と尋ねている。よって、男性は自分が仕事に必要な免許を持っているかどうかを心配していると判断できるので、(C)が正解。be concerned about ～「～について心配している」。required「必須の」、license「免許、認可」。
(A) provide「～を用意する」、tool「道具」。
(D) process「～を処理する」、payment「支払い」。

Words & Phrases
be interested in ～ ～に関心がある   auto 自動車 ★automobileの略   part 部品
the fact that ～ ～という事実   full-time 常勤の   look for ～ ～を探す   keep up with ～ ～に遅れずについていく
expectation 期待   important 重要な   within ～以内に   certify ～ as … ～を…として認定する
commercial 商業用の   regular 通常の   driver's license 運転免許証
～ is all you need （あなたが）必要なのは～だけです ★直訳は「～があなたが必要とするところの全てです」

Questions 38 through 40 refer to the following conversation.

M Patricia, ❶I know you just came back from a negotiation meeting with the company we're merging with. ❷Has it been decided which company's name will be used once we've merged?

W Actually, ❸we're going to go with a new name: Timvale's Stores. ❹It's a combination of the existing company names—Tim's Natural Foods, and Valeton Supermarkets.

M That's a clever idea. Oh, and ❺are there plans for a new logo? ❻I'd be happy to design one.

問題38-40は次の会話に関するものです。

Patricia、当社が合併予定の会社との交渉会議から戻ってこられたところですよね。合併したらどちらの社名が使われることになるか、決定されましたか。

実は、私たちはTimvale's Stores社という新名称でいく予定です。今ある社名——Tim's自然食品社とValetonスーパーマーケット——を組み合わせたものです。

それは賢いアイデアですね。ああ、それから、新しいロゴの構想はありますか。私は喜んでそれをデザインしますよ。

38 What are the speakers mainly discussing?

(A) A business merger
(B) A hiring event
(C) A training process
(D) A building renovation

話し手たちは主に何について話し合っていますか。

(A) 会社の合併
(B) 雇用イベント
(C) 研修の過程
(D) 建物の改装

正解 A 男性は❶「あなたは、当社が合併予定の会社との交渉会議から戻ってきたところだね」と女性に言った後、❷で、合併後に使われる社名について尋ねている。これに対し、女性は❸で、採用予定の新社名を伝え、以降でも合併に関連した話を続けている。よって、(A)が正解。mainly「主に」。business「会社、店」、merger「合併」。
(B) hiring「雇用」。
(C) training「研修」、process「過程、進行」。
(D) renovation「改装」。

39 What will Timvale's Stores most likely sell?

(A) Clothing
(B) Food
(C) Electronics
(D) Sporting goods

Timvale's Stores社は何を販売すると考えられますか。

(A) 衣料品
(B) 食品
(C) 電子機器
(D) スポーツ用品

正解 B 合併後の社名について尋ねられた女性は、❸で、Timvale's Stores社という新名称になる予定だと述べた後、❹「今ある社名——Tim's自然食品社とValetonスーパーマーケット——を組み合わせたものだ」と、新名称の由来を教えている。現在の名称から両社とも食品を扱う会社と判断でき、合併後のTimvale's Stores社も同様の業種と考えられるので、(B)が正解。
(A) clothing「衣料品」。
(C) electronics「電子機器」。
(D) goods「商品、品物」。

40 What does the man offer to do?

(A) Reserve a room
(B) Write a press release
(C) Contact a local official
(D) Design a logo

男性は何をすると申し出ていますか。

(A) 部屋を予約する
(B) 報道発表文書を作成する
(C) 地元の当局者に連絡する
(D) ロゴをデザインする

正解 D 男性は、新社名について聞いた後、❺で、新しいロゴの構想があるかと尋ね、続けて❻「私は喜んでそれをデザインする」と申し出ている。❻のoneはa logoを表しているため、(D)が正解。
(A) reserve「～を予約する」。
(B) press release「報道発表、プレスリリース」。
(C) official「当局者、役人」。

Words & Phrases
negotiation 交渉　merge with ～ ～と合併する　decide ～を決定する
once いったん～すると　actually 実は　go with ～ ～の線でいく、～に決める　combination 組み合わせ
existing 既存の　natural food 自然食品　clever 賢い、気の利いた　idea アイデア、考え　plan 構想
logo ロゴ　be happy to do 喜んで～する

Questions 41 through 43 refer to the following conversation with three speakers.

W Hiroshi, Alonso. ❶The tanks in the shark exhibit are due for water testing today. ❷Alonso, do you know how to do the testing?

M ❸I've watched other people do it with the sea turtle tanks, but I've never done it myself before. Hiroshi, can you help me with that?

M Sure. Then we can split the cleaning tasks.

W Sounds great. ❹Try to finish with that by one o'clock, and let me know if you need extra help. ❺I'll need you both for tours this afternoon. We have a large group coming from San Diego.

問題41-43は3人の話し手による次の会話に関するものです。

Hiroshi、Alonso。サメ展示場の水槽は今日、水質検査の予定です。Alonso、あなたは検査の仕方を知っていますか。

他の人がウミガメの水槽でするのを見たことはありますが、これまでに自分でしたことはありません。Hiroshi、それに関して私を手伝ってもらえますか。

もちろんです。その後、私たちは清掃作業を分担すればいいですね。

いいと思います。1時までにそれを完了するようにして、追加の人手が必要なら私に知らせてください。今日の午後の見学ツアーのために、あなたたち2人ともが必要になります。サンディエゴから大人数の団体が来館するのです。

---

41 Where do the speakers most likely work?

(A) At an aquarium
(B) At a pet store
(C) At a botanical garden
(D) At a farm

話し手たちはどこで働いていると考えられますか。

(A) 水族館
(B) ペットショップ
(C) 植物園
(D) 農場

正解 A 女性は❶「サメ展示場の水槽は今日、水質検査の予定だ」と男性2人に声を掛け、❷で1人目の男性に、検査方法を把握しているか尋ねている。また、❺では予定されている見学ツアーに言及している。以上より、3人は水族館で働いていると考えられる。aquarium「水族館」。
(B) 生き物への言及はあるが、団体客のための見学ツアーが行われると述べられているので不適切。
(C) botanical garden「植物園」。
(D) farm「農場」。

---

42 What task does Alonso say he has never done before?

(A) Heater adjustments
(B) Plant fertilization
(C) Water testing
(D) Animal feeding

Alonsoは、これまでに何の作業をしたことがないと言っていますか。

(A) 暖房装置の調節
(B) 植物への施肥
(C) 水質検査
(D) 動物への給餌

正解 C ❷で、水質検査の方法を知っているかとAlonsoに対して女性が尋ね、Alonsoは❸「他の人がウミガメの水槽でするのを見たことはあるが、これまでに自分でしたことはない」と、水質検査の作業が未経験であることを伝えている。よって、(C)が正解。
(A) heater「暖房装置」、adjustment「調節」。
(B) plant「植物」、fertilization「施肥」。
(D) feeding「給餌」。

---

43 Why do the men need to finish their tasks by 1:00?

(A) They have a lunch break.
(B) They have to give some tours.
(C) They have to conduct an inspection.
(D) A facility is closing early.

男性たちはなぜ、1時までに自分たちの作業を終える必要があるのですか。

(A) 彼らは昼休憩を取る。
(B) 彼らは見学ツアーを行わなければならない。
(C) 彼らは検査を実施しなければならない。
(D) 施設が早く閉まる予定である。

正解 B 女性は❹で1時までに作業を終えるよう男性たちに言った後、❺「今日の午後の見学ツアーのために、あなたたち2人ともが必要になる」と伝えている。よって、男性たちは見学ツアーを行うために1時までに作業を終える必要があると判断できるので、(B)が正解。
(A) lunch break「昼休み」。
(C) 水質検査は1時までに終えるべき作業であり、その後の予定ではない。conduct「～を実施する」、inspection「検査」。
(D) facility「施設、設備」、close「終業する」。

Words & Phrases

tank 水槽　shark サメ　exhibit 展示　be due for ~ ～の予定である　testing 検査
sea turtle ウミガメ　myself 自分で　help ~ with … …に関して～を手伝う　split ～を分担する、～を分ける
cleaning 清掃　try to do ～しようと努める　finish with ~ ～を完了する　extra 追加の　tour 見学ツアー

Questions 44 through 46 refer to the following conversation.

W David, I just talked to the manager of Benton Department Store. ❶There's been a change, so the grand opening of their new location will now be on April tenth, not April third.

M But ❷we've already printed more than half of the posters and promotional materials they requested.

W I know. The manager's going to send us the proofs with the new information and ❸agreed to pay for the extra printing work. But ❹everything needs to be ready by tomorrow.

M Well, ❺I thought we wouldn't have much work to do tonight, so Linda's the only one scheduled to come in.

W OK, I'll start making some calls.

問題44-46は次の会話に関するものです。

David、私はたった今、Benton百貨店の支配人と話をしました。変更があって、先方の新店舗のオープン記念イベントは、4月3日ではなく4月10日になります。

でも、私たちはすでに、先方が依頼したポスターや宣伝資材の半数以上を印刷してしまいました。

分かっています。支配人は新しい情報が載っている校正刷りを送ってくれるそうで、追加の印刷作業代を支払うことに同意してくれました。でも、明日までに全部仕上がっている必要があります。

ええと、今夜する作業はあまりないだろうと思っていたので、出勤予定なのはLindaだけです。

分かりました、幾つか電話をかけ始めることにします。

44 What has changed about an event?
(A) The date
(B) The location
(C) The time
(D) The cost

イベントについて何が変更になりましたか。
(A) 日程
(B) 場所
(C) 時間
(D) 費用

正解 **A** 女性は、Benton百貨店の支配人と話をしたところだと話を切り出してから、❶「変更があって、先方の新店舗のオープン記念イベントは、4月3日ではなく4月10日になる」と日程の変更を知らせている。❶のnowは「今や〜」という意味で、変更になったことを強調して伝えている。
(B) (C) いずれも変更点として言及されていない。
(D) 追加作業分の支払いについて言及はあるが、イベントの変更点ではない。cost「費用」。

45 Where do the speakers most likely work?
(A) At a restaurant
(B) At a print shop
(C) At an art gallery
(D) At an event planning agency

話し手たちはどこで働いていると考えられますか。
(A) レストラン
(B) 印刷所
(C) 画廊
(D) イベント企画代理店

正解 **B** イベントの変更点を聞いた男性は、❷で、依頼されたポスターや宣伝資材の半数以上を印刷してしまったと述べている。また、女性は❸で、追加の印刷作業代の支払いに顧客の同意を得たことを知らせている。よって、2人は印刷所で働いていると判断できる。print shop「印刷所」。
(C) art gallery「画廊、美術館」。
(D) planning「企画立案」、agency「代理店」。

46 What does the man mean when he says, "Linda's the only one scheduled to come in"?
(A) Linda is responsible for creating the schedule.
(B) Linda has been trained to do certain tasks.
(C) There is an error on the schedule.
(D) More workers are needed.

"Linda's the only one scheduled to come in"という発言で、男性は何を意図していますか。
(A) Lindaは予定作成の責任者である。
(B) Lindaは、特定の作業ができるよう研修を受けた。
(C) 予定表に誤りがある。
(D) もっと多くの作業者が必要である。

正解 **D** ❹で、明日までに全部仕上がっている必要があると告げる女性に対し、男性は❺「今夜する作業はあまりないだろうと思っていたので」と理由を述べてから、下線部の発言で、出勤予定なのはLindaのみだと知らせている。よって、男性は、今夜行う追加作業のためにもっと多くの作業者が必要だと暗に伝えていると判断できる。
(A) be responsible for 〜「〜に責任がある」、create「〜を作成する」。
(B) train 〜 to do「…できるよう〜を教育する」、certain「特定の」。

Words & Phrases
manager 支配人　department store 百貨店
grand opening オープン記念イベント、グランドオープン　location 場所、所在地　print 〜を印刷する
more than 〜 〜よりも多く　promotional 宣伝の、販売促進の　material 資材、資料　request 〜を要望する
proofs 校正刷り　agree to do 〜することに同意する　pay for 〜 〜の代金を支払う　extra 追加の、余分の
(be) scheduled to do 〜することが予定されている　come in 出勤する　start doing 〜し始める　make a call 電話をかける

Questions 47 through 49 refer to the following conversation.

問題47-49は次の会話に関するものです。

W ❶Someone from the movie studio called about getting a copy of the script. **Are we finished with the final draft?**

映画スタジオの方が、台本の入手について電話してきました。私たちは最終稿を完成させていますか。

M No, I'm afraid ❷some of the scenes have to be rewritten.

いいえ、あいにく一部のシーンは書き直しが必要です。

W Well, ❸I'm concerned that'll cause a delay in production if it takes much longer. **When do you think the final draft will be ready?**

うーん、それに大幅に長く時間がかかった場合、製作の遅れにつながることが心配です。最終稿はいつ用意できると思いますか。

M I don't know. ❹I've scheduled a meeting with the writers today to check on their progress. I'll forward you the details so you can join.

分かりません。進捗を確かめるため、今日、執筆者たちとの会議の予定を組んでいます。あなたも同席できるよう、詳細を送ります。

---

47 Which industry do the speakers most likely work in?

(A) Fashion
(B) Real estate
(C) Tourism
(D) Entertainment

話し手たちはどの業界で働いていると考えられますか。

(A) ファッション
(B) 不動産
(C) 観光
(D) エンターテインメント

正解 D 女性は❶「映画スタジオの人が、台本の入手について電話してきた」と話を切り出し、続けて台本の進捗について男性に確認している。また、男性は❷でシーンの書き直しに言及し、その後も2人は製作の遅延の可能性などについて話している。よって、2人は映画製作関連のエンターテインメント業界で働いていると考えられる。entertainment「エンターテインメント、娯楽」。
(B) real estate「不動産」。
(C) tourism「観光業」。

48 What is the woman concerned about?

(A) The quality of a product
(B) The effect on the environment
(C) An increase in costs
(D) A delay in production

女性は何について心配していますか。

(A) 製品の品質
(B) 環境への影響
(C) 諸経費の増加
(D) 製作の遅れ

正解 D 台本が一部書き直しの必要があると知った女性は、❸「それに大幅に長く時間がかかった場合、製作の遅れにつながることが心配だ」と懸念点を伝えている。よって、(D)が正解。be concerned about ～「～について心配している」。
(A) quality「質」、product「製品」。
(B) effect「影響」、environment「環境」。
(C) increase「増加」、costs「諸経費」。

49 What does the man say he did?

(A) He bought some supplies.
(B) He tested some equipment.
(C) He scheduled a meeting.
(D) He read some reviews.

男性は何をしたと言っていますか。

(A) 彼は必需品を購入した。
(B) 彼は機器のテストをした。
(C) 彼は会議の予定を組んだ。
(D) 彼はレビューを読んだ。

正解 C 男性は、台本の最終稿の仕上がり時期について分からないと答えた後、❹「進捗を確かめるため、今日、執筆者たちとの会議の予定を組んでいる」と、会議を設定したことを知らせている。よって、(C)が正解。
(A) supplies「必需品」。
(B) test「～のテストをする」、equipment「機器」。
(D) review「レビュー、批評」。

Words & Phrases

movie studio 映画スタジオ script 台本 be finished with ～ ～を終えている
final draft 最終稿 I'm afraid (that) ～ あいにく～だ、残念ながら～だと思う scene (映画などの)シーン
rewrite ～を書き直す be concerned (that) ～ ～ということを心配している cause ～を引き起こす delay 遅延
production 製作 take ～(時間)がかかる schedule ～の予定を組む check on ～ ～を確かめる progress 進捗
forward ～ … ～に…を送る、～に…を転送する details 詳細情報

Questions 50 through 52 refer to the following conversation.

問題50-52は次の会話に関するものです。

M Heidi, ❶is everything on the truck?

Heidi、全部トラックに積まれていますか。

W ❷Yes, we're finished here. And let's see what our next job is. OK, so ❸we're driving to New York to help a second family box and load their possessions onto this same truck before we transport them.

はい、ここの作業は終わっています。ですので、私たちの次の作業が何か確認しましょう。よし、ええと、私たちはニューヨークまで運転して、2件目の家族の家財道具の箱詰めとこの同じトラックへの積み込みを手伝ってから、それらを運ぶことになっています。

M ❹In that case, we should shift all of these items to the back of the truck, so they won't get mixed up with the next customer's possessions.

それなら、これらの物品は全てトラックの奥に移動させた方がいいですね。そうすると次の顧客の家財道具と混同しないでしょうから。

W Actually, ❺I think we should keep the furniture on either side of the truck and the boxes in the middle to balance the load.

実のところ、積み荷のバランスを取るため、家具をトラックのどちらの側にも載せ、箱を中央に載せた方がいいと思います。

50 What does the woman confirm to the man?

(A) A job has been completed.
(B) Some workers have arrived.
(C) Some equipment is available.
(D) A vehicle has been repaired.

女性は男性に対して何を確かだと言っていますか。

(A) 作業が完了している。
(B) 作業員が到着している。
(C) 機器が利用可能である。
(D) 車両が修理された。

正解 A ❶で、全てトラックに積まれているかと尋ねる男性に対し、女性は❷で、Yesと肯定し、現在地での作業が終了していることを伝えている。よって、作業が完了した状態であることを現在完了形で表している(A)が正解。confirm「~を確かだと言う、~を確証する」。
(B) worker「作業員」、arrive「到着する」。
(C) equipment「機器」、available「利用できる」。
(D) vehicle「車両」、repair「~を修理する」。

51 What type of business do the speakers most likely work for?

(A) A furniture factory
(B) A car dealership
(C) A home appliance store
(D) A moving company

話し手たちはどんな種類の会社に勤務していると考えられますか。

(A) 家具工場
(B) 車の販売代理店
(C) 家庭用電化製品店
(D) 引越会社

正解 D 女性は❸「私たちはニューヨークまで運転して、2件目の家族の家財道具の箱詰めとこの同じトラックへの積み込みを手伝ってから、それらを運ぶことになっている」と、荷造りや運搬作業について述べている。その後も2人はトラックの積み荷の位置について話し合っている。よって、2人は引越会社に勤務していると判断できる。business「会社、事業者」。moving「引っ越し」。
(A) 家具への言及はあるが、工場に関することは述べられていない。
(B) dealership「販売代理店」。
(C) home appliance「家庭用電化製品」。

52 What do the speakers disagree about?

(A) When to take a break
(B) How to arrange some items
(C) What price to charge
(D) How long a delivery will take

話し手たちは何について意見が食い違っていますか。

(A) 休憩を取るべき時
(B) 物品の配置方法
(C) 請求すべき金額
(D) 配達の見込み所要時間

正解 B 男性は❹で、荷物の混同を避けるために今ある物品を全てトラックの奥に移動させることを提案しているのに対し、女性は❺で、「積み荷のバランスを取るため、家具をトラックのどちらの側にも載せ、箱を中央に載せた方がいいと思う」と述べており、積み荷の位置について2人の意見が異なっている。よって、(B)が正解。disagree「意見が食い違う」。arrange「~を配置する」。
(A) take a break「休憩を取る」。
(C) price「価格」、charge「~を請求する」。

Words & Phrases

be finished 終わっている　drive to ~ ~へ車で行く　box ~を箱に詰める　load ~を積む　possessions 所有物、財産　transport ~を輸送する　in that case その場合　shift ~を移動させる　item 物品　back 奥、後部　get mixed up with ~ ~と混ざる　furniture 家具　either 〈2つで1対の語と共に〉どちらの~も　middle 中央部　balance ~のバランスを取る　load 積み荷

Questions 53 through 55 refer to the following conversation.

🇨🇦 M Zoya, I've reviewed the quarterly report from the sales group for our line of sports shoes. ❶Our company's attracted a large number of new customers. I'm impressed.

🇬🇧 W Well, I spent a lot of time putting together my advertising team.

🇨🇦 M Now—the report also indicates that we've had more returns as well. ❷Customers who are more serious runners have complained that there isn't enough arch support in the running shoes.

🇬🇧 W You know, we make arch-support inserts, and most of our stores carry them. ❸I'll make sure we ship them to every retail location.

問題53-55は次の会話に関するものです。

Zoya、当社の運動靴シリーズに関する販売グループの四半期報告書を詳しく見ました。当社は大勢の新規顧客を引き付けていますね。私は感心しています。

ええ、私は自分の広告チームをまとめるのに膨大な時間を費やしました。

ところで――その報告書は、返品も同様に増えていることを示しています。より熱心なランナーの顧客たちは、ランニングシューズのアーチサポートが十分ではないと不満を言っています。

ご存じの通り、当社はアーチサポートの中敷きを作っており、当社の店舗の大半がそれらを取り扱っています。必ずそれらを各小売店舗に出荷するようにします。

---

53 Why does the woman say, "I spent a lot of time putting together my advertising team"?
- (A) To explain a success
- (B) To express surprise
- (C) To recommend a policy change
- (D) To complain about a management decision

女性はなぜ "I spent a lot of time putting together my advertising team" と言っていますか。
- (A) 成功の理由を説明するため
- (B) 驚きを表明するため
- (C) 方針変更を勧めるため
- (D) 経営陣の決定について不満を言うため

正解 A 男性は四半期報告書を見て、❶「当社は大勢の新規顧客を引き付けている。私は感心している」と褒めている。これに対し、女性は下線部の発言で、自分が広告チームをまとめるのに膨大な時間を費やしたと言っているので、女性は販売業績が好調な理由を説明しているのだと判断できる。explain「～の理由を説明する」。
- (B) express「～を表明する」、surprise「驚き」。
- (C) recommend「～を推奨する」、policy「方針」。
- (D) complain about ~「～について不満を言う」、management「経営陣」、decision「決定」。

54 What problem does the man mention?
- (A) Inaccurate inventory
- (B) Material shortages
- (C) Customer complaints
- (D) A lack of qualified staff

男性はどんな問題について述べていますか。
- (A) 不正確な在庫目録
- (B) 材料の不足
- (C) 顧客の不満
- (D) 適任の従業員の不足

正解 C 男性は返品の増加に触れた後、❷「より熱心なランナーの顧客たちは、ランニングシューズのアーチサポートが十分ではないと不満を言っている」と顧客からの不満に言及している。complaint「不満、クレーム」。
- (A) inaccurate「不正確な」、inventory「在庫目録」。
- (B) material「材料」、shortage「不足」。
- (D) lack「不足」、qualified「適任の、資格のある」。

55 What does the woman offer to do?
- (A) Coordinate some shipments
- (B) Contact a design specialist
- (C) Look for a new vendor
- (D) Organize some training sessions

女性は何をすることを申し出ていますか。
- (A) 出荷品の手配をする
- (B) 設計の専門家に連絡する
- (C) 新しい販売業者を探す
- (D) 研修会を計画する

正解 A 女性は自社のアーチサポートの中敷きに言及し、❸「必ずそれらを各小売店舗に出荷するようにする」と申し出ている。❸のthemはarch-support insertsを指す。この内容をcoordinate「～をまとめ上げる、～の調整を行う」とshipment「出荷(品)」を用いて表した(A)が正解。
- (B) design「設計」、specialist「専門家」。
- (C) look for「～を探す」、vendor「販売業者」。
- (D) organize「～(企画・催し)を計画する」。

Words & Phrases

review ～を精査する　　quarterly 四半期の　　line 製品シリーズ　　attract ～を引き付ける
a large number of ~ 多数の～　　impress ～を感動させる、～に感銘を与える　　spend ~ doing ～を…するのに費やす
put together ~ ～をまとめる　　indicate that ~ ～ということを示す　　returns 返品　　as well 同様に　　serious 本気の
complain that ~ ～であると不満を言う　　arch support アーチサポート　　★arch「土踏まず」の部分を支える芯材
insert 挿入物　　carry ～(商品)を取り扱う　　make sure (that) ~ 必ず～であるようにする　　ship ～を出荷する

TEST2 PART 3

Questions 56 through 58 refer to the following conversation with three speakers.

問題56-58は3人の話し手による次の会話に関するものです。

M Noriko and Helen, ❶I have something exciting to tell you. ❷Jones Accounting has expressed serious interest in acquiring our firm. And our asking price won't be a problem.

NorikoとHelen、あなたたちに伝えるとてもうれしいことがあります。Jones会計事務所が当社を買収することに真剣な関心を表明しています。さらに、当社の提示価格も問題にはならないようです。

W That's great, but—Jones Accounting? Isn't their headquarters in London?

それは素晴らしい、でも——Jones会計事務所ですか。そこの本社はロンドンにあるのではないですか。

W Yes, ❸we'll have to move our office to London if Jones acquires us, won't we? ❹I'm not sure our staff would want to make that commute.

そう、Jones事務所が当社を買収すれば、当社のオフィスをロンドンに移転しなければならなくなりますよね？うちの従業員がそんな通勤をしたがるかは分かりませんよ。

W ❺I agree.

同感です。

M Well, a lot of our work can be done remotely. If we decide to go through with the acquisition, I can put together a presentation for our staff. ❻Would you two be willing to look it over and let me know what you think?

そうですね、私たちの業務の多くは遠隔でもできます。当社がこの買収をやり通すことにした場合は、私が従業員向けの説明を取りまとめようと思います。あなたたちお2人はそれに目を通した上で考えを教えてくれますか。

56 What news does the man share?

(A) The company may be purchased.
(B) Research funding has been approved.
(C) A client wants to buy additional services.
(D) A new CEO was hired.

男性はどんな知らせを伝えていますか。

(A) 会社が買収される可能性がある。
(B) 研究のための資金調達が承認された。
(C) 顧客が追加のサービスの購入を望んでいる。
(D) 新しい最高経営責任者が雇用された。

正解 A 男性は❶で女性2人に対して、うれしい知らせがあると前置きした後、❷「Jones会計事務所が当社を買収することに真剣な関心を表明している」と述べている。よって、話し手たちの会社をthe companyと表し、❷のacquiringをpurchase「～を買収する」を用いて表現した(A)が正解。share「～を伝える」。
(B) funding「資金調達」、approve「～を承認する」。
(D) CEO「最高経営責任者（chief executive officerの略）」、hire「～を雇用する」。

57 Why are the women concerned?

(A) A process is too complicated.
(B) A cost may increase.
(C) A location is inconvenient.
(D) An audit deadline is approaching.

女性たちはなぜ心配しているのですか。

(A) 手続きが複雑過ぎる。
(B) 費用が増す可能性がある。
(C) 場所が不便である。
(D) 会計監査の期限が近づいている。

正解 C 2人目の女性は❸で、買収された場合、オフィスをロンドンに移転する必要があるだろうと指摘した後、❹「うちの従業員がそんな通勤をしたがるかは分からない」と場所についての懸念点を伝え、1人目の女性が❺でそれに同意している。よって、(C)が正解。inconvenient「不便な」。
(A) process「手続き」、complicated「複雑な」。
(D) audit「会計監査」、deadline「最終期限」、approach「近づく」。

58 What does the man want the women to do?

(A) Update a schedule
(B) Sign some documents
(C) Provide some feedback
(D) Check an industry requirement

男性は、女性たちに何をしてほしいと思っていますか。

(A) 予定表を更新する
(B) 書類に署名する
(C) 意見を提供する
(D) 業界の要件を確認する

正解 C 2人の懸念を聞いた男性は、買収を進める場合は、自分が従業員向けの説明を取りまとめると伝えた後、❻「あなたたち2人はそれに目を通した上で考えを教えてくれるか」と女性たちに頼んでいる。よって、❻のlet me know what you thinkをprovide some feedbackと表している(C)が正解。provide「～を提供する」。
(A) update「～を更新する」。
(B) sign「～に署名する」、document「書類」。
(D) industry「業界」、requirement「要件」。

Questions 59 through 61 refer to the following conversation.

問題59-61は次の会話に関するものです。

🇬🇧 W Welcome to Frank's Lumber Yard. How can I help you?

Frank's木材販売店へようこそ。どのようなご用件でしょうか。

🇦🇺 M Hi, ❶I'm preparing to build a wooden dining table for a client who placed a custom order, and I need a large slab of oak.

こんにちは、私は、特注をした顧客用の木製ダイニングテーブルを作る準備をしているところで、オーク材の大きな平板が1枚必要なのです。

🇬🇧 W OK, I can show you what we have.

かしこまりました、当店の在庫をお見せいたしますね。

🇦🇺 M Great, and ❷my client would prefer wood that has been produced using environmentally sustainable methods.

いいですね、それから、私の顧客は環境面で持続可能な方法で生産された木材を望んでいます。

🇬🇧 W ❸We usually carry reclaimed lumber, but we don't have any in stock right now. ❹I'm sorry about that. Can you wait a week?

当店は通常、再生木材を取り扱っていますが、ちょうど今は在庫を切らしております。申し訳ございません。1週間お待ちいただけますか。

59 Who most likely is the man?

(A) An engineer
(B) A forest ranger
(C) A restaurant owner
(D) A furniture maker

男性は誰だと考えられますか。

(A) 技師
(B) 森林監視員
(C) レストランの所有者
(D) 家具製作者

正解 **D** 木材販売店へ来店している男性は、❶「私は、特注をした顧客用の木製ダイニングテーブルを作る準備をしているところで、オーク材の大きな平板が1枚必要だ」と希望の木材の種類を伝えている。このことから、男性は家具の製作者だと考えられる。furniture「家具」、maker「製作者、製造業者」。
(A) engineer「技師、エンジニア」。
(B) forest ranger「森林監視員」。
(C) owner「所有者、オーナー」。

60 What does the man say is important about a product?

(A) That it is affordable
(B) That it is durable
(C) That it is environmentally friendly
(D) That it is easy to use

男性は、製品について何が大切だと言っていますか。

(A) 金銭的に手頃であること
(B) 耐久性があること
(C) 環境に優しいこと
(D) 使用しやすいこと

正解 **C** 男性は希望の木材の種類を述べた後、❷「私の顧客は環境面で持続可能な方法で生産された木材を望んでいる」と、製品について要望を述べている。❷のenvironmentally sustainableをenvironmentally friendly「環境に優しい」と表した(C)が正解。
(A) affordable「金銭的に手頃な」。
(B) durable「耐久性のある」。

61 Why does the woman apologize?

(A) A delivery service is not offered.
(B) A storage area is far away.
(C) An item is unavailable.
(D) A price tag is incorrect.

女性はなぜ謝っているのですか。

(A) 配達サービスが提供されていない。
(B) 保管場所が遠く離れている。
(C) 品物の在庫がない。
(D) 値札が誤っている。

正解 **C** 環境面で持続可能な方法で生産された木材を希望する男性に対し、女性は❸「当店は通常、再生木材を取り扱っているが、ちょうど今は在庫を切らしている」と伝えた後、❹で謝罪している。よって、❸のreclaimed lumberをan item「ある品物」と、在庫がない状態をunavailable「入手不可能な」と表している(C)が正解。apologize「謝罪する」。
(A) delivery「配達」、offer「〜を提供する」。
(B) storage「保管」、area「場所」。
(D) price tag「値札」、incorrect「誤った」。

Words & Phrases

lumber yard　材木置き場　　prepare to *do*　〜する準備を行う　　build　〜を作る
wooden　木製の　　place a custom order　特別注文をする　　slab　平板　　oak　オーク材　　prefer　〜の方を好む
produce　〜を生産する　　environmentally　環境面で　　sustainable　持続可能な　　method　方法
carry　〜(商品)を取り扱う　　reclaim　〜を再生利用する　　lumber　木材　　in stock　在庫があって

Questions 62 through 64 refer to the following conversation and weather report.

問題62-64は次の会話と天気予報に関するものです。

W Well, it looks like we're going to be busy on the farm today covering up the crops! ❶It's supposed to drop to negative twelve degrees tomorrow.

さて、今日は農場で作物を覆うのに忙しくなりそうですね! 明日はマイナス12度にまで下がる見通しです。

M ❷I saw that. It sounds like tomorrow would be a good day for me to go to the bank. But we've got a lot to do to get the crops covered today.

私もそれを見ました。明日は私にとって、銀行へ行くのにちょうどいい日になりそうです。でも、私たちは今日、作物を覆うのにすべきことがたくさんありますね。

W ❸I knew it was a risk to plant some of these vegetables when we did. ❹Now I'm wishing we had waited until later.

これらの野菜の一部を植えたとき、リスクがあると分かっていました。今は、もっと後まで待てばよかったと思っています。

M Well, lesson learned. ❺Let's start by collecting all of our tarps so we can just drape them over the plants when it's time.

まあ、教訓を学びましたね。その時になったら野菜に覆いを掛けるだけで済むよう、当園の防水シートを全て集めることから取り掛かりましょう。

Temperatures (°C)		
	High	Low
Monday	2°	-1°
Tuesday	2°	-1°
Wednesday	2°	-12°
Thursday	-1°	-3°
Friday	9°	2°

気温（セ氏）		
	最高気温	最低気温
月曜日	2°	−1°
火曜日	2°	−1°
水曜日	2°	−12°
木曜日	−1°	−3°
金曜日	9°	2°

62 Look at the graphic. When does the man plan to go to the bank?

(A) Monday
(B) Tuesday
(C) Wednesday
(D) Thursday

図を見てください。男性はいつ銀行へ行くつもりですか。

(A) 月曜日
(B) 火曜日
(C) 水曜日
(D) 木曜日

63 What does the woman regret doing?

(A) Choosing a certain piece of equipment
(B) Planting some crops so early
(C) Cutting branches from a tree
(D) Not watering plants well enough

女性は何をしたことを後悔していますか。

(A) 特定の機器を選択したこと
(B) 早々と作物を植えたこと
(C) 木から枝を切り落としたこと
(D) 植物に十分に水やりをしなかったこと

64 What does the man suggest doing?

(A) Gathering materials
(B) Making a new calendar
(C) Looking at different locations
(D) Harvesting everything possible

男性は何をすることを提案していますか。

(A) 資材を集めること
(B) 新しい日程表を作成すること
(C) さまざまな場所を調べること
(D) 可能な限り全てを収穫すること

Words & Phrases

weather report 天気予報　it looks like ～　～のようである　busy *doing* ～するのに忙しい
cover up ～　～を覆う　crops 作物、収穫物　be supposed to *do* ～することになっている　drop to ～ ～まで下がる
negative マイナスの、負の　degree （温度などの）度　it sounds like ～ ～のように思われる
have got ＝ have ★主に英国語圏で使用される口語　get ～ … ～を…の状態にする　covered 覆われた　risk 危険
plant ～を植える　wish (that) ～ 〈仮定法で過去完了の節を続けて〉～していたらよかったのにと思う　lesson 教訓
collect ～を集める　tarp 防水シート　drape ～ over … ～を…に覆いかぶせる　plant 植物
when it's time 時機が来たら

天気予報 temperature 気温、温度　℃ セ氏～度　★degree Celsiusの意味の記号で、温度の単位

Questions 65 through 67 refer to the following conversation and product samples.

M Welcome to Yamada Décor and Building Supplies. Can I help you with anything?

W Yeah, ❶I own Maria's Café. ❷I'm adding a new dining room to the restaurant, and I'd like to see some wallpaper options.

M Of course. ❸There's one wallpaper brand I recommend. ❹It's easier to clean than most other brands.

W Perfect. I'm sure we'll need to clean up food stains from time to time.

M Here are some samples. The sunflower pattern is very popular.

W Actually, ❺I like this one with the city buildings. The price may be a bit high for my budget though.

問題65-67は次の会話と製品見本に関するものです。

Yamada室内装飾用品・建築用品店へようこそ。何かご用件を承りましょうか。

お願いします、私はMaria'sカフェを所有しています。レストランに新しいダイニングルームを増設する予定でして、壁紙の選択肢を幾つか見たいと思っています。

かしこまりました。お薦めの壁紙のブランドが1つございます。それは、他の大半のブランドよりも掃除が簡単なのです。

理想的ですね。きっと、時折食べ物の染みをきれいに落とす必要が出てくるでしょうから。

こちらが見本です。ヒマワリの柄が大変人気があります。

実は、私は都市の建物が描かれているこちらのものが好きです。もっとも、その値段は私の予算に対して少し高いかもしれませんが。

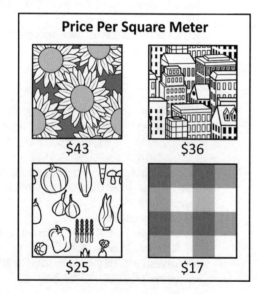

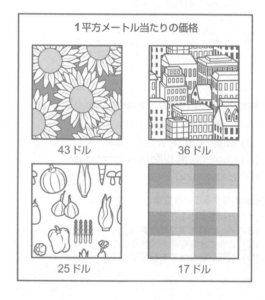

65 Who is the woman?

    (A) A painter

    (B) A restaurant owner

    (C) An interior designer

    (D) A real estate agent

女性は誰ですか。

    (A) 画家

    (B) レストランの所有者

    (C) 室内装飾家

    (D) 不動産業者

正解 B 用件を尋ねられた女性は、❶「私はMaria'sカフェを所有している」と自己紹介している。その後も❷で、レストランにダイニングルームを増設する予定であることを話している。よって、(B)が正解。owner「所有者、オーナー」。
(A) painter「画家」。
(C) 室内装飾用品店で壁紙の柄について話しているが、女性本人がデザイナーだという情報はない。interior designer「室内装飾家、インテリアデザイナー」。
(D) real estate agent「不動産業者」。

66 Why does the man recommend a product brand?

    (A) It is discounted.

    (B) It has bright colors.

    (C) It is made from recycled materials.

    (D) It is easy to clean.

男性はなぜ、ある製品ブランドを推薦しているのですか。

    (A) 割引されている。

    (B) 鮮やかな色彩である。

    (C) 再生資材からできている。

    (D) 掃除がしやすい。

正解 D 壁紙の選択肢を見たいと希望を伝える女性に対し、男性はOf course.と快諾してから、❸でお薦めの壁紙のブランドが1つあると述べている。男性は続けて、❹「それは、他の大半のブランドよりも掃除が簡単だ」とその特長を伝えているので、(D)が正解。
(A) discount「〜を割引して売る」。
(B) bright「鮮やかな」、color「色彩」。
(C) be made from 〜「〜(原料)からできている」、recycled materials「再生資材」。

67 Look at the graphic. What is the price of the pattern the woman prefers?

    (A) $43

    (B) $36

    (C) $25

    (D) $17

図を見てください。女性が好ましいと思っている柄の価格は幾らですか。

    (A) 43 ドル

    (B) 36 ドル

    (C) 25 ドル

    (D) 17 ドル

正解 B 壁紙の製品見本を見せ、ヒマワリの柄が人気であると述べる男性に対し、女性は❺「私は都市の建物が描かれているこちらのものが好きだ」と自分の好みを伝えている。製品見本の図を見ると、都市の建物を描いた柄の価格は1平方メートル当たり36ドル。よって、(B)が正解。prefer「〜をより好む」。
(A) 男性が推薦している柄の価格だが、女性はその柄を好みだとは言っていない。
(C) (D) いずれも話題に上っていない柄の価格。

Words & Phrases

sample 見本　　décor 室内装飾　　building 建築、建物　　supplies 用品、備品
help 〜 with … …に関して〜を手伝う　　own 〜を所有する　　café カフェ、喫茶店　　add 〜を追加する
wallpaper 壁紙　　option 選択肢　　recommend 〜を推薦する　　perfect 理想的な、完璧な
clean up 〜 〜をすっかりきれいにする　　stain 染み、汚れ　　from time to time 時折　　sunflower ヒマワリ
pattern 柄、模様　　a bit 少し　　budget 予算　　though もっとも〜ではあるが

製品見本 per 〜当たり　　square meter 平方メートル

Questions 68 through 70 refer to the following conversation and agenda.

W ❶I can't believe Insook Chung will be here at our bookstore on Saturday to talk about her new novel. I'm so excited!

M Me too. She's such a famous author; ❷I'm sure we'll sell a lot of copies of her book during the event.

W That reminds me—❸the extra copies we ordered for Saturday haven't been displayed yet. ❹I'll unpack the boxes after lunch.

M Oh, before you leave for lunch, ❺could you please look at the agenda for the event? Does everything look OK?

W Hmm. ❻I don't think two twenty to two thirty will be enough time; that's only ten minutes. I think it needs to be at least twice as long.

問題68-70は次の会話と予定表に関するものです。

土曜日に、Insook Chung さんが新刊小説について講演しに当書店に来るなんて信じられません。とても楽しみです！

私もです。彼女は非常に有名な作家ですから、きっと、イベントの間には彼女の本がたくさん売れるでしょうね。

それで思い出しました——私たちが土曜日に備えて発注した追加冊数分がまだ陳列されていません。私は昼食後にその箱を開けようと思います。

ああ、昼食に出る前にイベントの予定表を見ていただけますか。万事大丈夫そうですか。

うーん。2時20分から2時30分というのは十分な時間ではないと思います。それだとわずか10分ですから。少なくとも2倍の長さにする必要があると思います。

Agenda	
Introductions	2:05–2:20 P.M.
Live Reading	2:20–2:30 P.M.
Question-and-Answer Session	2:30–2:55 P.M.
Social Time and Refreshments	2:55–3:30 P.M.

予定表	
紹介	午後2時5分～2時20分
朗読実演	午後2時20分～2時30分
質疑応答の部	午後2時30分～2時55分
親睦の時間および軽食	午後2時55分～3時30分

68 Where do the speakers work?

    (A) At a bookstore
    (B) At a café
    (C) At a theater
    (D) At a library

話し手たちはどこで働いていますか。

    (A) 書店
    (B) カフェ
    (C) 劇場
    (D) 図書館

正解 A 女性は❶「土曜日に、Insook Chung さんが新刊小説について講演しに当書店に来るなんて信じられない」と述べており、男性も❷で、イベント開催中における店でのChungさんの本の売れ行きについて予測を立てている。これらのことから、2人は書店で働いていると判断できる。
(D) 書物と関連する話題だが、書籍の販売について述べられているので不適切。

69 What does the woman say she will do after lunch?

    (A) Send some invitations
    (B) Hang up some posters
    (C) Print some event tickets
    (D) Unpack some boxes

女性は昼食後に何をすると言っていますか。

    (A) 招待状を発送する
    (B) ポスターを掛ける
    (C) イベントのチケットを印刷する
    (D) 箱を開ける

正解 D 女性は❸で、土曜日に備えて発注した追加冊数分がまだ陳列されていないと述べた後、❹「私は昼食後にその箱を開けようと思う」と伝えている。よって、(D)が正解。
(A) invitation「招待状」。
(B) hang up ～「～を掛ける」、poster「ポスター」。

70 Look at the graphic. What agenda item does the woman suggest extending?

    (A) Introductions
    (B) Live Reading
    (C) Question-and-Answer Session
    (D) Social Time and Refreshments

図を見てください。女性は、どの予定事項の時間を延ばすことを提案していますか。

    (A) 紹介
    (B) 朗読実演
    (C) 質疑応答の部
    (D) 親睦の時間および軽食

正解 B ❺で、女性にイベントの予定表を見るよう頼み、万事大丈夫そうかと尋ねる男性に対し、女性は❻「2時20分から2時30分というのは十分な時間ではないと思う。それだとわずか10分だ。少なくとも2倍の長さにする必要があると思う」と意見を伝えている。予定表を見ると、2時20分から2時30分の時間枠に設定されているのは朗読実演なので、女性が時間の延長を提案しているのはこの予定事項だと分かる。item「事項、項目」、extend「～を延ばす」。
(A) (C) (D) いずれも、2時20分から2時30分の時間枠に設定されている予定事項ではない。

TEST 2 PART 3

| **Words & Phrases** | agenda 予定表、議事日程　author 作家　copy 冊、部　remind ～に思い出させる |

extra 追加の　order ～を発注する　display ～を陳列する　unpack ～を開けて中身を取り出す　enough 十分な
at least 少なくとも、最低でも　twice 2倍

予定表　introductions 紹介　live 生の　reading 朗読　question-and-answer session 質疑応答の部
    social 親睦の　refreshments 軽い飲食物

Questions 71 through 73 refer to the following broadcast.

問題71-73は次の放送に関するものです。

 W

Welcome back to the Channel 5 Evening News. I'm your host, Satomi Sato, and ❶today we're on location at the Springfield Arena. ❷Tonight is the final game of the basketball championship, and everyone's excited to see which team is going to take home the trophy. I'm here, outside of the ticket office, and there's a long line of people waiting to buy tickets. ❸I'm going to talk to several of the attendees now to hear what they think was the highlight of the season.

Channel 5 の夜のニュースへ再びようこそ。司会者のSatomi Satoです。本日はSpringfield競技場で野外収録中です。今夜はバスケットボール選手権大会の決勝戦で、どちらのチームが地元にトロフィーを持ち帰ることになるのか目にしようと、誰もが興奮しています。私はここ、チケット売り場の外にいまして、チケットを買おうと待っている人々の長い列があります。今から、来場者の何人かと話をして、今シーズンのハイライトが何だったと思うかお聞きしようと思います。

---

71 Where is the speaker?

(A) At an arena
(B) At a museum
(C) At a train station
(D) At a community center

話し手はどこにいますか。

(A) 競技場
(B) 博物館
(C) 鉄道駅
(D) コミュニティーセンター

正解 **A** 話し手は、自分が夜のニュースの司会者であると名前を述べてから、❶「本日はSpringfield競技場で野外収録中だ」と現在の状況を伝えている。よって、(A)が正解。
(B) (C) ticket officeから連想され得る点に注意。
(D) community center「コミュニティーセンター（地域社会の活動のための施設）、公民館」。

---

72 According to the speaker, why are people excited?

(A) A famous musician will perform.
(B) A championship game will be played.
(C) A new exhibition will open.
(D) A construction project will be completed.

話し手によると、人々はなぜ興奮しているのですか。

(A) 有名な音楽家が演奏する。
(B) 決勝戦が行われる。
(C) 新しい展示会が始まる。
(D) 建設事業が完了する。

正解 **B** 話し手は自分が競技場にいることを伝えた後、❷「今夜はバスケットボール選手権大会の決勝戦で、どちらのチームが地元にトロフィーを持ち帰ることになるのか目にしようと、誰もが興奮している」とリポートしている。よって、(B)が正解。championship game「決勝戦」。
(A) musician「音楽家」、perform「演奏する」。
(C) exhibition「展示会」、open「始まる」。
(D) construction「建設」、project「事業、計画」、complete「〜を完了させる」。

---

73 What will the speaker do next?

(A) Conduct some interviews
(B) Walk around a building
(C) Give away some tickets
(D) Explain a contest

話し手は次に何をしますか。

(A) インタビューを行う
(B) 建物内を歩き回る
(C) チケットを配る
(D) コンテストについて説明する

正解 **A** 話し手は、チケット購入の行列に言及した後、❸「今から、来場者の何人かと話をして、今シーズンのハイライトが何だったと思うか聞こうと思う」と、これからの流れを伝えている。よって、この内容をconduct some interviewsと表した(A)が正解。conduct「〜を行う」。
(B) walk around 〜「〜をあちこち歩き回る」。
(C) give away 〜「〜（賞品など）を配る」。
(D) contest「コンテスト、競争」。

Words & Phrases

broadcast 放送　Welcome back to 〜　〜へお帰りなさい　channel チャンネル
host 司会者　on location 野外収録中で、ロケの最中で　arena 競技場　final game 決勝戦
championship 選手権大会、決勝戦　be excited to do 〜することに興奮している　take home 〜　〜を家に持って帰る
trophy トロフィー、優勝記念品　outside of 〜　〜の外に　ticket office チケット売り場　wait to do 〜するのを待つ
several 数人、数個　attendee 出席者、参加者　highlight ハイライト、目玉　season （運動競技などの）シーズン、時期

Questions 74 through 76 refer to the following excerpt from a meeting.

問題74-76は次の会議の抜粋に関するものです。

🇨🇦 M

Good morning, everyone. ❶You've no doubt heard the good news about the big contract we signed with the Dankin Foods Corporation last week. We'll be handling all their graphic arts needs. ❷The first thing Dankin wants us to do is update the package design for all their products. ❸This is something that Diego has a lot of experience with, so I'm going to put him in charge of the project. He'll be looking for input from the rest of you, of course. ❹Please make sure your online calendars are updated so that he can schedule team meetings.

おはようございます、皆さん。皆さんはきっと、当社が先週Dankin食品社と結んだ大口契約についての吉報をお聞き及びでしょう。当社は、先方のグラフィックアートのニーズ全てに対応することになります。Dankin社が当社にまず第一に求めているのは、先方の全製品の包装デザインを新しくすることです。これはDiegoが経験豊富な分野なので、私は彼にプロジェクトの責任者を任せるつもりです。当然ながら、彼は、残りの皆さんからの意見を求めることになるでしょう。彼がチーム会議の予定を組むことができるよう、皆さんのオンライン日程表が最新の状態になっているようにしておいてください。

74 What did the company do last week?
(A) It adopted a new inventory system.
(B) It hosted a professional conference.
(C) It signed an important contract.
(D) It hired several employees.

会社は先週、何をしましたか。
(A) 新しい在庫管理システムを採用した。
(B) 専門家の協議会を主催した。
(C) 重要な契約を結んだ。
(D) 数名の従業員を雇用した。

正解 C 話し手は聞き手にあいさつした後、❶で、話し手たちの会社が先週取り交わしたDankin食品社との大口契約に言及している。よって、❶のthe big contractをan important contractと表している(C)が正解。important「重要な」。
(A) adopt「～を採用する」、inventory「在庫目録」。
(B) host「～を主催する」、professional「専門職の」、conference「協議会、会議」。
(D) hire「～を雇用する」。

75 According to the speaker, what does Diego have experience with?
(A) Computer repair
(B) Package design
(C) Public speaking
(D) Travel planning

話し手によると、Diegoには何の経験がありますか。
(A) コンピューターの修理
(B) 包装デザイン
(C) 人前で話すこと
(D) 旅行の計画立案

正解 B 話し手は、❷で、Dankin食品社が全製品の包装デザインを新しくすることを求めていると伝えている。続けて❸「これはDiegoが経験豊富な分野だ」と言っている。❸のThisは前文の❷で言及されている包装デザインのことを指すと考えられるので、(B)が正解。
(A) repair「修理」。
(C) public speaking「人前で話すこと、演説」。
(D) planning「計画を立てること」。

76 What does the speaker ask the listeners to do?
(A) Clean up their work areas
(B) Place a supply order
(C) Complete a registration form
(D) Update their calendars

話し手は、聞き手に何をするよう頼んでいますか。
(A) 作業場所をきれいに片付ける
(B) 備品の注文をする
(C) 登録用紙に漏れなく記入する
(D) 自分の日程表を最新の状態にする

正解 D 話し手は、プロジェクトの責任者を任せる予定のDiegoという人物が聞き手たちからの意見を求めるだろうと伝えた後、❹「彼がチーム会議の予定を組むことができるよう、皆さんのオンライン日程表が最新の状態になっているようにしておいてください」と聞き手に頼んでいる。
(A) clean up ～「～をきれいに片付ける」、area「場所」。
(B) place an order「注文する」。
(C) complete「～に漏れなく記入する」、registration「登録」。

Words & Phrases
no doubt きっと　good news 吉報　sign a contract with ～ ～と契約を結ぶ　corporation 会社　handle ～に対処する　graphic arts グラフィックアート　needs ニーズ、要望　update ～を新しくする、～を更新する　package 包装　have experience with ～ ～の経験がある　put ～ in charge of … ～に…の責任を持たせる　look for ～ ～を求める　input 意見提供、アイデア　the rest その他の人々・もの　make sure (that) ～ 必ず～であるようにする

Questions 77 through 79 refer to the following announcement. 問題77-79は次のお知らせに関するものです。

🇺🇸 w

Thanks for shopping at Southend! ❶Available on our shelves for the first time today is a new line of cookware. ❷This stunning collection of copper pots and pans is unique in that it was originally designed by Southend for celebrity chef Jerome Travers. ❸He requested a cookware set to use with induction stove tops. Now it's available to you! ❹If you'd like to see it in action, head to the area near the entryway. ❺Our sales associates will be demonstrating its use starting in fifteen minutes.

Southendでお買い物いただきありがとうございます！本日初めて当店の棚からお買い求めいただけるのは、調理器具の新シリーズです。銅の深鍋や平鍋のこの見事なコレクションは、もともとは有名シェフのJerome TraversのためにSouthendによって設計されたという点で、他にはないものです。彼は、IHこんろ上で使用するための調理器具セットを要望しました。今、それが皆さまにお買い求めいただけるのです！使用中の様子をご覧になりたい方は、入口通路近くのスペースへお向かいください。15分後より、当店の販売員がその使用法を実演説明いたします。

---

77 Where does the announcement most likely take place?

(A) At a convention center
(B) At a farmers market
(C) At a kitchen supply store
(D) At a cooking school

お知らせはどこで行われていると考えられますか。

(A) コンベンションセンター
(B) 農産物直売所
(C) 台所用品店
(D) 料理学校

正解 C 話し手は、来店に対するお礼を述べた後、❶で、今日から購入可能な調理器具の新シリーズに言及し、以降でその製品について紹介している。よって、このお知らせは台所用品を販売する店で行われていると考えられる。supply「用品」。
(A) convention center「コンベンションセンター（会議や博覧会のための建物）」。
(B) farmers market「（農産物の）産地直売所」。

---

78 According to the speaker, what is unique about some cookware?

(A) It is available in a variety of colors.
(B) It was handcrafted by local artisans.
(C) It is manufactured from recycled metal.
(D) It was created for a famous chef.

話し手によると、ある調理器具について何が独特ですか。

(A) さまざまな色で売られている。
(B) 地元の職人によって手作業で作られた。
(C) 再生金属から製造されている。
(D) 有名なシェフのために作られた。

正解 D 話し手は調理器具の新シリーズに言及してから、❷「銅の深鍋や平鍋のこの見事なコレクションは、もともとは有名シェフのJerome TraversのためにSouthendによって設計されたという点で、他にはない」と製品の独自性を説明している。加えて❸で、設計にあたってのシェフの要望を述べている。よって、(D)が正解。
(A) a variety of ～「さまざまな～」。
(B) handcraft「～を手作業で作る」、artisan「職人」。
(C) manufacture「～を製造する」、recycled「再生利用された」、metal「金属」。

---

79 What will happen in fifteen minutes?

(A) An author will sign cookbooks.
(B) A promotional sale will end.
(C) A contest winner will be announced.
(D) A product will be demonstrated.

15分後に何が起こりますか。

(A) 著者が料理本にサインする。
(B) 販売促進のセールが終了する。
(C) コンテストの優勝者が発表される。
(D) 製品が実演説明される。

正解 D 話し手は調理器具について、❹で、実際に使われている様子を見たい場合には入口通路近くのスペースへ向かうよう聞き手に促した後、❺「15分後より、当店の販売員がその使用法を実演説明する」と知らせている。
(A) author「著者」、sign「～にサインする」、cookbook「料理本」。
(B) promotional「販売促進の」。
(C) contest「コンテスト、大会」、winner「優勝者」、announce「～を発表する」。

Words & Phrases

announcement お知らせ　　shop 買い物する　　shelves 棚　★shelfの複数形
for the first time 初めて　　cookware 調理器具　　stunning 見事な、驚くべき　　copper 銅　　pot 深鍋　　pan 平鍋
unique 唯一無二の、独特な　　in that ～ ～という点において　　originally もともとは、当初は　　celebrity 有名人
induction stove IH（＝induction heating）こんろ　★電磁加熱式のこんろ。inductionは「誘導（電気・磁気がその電場・磁場内にある物体に及ぼす作用）」　　stove top こんろの上部　　in action 作動中で　　head to ～ ～へ向かう　　entryway 入口通路
sales associate 販売員　　demonstrate ～を実演説明する　　use 使用法　　in ～（時間・期間）後に

Questions 80 through 82 refer to the following talk.

🇬🇧 w

OK, crew. I'm really excited. ❶This is our last week of filming this nature documentary for Salterland Television Network. And ❷the rare parrot that we've been monitoring has eggs that are ready to hatch at any minute. Remember, we only have one chance to get this right. ❸Claudine, can you go back to the van and get the tripod for my camera? It's under the blanket on the back seat. Here are the keys.

問題80-82は次の話に関するものです。

さて、クルーの皆さん。私はとても興奮しています。これが、Salterlandテレビネットワークのためのこの自然ドキュメンタリー撮影の最終週です。しかも、私たちが見守り続けている希少なオウムは、今すぐにでもかえりそうな卵を抱えています。いいですか、これをうまくやる機会は一度しかありません。Claudine、ワゴン車に戻って、私のカメラの三脚を取ってきてくれますか。後部座席の毛布の下にあります。これが鍵です。

80 What is the talk mostly about?

(A) Filming a documentary
(B) Photographing some artwork
(C) Planning an advertising campaign
(D) Organizing a nature tour

話は主に何についてのものですか。

(A) ドキュメンタリーを撮影すること
(B) 芸術作品を写真撮影すること
(C) 広告キャンペーンを立案すること
(D) 自然散策ツアーを主催すること

正解 A　話し手は❶「これが、Salterlandテレビネットワークのためのこの自然ドキュメンタリー撮影の最終週だ」と述べている。その後は希少なオウムの様子に言及し、撮影に必要な機材について伝えているので、(A)が正解。mostly「主に」。
(B) カメラへの言及はあるが、artwork「芸術作品」は話題に出ていない。photograph「〜の写真撮影をする」。
(C) plan「〜の計画を立てる」、advertising「広告」、campaign「キャンペーン、組織的活動」。
(D) organize「〜を主催する」。

81 What does the speaker imply when she says, "we only have one chance to get this right"?

(A) Several mistakes have already been made.
(B) The listeners need to be prepared.
(C) Previous tasks were less important.
(D) Experienced staff should be in charge.

"we only have one chance to get this right" という発言で、話し手は何を示唆していますか。

(A) すでに幾つかの間違いが犯されている。
(B) 聞き手は準備ができている必要がある。
(C) 以前の作業の方が重要度が低かった。
(D) 経験豊かなスタッフが指揮を執るべきである。

正解 B　話し手は、自然ドキュメンタリー撮影の最終週だと述べ、❷「私たちが見守り続けている希少なオウムは、今すぐにでもかえりそうな卵を抱えている」と伝えている。続けて、下線部の発言で、これをうまくやる機会は一度しかないと念を押している。つまり話し手は、貴重な撮影機会を逃さないよう、撮影クルーである聞き手に準備万端であることを求めていると判断できる。prepared「準備のできた」。
(A) make a mistake「間違いを犯す」。
(C) previous「以前の」、task「作業、仕事」。
(D) experienced「経験豊かな」、staff「スタッフ、従業員」、in charge「管理して」。

82 What does the speaker ask Claudine to do?

(A) Repair a camera
(B) Adjust the sound on a television
(C) Get some equipment out of a vehicle
(D) Review some documents

話し手はClaudineに何をするよう頼んでいますか。

(A) カメラを修理する
(B) テレビの音を調節する
(C) 車両から機材を取ってくる
(D) 文書を精査する

正解 C　話し手は、❸「Claudine、ワゴン車に戻って、私のカメラの三脚を取ってきてくれるか」とClaudineという人物に頼み、続けて三脚の場所を伝えている。よって、(C)が正解。equipment「機材、器具」、vehicle「車両」。
(B) adjust「〜を調節する」。
(D) review「〜を精査する」、document「文書」。

TEST 2　PART 4

Words & Phrases

crew　(技術的な作業を行う)一団、班　　excited　興奮して　　film　〜を撮影する
documentary　ドキュメンタリー、記録映像作品　　network　ネットワーク、放送網　　rare　希少な　　parrot　オウム
monitor　〜をモニターする、〜を監視する　　be ready to do　今にも〜しそうである　　hatch　(卵が)かえる
at any minute　今すぐにでも　　remember　いいですか、念のために言っておきますが　　get 〜 right　〜を正しく行う
van　ワゴン車、バン　　tripod　(カメラなどの)三脚　　blanket　毛布　　back seat　(自動車の)後部座席

Questions 83 through 85 refer to the following excerpt from a meeting.

問題83-85は次の会議の抜粋に関するものです。

M

Thanks for attending this management meeting. ❶You may have seen from the agenda that the responses to our employee questionnaire are in. ❷For the most part, comments were positive—staff members indicated that they're happy working at our bank. However, ❸many recent hires noted challenges they encountered when they first started, especially with learning to use our computer system. ❹Given these concerns, I've set a goal of updating our training program to make it more effective. ❺Our next agenda item is the annual report, which will be coming out on Friday. ❻I'd like you all to take some time to review it before our next management meeting. We'll discuss it then.

この経営会議にご出席いただきありがとうございます。皆さんは議題から、当社の従業員向けアンケートへの回答が集まっていることにお気付きかもしれません。大部分においては、意見は肯定的なものでした——従業員は、当銀行での勤務に満足していることを示してくれました。しかし、多数の新入社員は、勤務開始時に直面した課題、とりわけ当社のコンピューターシステムの使い方の習得に関するものについて指摘しました。これらの懸念点を考慮し、私は、当社の研修プログラムをより効果的なものにするために改編するという目標を設定しました。私たちの次回の議題項目は年次報告書で、それは金曜日に発表される予定です。皆さんには、次回の経営会議までにそれを精査する時間を取っていただきたいと思います。当日、それについて話し合いますので。

---

83 What is the speaker mainly discussing?

(A) The concerns of a client
(B) The results of a survey
(C) A work-space reorganization plan
(D) An employee benefits package

話し手は主に何について話していますか。

(A) 顧客の関心事
(B) アンケート調査の結果
(C) 作業スペースの再編計画
(D) 従業員の福利厚生

正解 B　話し手は❶「皆さんは議題から、当社の従業員向けアンケートへの回答が集まっていることに気付いているかもしれない」と話を切り出し、❷ではアンケートで得た肯定的な意見に、❸ではその否定的な意見に言及している。よって、(B)が正解。result「結果」、survey「アンケート調査」。
(C) work-space「作業スペースの、仕事場の」、reorganization「再編」。
(D) benefits package「福利厚生」。

---

84 What goal does the speaker mention?

(A) Reducing operating expenses
(B) Attracting more clients
(C) Upgrading some technology
(D) Improving a training program

話し手はどんな目標について述べていますか。

(A) 運営費を削減すること
(B) より多くの顧客を引き付けること
(C) テクノロジーの性能を高めること
(D) 研修プログラムを改善すること

正解 D　話し手は❸で、新入社員が指摘した点に触れた後、❹「これらの懸念点を考慮し、私は、当社の研修プログラムをより効果的なものにするために改編するという目標を設定した」と述べている。よって、(D)が正解。improve「～を改善する」。
(A) reduce「～を削減する」、operating expenses「運営費、営業経費」。
(C) upgrade「～の性能を高める、～をグレードアップする」、technology「テクノロジー、科学技術」。

---

85 What are the listeners expected to do before the next meeting?

(A) Greet new employees
(B) Provide some feedback
(C) Finalize a supply order
(D) Review an annual report

聞き手は次の会議までに何をするよう期待されていますか。

(A) 新入社員にあいさつする
(B) 意見を提供する
(C) 備品の注文を最終決定する
(D) 年次報告書を精査する

正解 D　話し手は❺で、次回の議題である年次報告書に言及した後、❻「皆さんには、次回の経営会議までにそれを精査する時間を取ってもらいたいと思う」と聞き手に求めている。❻のitは the annual reportを指すので、(D)が正解。
(A) greet「～にあいさつする」。
(B) provide「～を提供する」、feedback「意見、感想」。
(C) finalize「～を最終決定する」。

Words & Phrases

response　回答　　questionnaire　アンケート　　for the most part　大部分は
positive　肯定的な　　indicate that ～　～ということを示す　　be happy doing　～することに満足している
hire　新雇用者、被雇用者　　note　～について指摘する、～に言及する　　challenge　難題　　encounter　～に直面する
especially　とりわけ　　learn to do　～できるようになる　　given　～を考慮すると　　concern　懸念事項、関心事
set　～を設定する　　effective　効果的な　　annual　年次の、年1回の　　come out　発表される　　review　～を精査する

Questions 86 through 88 refer to the following telephone message.

問題86-88は次の電話のメッセージに関するものです。

🇺🇸 w

Hi, ❶I've just finished inspecting the Hamstead home that you'd like to turn into an office for your insurance business. The building seems to be well-suited for your needs. But ❷it is listed on the local historic registry for its architectural significance. ❸You'll need to be careful to hire an architect who knows all the regulations around preserving historic architecture. And ❹you'll need to get a renovation permit from the city's historic preservation department. ❺I can help you with the paperwork for that when you're ready.

こんにちは、私はたった今、あなたが保険事業のオフィスへの転換を望んでいらっしゃるハムステッドの住宅を点検し終えたところです。この建物は、あなたのニーズに適していると思われます。ただ、そこは建築上の重要性から地域の史跡登録簿に記載されています。あなたは、歴史的建造物の保全に関連する全ての条例を把握している建築家を雇うよう注意する必要があるでしょう。それから、市の史跡保存課から改修許可証を得る必要があります。私はあなたのご用意が整い次第、その書類事務をお手伝いできます。

86 What most likely is the speaker's job?

(A) Accountant
(B) Building inspector
(C) Insurance salesperson
(D) Landscaper

話し手の仕事は何だと考えられますか。

(A) 会計士
(B) 建物の検査官
(C) 保険外交員
(D) 造園家

正解 B 話し手は❶で、聞き手に要望された住宅の点検作業を完了したことを知らせ、以降では、その建物が聞き手のニーズに合致していること、および改修する上での注意点を説明している。よって、話し手は建物の検査をする仕事をしていると考えられる。inspector「検査官」。
(A) accountant「会計士」。
(C) salesperson「外交販売員」。
(D) landscaper「造園家」。

87 What does the speaker advise the listener to be careful doing?

(A) Registering a new car
(B) Finding an architect
(C) Putting up a fence
(D) Reading some regulations

話し手は、聞き手に対して何をすることに注意するよう助言していますか。

(A) 新車を登録すること
(B) 建築家を見つけること
(C) 柵を建てること
(D) 条例を読むこと

正解 B 話し手は、聞き手が改修を望んでいる住宅について、❷で、その建物が地域の史跡登録簿に記載されている事実を挙げ、❸「あなたは、歴史的建造物の保全に関連する全ての条例を把握している建築家を雇うよう注意する必要があるだろう」と助言している。つまり、建築家を探す際に注意するよう述べているので、(B)が正解。advise ~ to do「~に…するよう助言する」、be careful doing「~することに注意する」。
(A) register「~を登録する」。
(C) put up ~「~を建てる」、fence「柵」。
(D) 話し手は聞き手自身が条例を把握するようには助言していない。

88 What does the speaker offer to help with?

(A) Filing for a permit
(B) Providing a meeting space
(C) Painting a house
(D) Setting up some computers

話し手は何に関して手伝うことを申し出ていますか。

(A) 許可証を申請すること
(B) 打ち合わせ用のスペースを用意すること
(C) 住宅を塗装すること
(D) コンピューターをセットアップすること

正解 A 話し手は、建築家選定に際しての注意点を述べた後、❹「市の史跡保存課から改修許可証を得る必要がある」と伝え、続く❺で、その書類事務の手伝いを申し出ている。よって、(A)が正解。file for ~「~の申請をする」。
(B) provide「~を用意する」。
(C) paint「~を塗装する」。
(D) set up ~「~をセットアップする、~を使える状態にする」。

Words & Phrases

inspect　~を点検する　　turn ~ into …　~を…に変える　　insurance　保険
seem to be ~　~のようだ　　be well-suited for ~　~に適切である、~にぴったりである
be listed on ~　~（目録など）に載っている　　historic　歴史上重要な　　registry　登録簿、登記簿　　architectural　建築上の
significance　重要性　　be careful to do　~するよう注意する　　regulations　条例　　preserve　~を保存する
architecture　建造物、建築　　permit　許可証　　preservation　保存　　paperwork　書類事務、必要書類

TEST 2 PART 4

Questions 89 through 91 refer to the following instructions.

🇨🇦 M

Good morning, everyone. ❶Each of you has experience writing code to develop computer software as part of your duties here at the company. So, we're glad ❷you've agreed to assist in the process for selecting new computer programmers to hire. ❸For the initial screening, you'll be calling the job candidates and asking them questions to assess their technical knowledge. Now, ❹it's been suggested that corresponding with the candidates via e-mail would be easier, but you can learn a lot from talking to someone.

問題89-91は次の説明に関するものです。

皆さん、おはようございます。皆さんお一人お一人が、当社での職務の一環として、コンピューターソフトウエアを開発するためのコードを書く経験をお持ちです。ですから、新しいコンピュータープログラマーを雇用する選考過程を手伝うことに皆さんが同意してくれて、私たちはうれしく思っています。一次選考では、皆さんは採用志望者に電話して、技術的な知識を評価するための質問をしてもらうことになっています。ところで、志望者とEメールでやりとりする方が簡単だろうということが提案されてきましたが、人は誰かと話すことで多くを知ることができるものです。

89 What area do the listeners most likely work in?

(A) Law
(B) Finance
(C) Technology
(D) Publishing

聞き手はどのような分野で働いていると考えられますか。

(A) 法律
(B) 金融
(C) テクノロジー
(D) 出版

正解 **C** 話し手は❶「皆さん一人一人が、当社での職務の一環として、コンピューターソフトウエアを開発するためのコードを書く経験を持っている」と述べている。よって、聞き手はソフトウエアの開発職だと考えられるので、(C)が正解。area「分野」。technology「テクノロジー」。
(B) finance「金融、財務」。

90 What will the listeners participate in?

(A) A staff picnic
(B) An intern orientation
(C) A research experiment
(D) A hiring selection

聞き手は何に参加する予定ですか。

(A) 従業員ピクニック
(B) インターン説明会
(C) 研究実験
(D) 採用選考

正解 **D** 話し手は、❷「新しいコンピュータープログラマーを雇用する選考過程を手伝うことに皆さんが同意してくれた」と述べ、❸で、聞き手が行う一次選考の内容を説明している。よって、(D)が正解。participate in ~「~に参加する」。hiring「採用、雇用」、selection「選び出すこと」。
(B) intern「インターン」、orientation「説明会」。
(C) research「研究」、experiment「実験」。

91 Why does the speaker say, "you can learn a lot from talking to someone"?

(A) To recommend consulting an expert
(B) To encourage attendance at a company party
(C) To reject a suggestion about a process
(D) To express surprise about a staff member's background

話し手はなぜ "you can learn a lot from talking to someone" と言っていますか。

(A) 専門家に相談することを推奨するため
(B) 会社の集まりへの出席を促すため
(C) 過程に関する提案を却下するため
(D) ある従業員の経歴について驚きを表明するため

正解 **C** 話し手は❸で、一次選考として聞き手が志望者と電話でやりとりする予定だと述べ、❹「志望者とEメールでやりとりする方が簡単だろうということが提案されてきた」と言った後、but「しかし」に続けて、下線部の発言で直接会話するメリットを伝えている。よって話し手は、選考過程における❹の提案を退けるためにこの発言をしていると判断できる。reject「~を却下する、~を拒絶する」、suggestion「提案」。
(A) recommend doing「~することを推奨する」、consult「~と相談する」、expert「専門家」。
(B) encourage「~を促す」、attendance「出席」、party「社交的な集まり、パーティー」。
(D) express「~を表明する」、background「経歴」。

Words & Phrases
instructions 説明、指示　experience 経験　develop ~を開発する　as part of ~ ~の一環として　duties 職務　assist in ~ ~を手伝う　process 過程　select ~を選び出す　initial 最初の　screening 選考、ふるい分け　candidate 志望者、候補者　assess ~を評価する　technical 技術的な　knowledge 知識　correspond with ~ （Eメールや手紙などで）~とやりとりする　via ~によって

Questions 92 through 94 refer to the following talk.

問題92-94は次の話に関するものです。

🇦🇺 M

❶Thank you for inviting me to Bradford's Bookstore to speak about my book *Will Travel for Mushrooms—An Amateur's Experience*. ❷Last year, I spent three weeks in Japan hunting for the matsutake mushroom, a highly prized delicacy there. I had an exceptional time foraging in Japan's beautiful forests. Of course, you can learn more about this experience by purchasing my book. Now, I belong to the Bradford mushroom hunters club. ❸There are many varieties of mushrooms found in this area. They are delicious. ❹If you don't believe me, I brought some of what we found this morning.

拙著『いざキノコ探しの旅へ――ある愛好家の体験』について講演するためにBradford's書店へ私をお招きいただき、ありがとうございます。昨年、私は日本に3週間滞在し、現地で珍重されているごちそうであるマツタケを探し求めました。私は、日本の美しい森で食べ物を探し回るという特別な時間を過ごしました。もちろん、拙著をご購入いただくことによって、皆さんはこの体験についてさらに詳しくお知りになれます。さて、私はBradfordキノコ狩り同好会に所属しています。この地域では実に多種多様なキノコが見つかります。みんなとてもおいしいんですよ。もし皆さんが私の言うことを信じられなければと思い、私たちが今朝見つけたものを幾つか持参しました。

92 Where is the speaker?

(A) At a library
(B) At a community garden
(C) At a town plaza
(D) At a bookstore

話し手はどこにいますか。

(A) 図書館
(B) 市民農園
(C) 町の広場
(D) 書店

正解 D 話し手は冒頭で、❶「拙著について講演するためにBradford's書店へ私を招いてくれて、ありがとう」と述べているので、(D)が正解。
(B) community garden「市民農園（農家ではない市民が非営利的に栽培活動を行っている農地）」。
(C) plaza「広場」。

93 What did the speaker do last year?

(A) He traveled to another country.
(B) He opened a restaurant.
(C) He received an award.
(D) He applied for a grant.

話し手は昨年、何をしましたか。

(A) 彼は別の国に旅行した。
(B) 彼はレストランを開店した。
(C) 彼は賞を受け取った。
(D) 彼は助成金の申請をした。

正解 A 話し手は❷「昨年、私は日本に3週間滞在し、現地で珍重されているごちそうであるマツタケを探し求めた」と述べている。よって、❷のJapanをanother countryと表している(A)が正解。
(C) award「賞」。
(D) apply for ～「～の申請をする」、grant「助成金」。

94 What does the speaker mean when he says, "I brought some of what we found this morning"?

(A) The listeners should help him pack some materials.
(B) The listeners should try a sample.
(C) A problem is urgent.
(D) A larger container is advised.

"I brought some of what we found this morning" という発言で、話し手は何を意図していますか。

(A) 聞き手は、彼が資材を容器に詰めるのを手伝うべきである。
(B) 聞き手は試食するべきである。
(C) ある問題が差し迫っている。
(D) より大きい容器が推奨される。

正解 B 話し手は、キノコ狩り同好会に所属していると伝え、❸「この地域では実に多種多様なキノコが見つかる。みんなとてもおいしい」と述べている。続けて❹で、聞き手がもし自分の発言を信じられないならと言った後、下線部の発言で、見つけたキノコを幾つか持ってきたことを伝えている。つまり、話し手は、この地域のキノコが本当に美味なのか確かめたいなら試食してほしいと聞き手を促しているのだと判断できる。
(A) help ～ do「～が…するのを手伝う」、pack「～を容器に詰める」、material「資材、材料」。
(C) urgent「急を要する」。
(D) container「容器」、advise「～を推奨する」。

Words & Phrases

mushroom キノコ　amateur 愛好家、素人　experience 体験
spend ～ doing …するのに～(時間)を使う　hunt for ～ ～を探し求める　highly 大いに　prized 貴重な
delicacy ごちそう、珍味　exceptional 特別な、異例な　forage 食糧を探し回る　belong to ～ ～に所属する
hunter 狩りをする人　club 同好会　varieties of ～ 多種多様な～　delicious 美味な　believe ～の言うことを信じる

133

Questions 95 through 97 refer to the following tour information and map.

問題95-97は次のツアー案内と地図に関するものです。

🇨🇦 M

❶On behalf of Jackson Tours, I apologize for this slight interruption in today's tour of Music City! ❷We have a flat tire, but the bus driver will be able to repair it within the hour. So let's use this as an opportunity to walk a bit. ❸I was glad to see that everyone enjoyed the visit to Clarksville Records a few minutes ago. You asked so many great questions. Now, ❹we're heading over to our next site on the list of historic music sites. As we walk, ❺here's an interesting fact I'll share with you about Music City. ❻Did you know that we manufacture more guitars here than anywhere else in the country?

Jacksonツアー社を代表し、本日のMusic Cityツアーのこのわずかな中断についておわび申し上げます。タイヤがパンクしてしまっているのですが、バスの運転手は1時間以内にそれを修理することができるでしょう。ですから、これをちょっと歩くための機会として活用しましょう。私は、皆さんが数分前のClarksvilleレコード社の訪問をお楽しみいただけたことが分かってうれしく思いました。皆さんはたくさん素晴らしいご質問をされましたね。さて、私たちは歴史的音楽名所のリストの次の場所へと向かっているところです。歩きがてら、皆さんにお伝えしたいMusic Cityに関する興味深い事実があります。ここでは国内の他のどこよりも多くのギターが製造されているということをご存じでしたか?

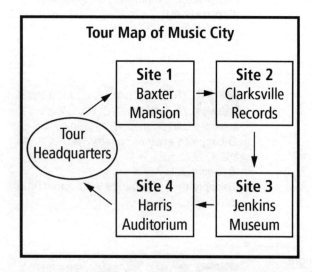

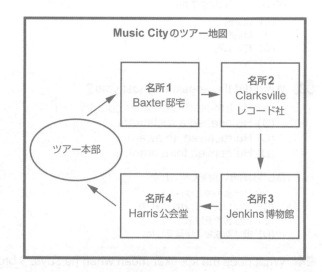

95 What problem does the speaker mention?

    (A) A road is busy with traffic.

    (B) A tire must be fixed.

    (C) An item was left behind.

    (D) A bus made a wrong turn.

話し手はどんな問題について述べていますか。

    (A) 道路の交通量が多い。

    (B) タイヤが修理されなければならない。

    (C) 物が置き忘れられた。

    (D) バスが曲がる場所を間違えた。

正解 B 話し手は❶で、ツアーの一時中断を謝罪してから、❷「タイヤがパンクしてしまっているのだが、バスの運転手は1時間以内にそれを修理することができるだろう」と伝えている。よって、この内容をA tireを主語にした受動態の文で表現している(B)が正解。fix「～を修理する」。
(A) be busy with ～「～でごった返している」、traffic「交通(量)」。
(C) leave ～ behind「～を置き忘れる、～を置き去りにする」。
(D) make a wrong turn「曲がる場所を間違える」。

96 Look at the graphic. Which site are the listeners going to now?

    (A) Site 1

    (B) Site 2

    (C) Site 3

    (D) Site 4

図を見てください。聞き手は今、どの名所に向かっているところですか。

    (A) 名所1

    (B) 名所2

    (C) 名所3

    (D) 名所4

正解 C ツアーの案内をしている話し手は、❸で、皆が数分前のClarksvilleレコード社の訪問を楽しめたことがうれしかったと感想を述べた後、❹で、次の名所へ向かっていることを伝えている。ツアー行程を示した地図を見ると、Clarksvilleレコード社の次に訪れることになっている場所は、名所3のJenkins博物館。よって、(C)が正解。
(A) (D) いずれの名所についても言及されていない。
(B) 数分前に訪れた名所として言及されている。

97 What fact does the speaker share about Music City?

    (A) It is over two hundred years old.

    (B) It is the birthplace of a famous singer.

    (C) Public concerts are held there weekly.

    (D) A large number of guitars are produced there.

話し手は、Music Cityについてどんな事実を伝えていますか。

    (A) そこには200年以上の歴史がある。

    (B) そこは有名な歌手の生誕地である。

    (C) そこでは毎週、公開コンサートが開かれている。

    (D) そこでは多数のギターが製造されている。

正解 D 話し手は、❺で、Music Cityに関する興味深い事実があると前置きし、❻「ここでは国内の他のどこよりも多くのギターが製造されているということを知っていたか」と、疑問形式で事実を伝えている。❻にあるhereはin Music Cityを表している。manufactureをproduceという語を用いて言い換えている(D)が正解。a large number of ～「多数の～」、produce「～を製造する」。
(B) birthplace「生誕地」、singer「歌手」。
(C) public「公開の、大衆の」。

Words & Phrases

on behalf of ～　～を代表して　　apologize for ～　～を謝罪する　　slight　わずかな
interruption　中断　　flat tire　パンクしたタイヤ　　repair　～を修理する　　within　～以内に
use ～ as …　～を…として活用する　　opportunity　機会　　a bit　少し　　visit　訪問、見物　　head over to ～　～へ向かう
site　(重要出来事が起こった)場所　　historic　歴史上重要な　　interesting　興味深い　　fact　事実
share ～ with …　～(情報など)を…に伝える　　manufacture　～を製造する　　anywhere　どこか　　else　他に

地図　headquarters　本部、本社　　mansion　邸宅　　museum　博物館　　auditorium　公会堂

Questions 98 through 100 refer to the following excerpt from a meeting and menu.

 w

Hi, everyone. Thanks for coming to the bakery a bit early. I just wanted to give you some quick updates. ❶We're going to start charging extra for our layer cakes. Their ingredients are more costly for us. ❷I'll update the menu later this week with that price change. Also, ❸Yuri called to say he's sick, so please let me know if any of you can cover his shift tomorrow morning. As for today, ❹I noticed that the floor in the back of the store is getting a bit dirty. ❺I'd like someone to give it a thorough mopping later. That's all for now. OK, let's open the bakery.

問題98-100は次の会議の抜粋とメニューに関するものです。

どうも、皆さん。少し早めにベーカリーへ来てくれてありがとう。ちょっと皆さんに手短に最新情報を伝えたかったのです。当店はレイヤーケーキを値上げする予定です。その材料が当店にとって以前より費用がかさむようになってきているのです。私は今週後半に、その価格変更に合わせてメニューを新しくするつもりです。また、Yuriが電話で体調が悪いと言ってきたので、皆さんのうちのどなたかが明日の午前中の彼のシフトを代わりに務めることができれば、私に知らせてください。今日に関しては、店の奥の床が少し汚れてきていることに気が付きました。後でどなたかに、そこを徹底的にモップ掛けしてもらいたいと思います。差し当たっては以上です。それでは、ベーカリーを開店しましょう。

  Dacey's Bakery

(1) Assorted Cookies: $18/dozen

(2) Assorted Muffins: $20/dozen

(3) Fruit Pies: $22/pie

(4) Layer Cakes: $18/cake

Dacey'sベーカリー

(1) クッキーの詰め合わせ：1ダースにつき18ドル

(2) マフィンの詰め合わせ：1ダースにつき20ドル

(3) フルーツパイ：パイ1個につき22ドル

(4) レイヤーケーキ：ケーキ1個につき18ドル

98 Look at the graphic. Which line of the menu will be changed?

    (A) Line 1
    (B) Line 2
    (C) Line 3
    (D) Line 4

図を見てください。メニュー中のどの行が変更になりますか。

    (A)　1行目
    (B)　2行目
    (C)　3行目
    (D)　4行目

正解 D 話し手は、❶「当店はレイヤーケーキを値上げする予定だ」と知らせ、❷「私は今週後半に、その価格変更に合わせてメニューを新しくするつもりだ」と伝えている。図を見ると、(1)から(4)までの計4品が記載されており、レイヤーケーキはこのメニューのうちの4行目に位置している。よって、(D)が正解。
(A) (B) (C) いずれの行に位置しているメニュー品についても言及されていない。

---

99 Why will Yuri not come to work tomorrow?

    (A) He is feeling unwell.
    (B) He has to take his car to an auto shop.
    (C) He will be starting a new job.
    (D) He will be attending a family event.

Yuriはなぜ、明日出勤しない予定なのですか。

    (A)　彼は具合が悪い。
    (B)　彼は自分の車を自動車店へ持っていかなければならない。
    (C)　彼は新しい仕事を始めることになっている。
    (D)　彼は家族の行事に参加することになっている。

正解 A 話し手は、❸「Yuriが電話で体調が悪いと言ってきたので、皆さんのうちのどなたかが明日の午前中の彼のシフトを代わりに務めることができれば、私に知らせてください」と聞き手に頼んでいる。よって、❸のhe's sickをHe is feeling unwell.と表している(A)が正解。unwell「具合が悪い」。
(B) auto「自動車」。
(D) attend「～に参加する」、event「行事」。

---

100 What does the speaker say about the back of the store?

    (A) The door must be locked every night.
    (B) The floor needs to be cleaned.
    (C) Some boxes need to be unpacked.
    (D) Some fans should be plugged in.

話し手は店の奥について何と言っていますか。

    (A)　ドアが毎晩施錠されなければならない。
    (B)　床が掃除される必要がある。
    (C)　箱が開梱される必要がある。
    (D)　換気扇がコンセントに接続されるべきである。

正解 B 話し手は❹で、店の奥の床が汚れてきていることに気付いたと言ってから、❺「後で誰かに、そこを徹底的にモップ掛けしてもらいたい」と伝えている。❺のitはthe floor in the back of the storeを指している。よって(B)が正解。
(A) lock「～を施錠する」。
(C) unpack「～(箱・荷物など)を開ける、～の梱包を解く」。
(D) fan「換気扇、ファン」、plug in ～「～のプラグをコンセントに接続する」。

TEST 2 PART 4

Words & Phrases

a bit　少し　　give ～ an update　～に最新情報を伝える　　quick　手短な
start *doing*　～し始める　　charge ～ for …　…の代金として～を請求する　　extra　割増料金
layer cake　レイヤーケーキ　★クリームやジャムなどを挟んで層状にしたスポンジケーキ　　ingredient　材料
costly　高くつく、費用のかかる　　update　～を新しくする、～を更新する　　sick　体調が悪い
cover *one's* shift　～のシフトの代わりを務める　　as for ～　～に関しては　　notice that ～　～ということに気が付く
back　奥　　dirty　汚れた　　give ～ a mopping　～をモップで拭く　　thorough　徹底的な　　for now　差し当たり
メニュー　assorted　詰め合わせた　　dozen　ダース、12個　　muffin　マフィン

PART 5

101 Please send a copy of ------- résumé to the hiring committee.

    (A) you
    (B) yours
    (C) yourself
    (D) your

あなたの履歴書を1部、雇用委員会に送ってください。

    (A) あなた
    (B) あなたのもの
    (C) あなた自身
    (D) あなたの

正解 D 選択肢は全て二人称の人称代名詞。空所の前に前置詞ofがあり、後ろには名詞résumé「履歴書」が続いている。空所には名詞を修飾する所有格の(D)「あなたの」が適切。committee「委員会」。
(A) 主格または目的格。
(B) 所有代名詞。
(C) 再帰代名詞。

102 Gnome Bicycle's employee turnover rate has been quite steady ------- the past year.

    (A) toward
    (B) over
    (C) rather
    (D) if

Gnomeサイクル社の従業員離職率は、この1年間にわたって、ほとんど変わりませんでした。

    (A) ～の方へ
    (B) ～にわたって
    (C) むしろ
    (D) もし～なら

正解 B 空所の前までは「Gnomeサイクル社の従業員離職率はほとんど変わらなかった」という意味であり、この部分だけで文として成り立つので、空所以降は修飾語句になる。空所の後ろはthe past yearという名詞句なので、空所には前置詞が入る。(B) over「～にわたって、～の間」を入れると、over the past year「この1年にわたって」が、従業員離職率が変わらなかった期間を表すことになり、意味が通る。turnover「離職(率)」、rate「比率」、quite「非常に、かなり」、steady「変わらない、安定した」。
(A) 前置詞だが、意味が通らない。
(C) 副詞。
(D) 接続詞。

103 Mainer Soft, Inc., offers a selection of video games, which are only ------- through its Web site.

    (A) sale
    (B) sell
    (C) sold
    (D) sells

Mainerソフト社はえり抜きのテレビゲームを売り出しており、それは同社のウェブサイトを通してのみ販売されています。

    (A) 販売
    (B) ～を売る
    (C) 売られて
    (D) ～を売る

正解 C カンマに続くwhichはa selection of video gamesを先行詞とする関係代名詞であり、which以降は、「そのテレビゲームはMainerソフト社のウェブサイトだけで-------である」という意味。空所の前にはbe動詞があるので、過去分詞の(C) soldを入れると受動態を形成して「売られている」となり、テレビゲームに説明を加える形として適切。offer「～を売り出す」、a selection of ～「えり抜きの～、精選された～」、video game「テレビゲーム」、through「～を通して」。
(A) 名詞。on saleなら可。
(B) 動詞の原形、(D) 動詞の三人称単数現在形。いずれもbe動詞には続かない。

104 Changes to the travel reimbursement process will be explained at this month's staff -------.

(A) level
(B) schedule
(C) proposal
(D) meeting

出張精算手順の変更が、今月のスタッフ会議で説明されます。

(A) レベル
(B) スケジュール
(C) 提案
(D) 会議

> **正解 D** 主語は文頭からprocessまでで、述語動詞はwill be explained。reimbursementとは、会社などで従業員が立て替え払いした経費などを精算・払い戻しすることであり、その手順に変更があるため説明が行われるというのがこの文の内容。(D) meeting「会議」を入れると、手順の変更が今月のスタッフ会議で説明されるということになり、意味が通る。process「手順、やり方」、explain「〜を説明する」。

105 Stillman Canning creates stews and soups using a ------- family recipe.

(A) trust
(B) trusted
(C) trusts
(D) trusting

Stillman缶詰製造社は、信頼できる家伝のレシピを使用して、シチューやスープを作り出しています。

(A) 〜を信頼する
(B) 信頼されている
(C) 〜を信頼する
(D) 信じやすい

> **正解 B** 選択肢は動詞trust「〜を信頼する」と、その変化した形。空所の前に不定冠詞aがあり、後ろにはfamily recipeという名詞句が続くので、空所にはその名詞句を修飾する語が入る。形容詞の働きを持つ(B) trusted「信頼されている」を入れると意味が通る。canning「缶詰製造」、stew「シチュー」、family recipe「家族に伝わる調理法」。
> (A) 動詞の原形または名詞。
> (C) 動詞の三人称単数現在形または名詞の複数形。
> (D) 現在分詞から転じた形容詞。名詞句を修飾することはできるが、意味の通る文にならない。

106 In its first week ------- operation, Sabon Hairstyling Salon had about 150 customers.

(A) of
(B) to
(C) as
(D) by

Sabonヘアスタイリング・サロンは、営業第1週に約150人の客を迎えました。

(A) 〜の
(B) 〜へ
(C) 〜として
(D) 〜によって

> **正解 A** 選択肢は全て前置詞の働きを持つ語。空所の前後のits first weekとoperationをつなぐには「〜の…」を表す(A) ofが適切。itsはitの所有格であり、主語のSabon Hairstyling Salonを指すので、In its first week of operationで「Sabonヘアスタイリング・サロンの営業第1週に」という意味になる。operation「営業、操業」、customer「客」。

107 Ekari Industries is proud to announce its ------- merger with Bogin Enterprises.

- (A) whole
- (B) external
- (C) upcoming
- (D) serious

Ekari産業社は、近く行われるBogin事業社との合併を発表することを光栄に思います。

- (A) 全体の
- (B) 外部の
- (C) 近づきつつある
- (D) 真剣な

正解 C 選択肢は全て形容詞の働きを持つ語。空所の前はitの所有格のitsで「Ekari産業社の」を表し、後ろにはmerger with Bogin Enterprises「Bogin事業社との合併」という名詞句があるので、この名詞句を適切に修飾するものを選ぶ。(C) upcoming「近づきつつある」を入れると意味が通る。be proud to do「~することを光栄に思う」、announce「~を発表する」、enterprise「企業、会社」。

---

108 All letters and packages are shipped in locked containers to ensure safe -------.

- (A) deliver
- (B) delivers
- (C) delivered
- (D) delivery

全ての手紙と小包は、安全な配達を確実なものにするため、鍵の掛かったコンテナに入れて輸送されます。

- (A) ~を配達する
- (B) ~を配達する
- (C) ~を配達した
- (D) 配達

正解 D 選択肢は動詞deliver「~を配達する」と、その変化した形や派生語。to ensure safe ------- は「安全な ------- を確実なものにするために」という意味。ensure「~を確実なものにする」は他動詞であり目的語が必要なので、空所には形容詞safeに修飾される名詞が入る。名詞の(D) delivery「配達」が適切。package「小包」、ship「~を輸送する」、lock「~に鍵を掛ける」、container「コンテナ、容器」。
(A) 動詞の原形。
(B) 三人称単数現在形。
(C) 過去形または過去分詞。

---

109 This year, ------- three million passengers across China boarded domestic flights the day before the holiday weekend.

- (A) almost
- (B) often
- (C) more
- (D) far

今年、中国全土で300万人近い乗客が、祝日と重なる週末の前日に国内線の便に搭乗しました。

- (A) ほとんど
- (B) しばしば
- (C) より多い
- (D) ずっと

正解 A 空所に何も入れなくても文として成り立つので、ここには修飾語が入る。数詞three million「300万の」を修飾する副詞の(A) almost「ほとんど」が適切。almost three millionで「300万人近い」という意味になる。passenger「乗客」、across「~の至る所で」、board「~に乗る」、domestic「国内の」、flight「飛行機の便、フライト」、holiday weekend「祝日と重なる週末」。
(B) 頻度を示す副詞なので不適切。
(C) more thanなら可。
(D) 副詞としては程度や比較級などを修飾するので不適切。

110 By the end of the workshop, participants will have a ------- understanding of how to request financial aid.

(A) hard
(B) full
(C) best
(D) busy

講習会が終わるまでに、参加者は、資金援助を依頼する方法について完全に理解しているでしょう。

(A) 難しい
(B) 完全な
(C) 最良の
(D) 忙しい

正解 B 選択肢は全て形容詞の働きを持つ語。空所の前には不定冠詞a、後ろにはunderstanding of how to request financial aid「資金援助を依頼する方法の理解」という名詞句があるので、空所にはこの名詞句を適切に修飾する語が入る。(B) full「完全な」を入れると、「資金援助を依頼する方法の完全な理解」となって意味が通る。participant「参加者」、financial aid「資金援助、奨学金」。

---

111 Removing personal items from the floor of your workstation will ------- facilitate tomorrow's carpet cleaning.

(A) greatness
(B) greats
(C) great
(D) greatly

ご自分の作業場所の床から私物を撤去していただくことで、明日のカーペット清掃が非常に容易になります。

(A) 偉大さ
(B) 要人
(C) 偉大な
(D) 非常に

正解 D 主語はRemoving ...... workstation「あなたの作業場所の床から私物を撤去すること」で、will facilitateが述語動詞。空所に何も入れなくても文として成り立つので、ここには修飾語が入る。動詞facilitate「〜を容易にする、〜を楽にする」を修飾する副詞の(D) greatly「非常に、大いに」が適切。remove「〜を取り除く」、personal item「私物」、workstation「個人の作業場所、オフィス内の各自の仕事机」。
(A) (B) 名詞。
(C) 形容詞または名詞。

---

112 Audience members are asked to resist looking at their phones because presenters find it -------.

(A) distraction
(B) distract
(C) distractible
(D) distracting

発表者の気が散るので、聴衆は携帯電話を見るのを控えるように求められています。

(A) 気を散らすこと
(B) 〜(気など)を散らす
(C) 注意散漫な
(D) 気を散らすような

正解 D 選択肢は動詞distract「〜(気など)を散らす」と、その変化した形や派生語。文頭からphonesまでが主節で「聴衆は携帯電話を見るのを控えるように求められている」という意味。because以降がその理由となる。find 〜 …で「〜を…と思う」という意味になり、〜には目的語となる名詞、…には形容詞が入る。よって、空所に形容詞の(D) distracting「気を散らすような」を入れると、発表者にとってit(＝聴衆が携帯電話を見ること)が集中の妨げになることを表し、意味が通る。audience member「聴衆、観客」、be asked to do「〜するように求められている」、resist doing「〜することを我慢する」、presenter「発表者」。
(A) 名詞。
(B) 動詞の原形。
(C) 形容詞だが、意味が通らない。

113 Hospital officials met with the architects ------- received an overview of the design of the new maternity center.

(A) either
(B) instead
(C) or
(D) and

病院の職員は建築家に会い、新しい産科センターの設計の概要を受け取りました。

(A) どちらか
(B) その代わりに
(C) あるいは
(D) そして

正解 D 主語はHospital officials、述語動詞はmet。空所の後ろにも動詞receivedがあり、receivedの主語もHospital officialsだと考えられるので、空所には並列させる接続詞の(D) and「そして」が適切。official「職員」、architect「建築家、建築技師」、overview「概要」、maternity「産科病院、産院」。

114 Anyone planning to ------- for a pharmacy degree program should consider gaining laboratory work experience.

(A) require
(B) vote
(C) apply
(D) complete

薬学の学位課程への申し込みを計画している人は誰でも、研究所での作業経験を積むことを検討するべきです。

(A) ～を必要とする
(B) 投票する
(C) 申し込む
(D) ～を完了する

正解 C 文頭からprogramまでが主語に当たり、planning ...... programの部分がAnyoneを後ろから修飾している。should以降は、「研究所での作業経験を積むことを検討するべきだ」という意味。空所には前置詞forが続いているので、(C) applyを入れてapply for ～「～に申し込む」とすると、主語が「薬学の学位課程に申し込むつもりの人は誰でも」となって、意味が通る。plan to do「～する計画である」、pharmacy「薬学」、degree「学位」、consider「～を検討する」、gain experience「経験を積む」、laboratory「研究所、研究室」。

115 Even first-time Pictafix subscribers can use the software to create photo collages nearly -------.

(A) increasingly
(B) effortlessly
(C) recently
(D) especially

Pictafixを初めて契約する方でも、このソフトウエアを使って写真のコラージュをほとんど苦労せずに作成できます。

(A) ますます
(B) 苦労せずに
(C) 最近
(D) 特に

正解 B 選択肢は全て副詞。文頭からcollagesまでは「Pictafixを初めて契約する人でも、このソフトウエアを使って写真のコラージュを作成できる」という内容であり、空所の直前のnearly「ほとんど」は空所の副詞を修飾すると考えられる。createを修飾する副詞として(B) effortlessly「苦労せずに」を入れると意味が通る。even「～でさえ」、first-time「初めての」、subscriber「(サービスの)契約者、(新聞・雑誌の)定期購読者」、collage「コラージュ(写真などの一部を切り取ったものを貼り合わせて作る作品)」。

116 The company's production issues were further ------- by an unexpected power outage.

    (A) complicate
    (B) complicated
    (C) complication
    (D) complicating

その会社の製造における問題は、想定外の停電によってさらに複雑化しました。

    (A) 〜を複雑にする
    (B) 複雑化された
    (C) 複雑化
    (D) 複雑にするような

正解 **B** 選択肢は動詞complicate「〜を複雑にする」と、その変化した形や派生語。主語は文頭からissuesまで。空所の前にはbe動詞と副詞further「さらに」、空所の後ろにはby an unexpected power outage「想定外の停電によって」とある。過去分詞の(B) complicated「複雑化された」を入れると、were complicated「複雑化した」という意味の受動態になり、適切。production「製造、生産」、issue「問題、問題点」、unexpected「予期しない」、power outage「停電」。
(A) 動詞の原形。
(C) 名詞。名詞はbe動詞に続けられるが意味が通らない。
(D) 現在分詞または動名詞。ここでは空所に続くby以降で行為者が示されているので不適切。

117 The board of directors at Ginishi Estate Investments is awaiting shareholder approval ------- acquiring more properties.

    (A) because
    (B) providing
    (C) before
    (D) though

Ginishi地所投資社の取締役会は、さらなる不動産を取得する前に株主の承認を待っています。

    (A) 〜なので
    (B) 〜という条件で
    (C) 〜の前に
    (D) 〜だが

正解 **C** 空所の前は「Ginishi地所投資社の取締役会は、株主の承認を待っている」という意味で、これだけで文として成り立つので、空所以降は修飾語句と考えられる。空所の後ろのacquiring more properties「さらなる不動産を取得すること」は名詞句なので、空所には前置詞が入る。前置詞の働きを持つ(C) before「〜の前に」が意味の上からも適切。board of directors「取締役会」、await「〜を待つ」、shareholder「株主」、approval「承認、許可」、acquire「〜を取得する、〜を入手する」、property「不動産、資産」。
(A) (B) 接続詞、(D) 接続詞または副詞。いずれも名詞句のみは続かない。

118 ------- assistant will be in the office today, but they can be contacted by e-mail.

    (A) Many
    (B) Other
    (C) Neither
    (D) None

今日はどちらのアシスタントも事務所にいませんが、彼らとはEメールで連絡を取ることが可能です。

    (A) 多くの
    (B) 他の
    (C) どちらも〜ない
    (D) 誰一人〜ない

正解 **C** 空所には、続く名詞assistantを修飾する語が入ると考えられる。assistantが単数形なので、単数形の名詞の前に置くことができる(C) Neither「(2人のうちの)どちらも〜ない」が適切。
(A) 単数形の名詞は修飾しない。
(B) 冠詞などがない場合は、原則として単数形の名詞を修飾しない。
(D) None of the assistantsなど、別の言い方にする必要がある。

119 Brynextech now has manufacturing ------- on both the east and west coasts.

(A) facilities
(B) selections
(C) performances
(D) revisions

Brynextech社は現在、東海岸と西海岸の両方に、製造施設を所有しています。

(A) 施設
(B) 選択
(C) 演技
(D) 改訂

正解 **A** 選択肢は全て名詞。文頭から空所までの部分は、「Brynextech社は現在、製造-------を持っている」という意味。空所の後ろは、「東海岸と西海岸の両方に」の意味。企業が東海岸と西海岸の両方に所有し得るもので、manufacturing「製造(の)」と共に名詞句を作る語として適切なのは、(A) facilities「施設」。

120 Cowan Company is usually filled with the sound of people talking ------- in its research library.

(A) during
(B) despite
(C) among
(D) except

Cowan社は通常、研究図書館の中を除いて、人々の話し声で満たされています。

(A) ～の間に
(B) ～にもかかわらず
(C) ～の中で
(D) ～を除いて

正解 **D** 選択肢は全て前置詞の働きを持つ語。前置詞の後には通常は名詞(句)が続くが、ここではin its research library「その研究図書館の中で」という副詞句が続いている。(D) except「～を除いて」には、副詞句や副詞節を伴って使う用法があるので、これが適切。図書館内以外の職場環境について述べる内容になり、意味の上でも自然な文になる。be filled with ～「～で満たされている、～でいっぱいの」、sound of people talking「人々の話し声」、research library「研究図書館(あるテーマに関して重点的な研究調査が可能な図書館)」。

121 To predict erosion, geologists ------- the water absorption rate of soil near the mountain range.

(A) monitor
(B) practice
(C) surround
(D) occupy

土壌浸食を予測するため、地質学者は山岳地帯近くの土壌の吸水率を監視しています。

(A) ～を監視する
(B) ～の練習をする
(C) ～を取り囲む
(D) ～を占有する

正解 **A** 選択肢は全て動詞の働きを持つ語。主語はgeologists「地質学者たち」。空所には、述語動詞となり、空所に続く名詞句 the water absorption rate of soil「土壌の吸水率」を目的語とする語が入る。(A) monitor「～を監視する」が適切。predict「～を予測する」、erosion「浸食」、water absorption rate「吸水率」、soil「土壌、土」、mountain range「山岳地帯、山脈」。

122 Returns of merchandise with original tags and receipts are ------- accepted for up to 30 days after purchase.

(A) general
(B) generally
(C) generalize
(D) generalized

元のタグとレシートのある商品の返品は、一般的に、購入から30日後まで応じられます。

(A) 一般的な
(B) 一般的に
(C) 〜を一般化する
(D) 一般化された

正解 **B** この文の述語動詞は受動態のare accepted「応じられる、受け入れられる」。空所はそれに挟まれているので、述語動詞を修飾する副詞が入ると考えられる。副詞の(B) generally「一般的に」が適切。returns「返品」、merchandise「商品」、original「元の」、tag「タグ、札」、receipt「レシート」、up to 〜「〜まで」、purchase「購入」。
(A) 形容詞。
(C) 動詞の原形。
(D) 過去形または過去分詞。

123 The visiting delegation will join the CEO for refreshments after they finish the factory -------.

(A) toured
(B) tourism
(C) tourist
(D) tour

来訪する代表団は、工場見学を終えた後、CEOと一緒に軽食をとる予定です。

(A) 見学された
(B) 観光業
(C) 観光客
(D) 見学

正解 **D** 文頭からrefreshmentsまでが主節で、after they finish the factory -------「彼らが工場-------を終えた後で」が従属節。(D) tour「見学」を入れると、空所の前の名詞factoryと共にfactory tour「工場見学」という名詞句となって意味が通る。delegation「代表団」、join 〜 for …「〜と一緒に…をする」、CEO「最高経営責任者（chief executive officerの略）」、refreshments「軽食」。

124 Cost should not be the only factor taken into account ------- choosing a contractor for a renovation.

(A) back to
(B) when
(C) between
(D) in part

改修工事の請負業者を選定する際、コストを唯一の検討要素とすべきではありません。

(A) 〜に戻って
(B) 〜するとき
(C) 〜の間に
(D) 部分的に

正解 **B** 空所の前の部分は、「コストは考慮される唯一の要素であるべきではない」という意味。これだけで文として成り立つので、空所以降は修飾語句になると考えられる。接続詞の(B) when「〜するとき」を入れると、空所以降が「改修工事の請負業者を選定するときには」となって意味が通る。接続詞の後には〈主語＋動詞〉の形が続くのが原則だが、このwhen choosingは、when you are choosingまたはwhen you chooseを省略したもの、あるいは分詞構文の意味を明確にするために接続詞を入れたものと解釈できる。factor「要素」、take 〜 into account「〜を考慮する」、contractor「請負業者」、renovation「改修工事」。

125 We could reserve the auditorium; -------, we could consider meeting in one of the larger conference rooms.

    (A) alternatively
    (B) immediately
    (C) in particular
    (D) such as

私たちは講堂を予約してもいいでしょう。あるいは、大会議室の一つに集まることを検討してもいいでしょう。

    (A) あるいは
    (B) 即座に
    (C) 特に
    (D) ～のような

正解 A 空所の前の部分では講堂を予約することを提案しており、空所の後ろでは会議室に集まることを提案している。(A) alternatively「あるいは、その代わりに」を入れると、空所の後ろの部分が前の部分の代案となって、意味が通る。We could do ～ は「～してもいいでしょう」という提案の表現。reserve「～を予約する」、auditorium「講堂」、consider doing「～することを検討する」、meet「集まる、会合する」、conference room「会議室」。

---

126 By requiring the ------- inspection of all assembly-line machines, the new policy will help improve workplace safety.

    (A) periodic
    (B) period
    (C) periodically
    (D) periods

全ての組立ラインの機械の定期点検を義務化することによって、新方針は作業場の安全性を改善する助けとなるでしょう。

    (A) 定期的な
    (B) 期間
    (C) 定期的に
    (D) 期間

正解 A 空所の前には定冠詞theがあり、後ろには名詞のinspection「点検」があるので、空所にはinspectionを修飾する語が入ると考えられる。形容詞の(A) periodic「定期的な」が適切。require「～を義務化する」、assembly-line「組立ラインの」、policy「方針」、help do「～する助けとなる」、improve「～を改善する」、workplace「作業場、職場」、safety「安全性」。
(B) (D) 名詞。名詞の形容詞的用法により名詞が2つ続いて名詞句を作ることはあるが、ここでは意味が通らない。
(C) 副詞。

---

127 The company, which Mr. Sato initially operated out of his own home, was ------- sold for several billion yen.

    (A) tightly
    (B) subsequently
    (C) severely
    (D) evenly

その会社は、当初Satoさんが自宅で運営していましたが、後に数十億円で売却されました。

    (A) きつく
    (B) 後に
    (C) 厳しく
    (D) 平等に

正解 B 選択肢は全て副詞。カンマで挟まれた関係代名詞節が文の主語The companyを説明し、「その会社は、当初Satoさんが自宅で運営していたが」という意味になる。述語動詞はwas sold。空所に(B) subsequently「後に」を入れると、関係代名詞節中のinitially「当初、初めは」と対比され、会社は後に売却されたということになって意味が通る。operate「～を運営する」。
(A) (C) (D) 意味の通る文にならない。

128 In the interest of -------, product designer Yu Cai will remain the team lead until the project is completed.

(A) continue
(B) continuity
(C) continuous
(D) continuously

継続性を確保するため、製品デザイナーのYu Caiさんはそのプロジェクトが完了するまでチームリーダーにとどまります。

(A) 〜を続ける
(B) 継続性
(C) 継続的な
(D) 連続的に

正解 B in the interest of 〜は「〜の(利益の)ため」という意味で、後ろには名詞が続く。選択肢中の唯一の名詞である(B) continuity「継続性」が適切。remain 〜「〜のままである」、lead「リーダー、先頭」、be completed「完了する」。
(A) 動詞の原形。
(C) 形容詞。
(D) 副詞。

129 Owing to their ------- of hot, dry climates, evergreens like the Arizona cypress grow well in drought-prone areas.

(A) tolerance
(B) abundance
(C) performance
(D) allowance

アリゾナイトスギのような常緑樹は、暑く乾燥した気候に対する耐性のおかげで、渇水の起こりやすい地域でよく育ちます。

(A) 耐性
(B) 豊富
(C) 性能
(D) 許容

正解 A 選択肢は全て名詞。主語はevergreens like the Arizona cypressで、述語動詞はgrow。evergreens以降は、「アリゾナイトスギのような常緑樹は渇水の起こりやすい地域でよく育つ」という意味。文頭からclimatesまでは文全体を副詞的に説明する修飾句であり、owing to 〜は「〜のため」という意味で、理由を表す。tolerance of 〜で「〜に対する耐性」を意味するので、(A) tolerance「耐性」を入れると「暑く乾燥した気候に対する耐性のおかげで」となり、意味が通る。climate「気候」、evergreen「常緑樹」、cypress「イトスギ」、drought-prone「渇水の起こりやすい」。

130 Alvin Parno's insightful column about the crisis in the international trade situation is very -------.

(A) attractive
(B) comfortable
(C) informative
(D) wealthy

Alvin Parnoさんの国際貿易情勢における危機に関する洞察力に満ちたコラムは、非常に有益です。

(A) 魅力的な
(B) 心地よい
(C) 有益な
(D) 裕福な

正解 C 選択肢は全て形容詞。文頭からsituationまでが主語に当たり、「Alvin Parnoさんの国際貿易情勢における危機に関する洞察力に満ちたコラム」という意味。これを形容するのに最も適切なのは、(C) informative「有益な、役立つ情報を提供する」。insightful「洞察力のある」、column「(新聞・雑誌などの)コラム・欄」、crisis「危機」、trade「貿易」、situation「情勢、状況」。
(A)「魅力的な」という意味だが、内容よりも見た目に対して使われることが多い。

TEST 2 PART 5

147

PART 6

Questions 131-134 refer to the following notice.

Lost and Found

❶ If you think you may have lost an item in one of our ------- , we advise you to contact our Lost and
              131.

Found desk at 973-555-0147. Alternatively, you may send an e-mail to help@finnwayairport.com.

Include a description of your item and the date you lost it at the airport. We will ------- within
                                                132.

48 hours. Items are kept at Lost and Found for 90 days. ------- .
                                         133.

❷ Note, however, that any inquiries involving either missing checked baggage or an item that you

------- on an aircraft should be directed to the airline you traveled with.
134.

問題131-134は次のお知らせに関するものです。

遺失物取扱所

もし、当社の旅客ターミナルの一つで落とし物をされたかもしれないとお思いなら、遺失物取扱所に 973-555-0147 までご連絡くださるようお勧めします。あるいは、help@finnwayairport.com までEメールをお送りくださっても結構です。お探しの品物の説明と、それを空港で紛失した日にちを含めてください。48 時間以内にお返事いたします。品物は、遺失物取扱所で 90 日間保管されます。*この期間を過ぎると、ほとんどの品物は地元の慈善団体に寄付されます。

ただし、紛失した機内預入手荷物や、お客さまが機内に置き忘れたかもしれない品物に関するお問い合わせは全て、ご利用になった航空会社までお願いします。

*問題 133 の挿入文の訳

131
(A) shopping carts
(B) terminals
(C) fitting rooms
(D) taxis

(A) ショッピングカート
(B) ターミナル
(C) 試着室
(D) タクシー

正解 **B** 　選択肢は全て名詞。空所を含む文は、「もしあなたが、当社の-------の一つで落とし物をしたかもしれないと思うなら、遺失物取扱所に 973-555-0147 まで連絡するよう勧める」という意味。❶ 3 行目に Include ...... at the airport.「あなたの品物の説明と、それを空港で紛失した日にちを含めてください」とあるので、空港内での落とし物について述べていると分かる。(B) terminals「ターミナル」を入れると、our terminals が「当社の旅客ターミナル」を表すことになり、文脈に合う。
(A) (C) (D) いずれも文脈に合わない。

132
(A) respond
(B) depart
(C) watch
(D) begin

(A) 返答する
(B) 出発する
(C) 見守る
(D) 始まる

正解 **A** 　選択肢は全て動詞の働きを持つ語。空所を含む文の直前の 2 文で、E メールに探し物の説明と紛失した日にちを書いて送るように、と述べられている。空所に (A) respond「返答する」を入れると、E メールを受け取ってから 48 時間以内に返答することになり、文脈に合う。
(B) (C) (D) いずれも文脈に合わない。

133
(A) They are renewed monthly.
(B) During this time, they are discarded.
(C) A claim may be submitted by each passenger.
(D) After this time, most items are donated to local charities.

(A) それらは毎月、一新されます。
(B) この期間に、それらは処分されます。
(C) それぞれの乗客から請求が出されるかもしれません。
(D) この期間を過ぎると、ほとんどの品物は地元の慈善団体に寄付されます。

正解 **D** 　空所の直前の文の Items are kept at Lost and Found for 90 days. は、「品物は、遺失物取扱所で 90 日間保管される」という意味。空所に (D) を入れると、this time「この期間」が直前の文の 90 days を指して、90 日の保管期間を過ぎるとどうなるかを説明するという自然な流れになる。donate「~を寄付する」、charity「慈善団体、慈善事業」。
(A) 品物は 90 日間保管されることが説明されており、毎月一新はされない。renew「~を一新する、~を更新する」。
(B) 直前で品物は 90 日間保管されると述べられているので、その期間に処分されるという内容は前文と矛盾する。discard「~を処分する、~を捨てる」。
(C) claim「請求」、submit「~を提出する」、passenger「乗客」。

134
(A) must be leaving
(B) were leaving
(C) was left
(D) may have left

＊選択肢の訳は省略

正解 **D** 　動詞 leave「~を置き忘れる」の適切な形を選ぶ。空所を含む an item that you ------- on an aircraft は「あなたが機内に ------- 品物」という意味であり、空所に過去の推量を表す (D) may have left を入れると、「機内に置き忘れたかもしれない品物」という意味になる。その前にある名詞句 missing checked baggage「紛失した機内預入手荷物」と共に involving の目的語となって、紛失した機内預入手荷物や、機内に置き忘れた可能性のある品物についての問い合わせは、利用した航空会社宛てに行うよう注意を促す内容となる。
(A) 〈助動詞＋進行形〉、(B) 過去進行形。ここでの leave は「~を置き忘れる」という意味なので、進行形は意味が通らない。
(C) 過去形の受動態。主語の you と動詞が一致せず、意味も通らない。

Questions 135-138 refer to the following e-mail.

To: All Employees
From: Holly Grimes
Subject: Dress Code
Date: 1 May

Dear Forestport Consulting Staff,

① Beginning on 28 May, the Forestport Consulting Company ------- a new, more relaxed dress-code
135.
policy. Business-casual work attire will be allowed in the office except when meeting with clients.
-------, business-casual attire includes dress slacks and khaki trousers, skirts and dresses, and
136.
blouses and collared shirts. -------. Remember, this policy is intended to promote a comfortable
137.
but professional working environment to further support ------- productivity. If you have any
138.
questions, please consult Human Resources.

Thank you,

Holly Grimes
Chief Executive Officer

問題135-138は次のEメールに関するものです。

受信者：従業員各位
送信者：Holly Grimes
件名：服装規定
日付：5月1日

Forestportコンサルティング社のスタッフの皆さん

5月28日開始で、Forestportコンサルティング社はより緩やかな新しい服装規定方針を制定します。顧客と面会する場合を除いて、ビジネスカジュアルの仕事服がオフィス内で認められることになります。参考までに、ビジネスカジュアルの服装には、ドレススラックスやカーキ色のズボン、スカートやワンピース、それにブラウスや襟付きのシャツが含まれます。*ジーンズやTシャツ、袖なしのシャツは適切ではありません。この方針は、当社の生産性をさらに支援するための、快適ながらもプロ意識の高い労働環境の促進を意図したものであることをお忘れなく。何か質問がありましたら、人事部までご連絡ください。

よろしくお願いします。

Holly Grimes
最高経営責任者

*問題137の挿入文の訳

Expressions

be intended to do 「～することを意図している、～するのが目的である」（①4～5行目）
This book is intended to introduce the basic grammatical structures of the language.
この本は、その言語の基本的文法構造を紹介することを目的としています。

135 (A) will be instituting
(B) will be instituted
(C) to be instituting
(D) had instituted

＊選択肢の訳は省略

正解 A 動詞institute「～（制度・規則など）を制定する」の適切な形を選ぶ。空所を含む文の主語はthe Forestport Consulting Companyで、a new, more relaxed dress-code policy「より緩やかな新しい服装規定方針」が他動詞instituteの目的語になると考えられる。このEメールの送信日は5月1日であり、❶1行目に「5月28日開始で」とある。また、❶2行目の方針の内容を示す文では、Business-casual work attire will be allowed「ビジネスカジュアルの仕事服が認められることになる」と、未来形で述べられている。よって、新しい服装規定方針が制定されるのは未来のことだと分かるので、未来進行形の (A) が適切。
(B) 未来形の受動態。文法的に不適切。
(C) to不定詞の進行形。空所には述語動詞が必要だが、to不定詞は述語動詞の役割を果たさないので不適切。
(D) 過去完了形。時制が合わない。

136 (A) For this reason
(B) In the same fashion
(C) For your reference
(D) Now that

(A) この理由で
(B) 同様に
(C) 参考までに
(D) 今や～なので

正解 C 空所の前の文では、ビジネスカジュアルの服装が認められるようになると述べられている。空所に続くbusiness-casual attire includes ...... collared shirtsは、「ビジネスカジュアルの服装には、ドレススラックスやカーキ色のズボン、スカートやワンピース、それにブラウスや襟付きのシャツが含まれる」という意味なので、(C) For your reference「参考までに」を入れると、前文のビジネスカジュアルの服装の例を具体的に説明する自然な流れとなる。
(B) このfashionは「方法、やり方」という意味。

137 (A) Your new uniforms should be arriving next Tuesday or Wednesday.
(B) Feedback about the updated policy should not be reviewed until next week.
(C) All staff should be prepared to explain the new policy to clients.
(D) Jeans, T-shirts, and sleeveless shirts are not appropriate.

(A) 皆さんの新しい制服は、次の火曜日か水曜日に届くはずです。
(B) 更新された方針についての意見は、来週まで検討されないはずです。
(C) スタッフの全員が、顧客に新しい方針を説明できるように準備しておくべきです。
(D) ジーンズやTシャツ、袖なしのシャツは適切ではありません。

正解 D ❶1～4行目の空所直前までに、新しい服装規定でビジネスカジュアルが認められるようになることと、ビジネスカジュアルに含まれる服装の例が説明されている。空所に (D) を入れると、逆に適切ではない服装の説明となり、流れとして自然。sleeveless「袖なしの」、appropriate「適切な」。
(A) uniform「制服」。
(B) 新しい方針について述べられているが、それに対する意見への言及はない。review「～を検討する」。

138 (A) their
(B) our
(C) her
(D) my

(A) 彼らの
(B) 私たちの
(C) 彼女の
(D) 私の

正解 B 選択肢は全て代名詞の所有格であり、空所には続く名詞productivityにかかる語が入る。空所を含む文では、方針制定の意図は労働環境をより良くすることであると述べられており、その目的として to further support ------- productivity「-------生産性をさらに支援するため」とある。このEメールは、CEOであるHolly Grimesさんが自社の従業員宛てに送ったものなので、(B) our「私たちの」を入れると、our productivity「当社の生産性」となり、文脈に合う。

TEST 2 PART 6

Words & Phrases

dress code　服装規定、ドレスコード　❶ relaxed　緩やかな、厳格でない　attire　服装　allow　～を認める
except　～を除いて　dress slacks　ドレススラックス　★スーツのスラックスなどのきちんとしたズボン
khaki trousers　カーキ色のズボン　★「チノパン」の意味でも使われる　dress　ワンピース、ドレス　promote　～を促進する
professional　専門性の高い、専門職の　working environment　労働環境　productivity　生産性　consult　～に相談する

Questions 139-142 refer to the following letter.

Dear Ms. Khan,

❶ Thank you for enrolling in the back pain management sessions at Bend Physical Therapy. We are excited to partner with you on your journey back to health. In the next week, you will receive your health kit. ------- .
139.

❷ Your personal trainer will be Coach Jenni. She will get in touch with you ------- . She will teach
140.
you exercises that hopefully will enable you ------- your back pain.
141.

❸ Should you have any questions, please consult our Web site or give ------- a call at
142.
863-555-0122.

Sincerely,

Melissa Agarwal
Bend Physical Therapy

問題139-142は次の手紙に関するものです。

Khan様

Bend理学療法社の腰痛対策セッションにご登録いただきありがとうございます。当社はあなたが健康を取り戻すための旅にご一緒できることをうれしく思います。来週、健康用具一式をお受け取りいただきます。*それには、ご家庭で使用するエクササイズマットと、ストレングスバンドが入っています。

あなたの専任トレーナーはJenniコーチになります。間もなく、彼女からご連絡を差し上げます。彼女はあなたの腰痛を取り除けるだろうと期待できる運動をお教えします。

もしご質問がありましたら、当社のウェブサイトをお調べになるか、863-555-0122まで当社にお電話ください。

敬具

Melissa Agarwal
Bend理学療法社

*問題139の挿入文の訳

Words & Phrases

❶ enroll in ~ ~に登録する、~に入会する   back pain 腰の痛み、背中の痛み   management 疾病管理
physical therapy 理学療法   partner with ~ ~とパートナーを組む   journey 旅   back to ~ ~に戻って
kit 用具一式 **❷** personal 個人専用の   trainer トレーナー   exercise 運動、エクササイズ
hopefully うまくいけば、願わくは   enable ~ to do ~が…することを可能にする
❸ Should you have ~, もしあなたに~があるなら ★If you should have ~, のIfが省略され、shouldが文頭に置かれた倒置表現
consult ~を調べる、~に相談する   give ~ a call ~に電話する

139
(A) It includes an exercise mat and a strength band for home use.
(B) Our clients often recommend our center to their colleagues.
(C) Please renew your payment option as soon as possible.
(D) Please submit this form by the due date, next Friday.

(A) それには、ご家庭で使用するエクササイズマットと、ストレングスバンドが入っています。
(B) 当社の顧客はしばしば、当センターを同僚の方々に薦めます。
(C) できるだけ早くお支払い方法の選択を更新してください。
(D) この申込用紙を、締切日である次の金曜日までに提出してください。

正解 **A**　❶ 1〜2行目から、手紙の受取人のKhanさんはBend理学療法社の腰痛対策セッションに登録したと分かる。続く空所直前の文は、「来週、あなたは健康用具一式を受け取るだろう」という意味。(A)を入れると、Itが前文のyour health kit「健康用具一式」を受け、用具一式の内容を説明する文となるので、流れとして自然。exercise mat「エクササイズマット」、strength band「ストレングスバンド、トレーニングチューブ（エクササイズ用のゴム製バンド）」。
(B) recommend「〜を推薦する」、colleague「同僚」。
(C) renew「〜を更新する」、option「選択、選択肢」。
(D) form「申込用紙」、due date「締切日」。

140
(A) temporarily
(B) shortly
(C) luckily
(D) similarly

(A) 一時的に
(B) 間もなく
(C) 幸運にも
(D) 同様に

正解 **B**　選択肢は全て副詞。空所を含む文は、「-------彼女はあなたに連絡するだろう」という意味。彼女というのは、直前の文の「あなたの専任トレーナーはJenniコーチになる」におけるJenniコーチを指している。空所を含む文の後に、「彼女はあなたに運動を教えるだろう」という内容が続く。空所に(B) shortly「間もなく」を入れると、❷ 1文目がコーチの紹介、2文目がコーチが間もなくすること、3文目がコーチが指導する内容を表し、自然な流れになる。
(A) (C) (D) いずれも文脈に合わない。

141
(A) to eliminate
(B) is eliminating
(C) has eliminated
(D) the elimination of

＊選択肢の訳は省略

正解 **A**　選択肢は動詞eliminate「〜を取り除く」の変化した形や派生語。空所を含む文のexercises that hopefully will enable you ------- your back painはthat以下がexercisesを修飾する関係代名詞節になっている。この節の中では、関係代名詞thatが主語の働き、will enableが述語動詞の働きをしている。空所にto不定詞の(A) to eliminateを入れると、enable 〜 to do「〜が…することを可能にする」という形になり、「運動があなたが腰痛を取り除くことを可能にする」という意味になるので適切。
(B) 現在進行形、(C) 現在完了形。いずれも主語に相当する語がないので文法的に不適切。
(D)「〜の除去」という意味だが、enableには「人」と「もの」という2つの目的語が続くことはないので不適切。

142
(A) it
(B) us
(C) mine
(D) them

(A) それに
(B) 私たちに
(C) 私のもの
(D) 彼らに

正解 **B**　選択肢は全て人称代名詞。give 〜 a callで「〜に電話する」という意味。(B) us「私たちに」を入れると、give us a callで「当社に電話してください」という意味になり、適切。
(A) itがour Web site「当社のウェブサイト」を指すことになり、不適切。

TEST2 PART 6

Expressions

get in touch with 〜　「〜と連絡を取る」（❷1行目）
I've been trying to get in touch with someone in customer service all morning.
私は午前中ずっと顧客サービス部の方と連絡を取ろうとしていました。

Questions 143-146 refer to the following press release.

FOR IMMEDIATE RELEASE

Media contact: Emiko Inoue, press officer <einoue@laurelhursttechnology.com>

❶ SEATTLE (July 20)—Laurelhurst Technology announced today the upcoming launch of Fabulan, its new online streaming platform. ------- . Each segment is to be at most five minutes long and filmed
143.
with smaller, handheld screen sizes in mind. Fabulan ------- will focus on home repairs, cooking
144.
tips, craft ideas, and other topics of common interest.

❷ Content developers ------- to the challenge presented by the limited format specifications.
145.
"Personally, I'm excited to produce my first Fabulan segment," said producer Jared Holm. "This format requires thinking even more ------- about how we present a topic. I'm eager to see what
146.
effect that has on my work."

問題143-146は次のプレスリリースに関するものです。

即日発表

メディア問い合わせ先：Emiko Inoue、広報担当 <einoue@laurelhursttechnology.com>

シアトル（7月20日）——Laurelhurstテクノロジー社は本日、同社の新しいオンライン・ストリーミング用プラットフォームである Fabulanの近日中のサービス開始を発表した。*それは、携帯電話用にフォーマットされた短いコンテンツを特徴とする。各番組は最長でも5分間で、小さめの、手のひらサイズの画面の大きさを念頭に撮影される。Fabulanの動画は、家の修繕、料理のコツ、工作のアイデア、その他の一般に興味を持たれるような話題に焦点を絞ったものになる。

コンテンツ開発者たちは、制約のあるフォーマット仕様によって生じる難題に向かって立ち上がろうとしている。「個人的に、私の最初の Fabulanの番組を制作することにわくわくしています」と、制作者のJared Holm氏は述べた。「このフォーマットは、われわれが一つの話題をどのように提示するかということについて、より一層クリエイティブな思考を要求します。それが私の作品にどんな影響を与えるのかをぜひ見てみたいと思います」。

*問題143の挿入文の訳

Words & Phrases

For Immediate Release　即日発表、即日解禁　★報道機関から一般への情報解禁日時の指定がない場合に使われる
media contact　メディア問い合わせ先　　press officer　広報担当者　❶ launch　新製品の売り出し
streaming　ストリーミング　★音声や動画をインターネット上で配信する際に、読み込みながら再生する方式
platform　プラットフォーム　★システムの基盤となる運用環境　　segment　番組、部分　　film　～を撮影する
with ～ in mind　～を念頭に置いて、～を考慮して　　handheld　手のひらサイズの、手で持てる　　focus on ～　～に焦点を絞る
repairs　修繕作業　　tip　こつ　　craft　手工芸品、クラフト　　topic　話題　　common　一般的な　❷ content　コンテンツ
developer　開発者　　challenge　難題、試練　　present　～（困難など）を生じさせる　　limited　制限のある、限られた
specifications　仕様、スペック　　personally　個人的に　　be excited to do　～することにわくわくしている
produce　～を創作する、～を作る　　producer　制作者　　present　～を提示する　　effect　影響　　work　作品

Expressions

be eager to do　「～したくてたまらない、～することを熱望している」（❷ 3～4行目）

Our new CEO is eager to enter the Asian market.
当社の新しいCEOは、アジア市場への参入に非常に意欲的です。

143

(A) Its exclusive music-related audio channels are very popular.

(B) The app is already installed on many top-rated smart televisions.

(C) It will feature short content that is formatted for mobile phones.

(D) Laurelhurst is known primarily for its child-friendly educational materials.

(A) それ専用の音楽関連の音声配信チャンネルはとても人気がある。

(B) そのアプリはすでに、人気のある多くのスマートテレビにインストールされている。

(C) それは、携帯電話用にフォーマットされた短いコンテンツを特徴とする。

(D) Laurelhurst 社は主に子ども向けの教材で知られている。

正解 C 空所直前の文で、Fabulanという名前の新しいオンライン・ストリーミング用プラットフォームが近日中にサービスを開始すると紹介されている。空所に(C)を入れると、It「それ」がFabulanを指して、Fabulanの特徴を説明する文になる。さらに、short content that is formatted for mobile phones「携帯電話用にフォーマットされた短いコンテンツ」が、空所直後の文「各番組は最長でも5分間で、小さめの、手のひらサイズの画面の大きさを念頭に撮影される」で具体的に補足されることになり、自然な流れとなる。feature「～を特徴とする」、format「～をフォーマットする、～の形式・体裁を整える」。
(A) まだサービスが始まっていないので「人気がある」というのは文脈に合わない。exclusive「専用の」、-related「～関連の」、audio channel「音声配信チャンネル」。
(B) アプリやスマートテレビについての言及はない。app「アプリ（applicationの略）」、install「～をインストールする」、top-rated「人気のある」。
(D) primarily「主として」、child-friendly「子ども向けの」、educational「教育的な」。

144

(A) signals
(B) fashions
(C) exhibits
(D) videos

(A) 信号
(B) 様式
(C) 展示品
(D) 動画

正解 D 選択肢は全て名詞の働きを持つ語。空所を含む文の直前で、「各番組は最長でも5分間で、小さめの、手のひらサイズの画面の大きさを念頭に撮影される」と、このプラットフォームで公開される番組の長さや最適な画面サイズについて説明されている。その内容に続くので、空所に(D) videos「動画」を入れると、Fabulanで配信される予定のコンテンツを具体的に紹介するという自然な流れとなる。
(A) (B) (C) いずれも文脈に合わない。

145

(A) will have risen
(B) would be rising
(C) are rising
(D) to be risen

＊選択肢の訳は省略

正解 C 動詞riseの適切な形を選ぶ。rise to ～で、「～（要求など）に応じて立ち上がる」という意味。この文の主語はContent developersで、空所には述語動詞が入る。空所の後のthe challenge presented by the limited format specifications「制約のあるフォーマット仕様によって生じる難題」は、❶で述べられた小さい画面向けの短い動画という仕様上の制約による難題を意味すると考えられる。Fabulanは近日開始されるサービスなので、その制約のあるフォーマットに立ち向かっていることを表すのに適切なのは、現在進行形の(C) are rising。続く❷2～4行目で、現在この難題に取り組んでいるコンテンツ開発者の一人として、Jared Holmという人物がFabulanで公開する初めての番組制作への意欲を述べる発言が続き、流れとして自然。
(A) 未来完了形。文脈に合わない。
(B) 〈推量の助動詞＋進行形〉。続けて開発者の発言が紹介されているので、推量の助動詞は文脈に合わない。
(D) to不定詞の受動態。述語動詞にならない。

146

(A) created
(B) creative
(C) creativity
(D) creatively

(A) 創造された
(B) 創造的な
(C) 創造性
(D) 創造的に

正解 D 空所を含む文の主語はThis format、述語動詞はrequires。述語動詞の目的語となる動名詞thinking「考えること」を修飾する副詞の(D) creatively「創造的に」を入れると、thinking even more creativelyが「より一層創造的に考えること」という意味になり、適切。
(A) 動詞の過去形または過去分詞。
(B) 形容詞。
(C) 名詞。

PART 7

Questions 147-148 refer to the following roadside sign.

FIVE STATES BARBECUE

❶ Turn left at the next traffic light.

❷ <u>Hot Sandwiches and Platters from $7</u>
- Texas Beef Brisket
- Missouri Pork Ribs
- Kentucky Grilled Chicken
- Carolina Pulled Pork
- California Roasted Vegetables

❸ Rated best restaurant 3 years in a row!

❹ Open for lunch from 11:00 A.M. to 3:30 P.M.

❺ CLOSED MONDAYS

問題147-148は次の道路沿いの看板に関するものです。

FIVE STATESバーベキュー店

次の信号で左折してください。

<u>ホットサンドイッチと大皿料理が7ドル〜</u>
- テキサス・ビーフブリスケット
- ミズーリ・ポークリブ
- ケンタッキー・グリルチキン
- カロライナ・プルドポーク
- カリフォルニア・ローストベジタブル

3年連続で最良のレストランと評価されました!

午前11時から午後3時30分までランチ営業

毎週月曜日定休

156

147 What is suggested about Five States Barbecue?

    (A) It offers breakfast.
    (B) It has many locations.
    (C) It is very popular.
    (D) It is open on Mondays.

Five States バーベキュー店について何が分かりますか。

    (A) 朝食を提供している。
    (B) 多くの店舗を持っている。
    (C) とても人気がある。
    (D) 毎週月曜日に開いている。

正解 C

❸に Rated best restaurant 3 years in a row「3年連続で最良のレストランと評価された」とあるので、Five States バーベキュー店はとても人気があると考えられる。よって、(C)が正解。
(A) ❹より、提供しているのは昼食のみと分かる。offer「～を提供する」。
(B) 店名に FIVE STATES BARBECUE「5つの州のバーベキュー」とあって❷のメニュー品目にそれぞれ州の名前が含まれているが、多くの店舗を持っているという記述はない。location「店舗」。
(D) ❺に「毎週月曜日定休」とある。

---

148 What is most likely true about the California menu item?

    (A) It comes with a salad.
    (B) It is served cold.
    (C) It contains no meat.
    (D) It is the most expensive item.

カリフォルニアというメニュー品目について正しいと考えられることは何ですか。

    (A) サラダが付いている。
    (B) 冷たい状態で出される。
    (C) 肉が入っていない。
    (D) 最も高価な品である。

正解 C

カリフォルニアというメニュー品目とは、❷6行目の California Roasted Vegetables「カリフォルニア・ローストベジタブル」のことを指している。肉類が含まれる他の品名と異なり、Roasted Vegetables という品名なので、野菜類のみを材料とする料理だと考えられる。よって、(C)が正解。menu item「メニュー品目（飲食店がメニューに載せている料理や飲み物）」。contain「～を含む」、meat「肉」。
(A) come with ～「～が付く」。
(B) roasted「焼かれた、あぶった」とあるので冷たいとは考えにくい。serve ～ …「～(飲食物など)を…の状態で出す」。
(D) ❷1行目に「7ドル～」との記載はあるが、それぞれの料理の価格は不明。expensive「高価な」。

Words & Phrases

roadside　道路沿いの　　sign　看板　　❶ traffic light　信号　　❷ platter　大皿料理
brisket　ブリスケット　★牛胸肉を野菜などと一緒にオーブンなどで火を通したもの
pork ribs　ポークリブ　★豚の背骨の部分の肉をバーベキューソースなどを付けてグリルしたもの　　grill　（直火や焼き網で）～を焼く
pulled pork　プルドポーク　★豚の塊肉に低温でじっくりと火を通し、細かくほぐしたもの　　roast　（オーブンや直火で）～を焼く
❸ rate ～ …　～を…と格付けする

Expressions

in a row　「連続して」（❸）

Real wages decreased four years in a row.
実質賃金は4年続けて減少しました。

Questions 149-150 refer to the following product usage instructions.

❶ **Drohol Lotion:** For minor skin irritation, itching, or rash. Safe for use on adults and children over twelve years old.

❷ **Directions:** Apply directly to the affected area twice a day for up to two weeks. Keep away from eyes and mouth. Store at room temperature (approximately 17–25 degrees Celsius). Protect lotion from freezing.

❸
Net weight 16 grams
Produced by Dojing Pharmaceuticals, Singapore

問題149-150は次の製品使用説明書に関するものです。

Drohol ローション：軽症の皮膚炎、かゆみ、または発疹に。成人および13歳以上の子どもに安全に使用可能。

使用法：最長2週間、1日2回、患部に直接塗ってください。目や口に近づけないようにしてください。室温で保管してください（およそ17～25℃）。ローションが凍結しないようにしてください。

正味重量16グラム
シンガポール、Dojing製薬会社製

149 What is the product intended to treat?

 (A) The hair
 (B) The eyes
 (C) The mouth
 (D) The skin

製品は何を手当てすることを目的としていますか。

 (A) 髪
 (B) 目
 (C) 口
 (D) 皮膚

| 正解 D | ❶ 1行目に、For minor skin irritation, itching, or rash.「軽症の皮膚炎、かゆみ、または発疹に」とあるので、(D)が正解。be intended to *do*「〜することを目的としている」、treat「〜を手当てする、〜を治療する」。 |

(B) (C) ❷ 1〜2行目に、「目や口に近づけないようにしなさい」とあり、目や口の手当ては想定されていない。

150 What are users instructed to do?

 (A) Keep the product from getting too cold
 (B) Apply the product once a day
 (C) Administer the product on adults only
 (D) Discard any of the product that is left after one year

使用者は何をするように指示されていますか。

 (A) 製品が冷たくなり過ぎないようにする
 (B) 製品を1日に1回塗る
 (C) 製品を成人にのみ塗布する
 (D) 1年後に残っている製品は全て処分する

| 正解 A | ❷ 2〜3行目に、およそ17〜25℃の室温で保管するよう書かれており、続く同3行目に、Protect lotion from freezing.「ローションが凍結しないようにしなさい」とあるので、(A)が正解。be instructed to *do*「〜するように指示される」。keep 〜 from *doing*「〜が…しないようにする」。 |

(B) ❷ 1行目で、1日に2回塗るよう指示されている。
(C) ❶ 1〜2行目に、13歳以上の子どもにも使用できることが記載されている。administer「〜を塗布する、〜を投与する」。
(D) 残った製品の処分については言及がない。discard「〜を処分する、〜を廃棄する」。

Expressions

protect 〜 from … 「〜を…から保護する」(❷ 3行目)

Please be sure to wrap these teacups in paper to protect them from being damaged.
破損しないように、これらのティーカップを必ず紙で包むようにしてください。

Questions 151-153 refer to the following article.

Bike Pedal Recall

❶ ABERDEEN (24 December)—Saorsa Mountain Bikes has recalled 5,000 bicycles sold in the United Kingdom between 9 October and 21 December. "This is a voluntary recall," said Jonathan Wakerman, spokesperson for Saorsa Mountain Bikes. "We have had a few cases where the plastic pedals cracked, and people could not complete their rides."

❷ No consumer injuries in the field have been reported, but recent additional testing by the manufacturer has revealed that too high a percentage of pedals are failing with normal use. Consumers are urged to bring their Saorsa Mountain Bike model 700XFT bicycles with plastic pedals to any authorised retail dealer, where aluminium replacement pedals will be installed at no cost to the owner.

問題151-153は次の記事に関するものです。

自転車ペダルのリコール

アバディーン（12月24日）——Saorsaマウンテンバイク社は10月9日から12月21日の間に英国で販売された自転車5,000台を回収した。「これは自主回収です」とSaorsaマウンテンバイク社の広報担当者Jonathan Wakermanは述べた。「プラスチック製ペダルにひびが入って、自転車に乗れなくなるケースが数件ありました」。

実際に使用中の消費者の負傷は報告されていないが、同メーカーによる最近の追加検査で、通常の使用でペダルが故障する割合が高過ぎることが明らかになった。消費者はプラスチック製ペダルの付いたSaorsaマウンテンバイク700XFTモデルの自転車をいずれかの公認小売店に持ち込むよう要請されており、そこで交換品のアルミニウム製ペダルが所有者に無償で取り付けられることになる。

Words & Phrases

pedal ペダル recall リコール、（欠陥商品などの）回収 ❶ mountain bike マウンテンバイク recall ～（欠陥商品など）を回収する the United Kingdom 英国 voluntary 自発的な、任意の spokesperson 広報担当者 crack ひびが入る ride 乗ること ❷ consumer 消費者 injury 負傷 in the field 実際に使われて、実地で report ～を報告する additional 追加の testing 検査 manufacturer メーカー、製造業者 reveal that ～ ～ということを明らかにする percentage 割合 fail 故障する normal 通常の be urged to do ～するように要請されている bring ～ to … ～を…に持ち込む authorised 公認の、認可された ★米国表記はauthorized retail dealer 小売業者 aluminium アルミニウム ★米国表記はaluminum replacement 交換 install ～を取り付ける at no cost 無料で owner 所有者

Expressions

a case where ～ 「～のケース、～の場合」（❶6～9行目）
There are several cases where this rule doesn't apply.
この規則が適用されないケースが幾つかあります。

151 What is the purpose of the article?

 (A) To introduce a new bicycle model
 (B) To discuss biking accessories
 (C) To issue a warning about a product
 (D) To explain how bicycles are designed

記事の目的は何ですか。

 (A) 新型モデルの自転車を紹介すること
 (B) 自転車付属品について詳しく述べること
 (C) ある製品について警告を発すること
 (D) 自転車がどのように設計されているのか説明すること

> **正解 C** 見出しと❶ 1～4行目より、この記事はSaorsaマウンテンバイク社による自転車の回収（リコール）について述べていると分かる。同6～9行目で、プラスチック製ペダルにひびが入るケースがあったと述べられ、続く❷ 1～5行目で、通常の使用でペダルが故障する割合が高過ぎることが分かったと書かれている。それゆえ、同5～7行目で、プラスチック製ペダルの付いた特定モデルの自転車を所有する消費者はそれを公認小売店に持ち込むよう要請されている。よって、記事の目的は製品について警告を発することだと考えられるので、(C)が正解。issue a warning「警告を発する」。
> (A) 自転車の特定のモデルへの言及はあるが、新型として紹介はされていない。introduce「～を紹介する」。
> (B) discuss「～について詳しく述べる」、biking accessory「自転車用付属品」。

152 What does the article indicate about the plastic pedals?

 (A) They make riders more comfortable.
 (B) They are usually less expensive.
 (C) They are commonly available.
 (D) They may break too easily.

記事はプラスチック製ペダルについて何を示していますか。

 (A) 乗り手をより快適にする。
 (B) 通例、より安価である。
 (C) 一般に入手可能である。
 (D) 壊れやす過ぎる可能性がある。

> **正解 D** ❶ 6～9行目で、プラスチック製ペダルにひびが入ったケースに言及があり、❷ 2～5行目に、recent additional testing by the manufacturer has revealed that too high a percentage of pedals are failing with normal use「同メーカーによる最近の追加検査で、通常の使用でペダルが故障する割合が高過ぎることが明らかになった」と書かれている。よって、プラスチック製ペダルが壊れやす過ぎる可能性があると分かるので、(D)が正解。
> (A) rider「乗り手」、comfortable「快適な、心地よい」。
> (C) commonly「一般に」、available「入手できる」。

153 What are some bicycle owners advised to do?

 (A) Purchase replacement parts
 (B) Take their bicycles to a dealership
 (C) Read a bicycle repair manual
 (D) Try out several bicycle models

一部の自転車の所有者は何をするように勧められていますか。

 (A) 交換用の部品を購入する
 (B) 自転車を販売代理店に持っていく
 (C) 自転車修理マニュアルを読む
 (D) 幾つかのモデルの自転車を試してみる

> **正解 B** ❷ 5～7行目に、Consumers are urged to bring their Saorsa Mountain Bike model 700XFT bicycles with plastic pedals to any authorised retail dealer「消費者はプラスチック製ペダルの付いたSaorsaマウンテンバイク 700XFTモデルの自転車をいずれかの公認小売店に持ち込むよう要請されている」と書かれており、続く同8～9行目で、アルミ製ペダルに無料交換してもらえると説明されている。よって、このモデルの所有者は自分の自転車を販売代理店に持っていくように勧められていることが分かるので、(B)が正解。be advised to do「～するように勧められている」。dealership「販売代理店」。
> (A) ❷ 8～9行目より、交換用のペダルは無償と分かる。part「部品」。
> (C) repair「修理」、manual「マニュアル」。
> (D) try out ～「～を試してみる」。

Questions 154-155 refer to the following text-message chain.

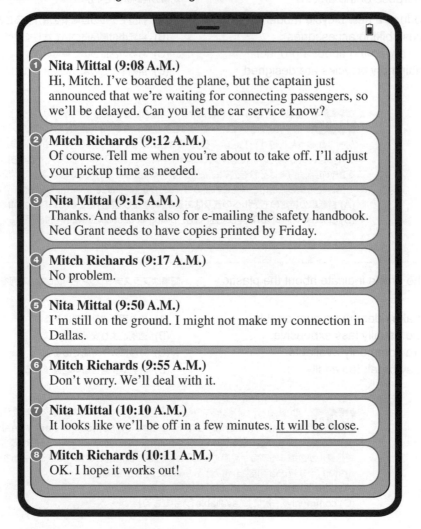

問題154-155は次のテキストメッセージのやりとりに関するものです。

Nita Mittal（午前9時08分）
こんにちは、Mitch。私は飛行機に乗りました。しかし、機長から乗り継ぎの乗客を待っているとのアナウンスがあったところなので、遅延しそうです。カーサービスに知らせてもらえますか。

Mitch Richards（午前9時12分）
もちろんです。離陸しそうになったら連絡してください。必要に応じて迎えの時間を調整します。

Nita Mittal（午前9時15分）
ありがとうございます。それに安全ハンドブックをEメールで送ってくれたこともありがとうございます。Ned Grantが金曜日までにコピーを印刷してもらう必要があるのです。

Mitch Richards（午前9時17分）
どういたしまして。

Nita Mittal（午前9時50分）
まだ地上にいます。ダラスでの乗り継ぎに間に合わないかもしれません。

Mitch Richards（午前9時55分）
心配しないでください。私たちが対処しますから。

Nita Mittal（午前10時10分）
数分後に離陸するようです。<u>際どいところでしょうね。</u>

Mitch Richards（午前10時11分）
分かりました。うまくいくことを願っています。

154 At 10:10 A.M., what does Ms. Mittal most likely mean when she writes, "It will be close"?

    (A) She might miss her next flight.
    (B) She will receive a document just in time to meet a deadline.
    (C) She thinks the airport in Dallas is conveniently located.
    (D) She plans to send another message soon.

午前 10 時 10 分に、"It will be close"という発言で、Mittal さんは何を意図していると考えられますか。

    (A) 彼女は次の便に間に合わないかもしれない。
    (B) 彼女は締め切りにちょうど間に合うように書類を受け取るだろう。
    (C) 彼女はダラスの空港が便利な場所にあると思っている。
    (D) 彼女はすぐに別のメッセージを送るつもりである。

> **正解 A** Mittal さんは、午前 9 時 08 分に❶で、搭乗した飛行機が遅延する見込みを Richards さんに伝え、午前 9 時 50 分に❺で、I'm still on the ground. I might not make my connection in Dallas.「まだ地上にいる。ダラスでの乗り継ぎに間に合わないかもしれない」と発言し、乗継便に乗り遅れる可能性を懸念している。その 20 分後の午前 10 時 10 分に❼で、「数分後に離陸するようだ」と述べてから下線部の発言をしている。close はこの文脈では「際どい」という意味と考えられるので、Mittal さんは自分が次の便に間に合うかが際どいと伝えていると判断できる。よって、(A) が正解。miss「~に間に合わない」、flight「航空機の便、フライト」。
> (B) document「書類」、in time to *do*「~するのに間に合って」、meet a deadline「締め切りに間に合う」。
> (C) be located「位置している」、conveniently「利便性よく」。

155 What will Mr. Richards probably do next?

    (A) E-mail a safety handbook
    (B) Ask Mr. Grant for copies of a document
    (C) Make hotel reservations for Ms. Mittal
    (D) Contact a car service

Richards さんはおそらく次に何をしますか。

    (A) 安全ハンドブックを E メールで送る
    (B) Grant さんに書類のコピーを要望する
    (C) Mittal さんのためにホテルを予約する
    (D) カーサービスに連絡する

> **正解 D** Mittal さんは❶で、自分の便が遅延するだろうと伝えた後、Can you let the car service know?「カーサービスに知らせてもらえるか」と依頼している。それに対して、Richards さんは❷で、Of course. と快諾し、Tell me when you're about to take off. I'll adjust your pickup time as needed.「離陸しそうになったら連絡してください。必要に応じて迎えの時間を調整する」と述べている。最終的に❼で、「数分後に離陸するようだ」と連絡する Mittal さんに対して、Richards さんは❽で、OK と応答しているので、この後 Richards さんはカーサービスに連絡するだろうと判断できる。よって、(D) が正解。contact「~に連絡する」。
> (A) ❸より、安全ハンドブックはすでに E メールで送られていると分かる。
> (B) ❸より、Grant さんが安全ハンドブックを印刷してもらう必要があると分かるが、Richards さんが Grant さんに対してコピーを頼むとは述べられていない。ask ~ for …「~に…を要望する」。
> (C) make a reservation「予約をする」。

Words & Phrases

❶ board　~(旅客機・船など)に乗り込む　　captain　機長　　announce that ~　~とアナウンスする、~と知らせる
connecting passenger　乗り継ぎの乗客　　be delayed　遅れる　　❷ be about to *do*　まさに~しようとしている
take off　離陸する　　adjust　~を調整する　　pickup　送迎の　　as needed　必要に応じて　　❸ e-mail　~を E メールで送る
safety handbook　安全ハンドブック　　❹ No problem　どういたしまして　　❺ on the ground　地上に
make *one's* connection　乗り継ぎに間に合う　　❼ be off　離陸する、出発する　　in a few minutes　数分後に
close　際どい、間一髪の　　❽ work out　うまくいく

Expressions

deal with ~　「~に対処する、~を扱う」(❻)

The problem should be dealt with through international cooperation.
その問題は国際的な協調を通じて対処されるべきです。

Questions 156-157 refer to the following instructions.

Caring for your Brewtime Supreme coffeemaker

❶ Machine cleaning: Your Brewtime Supreme coffeemaker is designed to last many years, providing you with delicious coffee day after day. For optimal performance, clean your Brewtime Supreme on a monthly basis. While commercial cleaning solutions are available, a 50-50 mixture of white vinegar and water may also be used. First, pour the cleaning solution into the coffeemaker's reservoir, switch the coffeemaker on, and allow half of the solution to drip into the carafe. Then, switch the coffeemaker off and wait 30 minutes for it to cool. Next, refill the reservoir with more of the solution, and allow the brewing process to finish. Finally, with water only, repeat the brewing process so that any remaining residue is washed away. Perform this action twice if necessary.

問題156-157は次の説明書に関するものです。

Brewtime Supreme コーヒーメーカーのお手入れ

機械洗浄：Brewtime Supremeコーヒーメーカーは、あなたに毎日おいしいコーヒーを提供しつつ、長年持ちこたえるように設計されています。最大限の性能を実現するためには、月に1回の頻度でBrewtime Supremeを洗浄してください。市販の洗浄液をご使用いただけますが、ホワイトビネガーと水を半分ずつ混ぜたものも使用できます。最初に、洗浄液をコーヒーメーカーの給水タンクに注ぎ、コーヒーメーカーのスイッチを入れ、洗浄液の半分がポットに落ちるようにしてください。そして、コーヒーメーカーのスイッチを切り、冷めるまで30分待ってください。次に、給水タンクにさらに洗浄液を補充して、抽出工程を終わらせてください。最後に、水だけで、全ての残留物が洗い流されるように抽出工程を繰り返してください。必要ならこの工程を2回行ってください。

156 For whom are the instructions most likely intended?

(A) Appliance retailers
(B) Product owners
(C) Product designers
(D) Repair technicians

説明書は誰を対象としていると考えられますか。

(A) 電化製品の小売業者
(B) 製品の所有者
(C) 製品の設計者
(D) 修理技師

正解 B 見出しに、Caring for your Brewtime Supreme coffeemaker「Brewtime Supreme コーヒーメーカーのお手入れ」とある。また、❶ 1～2 行目に、Your Brewtime Supreme coffeemaker is designed to last many years, providing you with delicious coffee day after day.「Brewtime Supreme コーヒーメーカーは、あなたに毎日おいしいコーヒーを提供しつつ、長年持ちこたえるように設計されている」と書かれている。ここでの your や you が説明書の対象者であり、Brewtime Supreme coffeemaker という製品を購入した所有者を指すと判断できるので、(B) が正解。be intended for ～「～を対象としている」。owner「所有者」。
(A) appliance「電化製品」、retailer「小売業者」。
(C) designer「設計者」。
(D) technician「技師」。

157 According to the instructions, how often should cleaning be performed?

(A) Every day
(B) Every two weeks
(C) Once a month
(D) Twice a year

説明書によると、洗浄はどのくらいの頻度で行われるべきですか。

(A) 毎日
(B) 2週間ごとに
(C) 1カ月に1度
(D) 1年に2度

正解 C ❶ 2～3 行目に、For optimal performance, clean your Brewtime Supreme on a monthly basis.「最大限の性能を実現するためには、月に1回の頻度で Brewtime Supreme を洗浄してください」とある。on a monthly basis を once a month と表している (C) が正解。
(B) every に数詞が続くと「～ごとに」という意味になる。

Expressions

wait for ～ to do 「～が…するのを待つ」（❶ 7行目）

All we can do is wait for the package to arrive.
私たちができることは荷物が届くのを待つことだけです。

Questions 158-160 refer to the following e-mail.

To:	All Employees
From:	Ken Ishibashi
Date:	11 June
Subject:	New procedure

1 The Tech Help Desk tends to receive a high number of service requests between the hours of 8:00 A.M. and 10:00 A.M. Our staff has the capacity to handle all of these within a reasonable time frame, but to improve efficiency we need your help in implementing a new procedure.

2 Going forward, employees must designate a priority level when submitting service requests. "Critical priority" designations will be reserved for problems that directly jeopardize our ability to meet client obligations. These requests will be acted on immediately by Help Desk staff members. The "high priority" designation should be used for issues that are preventing employees from doing their work. These issues will be handled within three hours, if possible. However, 60% of the requests we typically receive are for less time-sensitive issues and should be marked "standard priority." We will respond to these requests within 24 hours of submission. Finally, "low priority" requests will be addressed within three business days. Requests for software enhancements, for example, would fall under this last category.

3 As usual, the status of your service requests will be updated on the Tech Help Desk's Web site.

Thank you.

問題158-160は次のEメールに関するものです。

受信者：従業員各位
送信者：Ken Ishibashi
日付：6月11日
件名：新たな手続き

技術ヘルプデスクは午前8時から午前10時の時間帯に多数の業務依頼を受ける傾向があります。当チームのスタッフは妥当な時間内にこれらの全てに対処する能力を持っていますが、効率を改善するため、新たな手続きの実施に際して皆さんのご協力が必要です。

今後、従業員は業務依頼を提出する際に優先度を指定しなければなりません。「最重要優先度」の指定は、顧客への責務を果たす当社の能力を直ちに危うくする問題に取り置かれます。これらの依頼は、ヘルプデスクのスタッフによって即座に取り組まれます。「高優先度」の指定は、従業員が仕事をするのに支障を来す問題に使用されるものとします。これらの問題は、可能ならば3時間以内に対処されます。しかし、私たちが主として受ける依頼の60パーセントは時間の制約があまりない問題に関するものなので、「標準優先度」と記してください。私たちはこれらの依頼に対し、提出後24時間以内に対応します。最後に、「低優先度」の依頼は3営業日以内に対処されることになります。例えば、ソフトウエアの機能強化の依頼はこの最後の分類に入るでしょう。

いつもの通り、皆さんの業務依頼の状況は技術ヘルプデスクのウェブサイト上で更新されます。

よろしくお願いします。

Words & Phrases

procedure 手続き、手順　**1** tech help desk 技術ヘルプデスク　tend to *do* ～する傾向がある
a high number of ～ 多数の～　service request 業務依頼　capacity 能力　handle ～に対処する
reasonable 妥当な　time frame 時間枠、期間　efficiency 効率　help in *doing* ～する際の助力
implement ～を実行する　**2** going forward 今後、将来　designate ～を指定する　priority 優先度、優先
critical 極めて重大な　designation 指定　reserve ～ for … …のために～を取っておく　directly 直接に
jeopardize ～を危うくする　ability 能力　meet ～を果たす　obligation 責務、義務　act on ～ ～に取り組む
immediately 即座に　prevent ～ from *doing* ～が…するのを妨げる　typically 主として、概して
time-sensitive 時間的制約のある　mark ～ … ～に…と印を付ける　respond to ～ ～に対応する　submission 提出
address ～に対処する　enhancement 強化　fall under ～ ～(の分類)に入る

158 What challenge is the Tech Help Desk experiencing?

(A) It has been affected by team-member retirements.

(B) Its expenses have unexpectedly increased.

(C) It has a higher volume of work at certain times.

(D) Its software needs to be upgraded.

技術ヘルプデスクはどのような課題に直面していますか。

(A) チーム構成員の退職によって影響を受けている。

(B) 経費が思いがけなく増加している。

(C) 特定の時間帯に、より大量の仕事がある。

(D) ソフトウエアの改良が必要である。

正解 **C** ❶ 1〜2行目に、The Tech Help Desk tends to receive a high number of service requests between the hours of 8:00 A.M. and 10:00 A.M.「技術ヘルプデスクは午前8時から午前10時の時間帯に多数の業務依頼を受ける傾向がある」とある。続く同2〜4行目で、依頼に効率よく対処するために新たな手続きを実施すると述べられているので、午前8時から午前10時という特定の時間帯に仕事が集中するこ

とが技術ヘルプデスクの抱える課題と考えられる。よって、(C)が正解。challenge「課題、難題」。a high volume of 〜「大量の〜」、certain「特定の」。

(A) affect「〜に影響を与える」、retirement「退職」。

(B) expense「経費」、unexpectedly「思いがけなく」。

(D) ❷9〜10行目で言及されているソフトウエアの強化は、業務依頼の一例として挙げられているだけ。upgrade「〜を改良する」。

---

159 According to the e-mail, how are service requests changing?

(A) They must be submitted during specific hours.

(B) They must be categorized by the employees making them.

(C) Their assigned priority level must be approved by a manager.

(D) Their status will be posted on a Web site.

Eメールによると、業務依頼はどのように変わりますか。

(A) 特定の時間の間に提出されなければならない。

(B) それを行う従業員によって分類されなければならない。

(C) 割り当てられた優先度は部長によって承認されなければならない。

(D) 状況はウェブサイトに投稿される予定である。

正解 **B** ❶で業務依頼に効率的に対処するための新手続き導入の必要性が説明された後、❷1〜2行目に、Going forward, employees must designate a priority level when submitting service requests.「今後、従業員は業務依頼を提出する際に優先度を指定しなければならない」とある。優先度の指定とは、同2〜10行目より、依頼内容に応じて critical priority「最重要優先度」、high priority「高優先度」、standard priority「標準

優先度」、low priority「低優先度」のいずれかに分類することと分かる。よって、(B)が正解。categorize「〜を分類する」。

(A) 依頼を出す時間は限定されていない。specific「特定の」。

(C) 承認が必要とは述べられていない。assigned「割り当てられた」、approve「〜を承認する」。

(D) ❸に、いつもの通り業務依頼の状況はウェブサイトで更新されるとあるので、変更される点ではない。post「〜を投稿する」。

---

160 Within what time frame are the "standard priority" requests addressed?

(A) One hour

(B) Three hours

(C) One day

(D) Three days

「標準優先度」の依頼はどのくらいの期間内に対処されますか。

(A) 1時間

(B) 3時間

(C) 1日

(D) 3日

正解 **C** 「標準優先度」については❷6〜7行目で説明され、続けて同7〜8行目で「私たちはこれらの依頼に対し、提出後24時間以内に対応する」と書かれている。よって、(C)が正解。

(B) ❷4〜6行目より、可能な場合に3時間以内に対処するのは high priority「高優先度」。

(D) ❷8〜9行目より、3営業日以内に対処するのは low priority「低優先度」。

Expressions

if possible 「可能ならば」（❷6行目）

I would like to have you come to my office at ten o'clock tomorrow, if possible.
可能ならば、明日10時に私のオフィスに来ていただきたいのですが。

Questions 161-164 refer to the following notice.

Posted 12 March

Attention Dublin Transit riders:

❶ Dublin Transit is pleased to launch a new and improved Web site and app. — [1] —. In addition to having the ability to view entire transit schedules, you can now receive live route updates and purchase same-day tickets online. As always, information is available in English, Spanish, and French.

❷ If you have already purchased a ticket electronically and are ready to travel, simply print it out and bring it with you to the station or save the ticket to your mobile phone. — [2] —. Then scan the bar code that is on your ticket to open the gate at the entrance to your train platform. If you still need to purchase tickets, representatives at every station are available to serve you from 6:00 A.M. to 10:00 P.M. daily. — [3] —.

❸ To save money, commuters are reminded to buy weekly or monthly passes in advance. Please note that beginning on 1 April, commuters who purchase weekly or monthly passes will see a 4 percent cost increase. — [4] —. However, the price for the transit passes will continue to represent a cost savings over a daily ticket purchase.

問題161-164は次のお知らせに関するものです。

3月12日に掲示

ダブリン交通社の乗客の皆さまにお知らせ：

ダブリン交通社は、改良された新しいウェブサイトとアプリを公開することをうれしく思います。*革新的で使いやすい機能が両者に追加されました。全ての運行スケジュールが見られることに加えて、現在、リアルタイムの路線最新情報を得ることとオンラインで当日の切符を購入することができます。これまで通り、案内は英語、スペイン語、フランス語でご利用いただけます。

すでに電子媒体で切符を購入されていて、乗車のご用意ができている場合は、ただそれを印刷して駅までお持ちいただくか、切符をご自分の携帯電話に保存してください。そして切符にあるバーコードをスキャンして電車のプラットホームに通じる入り口のゲートを開けてください。まだ切符を購入される必要がある場合は、毎日午前6時から午後10時まで各駅の係員が応対いたします。

お金を節約するために、通勤通学のお客さまは前もって1週間または1カ月間の定期券を購入されますよう、改めてお知らせいたします。4月1日から、1週間または1カ月間の定期券を購入される通勤通学のお客さまは、4パーセントの値上げとなりますのでご留意ください。しかしながら、交通定期券の方が1日単位の切符の購入に比べて費用の節約となることは変わりません。

*問題164の挿入文の訳

161 What is a new feature on the Web site and app?

(A) Seat assignment confirmation
(B) Updated weather conditions
(C) Real-time transit updates
(D) Frequent-traveler rewards

ウェブサイトとアプリの一つの新しい機能は何ですか。

(A) 座席指定の確認
(B) 最新の天候状況
(C) リアルタイムの運行最新情報
(D) 頻繁な利用者への報奨

正解 C ❶1行目で、ダブリン交通社は新しいウェブサイトとアプリを公開すると述べている。続く同2〜3行目に、「全ての運行スケジュールが見られることに加えて、現在、リアルタイムの路線最新情報を得ることとオンラインで当日の切符を購入することができる」とあるので、ウェブサイトとアプリの新機能の一つは、リアルタイムの運行最新情報が得られることだと分かる。live route updatesをreal-time transit updatesと表している(C)が正解。feature「機能」。real-time「リアルタイムの」。
(A) seat assignment「座席指定」、confirmation「確認」。
(B) updated「最新の」、condition「状況」。
(D) frequent「頻繁な」、rewards（＝rewards program）「報奨（制度）」。

162 According to the notice, what is indicated about transit tickets?

(A) They must be stamped by a representative in the station office.
(B) They are scanned for entry to a train platform.
(C) They must be presented to a conductor upon boarding.
(D) They are intended for use by regular commuters only.

お知らせによると、交通機関の切符について何が示されていますか。

(A) 駅窓口の係員にスタンプを押されなければならない。
(B) 電車のプラットホームへの入場のためにスキャンされる。
(C) 乗車の際に車掌に提示されなければならない。
(D) 通常の通勤通学客専用である。

正解 B ❷3〜4行目に、「切符にあるバーコードをスキャンして電車のプラットホームに通じる入り口のゲートを開けてください」とある。よって、正解は(B)。entry「入場」。
(A) stamp「〜にスタンプを押す」。
(C) present「〜を提示する」、conductor「車掌」、upon boarding「乗車の際に」。
(D) be intended for 〜「〜向けである、〜を対象としている」。

163 What is NOT mentioned in the notice?

(A) Transit information is available in several languages.
(B) Station offices are open daily.
(C) A new transit station will open soon.
(D) Transit passes will cost more starting in April.

お知らせで述べられていないものは何ですか。

(A) 運行情報は幾つかの言語で利用可能である。
(B) 駅窓口は毎日開いている。
(C) 新しい乗換駅が間もなく開業する予定である。
(D) 交通定期券は4月から値上がりする予定である。

正解 C (A)については、❶3〜4行目に、「これまで通り、案内は英語、スペイン語、フランス語で利用可能」とある。(B)については、❷4〜6行目に、「まだ切符を購入する必要がある場合は、毎日午前6時から午後10時まで各駅の係員が応対する」とある。(D)については、❸2〜3行目に、「4月1日から、1週間または1カ月間の定期券を購入する通勤通学客は、4パーセントの値上げとなる」とある。新しい乗換駅の開業予定に関する言及はないので、(C)が正解。

164 In which of the positions marked [1], [2], [3], and [4] does the following sentence best belong?

"Innovative, user-friendly features have been added to both."

(A) [1]   (C) [3]
(B) [2]   (D) [4]

[1]、[2]、[3]、[4]と記載された箇所のうち、次の文が入るのに最もふさわしいのはどれですか。

「革新的で使いやすい機能が両者に追加されました」

正解 A 挿入文では、both「両者」に対して機能が追加されたことが述べられている。❶1行目に「ダブリン交通社は、改良された新しいウェブサイトとアプリを公開することをうれしく思う」とあるので、この直後の(A) [1]に挿入文を入れると、bothがウェブサイトとアプリの両者を指すことになり、前文の補足説明になる。また、続く同2〜3行目で新たな機能の具体例が述べられているので、追加された新機能を説明するという自然な流れになる。innovative「革新的な」、user-friendly「使いやすい」、add 〜 to …「〜を…に加える」。

Questions 165-167 refer to the following Web page.

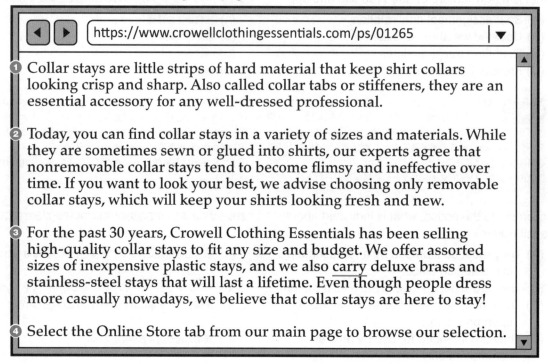

問題165-167は次のウェブページに関するものです。

https://www.crowellclothingessentials.com/ps/01265

襟芯はシャツの襟を常にぱりっとスマートな見た目にする硬質素材の小さな細長い一片です。襟用タブまたは補強芯とも呼ばれ、身だしなみのいい職業人であれば誰にとっても不可欠な服飾品です。

今日、多種多様なサイズと素材の襟芯が見られます。それらは時にシャツに縫い付けられたり接着剤で貼り付けられたりしていますが、当社の専門家たちは、取り外せない襟芯は時とともにもろくなり効果がなくなる傾向があるという考えで一致しています。もしあなたがご自分を最も魅力的に見せたいなら、当社は取り外し可能な襟芯だけを選ぶことをお勧めします。それはあなたのシャツをずっと真新しい見た目のままにしてくれるでしょう。

この30年間、Crowell服飾必需品社は、どんなサイズや予算にも合致する高品質な襟芯を販売してきました。当社は各種サイズの低価格なプラスチック製の襟芯を販売しておりますし、また一生長持ちする高級な真ちゅう製やステンレス製の襟芯も扱っております。最近では人々はよりカジュアルな服装をしていますが、当社は襟芯が日常に定着していると信じています!

当社の品ぞろえを閲覧するには、メインページからオンラインストアのタブを選択してください。

Words & Phrases

❶ collar 襟　stay 芯、支柱　strip 細長い一片　material 素材、材料　crisp ぱりっとした
sharp （服装が）スマートな、おしゃれな　tab タブ、服の垂れ飾り　stiffener 硬化・補強するもの、芯
essential 不可欠な　accessory 服飾品、装飾品　well-dressed 身なりのよい　professional 職業人
❷ a variety of ～ 多種多様な～　while ～だけれども　sew ～を縫う　glue ～を接着剤で貼り付ける
expert 専門家　agree that ～ ～という点で意見が一致する　nonremovable 取り外せない
tend to do ～する傾向がある　flimsy もろい　ineffective 効果がない　advise doing ～することを勧める
removable 取り外せる　fresh 新しい、出来たての　❸ clothing 衣服　essentials 必要不可欠なもの
high-quality 高品質な　fit ～に合う　budget 予算　offer ～を売り出す　assorted 各種の
inexpensive 低価格の　carry ～（商品）を取り扱う　deluxe 高級な　brass 真ちゅう
stainless-steel ステンレス製の　last 長持ちする、持ちこたえる　lifetime 生涯　dress casually カジュアルな服装をする
nowadays 最近は　believe that ～ ～ということを信じる　be here to stay 定着している、日常化する
❹ select ～を選択する　browse ～を閲覧する　selection 品ぞろえ

165 What is one purpose of the Web page?

    (A) To describe how to clean a high-quality garment

    (B) To announce a new price on a clothing accessory

    (C) To explain how collar stays changed over time

    (D) To persuade customers to purchase an item

ウェブページの一つの目的は何ですか。

    (A) 高品質な衣服をクリーニングする方法を説明すること

    (B) 服飾品の新しい価格を知らせること

    (C) 襟芯が時とともにどのように変化したのか説明すること

    (D) 顧客に品物を購入するよう促すこと

正解 D ❶では、襟芯という服飾品の特長を紹介している。続く❷では、一般によく見られる多様な襟芯について触れた後、取り外し可能な襟芯を薦めている。これらの情報に続き、❸では、Crowell服飾必需品社が30年にわたって高品質な襟芯を販売していることをうたい、❹で、Select the Online Store tab from our main page to browse our selection.「当社の品ぞろえを閲覧するには、メインページからオンラインストアのタブを選択してください」と述べ、自社の商品を薦めている。よって、ウェブページの一つの目的は、襟芯という商品の宣伝だと考えられるので、(D)が正解。persuade ~ to do「~に…するよう促す、~に…するように説得する」。
(A) describe「~を説明する」、garment「衣服」。

---

166 What is suggested about Crowell Clothing Essentials?

    (A) It manufactures casual shirts.

    (B) It sells removable collar stays.

    (C) It recently celebrated its grand opening.

    (D) It offers brass and steel buttons in its online store.

Crowell服飾必需品社について何が分かりますか。

    (A) カジュアルなシャツを製造している。

    (B) 取り外し可能な襟芯を販売している。

    (C) 最近オープン記念を祝った。

    (D) オンラインショップで真ちゅう製や鋼製のボタンを販売している。

正解 B 全体の内容から、このウェブページはCrowell服飾必需品社のものと分かる。❷1~4行目で、同社の専門家たちは取り外せない襟芯は時とともにもろくなって効果がなくなる傾向があると考えていることが述べられている。続く同4~5行目に、「もしあなたが自分を最も魅力的に見せたいなら、当社は取り外し可能な襟芯だけを選ぶことを勧める」とある。❸1~4行目では、同社はさまざまな襟芯を販売していることが述べられている。以上より、同社は取り外し可能な襟芯を販売していると判断できる。よって、(B)が正解。
(A) manufacture「~を製造する」。
(C) celebrate「~を祝う」、grand opening「オープン記念」。
(D) ❸3~4行目で真ちゅう製やステンレス製と言及されているのは襟芯であり、button「ボタン」ではない。steel「鋼鉄」。

---

167 The word "carry" in paragraph 3, line 3, is closest in meaning to

    (A) lift

    (B) sell

    (C) wear

    (D) take

第3段落・3行目にある "carry" に最も意味が近いのは

    (A) ~を持ち上げる

    (B) ~を販売する

    (C) ~を身に着ける

    (D) ~を持っていく

正解 B ❸1~2行目に、「この30年間、Crowell服飾必需品社は、どんなサイズや予算にも合致する高品質な襟芯を販売してきた」とある。続く同2~4行目の該当の語を含む文は、「当社は各種サイズの低価格なプラスチック製の襟芯を販売しており、また一生長持ちする高級な真ちゅう製やステンレス製の襟芯も-------」という意味。Crowell服飾必需品社は、豊富なサイズの低価格なプラスチック製から高価な真ちゅう製やステンレス製のものまで多種多様な襟芯を商品として取り扱っていることを述べている。よって、(B) sell「~を販売する」が正解。

Expressions

even though ~ 「~であるけれども」（❸4~5行目）

Even though I've done these presentations many times, I still get nervous when speaking in front of crowds.
私はこういったプレゼンを何度もしてきましたが、大勢の前で話すときはいまだに緊張します。

TEST 2 PART 7

Questions 168-171 refer to the following e-mail.

From:	Juan Romas
To:	All Staff; Conservancy Members
Sent:	Tuesday, April 21
Subject:	Questionnaire

Good morning,

❶ A performance evaluation of Walkinson Conservancy's executive director has been initiated by the board of directors and is currently being conducted by my department. — [1] —. All Conservancy staff and current members will be receiving a hard-copy version of the questionnaire form in the mail this week. An online version is also available on our Web site at walkinsonconservancy.org/ed-questionnaire.

❷ The questionnaire is anonymous unless you choose to include your name. — [2] —. There is room at the end of the form if you wish to expand on your answers with any additional thoughts.

❸ Please be aware that submissions will be read by every member of the board. These forms will become part of the executive director's personnel file, with the same privacy protections and restricted access as any employee's personnel file. — [3] —.

❹ The form must be submitted by 5 P.M. on Monday, May 10. — [4] —. If you are completing the paper version, please send it by mail, or put it in the interoffice mail in a sealed envelope marked: Executive Director Performance Evaluation, Human Resources.

❺ Thank you in advance for your participation.

Sincerely,

Juan Romas, Director of Human Resources

問題168-171は次のEメールに関するものです。

送信者：Juan Romas
受信者：全職員、自然環境保護団体会員
送信日：4月21日火曜日
件名：アンケート

おはようございます。

Walkinson自然環境保護団体事務局長の業績評価が理事会によって開始され、現在私の部署が実施しています。＊そのプロセスの一環として、アンケートが用意されました。全ての団体職員と現会員は、今週ハードコピー版のアンケート用紙を郵便で受け取ることになります。オンライン版も当団体ウェブサイトwalkinsonconservancy.org/ed-questionnaireで利用できます。

アンケートは、ご自分の名前を含めることを選択しない限り、匿名です。もしご自分の回答に追加のご意見を詳しく述べたければ、用紙の最後に余白があります。

提出されたものは理事会の全役員に閲覧されることにご留意ください。これらの用紙は、全職員の人事ファイルと同様のプライバシー保護とアクセス制限付きで事務局長の人事ファイルの一部となります。

用紙は5月10日月曜日午後5時までに提出されなければなりません。紙版に記入される場合は、郵送していただくか、人事部宛て・事務局長業績評価と書いて封をした封筒に入れて社内便で出してください。

ご協力にあらかじめお礼申し上げます。

敬具

人事部長、Juan Romas

＊問題171の挿入文の訳

168 Who started a performance-evaluation process at the organization?

(A) The board of directors
(B) The executive director
(C) The conservancy members
(D) The human resources department

誰が団体における業績評価のプロセスを開始しましたか。

(A) 理事会
(B) 事務局長
(C) 自然環境保護団体会員
(D) 人事部

正解 A	人事部長の Juan Romas さんが送信したEメールの ❶ 1～2 行目に、「Walkinson 自然環境保護団体事務局長の業績評価が理事会によって開始され、現在私の部署が実施している」とある。よって、(A)が正解。organization「団体」。	(B) 事務局長は業績評価を受ける人物。 (D) 人事部は、業績評価のプロセスを開始したのではなく、現在実施している部署。

169 What is true about the questionnaire?

(A) It should be completed and returned within a week.
(B) It can be completed on the Internet or on paper.
(C) It must be signed by the person submitting it.
(D) It will gather feedback on the organization's policies.

アンケートについて正しいことは何ですか。

(A) 1週間以内に全て記入して返送されるべきである。
(B) インターネット上または紙面上で全て記入することができる。
(C) 提出する人によって署名されなければならない。
(D) 団体の方針についての意見を集めることになる。

正解 B	❶ 3～5 行目に、「全ての団体職員と現会員は、今週ハードコピー版のアンケート用紙を郵便で受け取ることになる。オンライン版も当団体ウェブサイトで利用できる」と書かれているので、(B)が正解。 (A) このEメールの送信日が 4 月 21 日で、❹ 1 行目から提出期	限は 5 月 10 日。回答期間は 2 週間以上ある。within「～以内に」。 (C) ❷ 1 行目より、アンケートは匿名でもよいと分かる。sign「～に署名する」。 (D) アンケートは事務局長の業績評価に関するもの。gather「～を集める」、policy「方針」。

170 What is indicated about the personnel files of employees at the organization?

(A) They are updated annually.
(B) They are read by board members.
(C) They are used to determine promotions.
(D) They are kept private.

この団体の職員の人事ファイルについて何が示されていますか。

(A) 毎年更新される。
(B) 理事会の役員に読まれる。
(C) 昇進を決定するために使われる。
(D) 非公開にしておかれる。

正解 D	提出されたアンケート用紙について ❸ 1～3 行目に、「これらの用紙は、全職員の人事ファイルと同様のプライバシー保護とアクセス制限付きで事務局長の人事ファイルの一部となる」とあるので、この団体の職員の人事ファイルは、保護・アクセス制限のある非公開の状態だと判断できる。よって、(D)	が正解。keep ～ private「～を非公開の状態に保つ」。 (A) annually「毎年」。 (B) ❸ 1 行目で理事会の全役員に閲覧されるとあるのは提出されたアンケートであり、職員の人事ファイルではない。 (C) determine「～を決定する」、promotion「昇進」。

171 In which of the positions marked [1], [2], [3], and [4] does the following sentence best belong?

"As part of that process, a questionnaire has been prepared."

(A) [1]   (C) [3]
(B) [2]   (D) [4]

[1]、[2]、[3]、[4]と記載された箇所のうち、次の文が入るのに最もふさわしいのはどれですか。

「そのプロセスの一環として、アンケートが用意されました」

正解 A	挿入文はアンケートの準備が完了したことを述べるもの。挿入文中の that process「そのプロセス」に注目する。❶ 1～2 行目に、事務局長の業績評価が理事会によって開始され、現在、Romas さんの部署で実施していることが書かれている。この直後の (A) [1] に挿入文を入れると、that process が Walkinson 自然環境保護団体事務局長の業績評価を指すことになり、業績評価のプロセスの一部として今回のアンケートが用意されたという意味になる。また、続く同 3～5 行目のハードコピー版とオンライン版があるという内容がアンケートの追加の説明となり、自然な流れでつながる。prepare「～を用意する」。

Questions 172-175 refer to the following text-message chain.

Rita Carvallo (10:19 A.M.) Has Ms. Castelli decided on the type of wood she wants for her custom dining table and chairs?

Lawrence Bremen (10:21 A.M.) Not yet. She asked for samples and recommendations. I wanted to check with you first. Any suggestions?

Rita Carvallo (10:23 A.M.) It depends on her budget. She has to decide on either hardwood or softwood, and then if she wants the wood painted or stained.

Lawrence Bremen (10:25 A.M.) She wants a natural look, so not painted. Aren't softwoods too weak for tables and chairs?

Tom Ohrt (10:29 A.M.) They aren't, actually. Pine and cedar come from evergreen trees. They're naturally yellowish red, and our local suppliers always have them in stock.

Lawrence Bremen (10:31 A.M.) Good to know. What about hardwood?

Rita Carvallo (10:32 A.M.) Many clients love a hardwood's rich colors and textures. They look good with a dark stain or a natural finish.

Tom Ohrt (10:34 A.M.) Their grain patterns are beautiful, but they are more expensive because the trees grow slowly. Cherrywood might be a good choice because it resists scratches. It is also popular, so we have it in stock. There should be enough for Ms. Castelli's project if she chooses it.

Lawrence Bremen (10:36 A.M.) I'll run a sample by her. Thank you both!

問題172-175は次のテキストメッセージのやりとりに関するものです。

Rita Carvallo（午前10時19分）
Castelliさんは、オーダーメードのダイニングテーブルと椅子に使いたい木材の種類をお決めになりましたか。

Lawrence Bremen（午前10時21分）
まだです。彼女はサンプルとお薦めの品をご要望でした。私はまずあなた方に相談したかったのです。何か提案はありますか。

Rita Carvallo（午前10時23分）
彼女のご予算によります。彼女には、硬材か軟材か、そして木材にペンキを塗ってほしいか染色してほしいかを決めてもらわなくてはなりません。

Lawrence Bremen（午前10時25分）
彼女は自然な見た目を望んでいるので、ペンキ塗りはなしですね。軟材はテーブルや椅子には弱過ぎませんか。

Tom Ohrt（午前10時29分）
実際、そんなことはありません。松材や杉材は常緑樹から採れます。それらは自然に黄色がかった赤色で、当社の地元の供給業者は常に在庫を持っています。

Lawrence Bremen（午前10時31分）
それはいいことを聞きました。硬材はどうですか。

Rita Carvallo（午前10時32分）
多くの顧客が硬材の豊かな色と質感を気に入っています。濃色の染料や自然な仕上げで見栄えが良くなりますよ。

Tom Ohrt（午前10時34分）
硬材の木目柄は美しいですが、木がゆっくりと成長するのでより高価です。傷がつきにくいので桜材が良い選択かもしれません。人気もあるので、当社には在庫があります。Castelliさんがそれを選んだ場合、彼女の案件分は十分にあるはずです。

Lawrence Bremen（午前10時36分）
彼女にサンプルを見てもらうようにします。お2人ともありがとうございました！

172 What type of work do the writers do?

    (A) They maintain gardens.

    (B) They sell custom furniture.

    (C) They are financial advisors.

    (D) They work at a hardware store.

書き手たちはどのような仕事をしていますか。

    (A) 彼らは庭の整備をしている。

    (B) 彼らはオーダーメードの家具を販売している。

    (C) 彼らはファイナンシャルアドバイザーである。

    (D) 彼らは工具店で働いている。

> **正解 B** Carvalloさんが❶で、Has Ms. Castelli decided on the type of wood she wants for her custom dining table and chairs? 「Castelliさんは、オーダーメードのダイニングテーブルと椅子に使いたい木材の種類を決めたか」と尋ねている。それに対して、Bremenさんは❷で、Not yet. She asked for samples and recommendations. 「まだだ。彼女はサンプルとお薦めの品を要望した」と答えた後、やりとりの相手に木材の種類の提案を求めている。その後、Ohrtさんが加わり、Castelliさん向けの木材に関して、特性や在庫を含めて推薦すべき品を検討している。よって、書き手たちはオーダーメードの家具を販売していると考えられるので、(B)が正解。furniture「家具」。
> (A) maintain「～を整備する、～を維持する」。
> (C) financial advisor「ファイナンシャルアドバイザー」。

173 What is indicated about Ms. Castelli?

    (A) She prefers a natural look.

    (B) She is ordering cabinets.

    (C) She is mostly concerned about price.

    (D) She wants pinewood.

Castelliさんについて何が示されていますか。

    (A) 彼女は自然な見た目の方を好む。

    (B) 彼女はキャビネットを注文している。

    (C) 彼女はもっぱら価格を気にしている。

    (D) 彼女は松材を希望している。

> **正解 A** ❶より、Castelliさんとはオーダーメード家具の注文者と分かる。サンプルやお薦めの品を要望したという彼女について、Bremenさんは❹で、She wants a natural look, so not painted. 「彼女は自然な見た目を望んでいるので、ペンキ塗りはなしだ」という発言をしている。よって、(A)が正解。prefer「～をより好む」。
> (B) ❶より、注文しているのはダイニングテーブルと椅子。cabinet「キャビネット、収納棚」。
> (C) ❸に、「彼女の予算による」とあるが、Castelliさん自身が価格を気にしているという記述はない。be concerned about ～「～を気にする、～を心配する」、mostly「主に」。
> (D) ❺に松材への言及はあるが軟材の一例として特徴が述べられているだけであり、❷よりCastelliさんはどんな種類の木材にするかまだ決めていないと分かる。

Words & Phrases

❶ decide on ～　～に決める　　type　種類　　wood　木材　　custom　オーダーメードの、特別注文の
❷ ask for ～　～を求める　　recommendation　お薦めのもの　　check with ～　～に相談する　　suggestion　提案
❸ budget　予算　　either A or B　Aかそれともか　　hardwood　硬材　　softwood　軟材　　paint　～にペンキを塗る
stain　～を染色する　　❹ natural look　自然な見た目　　❺ actually　実は　　pine　松材　　cedar　ヒマラヤ杉材
come from ～　～からもたらされる　　evergreen tree　常緑樹　　yellowish　黄色がかった　　in stock　在庫があって
❻ What about ～?　～はどうですか　　❼ texture　質感　　stain　染料　　finish　仕上げ　　❽ grain　木目
pattern　柄、模様　　cherrywood　桜材　　choice　選択、選択肢　　resist　～に耐える、～に抵抗する　　scratch　傷
❾ run ～ by …　（意見を求めて）～を…に見せる、～を…に伝える

174 At 10:29 A.M., what does Mr. Ohrt most likely mean when he writes, "They aren't, actually"?

(A) He suggests a brighter color.
(B) He has no more samples left.
(C) He is not sure what wood to order.
(D) He believes that a softwood is suitable.

午前 10 時 29 分に、"They aren't, actually" という発言で、Ohrt さんは何を意図していると考えられますか。

(A) 彼はより明るい色を提案している。
(B) 彼にはもう見本が残っていない。
(C) 彼はどんな木材を注文するべきか分からない。
(D) 彼は軟材は適していると考えている。

正解 **D** Bremenさんが❹で、Aren't softwoods too weak for tables and chairs?「軟材はテーブルや椅子には弱過ぎないか」と尋ねており、❺のOhrtさんの下線部の発言はそれに応答するもの。下線部のTheyはsoftwoodsを指し、They aren't too weak, actually.「実際には弱過ぎるということはない」と答えていると考えられる。Ohrtさんは、続けて軟材が常緑樹を原料とすること、自然な色合いを持っていることや常に在庫があることなどの利点を述べているので、下線部の発言で、軟材はこれらの家具に適していると伝えていると判断できる。よって、(D)が正解。suitable「適している」。
(A) suggest「～を提案する」、bright「明るい」。
(B) no more ～「もう～はない」。
(C) sure「確信して」。

175 What is indicated about hardwood?

(A) It has lovely patterns.
(B) It is best used indoors.
(C) It is currently out of stock.
(D) It is difficult to carve.

硬材について何が示されていますか。

(A) 美しい模様がある。
(B) 屋内での使用に最も適している。
(C) 現在在庫がない。
(D) 彫るのが難しい。

正解 **A** Bremenさんが❻で、What about hardwood?「硬材はどうか」と尋ねているのに対し、Carvalloさんが❼で硬材の特徴を述べ、続けてOhrtさんが❽で、Their grain patterns are beautiful「それらの木目柄は美しい」と伝えている。よって、(A)が正解。lovely「美しい、素晴らしい」。
(B) indoors「屋内で」。
(C) ❽より、硬材の桜材は在庫が十分にあることが分かる。currently「現在」、out of stock「在庫がなくて」。
(D) carve「～を彫る」。

Expressions

depend on ～ 「～による、～次第である」(❸1行目)

Choosing the right computer depends on what you want to use it for.
適切なコンピューターの選択は、それを何に使いたいかによります。

Questions 176-180 refer to the following e-mail and article.

To:	Althea Kim <a.kim@busselton.gov>
From:	Sam Thompson <s.thompson@gpecproductions.com>
Date:	January 12
Subject:	Summary of our recent discussion

Hello Ms. Kim,

Here are the notes from today's discussion regarding the upcoming film shoot at the Hastings Bridge. Please review them and let me know if there is anything that I may have overlooked.

• Two weeks before filming, notices will be placed at both ends of the bridge to keep drivers informed.
• During the week of filming, March 8–15, the road will be barricaded one block from both ends of the bridge. Security personnel will be stationed at the barricades to help direct traffic.
• I will contact Nadia Sonder, the owner of a piece of land near the bridge's east entrance, to see whether she will rent it to us as a parking area for our trucks and equipment.
• If Ms. Sonder is unwilling, I will make an alternative arrangement, which is likely to be the parking lot of a movie theater, a theme park, or a grocery store. We would only need a little space in the corner, as our crew can pack our vehicles in pretty tightly, and we won't have any trailers with us, as all of our actors will be staying in town.

With our deepest gratitude,
Sam Thompson, Location Manager, GPEC Productions

Busselton To Host Movie Shoot

❶ BUSSELTON (January 23)—Hastings Bridge, which crosses the Lawrence River in Busselton, will be closed from 7:00 A.M. on March 8 to 7:00 P.M. on March 15 while a film production takes place. Those who routinely use the bridge are urged to plan alternate routes.

❷ Motorists should also be aware of the potential for increased pedestrian traffic in the area and take precautions accordingly. For the duration of the shoot, the film studio's vehicles and equipment will be stationed in an undeveloped area near the east end of the bridge.

❸ While residents may be frustrated by the inconveniences that accompany the film production's work in Busselton, Althea Kim, head of the city's Office of Tourism, points to the gains for local residents.

❹ "I appreciate the public's concerns, but the film's cast and crew will stay in the city's hotels and visit local restaurants as well as purchase other necessities," said Ms. Kim.

❺ Local officials estimate that the production could bring in as much as one million dollars to Busselton.

受信者：Althea Kim <a.kim@busselton.gov>
送信者：Sam Thompson <s.thompson@gpecproductions.com>
日付：1月12日
件名：最近の話し合いの概要

Kim様

以下は、近日中に行われるヘイスティングス橋での映画撮影に関する今日の話し合いの覚え書きです。これらを見直して、私が見落とした可能性のあるものがもし何かあればお知らせください。

・撮影2週間前に、車で通る人に知らせるために看板が橋の両端に設置される。
・撮影の週の3月8日〜15日の間、道路は橋の両端から1ブロックの所でバリケードでふさがれる。警備員が交通整理を行うためにバリケードの所に配置される。
・私が、橋の東側の入り口近くの区画の土地所有者であるNadia Sonderさんに連絡して、そこを当社のトラックや機材の駐車場として貸してくれるかどうか確認する。
・Sonderさんに受けてもらえない場合、私が代替となる手配を行う。映画館、テーマパーク、または食料雑貨店の駐車場となる見込み。当社のクルーは車両をかなりぴったり詰めることができるので、隅に少しのスペースが必要になるだけだろう。また、俳優は全員町に滞在するので、トレーラーは1台も使用しない。

どうぞよろしくお願いします。
GPEC製作会社　現場責任者　Sam Thompson

バッセルトンが映画撮影の場に

バッセルトン（1月23日）——バッセルトンのローレンス川にかかるヘイスティングス橋は、映画製作が行われる期間の3月8日午前7時から3月15日午後7時まで、閉鎖される予定である。いつも橋を利用している人々は、代替経路を計画するよう求められる。

自動車運転者はまた、同地域で通行人の往来が増える可能性があることを認識し、それに応じて予防策を講じるとよいだろう。撮影期間中、映画スタジオの車両や機材が橋の東端近くの未開発区画に置かれる予定である。

住民はバッセルトンでの映画製作作業に伴う不便さを不満に思うかもしれないが、市の観光局長であるAlthea Kimは地元住民にとっての利益を指摘する。

「私は市民の皆さんの懸念を認識していますが、映画の出演者やクルーは市のホテルに宿泊し、地元のレストランを訪れ、必需品などを購入するでしょう」とKim氏は述べた。

地元当局は、映画製作はバッセルトンに100万ドルもの収益をもたらすだろうと見積もっている。

176 What is the date of the meeting that Mr. Thompson attended?

(A) January 11
(B) January 12
(C) March 8
(D) March 15

Thompsonさんが出席した会議の日付はいつですか。

(A) 1月11日
(B) 1月12日
(C) 3月8日
(D) 3月15日

> **正解 B** Thompsonさんが送信したEメールである**1**の**❶** 1～2行目に、Here are the notes from today's discussion regarding the upcoming film shoot at the Hastings Bridge. 「以下は、近日中に行われるヘイスティングス橋での映画撮影に関する今日の話し合いの覚え書きだ」と書かれている。Eメールの日付欄に「1月12日」とあるので、会議もこの日だと分かる。(B)が正解。
> (C) (D) **1**の**❷**の2つ目の項目より、映画撮影の開始日と終了日。

177 What does Mr. Thompson mention in the e-mail?

(A) The identity of actors involved in a film shoot
(B) The urgency of choosing a setting for a movie scene
(C) A plan for controlling traffic near a bridge
(D) A need to rent trucks and equipment

Eメールで Thompsonさんは何を述べていますか。

(A) 映画撮影に関わっている俳優の身元
(B) 映画のシーンの舞台を選ぶ緊急性
(C) 橋の近くで交通整理をする計画
(D) トラックや機材を借りる必要性

> **正解 C** Eメール**1**の**❷**の2つ目の項目で、道路は橋の両端から1ブロックの所でバリケードでふさがれることが述べられ、続けてSecurity personnel will be stationed at the barricades to help direct traffic.「警備員が交通整理を行うためにバリケードの所に配置される」と書かれている。よって、(C)が正解。control traffic「交通整理をする」。
> (A) identity「身元」、involved in ～「～に関係して」。
> (B) urgency「緊急性」、setting「舞台」、scene「シーン、場面」。
> (D) **1**の**❷**の3つ目の項目にトラックと機材を留め置く場所を借りる案への言及はあるが、トラックと機材を借りるとは述べられていない。rent「～を借りる」。

178 What type of property does Ms. Sonder most likely own?

(A) A movie theater
(B) An amusement park
(C) An undeveloped field
(D) A grocery store

Sonderさんはどんな種類の不動産を所有していると考えられますか。

(A) 映画館
(B) 遊園地
(C) 未開発の草地
(D) 食料雑貨店

> **正解 C** Eメール**1**の**❷**の3つ目の項目に、「私が、橋の東側の入り口近くの区画の土地所有者であるNadia Sonderさんに連絡して、そこを当社のトラックや機材の駐車場として貸してくれるかどうか確認する」とある。記事**2**の**❷**4～7行目には、「撮影期間中、映画スタジオの車両や機材が橋の東端近くの未開発区画に置かれる予定だ」とある。**1**でa piece of land near the bridge's east entranceと言及されたSonderさんの所有する不動産は、**2**でan undeveloped area near the east end of the bridgeと表されていると考えられる。よって、(C)が正解。property「不動産」。field「草地、野原」。
> (A) (B) (D) **1**の**❷**の4つ目の項目より、Sonderさんが承諾しなかった場合の代替場所の候補として言及されている。

Expressions

be urged to do 「～するよう求められる、～するよう促される」(**2**の**❶**6～7行目)
Residents living near the river were urged to evacuate and seek higher ground.
その川の近くに住む住民は、避難して高台を目指すよう促されました。

179 In the article, the word "appreciate" in paragraph 4, line 1, is closest in meaning to

(A) acknowledge
(B) enjoy
(C) increase
(D) desire

記事の第4段落・1行目にある "appreciate" に最も意味が近いのは

(A) 〜を認識する
(B) 〜を楽しむ
(C) 〜を増やす
(D) 〜を強く望む

> **正解 A** 記事2の❶・❷で、映画撮影による橋の閉鎖に関連して住民の協力が呼び掛けられており、続く同❸では、「住民はバッセルトンでの映画製作作業に伴う不便さを不満に思うかもしれないが、市の観光局長であるAlthea Kimは地元住民にとっての利益を指摘する」と述べられている。続く同❹の該当の語を含むKimさんの発言は、「私は市民の皆さんの懸念-------が、映画の出演者やクルーは市のホテルに宿泊し、地元のレストランを訪れ、必需品などを購入するだろう」という意味。Kimさんは、住民の懸念に理解を示した上で、映画製作によって地域にもたらされるメリットを述べていると判断できるので、(A) acknowledge「〜を認識する」が正解。

180 What is suggested in the article about the city of Busselton?

(A) Its bridge has a walkway for use by people on foot.
(B) Its hotels are currently full.
(C) Its drinking water comes from the river.
(D) Its economy profits from the filming.

バッセルトン市についての記事で何が分かりますか。

(A) 同市の橋には徒歩の人々が使う歩道がある。
(B) 同市のホテルは現在満室である。
(C) 同市の飲料水は川から来ている。
(D) 同市の経済は撮影から利益を得る。

> **正解 D** 記事2の❸・❹で、バッセルトン市の観光局長Althea Kimさんが映画製作が地元に利益をもたらすと指摘していることが述べられている。続く同❺に、「地元当局は、映画製作はバッセルトンに100万ドルもの収益をもたらすだろうと見積もっている」とある。これらのことから、バッセルトン市の経済は映画撮影から利益を得ると見込まれていると分かるので、(D)が正解。economy「経済」、profit from 〜「〜から利益を得る」。
> (A) 橋の利用者や車での通行者への言及はあるが、歩道の有無は述べられていない。on foot「徒歩で」。
> (C) drinking water「飲料水」。

Words & Phrases

1 Eメール summary 概要　discussion 話し合い　❶ note 覚え書き、メモ　regarding 〜に関して　film shoot 映画撮影　review 〜を見直す、〜を精査する　may have *done* 〜したかもしれない　overlook 〜を見落とす　❷ filming 撮影　notice 看板　place 〜を置く　end 端　keep 〜 informed 〜に欠かさず知らせる　barricade 〜をバリケードでふさぐ　security personnel 警備員　station 〜を配置する　direct traffic 交通整理をする　★directは「〜に(方向などを)指示する」という意味　a piece of 〜 1区画の〜、1つの〜　land 土地　entrance 入り口　see whether 〜 〜かどうか確かめる　rent 〜を貸す　unwilling 気が進まない　make an arrangement 手配を行う　alternative 代替の　be likely to *do* 〜しそうである、〜する可能性が高い　parking lot 駐車場　theme park テーマパーク　grocery store 食料雑貨店　crew クルー、一団　pack 〜 in 〜を詰め込む　vehicle 車両　pretty かなり　tightly ぴったりと、きつく　trailer トレーラー　actor 俳優　gratitude 感謝　location manager 現場責任者　production 製作

2 記事 host 〜を催す　❶ cross 〜を横断する　those who 〜 〜する人々　routinely 日常的に　alternate 代わりの　❷ motorist 自動車運転者　be aware of 〜 〜を認識している　potential 可能性　pedestrian traffic 通行人の往来　take a precaution 予防策を講じる　accordingly それに応じて　for the duration of 〜 〜の間ずっと　undeveloped 未開発の　❸ resident 住民　be frustrated by 〜 〜にいらいらしている　inconvenience 不便さ　accompany 〜に伴って起こる　Office of Tourism 観光局　point to 〜 〜を指摘する　gain 利益、利点　❹ appreciate 〜を認識する　the public 一般市民　cast 出演者　*A* as well as *B* *A*および*B*　necessity 必需品　❺ official 当局者　estimate that 〜 〜と見積もる　bring in 〜 〜をもたらす　as much as 〜 〜もの

Questions 181-185 refer to the following packing slip and e-mail.

1 梱包票

Jardinar International
Rua da Nova 49
Funchal, 9000-720, Madeira, Portugal

❶ Order and Shipping Date: 12 February
Order Status: Paid

Ship To: Emmy Kirsch
Kirsch Garden Center
8 Boulevard Leon
L-1623 Luxembourg

❷ Item	Quantity
Autumn Beauty Marigold	24
Azorean Red Tomato (organic)	36
Classic Dill	12
Sweet Pea Mix	15
Blue Tarragon	15

❸ Questions about your order?
Reach us at www.jardinarinternational.pt or call 351-291-555-017.

2 E メール

To:	ekirsch@kirschgardencenter.lu
From:	lenasilvia@jardinarinternational.pt
Sent:	21 February, 8:23 A.M.
Subject:	Seed packet misprint

Dear Ms. Kirsch:

❶ I received the voice mail you left yesterday and checked into the matter. The seed packages you referred to did include a misprint. We had intended for the "organic" label to appear in the lower-right corner, but the printer inadvertently left it out. Unfortunately, we failed to spot the error before the packages were shipped.

❷ We are sending you, by express mail, several sheets of stickers labeled "organic" that you can affix to the lower-right corner of the seed packets so customers in your shop can be certain that they are buying organic seeds. We are also putting a credit of 25 euros on your account to make up for any inconvenience.

❸ Thank you for bringing the matter to our attention. Thank you, too, for your business over the years. We trust your customers will continue to be pleased with the seed varieties from Jardinar International.

Sincerely,

Lena Silvia, Customer Service Manager
Jardinar International

問題181-185は次の梱包票とEメールに関するものです。

Jardinarインターナショナル社
ルア・ダ・ノバ49番地
フンシャル、9000-720、マデイラ、ポルトガル

注文発送日：2月12日
注文状況：支払済

送り先：Emmy Kirsch様
　　　　Kirschガーデンセンター
　　　　レオン通り8番地
　　　　L-1623 ルクセンブルク

品物	数量
オータム・ビューティー・マリーゴールド	24
アゾリアン・レッド・トマト（有機栽培）	36
クラシック・ディル	12
スイートピー・ミックス	15
ブルー・タラゴン	15

ご注文についてご質問はございますか？
www.jardinarinternational.ptにて当社にご連絡いただくか、351-291-555-017にお電話ください。

受信者：ekirsch@kirschgardencenter.lu
送信者：lenasilvia@jardinarinternational.pt
送信日時：2月21日午前8時23分
件名：種の袋のミスプリント

Kirsch様

お客さまが昨日残されたボイスメールを受信し、問題を調査いたしました。お客さまが言及された種の包装に、確かにミスプリントが含まれていました。当社は「有機栽培」というラベルが右下隅に表示されるようにするつもりでしたが、印刷業者がうっかりそれを抜かしてしまいました。あいにく、当社は商品が発送される前に誤りを見つけることができませんでした。

当社は、貴店の顧客が有機栽培の種を購入しているのだと確信が持てるよう、種の袋の右下隅に貼っていただける「有機栽培」というシールのシート数枚を速達便でお送りいたします。また、当社はご迷惑をお掛けしたことのおわびとして、貴店の口座に25ユーロを入金させていただきます。

この度は問題点をご指摘いただきありがとうございました。また、長年にわたるお取引をありがとうございます。貴店の顧客の方々が引き続きJardinarインターナショナル社の多様な種子にご満足いただけると信じております。

敬具

Lena Silvia、顧客サービスマネージャー
Jardinarインターナショナル社

181 What is suggested about Jardinar International?

(A) It has a store in Luxembourg.
(B) It offers landscaping services.
(C) It sells its products to businesses.
(D) It provides gardening advice on its Web site.

Jardinarインターナショナル社について何が分かりますか。

(A) ルクセンブルクに店舗がある。
(B) 造園事業を提供している。
(C) 商品を店に販売している。
(D) ウェブサイトで園芸の助言をしている。

正解 C Jardinarインターナショナル社が発行している梱包票である**1**の**❶**の送り先にKirsch Garden Center「Kirschガーデンセンター」と記されている。また、Jardinarインターナショナル社がKirschさん宛てに送信したEメールである**2**の**❷** 2〜3行目に、so customers in your shop can be certain that they are buying organic seeds「貴店の顧客が有機栽培の種を購入しているのだと確信が持てるように」とある。よって、Jardinarインターナショナル社は商品をKirschさんの

所有する店に販売していると判断できるので、(C)が正解。business「店、企業」。
(A) **1**のヘッダー部分より、Jardinarインターナショナル社はポルトガルにあると分かる。ルクセンブルクにあるのは送り先のKirschガーデンセンター。
(B) offer「〜を提供する」、landscaping「造園」。
(D) provide「〜を与える」、gardening「園芸」、advice「助言」。

---

182 Which item in the order was mislabeled?

(A) Azorean Red Tomato
(B) Classic Dill
(C) Sweet Pea Mix
(D) Blue Tarragon

注文の中でどの品物がラベルに誤りがありましたか。

(A) アゾリアン・レッド・トマト
(B) クラシック・ディル
(C) スイートピー・ミックス
(D) ブルー・タラゴン

正解 A Eメール**2**の**❶** 1〜2行目で、Kirschさんの指摘通り種の包装にミスプリントがあったと伝え、続く同**❶** 2〜3行目で、We had intended for the "organic" label to appear in the lower-right corner, but the printer inadvertently left it out.「当社は『有機栽培』というラベルが右下隅に表示されるようにするつもりだったが、印刷業者がうっかりそれを抜かして

しまった」とラベルの誤りを説明している。梱包票**1**の**❷**の商品名が並んでいる中で "organic" というラベルが必要なのは上から2つ目のAzorean Red Tomato (organic)「アゾリアン・レッド・トマト(有機栽培)」なので、(A)が正解。 mislabel「〜に誤ったラベルを付ける」。

---

183 How did Ms. Silvia solve Ms. Kirsch's problem?

(A) By sending Ms. Kirsch some stickers
(B) By advising Ms. Kirsch to purchase an alternative product
(C) By providing Ms. Kirsch with new seed packets
(D) By reimbursing Ms. Kirsch for the cost of an item

SilviaさんはどのようにしてKirschさんの問題を解決しましたか。

(A) Kirschさんにシールを送ることによって
(B) Kirschさんに代わりの商品を購入するように助言することによって
(C) Kirschさんに新しい種の袋を提供することによって
(D) Kirschさんに品物の費用を返金することによって

正解 A Silviaさんとは、Eメール**2**の送信者であり、Jardinarインターナショナル社の顧客サービスマネージャー。Kirschさんの問題とは、同**❶** 1〜2行目で述べられている、注文した種の包装にミスプリントがあったことである。同**❷** 1〜3行目に、「当社は、貴店の顧客が有機栽培の種を購入しているのだと確信が持てるよう、種の袋の右下隅に貼ってもらえる『有機栽培』というシールのシート数枚を速達便で送る」とある。よ

って、SilviaさんはKirschさんにシールを送ることによって問題を解決したと分かるので、(A)が正解。solve「〜を解決する」。
(B) advise 〜 to do「〜に…するように助言する」、alternative「代わりの」。
(D) **2**の**❸** 3〜4行目に、おわびとして25ユーロを入金するとあるが、これは品物の費用の返金ではない。reimburse 〜 for …「〜に…を返金する」。

Expressions

make up for 〜 「〜の埋め合わせをする、〜を償う」(**2**の**❸** 4行目)
We have to make up for the lost time in a short period.
私たちは失った時間を短期間で埋め合わせなければなりません。

184 In the e-mail, the word "<u>matter</u>" in paragraph 3, line 1, is closest in meaning to

(A) idea
(B) issue
(C) amount
(D) material

Eメールの第3段落・1行目にある "matter" に最も意味が近いのは

(A) 考え
(B) 問題
(C) 総額
(D) 材料

> **正解 B** Eメール**2**の**❶**・**❷**で、ミスプリントの原因とその解決策、おわびが述べられている。続く同**❸**1行目の該当の語を含む文におけるbring 〜 to *one's* attentionは「〜を…に注目させる」という意味なので、この文では「------を私た
>
> ちに注目させてくれてありがとう」とお礼が述べられている。このmatterは、同**❶**1行目のmatterと同義のものであり、ミスプリントという問題をKirschさんが指摘してくれたことにお礼を述べていると考えられる。よって、(B) issue「問題」が正解。

---

185 What is indicated about Ms. Kirsch?

(A) She is a former employee of Jardinar International.
(B) She paid 25 euros for express shipping.
(C) She received a discount for ordering in bulk.
(D) She is a longtime customer of Jardinar International.

Kirschさんについて何が示されていますか。

(A) 彼女はJardinarインターナショナル社の元従業員である。
(B) 彼女は速達に25ユーロ支払った。
(C) 彼女は大量に注文して割引を受けた。
(D) 彼女はJardinarインターナショナル社の長年にわたる顧客である。

> **正解 D** JardinarインターナショナルがKirschさん宛てに送信したEメールである**2**の**❸**1〜2行目に、Thank you, too, for your business over the years.「また、長年にわたるお取引をありがとうございます」と書かれている。よって、KirschさんはJardinarインターナショナル社の長年にわたる顧客であると判断できるので、(D)が正解。longtime customer
>
> 「長年にわたる顧客」。
> (A) former「以前の」。
> (B) **2**の**❷**3〜4行目より、25ユーロはJardinarインターナショナル社がおわびとしてKirschさんの口座に入金すると述べられている金額。
> (C) discount「割引」、in bulk「大量に」。

---

packing slip　梱包票

1 梱包票　❶ shipping　発送　　order status　注文状況　　paid　支払いの済んだ
boulevard　大通り　★街路名に用いられる場合は語頭が大文字で表記される　　❷ quantity　数量
marigold　マリーゴールド　★キク科の一年草　　organic　有機栽培の
dill　ディル、イノンド　★セリ科の一年草。ハーブの一種　　sweet pea　スイートピー
tarragon　タラゴン　★キク科の多年草。ハーブの一種　　❸ reach　〜に連絡する

2 Eメール　seed　種　　packet　小袋　　misprint　ミスプリント
❶ voice mail　ボイスメール　★コンピューターを使って送信する音声伝言システム　　check into 〜　〜を調査する
matter　問題　　package　包装　　refer to 〜　〜に言及する　　include　〜を含む
intend for 〜 to *do*　〜に…させるつもりである　　label　ラベル　　appear　現れる　　lower-right　右下の
printer　印刷業者、プリンター　　inadvertently　うっかりと　　leave out 〜　〜を抜かす、〜を省く
unfortunately　あいにく　　fail to *do*　〜しそこなう、〜しない　　spot　〜に気付く　　❷ express mail　速達便
a sheet of 〜　1枚の〜　　sticker　シール、ステッカー　　label 〜 …　〜に…と表示する
affix 〜 to …　〜を…に貼る　　so (that) 〜 can …　〜が…できるように
be certain that 〜　〜ということを確信する　　credit　入金、貸勘定　　euro　ユーロ　　inconvenience　迷惑、不便
❸ attention　注意、注目　　business　取引　　over the years　長年にわたって
trust (that) 〜　〜ということを信じる　　continue to *do*　〜し続ける　　variety　種類、品種
customer service manager　顧客サービスマネージャー

Questions 186-190 refer to the following article, advertisement, and memo.

Changes on Main Street

❶ GORTON (4 August)—Shanitra Jones, director of the city's Small Business Coalition, welcomed two new businesses to Main Street during an outdoor ceremony last week. Both newcomers are occupying properties left vacant for over six months by previous businesses that closed down.

❷ Great Customisables has moved into the old Walt's Jewellery Mart space at 65 Main Street. Great Customisables offers merchandise such as hats, shirts, and totes that can be personalised with names, designs, and company logos.

❸ Fred Djirubal, the store's manager, said he looks forward to playing an active role in the Gorton community. "We love working with schools and charitable organisations by assisting with fund-raisers," he said.

❹ Café Arepa, an eatery specialising in Venezuelan cuisine, now occupies the space formerly held by Pizza Kings at 14 Main Street. "The Small Business Coalition is delighted to have Café Arepa there," Ms. Jones said. "Having a fine restaurant right in the middle of the shopping district will draw people in."

❺ Ms. Jones added that Hargrave Cleaning Services will be opening a branch office in downtown Gorton as soon as it can finalise the lease.

Hargrave Cleaning Services
Suite 220, Second Floor, 65 Main Street, Gorton

❶ We clean commercial properties throughout the Gorton area. Whether you're looking for regular daily or weekly cleaning or for a one-time deep cleaning, we can do it! Let us know what you need. We can come up with a plan just for you.

❷ October Deep Cleaning Special—20% off if scheduled before 31 October! For more information or to schedule an appointment, call 07 5550 6653.

MEMO

To: All employees of Ohanian Manufacturing
From: Facilities department
Date: 12 October
Re: This weekend

❶ Hargrave Cleaning Services will be here this weekend, 17–18 October, to perform a deep cleaning of the entire facility, including the break room. Carpets will be shampooed. Please remove all personal items from the floor in your office or cubicle and clear your desk. All food must be removed from the break-room refrigerator, and anything left there will be thrown away. Please make certain to complete these tasks before the end of the day on Friday, 16 October.

問題186-190は次の記事、広告、メモに関するものです。

メイン通りの変化

ゴートン（8月4日）——市の中小企業連合会会長のShanitra Jonesは、先週、野外式典で2つの新たな事業者をメイン通りに歓迎した。新規参入の両者は、閉業した以前の事業者が6カ月を超えて空いたままにしていた物件を使用する。

Great Customisablesはメイン通り65番地の旧Walt's Jewellery Martのスペースに入居してきた。Great Customisablesは、名前や図柄、会社のロゴを個別注文に合わせて入れることのできる帽子、シャツ、手提げバッグなどの商品を販売する。

同店の経営者のFred Djirubalはゴートン地域で積極的な役割を果たすことを楽しみにしていると言った。「当店は、資金集めのイベントを支援することで学校や慈善団体と協業することを大事にしています」と彼は述べた。

ベネズエラ料理を専門に扱う料理店のCafé Arepaは現在、Pizza Kingsが以前占有していたメイン通り14番地のスペースを使用している。「中小企業連合会はCafé Arepaを同地に迎えてうれしく思います」とJones氏は言った。「商業地区のちょうど真ん中に良いレストランがあると、人々を引き寄せることになるでしょう」。

Jones氏は、Hargrave清掃サービス社がリース契約をまとめられ次第、ゴートンの中心街に支店を開く予定であると付け加えた。

Hargrave清掃サービス社
2階220号室、メイン通り65番地、ゴートン

当社はゴートン全域の商業用不動産を清掃いたします。毎日または週1回の定期清掃をお求めであろうと1回限りの徹底清掃をお求めであろうと、当社は対応可能です！ご要望をお知らせください。お客さまのためだけのプランをご提案します。

10月の徹底清掃の特別提供——10月31日より前に予定を組んでいただければ、20パーセント割引！ さらなる情報もしくはご予約の設定には、07 5550 6653にお電話ください。

メモ

宛先：Ohanian製造社従業員各位
差出人：施設部
日付：10月12日
件名：今週末

Hargrave清掃サービス社が今週末の10月17～18日にこちらに来て、休憩室を含む施設全体の徹底清掃を行う予定です。カーペットは洗剤で洗浄されます。ご自分の執務室や作業区画の床から全ての私物を撤去して、机周りを片付けてください。休憩室の冷蔵庫から全ての食べ物が撤去されなければならず、そこに残っているものは全て処分されます。これらの作業を10月16日金曜日いっぱいまでに必ず完了するようにしてください。

186 According to the article, what is true about the building at 14 Main Street?

(A) It was owned by Mr. Djirubal.
(B) It is now a construction site.
(C) It houses the Small Business Coalition.
(D) It was empty for more than six months.

記事によると、メイン通り 14 番地の建物について正しいことは何ですか。

(A) Djirubal さんが所有していた。
(B) 現在は工事現場である。
(C) 中小企業連合会が入っている。
(D) 6 カ月を超える期間空いていた。

正解 D 記事**1**の**❶** 1～5 行目に、ゴートン市が 2 つの新たな事業者をメイン通りに迎えたと書かれている。1 つ目は Great Customisables で、同**❷**・**❸**で紹介され、2 つ目は Café Arepa で、同**❹**で紹介されている。同**❹** 1～4 行目より、メイン通り 14 番地は Café Arepa の所在地。同**❶** 5～7 行目に、Both newcomers are occupying properties left vacant for over six months by previous businesses that closed down.「新規参入の両者は、閉業した以前の事業者が 6 カ月を超えて空いたままにしていた物件を使用する」とある。つまり、Café Arepa が入居したメイン通り 14 番地の建物は、それまで 6 カ月を超える期間空いていたと分かる。(D)が正解。empty「空いている」、more than ～「～より多い」。
(A) Djirubal さんは、メイン通り 65 番地の建物に入居した Great Customisables の経営者。own「～を所有する」。
(B) **1**の**❹** 1～4 行目より、同地の建物には Café Arepa が入居していると分かるので、construction site「工事現場」ではない。
(C) 中小企業連合会の所在地は述べられていない。house「(建物が)～にスペースを提供する」。

---

187 Why is Ms. Jones pleased about the opening of a restaurant?

(A) She enjoys Venezuelan cuisine.
(B) She plans to host special events there.
(C) She thinks it will attract shoppers to the area.
(D) She expects it will employ many people from the community.

Jones さんはなぜレストランの開店を喜んでいますか。

(A) 彼女はベネズエラ料理が好きである。
(B) 彼女はそこで特別なイベントを主催するつもりである。
(C) 彼女はそれがその地域に買い物客を引き付けるだろうと考えている。
(D) 彼女はそれがその地域の多くの人々を雇用するだろうと期待している。

正解 C 記事**1**の**❶** 1～3 行目より、Jones さんとはゴートン市の中小企業連合会会長と分かる。開店するレストランとは、同**❹**で紹介されているベネズエラ料理を専門に扱う料理店の Café Arepa。Jones さんは、同**❹** 4～5 行目で、「中小企業連合会は Café Arepa を同地に迎えてうれしく思う」と歓迎し、続く同**❹** 6～8 行目で、Having a fine restaurant right in the middle of the shopping district will draw people in.「商業地区のちょうど真ん中に良いレストランがあると、人々を引き寄せることになるだろう」と述べている。つまり、Jones さんは Café Arepa の存在が買い物客をゴートン地域に引き付けるだろうと考えていることが分かる。draw people in を attract shoppers to the area と表している(C)が正解。be pleased about ～「～を喜んでいる」。attract ～ to …「～を…に引き付ける」、shopper「買い物客」。
(B) host「～を主催する」。
(D) employ「～を雇用する」。

---

188 What business is located in the same building as Hargrave Cleaning Services?

(A) Great Customisables
(B) Walt's Jewellery Mart
(C) Café Arepa
(D) Pizza Kings

どの店が Hargrave 清掃サービス社と同じ建物の中にありますか。

(A) Great Customisables
(B) Walt's Jewellery Mart
(C) Café Arepa
(D) Pizza Kings

正解 A Hargrave 清掃サービス社の広告**2**の住所欄に「メイン通り 65 番地」とある。記事**1**の**❷** 1～3 行目より、Great Customisables が同じメイン通り 65 番地に入居していることが分かるので、(A)が正解。be located in ～「～にある」。
(B) **1**の**❷** 1～3 行目より、メイン通り 65 番地にかつて入居していたのが Walt's Jewellery Mart と分かるが、Hargrave 清掃サービス社が入居するより前に閉業している。
(C) (D) **1**の**❹** 1～4 行目より、メイン通り 14 番地にかつて入居していたのが Pizza Kings で、そこに新たに入居してきたのが Café Arepa。

189 What is suggested about Ohanian Manufacturing?

    (A) It manufactures carpets.

    (B) It received a discount on a service.

    (C) Its facility was recently redecorated.

    (D) Its employees will be given a day off from work.

Ohanian 製造社について何が分かりますか。

    (A) 同社はカーペットを製造している。

    (B) 同社はあるサービスについて割引を受けた。

    (C) 同社の施設は最近改装された。

    (D) 同社の従業員は休日を1日与えられる予定である。

正解 B Ohanian 製造社の施設部が全従業員に宛てたメモ③の❶ 1～2 行目に、「Hargrave 清掃サービス社が今週末の 10 月 17～18 日にここに来て、休憩室を含む施設全体の徹底清掃を行う予定だ」とある。Hargrave 清掃サービス社の広告②の❷ 1 行目には、October Deep Cleaning Special — 20% off if scheduled before 31 October!「10 月の徹底清掃の特別提供――10 月 31 日より前に予定が組まれれば、20 パーセン ト割引」と書かれている。よって、Ohanian 製造社は清掃サービスについて 20 パーセントの割引を受けたと考えられるので、(B) が正解。discount「割引」。

(A) manufacture「～を製造する」。
(C) recently「最近」、redecorate「～を改装する」。
(D) day off「休日、休暇」。

190 What is the last day that employees of Ohanian Manufacturing can remove food from the refrigerator?

    (A) October 12

    (B) October 16

    (C) October 17

    (D) October 18

Ohanian 製造社の従業員が冷蔵庫から食べ物を撤去することができる最後の日はいつですか。

    (A) 10 月 12 日

    (B) 10 月 16 日

    (C) 10 月 17 日

    (D) 10 月 18 日

正解 B Ohanian 製造社のメモ③の❶ 4～5 行目に、「休憩室の冷蔵庫から全ての食べ物が撤去されなければならない」とある。同 6～7 行目には、Please make certain to complete these tasks before the end of the day on Friday, 16 October.「これらの作業を 10 月 16 日金曜日いっぱいまでに 必ず完了するようにしてください」と書かれている。よって、(B) が正解。

(A) ③の日付より、メモが掲示された日。
(C) (D) ③の❶ 1～2 行目より、清掃作業が行われる日付。

Questions 191-195 refer to the following e-mail, article, and Web page.

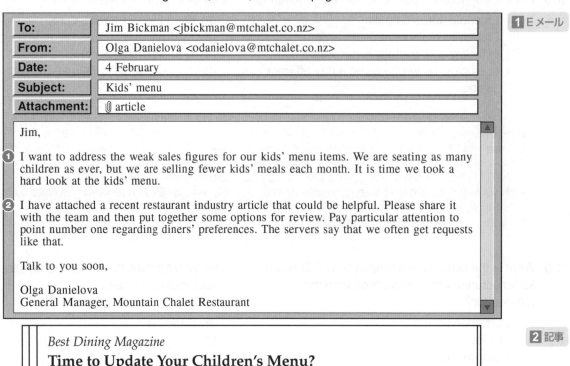

1 E メール

To:	Jim Bickman <jbickman@mtchalet.co.nz>
From:	Olga Danielova <odanielova@mtchalet.co.nz>
Date:	4 February
Subject:	Kids' menu
Attachment:	🖉 article

Jim,

1 I want to address the weak sales figures for our kids' menu items. We are seating as many children as ever, but we are selling fewer kids' meals each month. It is time we took a hard look at the kids' menu.

2 I have attached a recent restaurant industry article that could be helpful. Please share it with the team and then put together some options for review. Pay particular attention to point number one regarding diners' preferences. The servers say that we often get requests like that.

Talk to you soon,

Olga Danielova
General Manager, Mountain Chalet Restaurant

2 記事

Best Dining Magazine

Time to Update Your Children's Menu?

1 According to a recent *Best Dining Magazine* survey, restaurants need to make big changes to their children's menus if they want to appeal to young families. Diners preferred expanded kids' menu options in three main categories:

2 1. Seventy percent of respondents wanted menu options for children who are on special diets (e.g., vegetarian meals).

2. Eighty-seven percent of respondents requested options for healthier eating (e.g., fruits, vegetables, and grilled or baked poultry and fish).

3. Sixty-four percent of respondents said they would like to see more customizable kids' meals (e.g., choose-your-own toppings, sauces, and side items).

3 Interestingly, very few respondents (19 percent) requested lower prices.

3 ウェブページ

◀ ▶ http://www.foodloveblog.co.nz ▼

Goodbye, Chicken Nuggets; Hello, Kale Salad!

1 Chef Jim Bickman at Mountain Chalet has made dining out with kids a lot healthier—and more enjoyable—by updating the restaurant's kids' menu. On a recent visit, the parents and children at our table all gave the new menu items an excellent review.

2 One young diner was thrilled that he could choose to top his kale salad with grilled chicken, tofu, or fish. Similarly, another child loved that she could choose from three sauces and multiple meats to create a pasta dish. Old favorites like grilled cheese sandwiches are also still available.

3 While we relaxed at our table, we enjoyed playing tabletop games that the restaurant had recently introduced. The atmosphere and the food made for a wonderful dining experience. I highly recommend Mountain Chalet to all food lovers with kids.

問題191-195は次のEメール、記事、ウェブページに関するものです。

受信者：Jim Bickman <jbickman@mtchalet.co.nz>
送信者：Olga Danielova <odanielova@mtchalet.co.nz>
日付：2月4日
件名：子ども用メニュー
添付ファイル：記事

Jimさん

私は当店の子ども用メニュー品目の低調な売り上げに対処したいと思っています。相変わらず多くのお子さんを席に案内しているのに、子ども向け料理の売り上げは毎月減少しています。当店は子ども用メニューを厳しく見直してみてもよい時期です。

役に立つかもしれない最近のレストラン業界の記事を添付しました。それをチームで共有して、検討用の選択肢を幾つかまとめてください。食事客の好みに関する1つ目のポイントに特に注意を払ってください。給仕係が当店でしばしばそのような要望を受けると言っています。

近々お話ししましょう。

Olga Danielova
Mountain Chaletレストラン総支配人

『ベスト・ダイニング・マガジン』
子ども用メニューを更新すべき時期？

最近の『ベスト・ダイニング・マガジン』の調査によると、小さい子どもがいる家庭に訴求したいなら、レストランは子ども用メニューに大きな変更を加える必要がある。食事客は、3つの主な分類において、子ども用メニューの選択肢が拡充されることを希望した。

1. 70パーセントの回答者が、特別な食事制限をしている子どもたちのためのメニューの選択肢を望んだ（例えば、ベジタリアン向けの料理）。
2. 87パーセントの回答者が、より健康的な食事のための選択肢を求めた（例えば、果物、野菜、直火やオーブンで焼いた鶏肉や魚）。
3. 64パーセントの回答者が、カスタマイズ可能な子ども用の料理をもっと見てみたいと言った（例えば、自分で選べるトッピング、ソース、付け合わせ）。

興味深いことに、より低い価格を求めた回答者はごく少数（19パーセント）だった。

---

http://www.foodloveblog.co.nz

『さようなら、チキンナゲット、こんにちは、ケールサラダ！』

Mountain ChaletのシェフJim Bickmanは、レストランの子ども用メニューを更新することで、子どもと一緒の外食をずっとより健康的なもの——そしてより楽しいもの——にした。最近店を訪れた際に、私たちのテーブルの親と子どもの全員が新しいメニュー品目に最高の評価を与えた。

食事をしていた子どもの1人は、ケールサラダにトッピングとしてグリルチキンや豆腐、魚を選べるので喜んでいた。同様に、別の子どもは3つのソースと複数の肉から選んでパスタ料理を創作するのをとても気に入っていた。グリルチーズ・サンドイッチのような昔から人気のあるものも変わらず用意されている。

私たちはテーブルでくつろいでいる間、レストランが最近導入した卓上用ゲームをして楽しんだ。雰囲気と食べ物のおかげで素晴らしい食事体験となった。私はMountain Chaletを、子ども連れの全ての食いしん坊に強くお薦めする。

191 What most likely is Ms. Danielova's goal?

(A) To get better publicity for the restaurant
(B) To increase sales for a particular menu category
(C) To locate more suppliers of fresh food
(D) To resolve customer complaints more quickly

Danielovaさんの目標は何だと考えられますか。

(A) レストランがより良い評判を得ること
(B) 特定のメニュー分野の売り上げを伸ばすこと
(C) 生鮮食品の仕入れ先をもっと多く見つけること
(D) 顧客からの苦情をより迅速に解決すること

| 正解 B | Eメール**1**の送信者の署名より、DanielovaさんとはMountain Chaletレストランの総支配人と分かる。Danielovaさんは同**1** 1行目で、「私は当店の子ども用メニュー品目の低調な売り上げに対処したいと思っている」と書き、それ以降でも、子ども用メニューの見直しに言及して案をまとめるよう要請している。よって、Danielovaさんの目標は子ども用メニューという特定の分野の売り上げを伸ばすことだと考えられる | ので、(B)が正解。goal「目標」。increase「〜を増やす」。
(A) **3**のウェブページでレストランの良い評判を得ているが、Danielovaさんの目標として述べられているわけではない。publicity「評判」。
(C) locate「〜を見つける」、supplier「仕入れ先」、fresh food「生鮮食品」。
(D) resolve「〜を解決する」、complaint「苦情」。 |

192 In the e-mail, what is Mr. Bickman asked to do?

(A) Look at sales figures
(B) Meet with Ms. Danielova
(C) Arrange for additional seating
(D) Share an article with employees

Eメールで、Bickmanさんは何をするように求められていますか。

(A) 売上高を見る
(B) Danielovaさんと会う
(C) 追加の座席を手配する
(D) 記事を従業員に共有する

| 正解 D | BickmanさんはEメール**1**の受信者。**1**の**2** 1〜2行目に、「役に立つかもしれない最近のレストラン業界の記事を添付した。それをチームで共有して、検討用の選択肢を幾つかまとめてください」とある。Bickmanさんは、記事を他の従業員に共有するように求められているので、(D)が正解。 | (A) **1**の**1**で、子ども用メニューの売り上げに言及されているが、Bickmanさんは売上高を見るよう求められてはいない。
(B) meet with 〜「〜と会う」。
(C) arrange for 〜「〜を手配する」、additional「追加の」、seating「座席」。 |

193 What change mentioned in the article would address the issue Ms. Danielova feels is most important?

(A) Adding vegetarian meals
(B) Offering fresh fruits
(C) Making meals customizable
(D) Decreasing prices

記事で述べられているどのような変更が、Danielovaさんが最も重要だと感じる問題に対処することになりますか。

(A) ベジタリアン向けの料理を追加すること
(B) 新鮮な果物を提供すること
(C) 料理をカスタマイズ可能なものにすること
(D) 価格を下げること

| 正解 A | DanielovaさんはEメール**1**の**2** 1〜2行目で、子ども向けメニュー改善に役立ちそうな記事について述べた後、同**2** 2〜3行目で、「食事客の好みに関する1つ目のポイントに特に注意を払ってください」と書いている。記事**2**はDanielovaさんが添付した記事と考えられ、同**2**に調査結果が3点記載されている。その1つ目のポイントには、「70パーセントの回答者が、特別な食事制限をしている子どもたちのためのメニューの選択肢を望んだ（例えば、ベジタリアン向けの料理）」とある。よって、Danielovaさんが最も重要だと考えている問題について、 | 記事にあるようにベジタリアン向けの料理を追加することが対処の例になると判断できるので、(A)が正解。issue「問題」。add「〜を追加する」。
(B) 果物の記載があるのは、**2**の**2** 2つ目のポイント。
(C) 料理のカスタマイズについて記載があるのは、**2**の**2** 3つ目のポイント。
(D) **2**の**3**に、低価格を求める意見は少数とあるのみ。decrease「〜を低下させる」。 |

Expressions

〈it is time＋主語＋動詞の過去形〉 「もう〜してもよい頃だ」（**1**の**1** 2〜3行目）

It is time we made the final decision whether to carry out the plan or not.
私たちはその計画を実行するべきか否か、もう最終決定をしてもよい頃です。

194 To whom did Ms. Danielova direct her concerns?

    (A) A restaurant owner
    (B) A general manager
    (C) A chef
    (D) A server

Danielovaさんは誰に懸念を向けましたか。

    (A) レストランの所有者
    (B) 総支配人
    (C) シェフ
    (D) 給仕係

> **正解 C** Danielovaさんは Jim Bickmanさんに宛てたEメール**1**の**❶** 1～2行目で、レストランの子ども用メニューの売り上げが低調であるという懸念に触れ、同**❶** 2～3行目で、「当店は子ども用メニューを厳しく見直してみてもよい時期だ」と述べている。また同**❷** 1～2行目で、「検討用の選択肢を幾つかまとめてください」と求めている。Jim Bickmanさんは、ウェブページ**3**の**❶** 1行目より、Mountain Chaletレストランのシェフであることが分かるので、Danielovaさんはシェフである人物に懸念を向けたことになる。よって、(C)が正解。direct ～ to … 「～を…に向ける」、concern「懸念」。
> (B) **1**の署名より、総支配人はDanielovaさん。

195 According to the Web page, what is newly available at Mountain Chalet?

    (A) Chicken nuggets
    (B) Outdoor seating
    (C) Grilled cheese sandwiches
    (D) Tabletop games

ウェブページによると、Mountain Chaletで新たに利用できるのは何ですか。

    (A) チキンナゲット
    (B) 屋外座席
    (C) グリルチーズ・サンドイッチ
    (D) 卓上用ゲーム

> **正解 D** ウェブページ**3**の**❸** 1～2行目に、While we relaxed at our table, we enjoyed playing tabletop games that the restaurant had recently introduced. 「私たちはテーブルでくつろいでいる間、レストランが最近導入した卓上用ゲームをして楽しんだ」とある。よって、(D)が正解。newly「新たに」。
> (A) **3**のタイトルにチキンナゲットとあるのは、健康的な食事の象徴としてのケールサラダと対比させるためと考えられる。
> (C) **3**の**❷** 3～4行目より、昔から人気のあるメニューとして言及されているので、新たなものではない。

Words & Phrases

1 Eメール
attachment 添付ファイル   **❶** address ～(問題など)に取り組む   weak 低調な、弱い
sales figures 売上高、販売数量   menu item メニュー品目 ★飲食店がメニューに載せている料理や飲み物
seat ～を席に案内する、～を座らせる   as ～ as ever 相変わらず～   meal 料理、食事
take a hard look at ～ ～を厳しく見直す   **❷** attach ～を添付する   helpful 役立つ、有益な
share ～ with … ～を…と共有する   put together ～ ～をまとめる   option 選択肢   review 再検討
pay attention to ～ ～に注意を払う   particular 特別の   regarding ～に関して   diner 食事をする人
preference 好み、好みのもの   server 給仕係   general manager 総支配人

2 記事
dining 食事   **❶** make a change to ～ ～に変更を加える   appeal to ～ ～に訴える
young family 小さい子どもがいる家庭   prefer ～をより好む   expanded 拡大された   category 分類
❷ respondent 回答者   be on a special diet 特別な食事制限・療法をしている
e.g. 例えば ★英語のfor exampleに当たるラテン語exempli gratiaの略
vegetarian ベジタリアンの、菜食主義(者)の   healthy 健康的な   eating 食事
grill (直火や焼き網で)～を焼く   bake (オーブンなどで)～を焼く   poultry 鶏肉
would like to *do* ～したい   customizable カスタマイズ可能な   choose-your-own 自分で選べる
sauce ソース   side item 付け合わせ   **❸** interestingly 興味深いことに   few ほとんどない、わずかの

3 ウェブページ
chicken nugget チキンナゲット   kale ケール   **❶** chef シェフ   dine out 外食をする
enjoyable 楽しい   excellent 非常に優れた、素晴らしい   review 評価
❷ be thrilled that ～ ～ということに興奮している   choose to *do* ～することを選ぶ
top ～ with … ～に…を乗せる   tofu 豆腐   similarly 同様に   multiple 複数の   create ～を作る
pasta dish パスタ料理   favorite 人気のあるもの   **❸** relax くつろぐ   tabletop 卓上用の
introduce ～を導入する   atmosphere 雰囲気   make for ～ ～を作り出す   experience 体験
highly 強く   recommend ～を薦める   food lover 食べるのが好きな人、グルメ

Questions 196-200 refer to the following letter, e-mail, and utility bill.

September 15

Edward Maunce, Operations Manager
Bronski Solutions, Inc.
21 Woerdens Road
Martindale, IN 46176

Dear Mr. Maunce,

❶ Your company's monthly electricity charges fluctuated significantly over the past year. Many of our commercial customers with this kind of usage pattern have switched to Commercial SB billing. Under this plan, a company pays the same amount each month regardless of usage levels. This makes budgeting much easier. Contact me if your company is interested in Commercial SB billing.

❷ Also, please note that next month all customers will be subject to a small 1% rate increase. The revenue generated from this increase will fund important repairs to our power delivery infrastructure.

Sincerely,

Patrice Tsui

Patrice Tsui
Commercial Accounts Representative
Oaklawn Electric Supply

	E-mail
To:	Sunita Colman, Vice President of Operations
From:	Edward Maunce, Operations Manager
Date:	September 30
Subject:	Electricity service
Attachment:	📎 Service company letter - copy

Hello Sunita,

❶ Please take a moment to read the attached copy of a letter I just received. I like Ms. Tsui's suggestion, and I believe we should move forward with it. Do you agree? Looking back at our recent records, I notice we experienced a major jump in costs starting in the exact month our temporary interns first arrived and began working on those short-term projects.

Thanks,

Ed
Operations Manager, Bronski Solutions, Inc.

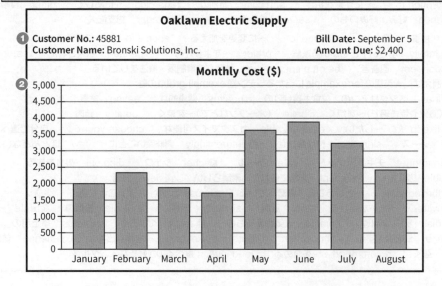

Oaklawn Electric Supply

❶ Customer No.: 45881
Customer Name: Bronski Solutions, Inc.

Bill Date: September 5
Amount Due: $2,400

❷ **Monthly Cost ($)**

(Bar chart showing monthly cost from January to August)
- January: 2,000
- February: 2,350
- March: 1,900
- April: 1,700
- May: 3,600
- June: 3,900
- July: 3,250
- August: 2,400

問題196-200は次の手紙、Eメール、公共料金請求書に関するものです。

9月15日

運用管理者　Edward Maunce様
Bronskiソリューションズ社
ウールデンズ通り21番地
マーティンデール、IN 46176

Maunce様

貴社の毎月の電気料金はこの1年間にわたって大きく変動しました。このような使用傾向のある当社の商用顧客の多くは、商用SB請求に切り替えています。このプランでは、企業は使用水準にかかわらず毎月同額を支払います。これにより予算管理がはるかに簡単になります。もし貴社が商用SB請求に興味がおありでしたら、私までご連絡ください。

また、来月全てのお客さまが1パーセントのわずかな値上げの対象となることにご注意ください。この値上げから生じる収益は、当社の電源供給用の基幹設備の重要な補修の資金に充てられます。

敬具

Patrice Tsui（署名）
Patrice Tsui
商用顧客担当者
Oaklawn電気供給会社

受信者：事業部長　Sunita Colman
送信者：運用管理者　Edward Maunce
日付：9月30日
件名：電力供給
添付ファイル：供給会社の手紙 － コピー

Sunitaさん

少しお時間を取って、添付の、私が先ほど受け取った手紙の写しを読んでください。私はTsuiさんの提案が気に入っており、当社はそれを進めるべきだと思います。同意されますか。当社の最近の記録を振り返ってみて、私は、一時的なインターン生が初出社して短期プロジェクトに取り組み始めたまさにその月から、当社の経費が大幅に増加したということに注目しています。

よろしくお願いします。

Ed
Bronskiソリューションズ社　運用管理者

Oaklawn電気供給会社

顧客番号：45881　　　　　　　　　　　　請求日：9月5日
顧客名：Bronskiソリューションズ社　　　　請求額：2,400ドル

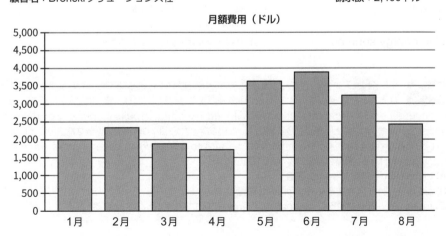
月額費用（ドル）

196 What is one purpose of the letter?

    (A) To apologize for a billing error
    (B) To promote ideas for reducing energy usage
    (C) To request payment for a past-due bill
    (D) To explain a new way of paying for services

手紙の一つの目的は何ですか。

    (A) 請求書の間違いを謝罪すること
    (B) エネルギー使用量を削減する案を推進すること
    (C) 支払期限を過ぎた請求書の支払いを求めること
    (D) 電力供給の新しい支払方法を説明すること

> **正解 D** 手紙❶は、Oaklawn電気供給会社の商用顧客担当者であるPatrice Tsuiさんが、Bronskiソリューションズ社の運用管理者であるEdward Maunceさんに送ったもの。同❶1~3行目で、Bronskiソリューションズ社の毎月の電気料金がこの1年間にわたって大きく変動しており、このような使用傾向のある商用顧客の多くが商用SB請求に切り替えていると述べている。続く同3~4行目で、「このプランでは、企業は使用水準にかかわらず毎月同額を支払う。これにより予算管理がはるかに簡単になる」と説明している。このように、手紙の一つの目的は電力供給の新しい支払方法を説明することなので、(D)が正解。
> (A) apologize for ~「~を謝罪する」、error「間違い」。
> (B) promote「~を推進する」、reduce「~を削減する」、energy「エネルギー」。
> (C) past-due「支払期限を過ぎた」。

197 What does Ms. Tsui suggest is a common concern among commercial customers?

    (A) Large variations in monthly bills
    (B) Long wait times for customer service
    (C) Frequent service disruptions
    (D) Corporate restrictions on electricity usage

Tsuiさんは、何が商用顧客の共通の懸念事項だと示唆していますか。

    (A) 月々の請求書における大きなばらつき
    (B) 顧客サービスの長い待ち時間
    (C) 頻繁な供給の中断
    (D) 電気使用に対する企業の規制

> **正解 A** Tsuiさんとは、手紙❶を書いたOaklawn電気供給会社の商用顧客担当者。同❶1~3行目で、電気料金が月によって大きく変動する傾向のある商用顧客の多くは、商用SB請求に切り替えていることを説明し、続く同3~4行目で、商用SB請求では、企業は使用量に関係なく毎月同額を支払うので予算管理がしやすくなる、と述べている。つまりTsuiさんは、月々の請求額が大きくばらつく企業の多くが毎月同額を支払うプランに変更していると述べることで、月々の請求額が大きく変動することが商用顧客の共通の懸念事項だと示唆していると言える。(A)が正解。common「共通の」、concern「懸念事項」。variation「変化量、変動」。
> (B) wait time「待ち時間」、customer service「顧客サービス」。
> (C) frequent「頻繁な」、disruption「中断」。

198 According to the letter, what will money from higher rates be used for?

    (A) To increase technicians' wages
    (B) To bid on new equipment
    (C) To pay for maintenance
    (D) To research alternative energy sources

手紙によると、料金の上昇から得るお金は何のために使われる予定ですか。

    (A) 技術者の賃金を引き上げるため
    (B) 新しい設備に入札するため
    (C) 補修の費用を支払うため
    (D) 代替エネルギー源を研究するため

> **正解 C** 手紙❶の❷1~2行目で、「また、来月全ての顧客が1パーセントのわずかな値上げの対象となることに注意してください」と料金の値上げに言及しており、続く同2~3行目で、The revenue generated from this increase will fund important repairs to our power delivery infrastructure.「この値上げから生じる収益は、当社の電源供給用の基幹設備の重要な補修の資金に充てられる」と書かれている。よって、important repairs to our power delivery infrastructureをmaintenance「補修、整備」と表している(C)が正解。
> (A) technician「技術者」、wage「賃金」。
> (B) bid on ~「~に入札する」、equipment「設備」。
> (D) research「~を研究する」、alternative energy「代替エネルギー」、source「源」。

199 What does Mr. Maunce think Bronski Solutions, Inc., should do?

(A) Choose Commercial SB billing
(B) Start an effort to reduce expenses
(C) Decrease the number of interns hired
(D) Stop being a client of Oaklawn Electric Supply

Maunceさんは、Bronskiソリューションズ社は何をするべきだと考えていますか。

(A) 商用SB請求を選択する
(B) 経費を削減する努力を始める
(C) 雇用するインターン生の数を減らす
(D) Oaklawn電気供給会社の顧客であることをやめる

正解 A Maunceさんとは、手紙**1**を受け取ったBronskiソリューションズ社の運用管理者であり、事業部長のSunita Colmanさんに宛てたEメールである**2**の送信者。Maunceさんは、Eメール**2**の**❶** 1〜2行目で、I like Ms. Tsui's suggestion, and I believe we should move forward with it. 「私はTsuiさんの提案が気に入っており、当社はそれを進めるべきだと思う」と述べている。Tsuiさんの提案とは、手紙**1**の**❶**で勧められた商用SB請求に切り替えることだと判断できるので、(A)が正解。
(B) effort「努力」、expense「経費」。
(C) the number of 〜「〜の数」、hire「〜を雇用する」。
(D) stop *doing*「〜するのをやめる」。

---

200 In what month were some temporary staff most likely hired?

(A) In May
(B) In June
(C) In July
(D) In August

臨時スタッフは何月に雇用されたと考えられますか。

(A) 5月
(B) 6月
(C) 7月
(D) 8月

正解 A Eメール**2**の**❶** 3〜5行目に、「当社の最近の記録を振り返ってみて、私は、一時的なインターン生が初出社して短期プロジェクトに取り組み始めたまさにその月から、当社の経費が大幅に増加したということに注目している」と書かれている。a major jump in costs「経費の大幅な増加」があった月は、公共料金請求書**3**の**❷**の棒グラフから、5月であることが分かる。よって、この月に一時的なインターン生、つまり臨時スタッフが雇用されたと判断できるので、(A)が正解。

Words & Phrases

utility bill 公共料金請求書

1 手紙 operations manager 運用管理者　〜, Inc. 〜社 ★incorporatedの略　**❶** electricity charge 電気料金
fluctuate 変動する　significantly 大きく　commercial customer 商用顧客、法人顧客　usage 使用
pattern 傾向　switch to 〜 〜に切り替える　billing 請求　amount 総額　level 水準、程度
budgeting 予算管理、予算編成　**❷** note that 〜 〜ということに注意する
be subject to 〜 〜を受ける、〜を免れない　rate increase 値上げ、料金上昇　revenue 収益
generate 〜を生み出す　fund 〜に資金を提供する　repair 補修　power delivery 電源供給
infrastructure 基幹設備、インフラ　commercial accounts representative 商用顧客担当者
electric supply 電気供給

2 Eメール vice president of operations 事業部長　service (電気・ガスなどの)供給　attachment 添付ファイル
❶ take a moment to *do* 時間を取って〜する　attached 添付の　suggestion 提案
move forward with 〜 〜を進める　look back at 〜 〜を振り返ってみる　record 記録
notice (that) 〜 〜ということに気付く　experience 〜を体験する　major 大きな　jump 急上昇
exact まさにその、正確な　temporary 一時的な、臨時の　intern インターン生
work on 〜 〜に取り組む　short-term 短期の

3 公共料金請求書 **❶** bill date 請求日　amount due 請求額

Expressions

regardless of 〜 「〜にかかわらず」（**1**の**❶**4行目）

The Personnel Department discussed the open entry system in order to hire a variety of people regardless of their background.
人事部は、経歴にかかわらず多様な人材を採用するために、自由応募制度について話し合いました。

CDトラック・特典音声ファイル 一覧表

● CD1

Test	Track No.	Contents
サンプル問題	1	タイトル
	2	Listening Test Directions/ Part 1 Directions
	3	Q1
	4	Part 2 Directions
	5	Q2, Q3
	6	Part 3 Directions
	7	Q4-6
	8	Q7-9
	9	Part 4 Directions
	10	Q10-12
TEST 1	11	Test 1
	12	Listening Test Directions/ Part 1 Directions
	13	Q1
	14	Q2
	15	Q3
	16	Q4
	17	Q5
	18	Q6
	19	Part 2 Directions
	20	Q7
	21	Q8
	22	Q9
	23	Q10
	24	Q11
	25	Q12
	26	Q13
	27	Q14
	28	Q15
	29	Q16
	30	Q17
	31	Q18
	32	Q19
	33	Q20
	34	Q21
	35	Q22
	36	Q23
	37	Q24
	38	Q25
	39	Q26
	40	Q27
	41	Q28
	42	Q29
	43	Q30
	44	Q31
	45	Part 3 Directions

Test	Track No.	Contents
TEST 1	46	Part 3 Q32-34 会話
	47	Q32-34 問題
	48	Q35-37 会話
	49	Q35-37 問題
	50	Q38-40 会話
	51	Q38-40 問題
	52	Q41-43 会話
	53	Q41-43 問題
	54	Q44-46 会話
	55	Q44-46 問題
	56	Q47-49 会話
	57	Q47-49 問題
	58	Q50-52 会話
	59	Q50-52 問題
	60	Q53-55 会話
	61	Q53-55 問題
	62	Q56-58 会話
	63	Q56-58 問題
	64	Q59-61 会話
	65	Q59-61 問題
	66	Q62-64 会話
	67	Q62-64 問題
	68	Q65-67 会話
	69	Q65-67 問題
	70	Q68-70 会話
	71	Q68-70 問題
	72	Part 4 Directions
	73	Q71-73 トーク
	74	Q71-73 問題
	75	Q74-76 トーク
	76	Q74-76 問題
	77	Q77-79 トーク
	78	Q77-79 問題
	79	Q80-82 トーク
	80	Q80-82 問題
	81	Q83-85 トーク
	82	Q83-85 問題
	83	Q86-88 トーク
	84	Q86-88 問題
	85	Q89-91 トーク
	86	Q89-91 問題
	87	Q92-94 トーク
	88	Q92-94 問題
	89	Q95-97 トーク
	90	Q95-97 問題
	91	Q98-100 トーク
	92	Q98-100 問題

● CD2

Test	Track No.	Contents
TEST 2	1	Test 2
	2	Listening Test Directions/ Part 1 Directions
	3	Q1
	4	Q2
	5	Q3
	6	Q4
	7	Q5
	8	Q6
	9	Part 2 Directions
	10	Q7
	11	Q8
	12	Q9
	13	Q10
	14	Q11
	15	Q12
	16	Q13
	17	Q14
	18	Q15
	19	Q16
	20	Q17
	21	Q18
	22	Q19
	23	Q20
	24	Q21
	25	Q22
	26	Q23
	27	Q24
	28	Q25
	29	Q26
	30	Q27
	31	Q28
	32	Q29
	33	Q30
	34	Q31
	35	Part 3 Directions
	36	Q32-34 会話
	37	Q32-34 問題
	38	Q35-37 会話
	39	Q35-37 問題
	40	Q38-40 会話
	41	Q38-40 問題
	42	Q41-43 会話
	43	Q41-43 問題
	44	Q44-46 会話
	45	Q44-46 問題
	46	Q47-49 会話

次ページの「音声を使った学習例の紹介」を参考に、問題に解答した後の学習用教材としてもご活用ください。

音声ダウンロードの手順▶本誌 p.3　　音声を使った学習例▶別冊 p.200

Test	Track No.	Contents
TEST 2	47	Part 3 Q47-49 問題
	48	Q50-52 会話
	49	Q50-52 問題
	50	Q53-55 会話
	51	Q53-55 問題
	52	Q56-58 会話
	53	Q56-58 問題
	54	Q59-61 会話
	55	Q59-61 問題
	56	Q62-64 会話
	57	Q62-64 問題
	58	Q65-67 会話
	59	Q65-67 問題
	60	Q68-70 会話
	61	Q68-70 問題
	62	Part 4 Directions
	63	Q71-73 トーク
	64	Q71-73 問題
	65	Q74-76 トーク
	66	Q74-76 問題
	67	Q77-79 トーク
	68	Q77-79 問題
	69	Q80-82 トーク
	70	Q80-82 問題
	71	Q83-85 トーク
	72	Q83-85 問題
	73	Q86-88 トーク
	74	Q86-88 問題
	75	Q89-91 トーク
	76	Q89-91 問題
	77	Q92-94 トーク
	78	Q92-94 問題
	79	Q95-97 トーク
	80	Q95-97 問題
	81	Q98-100 トーク
	82	Q98-100 問題

● 特典（ダウンロード）

Test	File No.	Contents
TEST 1	01	Part 5 Q101 問題
	02	Q102 問題
	03	Q103 問題
	04	Q104 問題
	05	Q105 問題
	06	Q106 問題
	07	Q107 問題
	08	Q108 問題

Test	File No.	Contents
TEST 1	09	Part 5 Q109 問題
	10	Q110 問題
	11	Q111 問題
	12	Q112 問題
	13	Q113 問題
	14	Q114 問題
	15	Q115 問題
	16	Q116 問題
	17	Q117 問題
	18	Q118 問題
	19	Q119 問題
	20	Q120 問題
	21	Q121 問題
	22	Q122 問題
	23	Q123 問題
	24	Q124 問題
	25	Q125 問題
	26	Q126 問題
	27	Q127 問題
	28	Q128 問題
	29	Q129 問題
	30	Q130 問題
	31	Part 6 Q131-134 問題
	32	Q135-138 問題
	33	Q139-142 問題
	34	Q143-146 問題
	35	Part 7 Q147-148 文書
	36	Q149-150 文書
	37	Q151-152 文書
	38	Q153-154 文書
	39	Q155-157 文書
	40	Q158-160 文書
	41	Q161-163 文書
	42	Q164-167 文書
	43	Q168-171 文書
	44	Q172-175 文書
	45-46	Q176-180 文書
	47-48	Q181-185 文書
	49-51	Q186-190 文書
	52-54	Q191-195 文書
	55-57	Q196-200 文書
TEST 2	58	Part 5 Q101 問題
	59	Q102 問題
	60	Q103 問題
	61	Q104 問題
	62	Q105 問題
	63	Q106 問題
	64	Q107 問題

Test	File No.	Contents
TEST 2	65	Part 5 Q108 問題
	66	Q109 問題
	67	Q110 問題
	68	Q111 問題
	69	Q112 問題
	70	Q113 問題
	71	Q114 問題
	72	Q115 問題
	73	Q116 問題
	74	Q117 問題
	75	Q118 問題
	76	Q119 問題
	77	Q120 問題
	78	Q121 問題
	79	Q122 問題
	80	Q123 問題
	81	Q124 問題
	82	Q125 問題
	83	Q126 問題
	84	Q127 問題
	85	Q128 問題
	86	Q129 問題
	87	Q130 問題
	88	Part 6 Q131-134 問題
	89	Q135-138 問題
	90	Q139-142 問題
	91	Q143-146 問題
	92	Part 7 Q147-148 文書
	93	Q149-150 文書
	94	Q151-153 文書
	95	Q154-155 文書
	96	Q156-157 文書
	97	Q158-160 文書
	98	Q161-164 文書
	99	Q165-167 文書
	100	Q168-171 文書
	101	Q172-175 文書
	102-103	Q176-180 文書
	104-105	Q181-185 文書
	106-108	Q186-190 文書
	109-111	Q191-195 文書
	112-114	Q196-200 文書

＊CDに収録の問題音声は全て、TOEIC®公式スピーカーによるものです。

＊特典音声は、CDとは別に収録したもので、標準的な北米発音を採用しています。

音声を使った学習例の紹介

『公式 TOEIC® Listening & Reading 問題集 9』は、付属 CD の音声の他、特典として TEST 1、2 のリーディングセクションの一部の音声を、スマートフォンや PC にダウンロードしてお聞きいただけます。以下に音声を使った公式問題集の学習法の一例をご紹介しますので、学習の参考になさってください。

準備するもの：別冊「解答・解説」（本書）、音声をダウンロードしたスマートフォンまたは PC

* Part 1 ～ 4 の音声は付属 CD でも聞くことができます。Part 5 ～ 7 の特典音声を含む全ての音声の利用は、abceed への会員登録（無料）とダウンロードが必要です。本誌 p. 3 の「音声ダウンロードの手順」に従ってサイトにアクセスし、『公式 TOEIC® Listening & Reading 問題集 9』をダウンロードしてください。リーディングの特典音声のスピードが速くて聞き取りが難しいと感じる方は、abceed のアプリなどのスピード調整機能を利用しましょう。初めのうちは 0.8 ～ 0.9 倍などで聞いてもいいでしょう。

Part 1、2

1. 「解答・解説」で正解の英文の意味内容を正しく理解する。
2. 音声を聞き、発音やイントネーションをまねて音読する（リピーティング）。最初はスクリプトを見ながら行い、慣れてきたらスクリプトを見ずに行う。

> Part 1 では写真を見ながら正解の描写文だけを、Part 2 では質問と正解の応答を、音読してみましょう。自分が発話しているつもりで音読すると、表現が定着しやすくなります。

Part 3、4

1. 「解答・解説」でスクリプトの英文と訳を確認。知らない語の意味や英文の内容を把握する。
2. スクリプトを見ながら会話やトークを聞く。発話と同じスピードで英文を目で追い、即座に意味を理解できるようになるまで繰り返す。
3. スクリプトを見ずに会話やトークを聞く。聞き取りづらい箇所や意味が理解できない箇所をスクリプトで確認し、再び音声だけで理解できるか挑戦する。

> Part 3 ではスピーカー同士の関係や会話の目的、Part 4 では場面やトークの趣旨をまず把握し、徐々に理解できる範囲を増やしていくつもりで、細部の情報まで聞き取るようにしましょう。

Part 5、6

1. 「解答・解説」で英文と訳を確認。知らない語の意味や英文の内容を把握する。
2. 本誌の TEST 1、2 の該当ページ(p.42-48 と p.84-90)のコピーを取り、音声を聞いて空所の語や文を書き取る。知っている語彙や文法の知識も用いて空所を埋め、書き取ったものと実際の英文を比較する。最後に、もう一度音声を聞く。

> 聞き取れない箇所は、飛ばしたりカタカナで書いたりしても構いません。音声だけに頼らず、語彙力や文法の知識を用いて挑戦してみましょう。Part 5 は短い文なので、ディクテーションをするのもよいでしょう。

Part 6、7

1. 「解答・解説」で英文と訳を確認。知らない語の意味や英文の内容を把握する。その際、読み方に迷った箇所に印を付けておく。
2. 音声を聞きながら英文を目で追い（初めはスピードを遅めにしても可）、英語の語順のまま理解できるようになることを目指す。分からなかった箇所は適宜、訳を確認する。
3. 1. で印を付けた、読み方に迷った箇所の言い方を確認する。
   例：数字や記号の言い方（日付、住所、飛行機の便名、価格、URL）など。

> 1. は構文や語彙の学習、2. は速読の学習です。2. では意味のまとまりを意識しながら英文を読み進めていくようにすると、取り組みやすいでしょう。3. は、実際の会話の際にも役立つので積極的に覚えるとよいでしょう。